A Walking Guide To The Superior Hiking Trail

Natural History, Scenery, and Other Trail Features

Ron Morton and Judy Gibbs

Rockflower Press

Knife River, Minnesota

Rockflower Press
Box 295
Knife River MN 55609
www.rockflowerpress.com

A Walking Guide To The Superior Hiking Trail
Natural History, Scenery, and Other Trail Features

Printed in the United States of America

Cover design by Steve Rodriques
Cover Photograph by Judy Gibbs

ISBN 0-9785998-0-2

Dedication

To Charlie, Sammy, and Rhubarb, our three constant trail companions. We doubt there is a page of this book that doesn't have at least one of your paw prints on it–and that's just how it should be!

Contents

The Walks

Walk Waypoints:

Individual walk waypoints are based on GPS locations, with the accuracy of the GPS unit varying from 10 to 80 feet–the average was about 32 feet. The waypoints for each hike are available for uploading to your GPS unit from Rockflower Press (www. rockflowerpress.com). For those who do not have or use a GPS unit, we have tried to tie the waypoints to prominent geographic, geological, or scenic features and, for the most part, this has made them easy to locate as you walk the trail.

Acknowledgements

We would both like to thank and gratefully acknowledge the Superior Hiking Trail Association, and their numerous volunteers who help keep this premier foot path in such excellent shape. Whether it is clearing fallen trees, laying boardwalk, rebuilding bridges, or any of the other trail maintenance jobs they do, as you walk along you can't help but notice and be grateful for their hard work—work that is truly a labor of love. Thank you one and all. For more information on this great organization visit their web site at www.shta.org.

Nancy Nelson spent many hours editing a preliminary draft of this book. She offered numerous suggestions for improvement, and her insight, dedication, and wonderful editing skills greatly influenced and improved the final version of this walking guide. Gale Coyer went through a copy of the manuscript and made helpful suggestions for improving the book. Her intimate knowledge of the Superior Hiking Trail provided us with valuable information on aspects of the trail that dealt with the Superior Hiking Trail Association.

Finally we would like to acknowledge, as well as pay tribute to, all the geologists and naturalists whose field work along the North Shore of Lake Superior provided us with the background information that turned this idea into reality.

Introduction

"The trail is the thing, not the end of the trail. Travel too fast and you miss all you are traveling for." Louis L'Amour

The shoreline of Lake Agnes is the perfect place to write the introduction for a book such as this: blue water, boreal forest with stately pines, wildflowers galore, rocky shoreline, and nice campsites. I was first here in the summer of 2003 when I walked over 140 miles of the Superior Hiking Trail with Walter Broughton, his two black labs, Nook and Stormy, and my wire-haired dachshund Charlie. It was here, along this lakeshore, I first thought about writing such a guidebook.

As Walter and I continued our walks, and I gave more thought to actually attempting such a project, I came to the conclusion there was no way I could do it alone. I needed the help of a naturalist, one willing to walk over 200 miles taking notes and making observations every step of the way, and one with whom I would still be on speaking terms at trails end. As it turned out I happened to know just the right person. Judy Gibbs and I had been teaching Elderhostel together for several years. I knew her knowledge of plants and trees and her ability to communicate this knowledge in common terms was just what such a guidebook needed. The other reason I considered her the person I wanted to walk the trail with goes back to our first Elderhostel together. It was at Nor'Wester Lodge on the Gunflint Trail and at the end of the week Judy packed up her stuff and set out alone to canoe from the lodge on Poplar Lake to Ely, Minnesota! I figured if she could undertake and complete a trip like that, then walking the hiking trail would be a "piece of cake." So one rainy October day I called Judy up, invited her to lunch, and explained what I had in mind. The rest is "trail history."

The essence of this walking guide is found in the quote at the start of the introduction. Over the years my usual way of hiking has been to travel fast, to get from start to finish as quickly as possible. With Judy I traveled to take a closer look. These two different approaches to the Hiking Trail can nicely be summed up by a story Judy likes to tell. It's the story of a hike I did with Walter, and was absolutely dreading having to repeat. I told Judy numerous times how awful this walk was: start out on a spectacular overlook then descend into swamp and cutover forest and stay there for mile after boring mile. Judy and I redid the hike. After we finished Judy asked me how I would now describe the walk. A bit differently, I told her. I think it would go something like this. After great views from anorthosite and diabase cliffs descend into a canyon full of lush green vegetation. The canyon opens into a series of small lakes with boundary water type views. Boardwalks take us past cattails and wild irises. Orchids abound, birds are in full song, and some of the views are reminiscent of Ansil Adams half-dome photographs.

Taking time to look closer turned a negative memory of a walk into one of the better walks on the trail. The difference in one's approach, "the trail" itself or "the end of the trail," makes all the difference to what is seen, experienced, and taken home when you do any of the 32 walks in this book.

Finally, this book is a chronicle of the walks Judy and I did along the Superior Hiking Trail. We spent a lot of time on each of the 32 walks but no matter how much time is spent on the trail there is no way to see everything. Some of what is seen will look different depending on the season and weather, so I am certain we have missed things. If you think our omissions are of a unique or truly interesting trail feature, or the result of a dramtic change in the trail itself, please let us now. Not only would we like to go out and see what we missed, but it would be an invaluable help in planning future editions of this book. You can contact either Judy or myself through Rockflower Press (www.Rockflowerpress.com).

Geological Time and the Superior Hiking Trail

This walking guide is, in part, about the geology of the Superior Hiking Trail– its rocks and landforms. In order to understand and appreciate these features they need to be placed in the context of geological time. Geological time is the foundation of modern geology. In fact, it is believed to be so important it has been called "the greatest contribution of the science of geology to modern western thought." Geological time gets this distinction for three reasons.

First, it allows geologists to place rocks, fossils, ice ages, ore deposits, mountain ranges, and a zillion other geological events and formations in the proper sequence so they can unravel and understand the evolution of our planet and the many different creatures that have called it home.

Second, geologic time shows us that earth processes and events take place over a great range of time periods. For example, mudslides and earthquakes last only a few seconds or minutes, volcanic eruptions a few hours or days, but the building of great mountains and the creeping of continents halfway around the world take tens of millions of years.

These different geological events, and a hundred others, come and go. Some fast, some slow, but over the long length of geological time the same land area, such as that of the Superior Hiking Trail, can be the scene of a wide variety of these events. Think about it, all the changes that have occurred along the length of the hiking trail over the long eons of geological time. Great volcanoes, more than once, raged, roared and ruled the land; hot springs exited onto ancient seafloors and flowed over barren landscapes bubbling with all kinds of minerals. Twice, great Alp-like mountains rose above what would become the Superior Hiking Trail and both times they ended up being washed to long gone seas.

Speaking of seas, this land has been covered by numerous oceans, each of which was filled with all sorts of strange creatures, most of whom are now extinct. Dinosaurs walked the length of the Superior Hiking Trail, and during the last Ice Age, there was more than a mile of ice above such places as Mt. Trudee, Crow Creek, and Carlton Peak. Wooly mammoths, giant beavers, and "dire" wolves lived here at the end of the last Ice Age.

When the ice melted away it left behind a brand new landscape, one formed and molded in the ice's own image. It was a landscape covered by thick deposits of glacial till and littered with glacial erratics. There were also many new lakes, both small and large.

It was running water over the last few thousand years, that did the final sculpting of the land the Superior Hiking Trail traverses. Streams along the North Shore flow from west to east following the slope or tilt of the lava flows into Lake

Superior. These streams cut down through the glacial deposits into the underlying lava flows, sedimentary, and intrusive rocks. In doing so the streams tended to follow zones of weakness in the bedrock, such as cracks and fractures, flow or bedding contacts, cooling joints, and tops of lava flows. Because of their opportunistic nature larger streams have been able to cut deep canyons and twisting gorges, and to uniquely sculpt the bedrock to form some of the more spectacular scenery along the North Shore and the Superior Hiking Trail.

The third reason geological time is important is because it tells us planet earth is not just old, it is ancient beyond imagination. It is all of 4.6 billion years old! 4.6 billion years, a length of time difficult to imagine let alone comprehend. In dealing with time, our frame of reference is relatively short. For most of us a hundred years is a long time, but take 500 or 1000 years and we're talking ancient history, many times *lost* history.

What we have here in the Lake Superior region is *really* ancient history. The rocks along the Superior Hiking Trail formed during what geologists call Precambrian time, a time that begins with the formation of the earth and ends with the start of the so-called Cambrian period, some 544 million years ago. Though this particular time break is a natural one, it is rather lopsided, for the Precambrian represents 88% of all geological time. It's natural because it represents the time when fossils, the remains of prehistoric life, first became abundant in sedimentary rocks. Before the Cambrian, fossils in rocks were few and far between. That doesn't mean there wasn't any life, just that life had not evolved to the point of being able to form or secrete hard skeletons that allowed preservation in sediment. Early life forms, for almost 4 billion years, had bodies that were soft and squishy, and thus nothing much on them to preserve.

Overall, Precambrian time is divided into what is called the Archean, the time from 2.5 billion years ago back to 4.0 billion, the age of the oldest known rock. The time between 2.5 billion and 544 million is called the Proterozoic. The rocks along the hiking trail are Proterozoic in age, varying from about two to one billion years old. Archean-age rocks occur beneath the Proterozoic rocks and are exposed in the Tower-Ely area (2.7 billon years) and around the town of Morton in central Minnesota (3.5 billion years).

So when you walk on the trail, no matter how long or how far, you become not only a time traveler, but one who occupies two different geological ages at the same moment. The rocks exposed along the Superior Hiking Trail represent part of the ancient history of our planet. Based on age dates they record over a billion years of geological events, events that began some 900 million years ago and extend back to 2.0 billion years. At the same time the immediate landscape you are walking over, and viewing in the distance, formed only after the last great ice sheet melted away some 12,000 years ago.

Young land, old rocks, and each a history book containing many different chapters that can be read, seen, and experienced as you use this guide to walk along the Superior Hiking Trail, a trail that truly winds its way through time.

Book Layout

Each of the 32 individual day walks is divided into three parts. These are:

One: **"Walk Logistics"** gives logistical information about the walk such as start and end points, directions on how to get to these places, walk distance and date Judy and I did the walk.

All of the walks, with the exception of the loop walks, were done walking from south to north on the trail. To get the most out of this guide we suggest you do the walks in the same direction. The distance of the walk is from waypoint one to the parking lot at the end of the walk and is based on GPS track logs. Walk distances do not include spur trails to overlooks unless so indicated.

The date(s) Judy and I walked a particular section are included so you will know the time of year we saw the flowers, buds, plants, and/or condition of the leaves described in the waypoint to waypoint section.

Two: **"Worth a Longer Look"** is a list of waypoints Judy and I found to be particularly interesting, scenic, unusual, and/or simply neat and special. Obviously, such places are partly in the eye and mind of the beholder, so if we missed a spot on the trail you consider special or unique or extra scenic we would like to know about it. You can contact either of us by e-mail at www.rockflowerpress.com.

Three: **"Waypoint-to-Waypoint"** describes the walk itself. In this section you will find detailed descriptions of trail conditions, what there is to see between waypoints, and what each individual waypoint is about. Trail conditions for each section are described under the waypoint number you are walking toward. So, to find out what the trail is like between waypoints 1 and 2 read the material in waypoint 2; conditions between 2 and 3 are found under waypoint 3 and so on.

Individual walk waypoints are based on GPS locations, with the accuracy of the GPS unit varying from 10 to 80 feet; the average was about 32 feet. The waypoints for each hike are available for uploading to your GPS unit from Rockflower Press (www. rockflowerpress.com). For those who do not have or use a GPS unit, we have tried to tie the waypoints to prominent geographic, geological, or scenic features and, for the most part, this has made them easy to locate as you walk the trail.

Maps: Two maps accompany each walk. One is a trail map that shows the GPS track of the walk, the locations of waypoints along the track, prominent geographic features, campsite locations (campsite symbol is adjacent to waypoint of the campsite), roads, and trailhead parking sites. The second map is an elevation profile showing the elevation of each waypoint, elevation change between waypoints, and the distance, in miles, between waypoints. When using these profiles please remember that elevations are in hundred foot intervals and distances between waypoints are not uniform. So a section of the trail that looks, on the profile, to be particularly steep may actually represent a 150 foot change over 1 mile–a very gentle climb! Elevations were determined by plotting the waypoints on USGS topographic maps.

Glossary: Geological terms and features are defined in glossary I at the back of the book, and are italicized the first time they are used or encountered in a given walk. In this regard we have tried to keep scientific jargon to a minimum, and have attempted to use everyday terms and analogies wherever possible. Glossary II gives brief descriptions of many of the plants and wildflowers observed along the trail and mentioned in the "waypoint-to-waypoint" section. These are also italicized the first time they are encountered in a given walk.

Trail Access: The Superior Hiking Trail is easily accessed from either Highway 61 or county and forestry roads that join Highway 61. The hiking trail also crosses seven of the state parks that are located on or close to the North Shore, and these also provide trail access.

Judy and I did all but the loop walks using two vehicles. We would leave one at the destination parking lot and then shuttle to the start point. If you only have one vehicle there are numerous other options. Some of these are: a) use the Superior Shuttle service (www.superiorshuttle.com), b) if staying at a lodge or resort many of these provide shuttle service to trail access points close to their establishment, c) store a bicycle at the end point and bike back to your car, d) friends, e) do part of a hike by walking to a waypoint on the trail, and then return along the same route using the guide book one way. By doing this you will get a different view of the landscape when walking in the opposite direction.

Please Do: The following is a list of please do's before you set out on a walk:

a) Read through the entire walk and use the glossaries to look up terms and definitions you may not be familiar with.

b) Wear sturdy walking shoes or hiking boots. The trail is root-crossed and boulder-strewn; it may also be wet and muddy in places. Walking Sticks are NOT prohibited.

c) Carry a raincoat.

d) Dress in or carry extra layers of clothing. The trail is close to a huge body of really cold water, and if the wind comes up or changes direction the temperature could rise or fall by many degrees.

e) Carry lots of water. More is better. Same goes for food–walking does make you hungry.

f) Take bug dope and sunscreen.

g) Carry a first aid kit, at least one that has band aids, antiseptic ointment, and ibuprofin or aspirin.

h) Take a camera.

i) If you have one, don't forget your GPS unit, extra batteries, and to upload the waypoints for the walk you are doing.

j) Just in case-a penlight, a pocketknife, and matches.

Finally, as we found written in one of the trail "happy" books, "with observant eyes, a kid's curiosity, and a desire to explore and learn I can think of no better place to meet nature and possibly, just possibly, come to know her." Amen, have fun, and good walking.

Map Key

P   Parking Area for Trail Head

●   Waypoints

～～ Outline of the Walking Trail

▲   Campsites

61   U.S. Highways (Highway 61)

5   County Roads

321 Forestry Roads

/   Other Roads

⬭   Lakes

/   Rivers

Superior Hiking Trail
Walk 1: Crow Creek

Walk Logistics

Start: Fors Road (County Road 301)

Getting There: Just past the Stewart River and Betty's Pies take Lake County Road 3 north for 2 miles. Turn left onto Fors Road (Lake County Road 301) and follow this for 0.3 miles. Parking lot is on the left.

End: West Castle Danger Road (County Road 106)

Getting There: Pass through the Silver Creek and Lafayette Bluff tunnels on Highway 61, cross Crow Creek, and at Castle Danger turn left onto Lake County Road 106 (West Castle Danger Road which becomes Silver Creek Township Road after 0.6 miles). Follow this for 2.4 miles, parking lot is on the right.

Walk Distance: 5.9 miles   **Date Walked:** May 25th, 2004

Worth a Longer Look:

Wilson's Creek: 4	Old Growth Forest: 12, 13, 16
Bloodroot Creek: 5	Encampment River: 15
Silver Creek Diabase: 8	Red Pine Overlook: 18
Frost Wedged Talus: 10	Crow Creek Valley: 21
Enchanted Forest: 12	Crow Creek Lavas: 23

Waypoint-to-Waypoint

One: Parking Lot off Fors Road (County Road 301)

Much like the breath of a glacier, the cold mist creeps across the parking lot, forcing us to put on fleece jackets. With the fog comes silence, a quiet that makes us talk in whispers. There is no wind. After four days of a steady breeze off the great ice machine called Superior, there is nothing to rustle the first leaves of spring or part the long fingers of grayness that swirl around us like smoke from a campfire.

This spring has been wet with rain steadily falling to fill bogs and swamps and make the woods dripping wet. The wetness adds to the color of the tree bark: dark, brownish-green of the aspen, dark gray to black of the maple, creamy white of the paper birch, and vibrant green of lichens and moss growing on the bark. The woods, according to Judy, are holding their breath waiting, waiting for the sun and warmth that will let them work their spring magic.

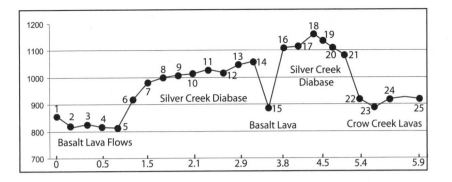

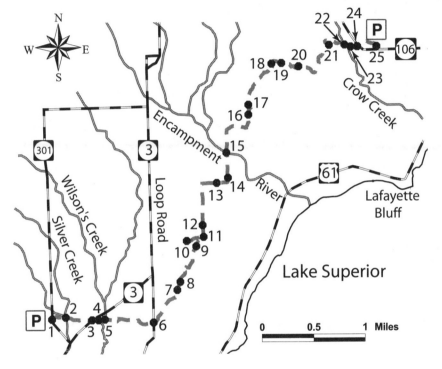

Two: Branch of Silver Creek

It's a short walk from the parking lot through a forest dominated by balsam fir, with a few balsam poplar and spruce trees, to a branch of Silver Creek. Along this section the forest is vibrating with the hopeful songs of the chipping sparrows, white-throated sparrows, blue-jay, chestnut-sided warbler, hermit thrush, and, above all the others the ovenbird with its tee-cher, tee-cher song.

Today Silver Creek is hopping, filled to the brim with tea-colored water that seems impatient to reach Lake Superior. The banks of the creek are lined

11

with long, grass-like leaves which, later in the summer, will have lilac-colored flowers. These are *wild onions*, and their small, pungent bulbs can be found just below the surface.

Three: County Road 3

Leaving the creek the trail is flat and wet, crossing two small creeks with bridges, as it continues east through a forest dominated by fir, spruce, and balsam poplar. Just before County Road 3 (waypoint 3) there is a large open field that represents an early and futile attempt to farm in this part of the world. Planted here are scotch pines. This tree is not native to this part of the world. It resembles red pine but has a more flaky and butterscotch-colored bark.

Four: Wilson's Creek

It's not far from the county road to Wilson's Creek (waypoint 4). Be careful here because the wooden steps down to the creek are slippery when wet. The creek bottom contains some nice yellow birch, and from the bridge the prominent red stream bank is impressive–steep and composed of *glacial till*. This red till is referred to as the Wilson's Creek Till.

The gravel bar on the north side of the creek is composed predominantly of reddish-colored *amygdaloidal* and *massive basalt* that form part of the *North Shore Volcanic Group*. Here the *amygdules* are filled by *quartz, calcite,* and a fibrous white *zeolite*.

Five: Bloodroot Creek

A short walk from Wilson's Creek the trail crosses another small creek Judy names "Bloodroot Creek" (waypoint 5). That's because *bloodroots* are everywhere, a thick blanket of small white flowers with 8-10 white petals. Bloodroot, a member of the poppy family, gets its name from the orange-colored juice that seeps from its roots when broken. The Ojibwe used the juice as a dye for clothing and blankets. The leaves of the bloodroot are enormous late in the summer. Their main function is to gather in the sun's energy, make sugar, and get this to the roots, which are dark orange in color. This is a short-lived flower, but one Judy always hopes to see, because for her it is the introduction to a new spring, and all the wildflowers that will follow.

Six: Wet and Boggy, Loop Road

After Bloodroot Creek the trail passes onto private land and is relatively flat, wet, and muddy. It is what Judy and I refer to as a "just walk and get it over with section." This particular "just walk" section is 0.4 miles long and has two features that almost redeem its soppy, blah aspect: *springbeauties* and white-flowered *wood anemones* or windflowers.

Heading gently uphill to Highway 3 (Loop Road, Township Road 613, and waypoint 6), Judy informs me the woods look "pregnant." "Everything is ready to pop," she says. "From the *starflowers*, *Canadian mayflower*, and *Mertensia* to the *Hepatica*, and large-flowered *bellwort*. All that's needed is warmth and sunshine."

Seven: MN DOT Stream and Bench Marker

The trail, composed partly of glacial till, goes through a small cedar grove then winds around the edge of a hill through a mixed forest of black ash, aspen, and alder to a small creek Judy christens Hare Creek. Hare Creek because, in her words, it is so apparent snowshoe hares have passed the winter here because most of the twigs have chewed off bark and there is heaps of bunny scat. Just beyond Hare Creek is a small spring, and a MN DOT Stream and Bench Marker that is waypoint 7. Immediately past this is a wide dirt road that provides a nice view of the Silver Creek Valley. This valley was nicknamed "wall street" in the 1940's because the townsfolk thought only rich people lived up here.

Judy tells me that, with imagination, we might hear the roar of the 747 jumbo jets taking off from Weidman International Airport situated about a mile to the west. At least that's the name on topographic maps for what is a small grass landing strip. According to Kyle Weidman "The tail-dragging airplanes we flew didn't need much of a strip. And, when it came time to get it licensed in the 70's for the construction business, we just figured to name it something for fun."

Eight: Silver Creek Diabase

From the road it's uphill over a trail composed of glacial till, to a moss-and-lichen-covered *outcrop* of *Silver Creek Diabase* (also see *diabase*), which is waypoint 8. The Silver Creek Diabase forms a prominent ridge that the hiking trail will follow until its steep descent into the Encampment River Valley. The ridge extends from Silver Cliff on Highway 61 (location of the Silver Cliff Tunnel) to the headwaters of the Gooseberry River, broken only where the Encampment River and Crow Creek have cut down through it. There are *blueberry* plants here, and you can see lots of new growth on the balsam fir trees.

Nine: Ginger Creek

The trail heads northeast past numerous small outcrops of Silver Creek Diabase, through a balsam fir and spruce forest, that is dense and dark in places. After crossing the old road to Beaver Bay arrive at "Ginger Creek" and waypoint 9.

Ginger Creek is lush with what else–*wild ginger*, a plant with large heart-shaped leaves and a reddish-brown cup-shaped flower hiding beneath the leaves. Also abundant here is *blue bead lily*. In the early spring the shiny green leaves of the bead lily taste like cucumber; later in the spring the plant will have bell-shaped yellow flowers and "not so good for you" blue berries atop a slender green stalk.

Ten: High Knob of Silver Creek Diabase

After Ginger Creek it's a short, steep climb to an open knob of Silver Creek Diabase (waypoint 10), which is lumpy and weathered to kibbles and bits (see *diabase weathering*). From here there is a nice view to the south and southeast of the Two Harbors area including Burlington Bay and a water tower. The diabase knob is close to the top of a steep cliff, a cliff with a huge pile of rock *talus* at its base. The talus formed from a process called *frost wedging*. This process breaks the rocks into fragments that then slide, roll, and/or tumble to the bottom of the cliff to be added to the growing pile of rock debris.

Eleven: Private Land

Heading northeast the trail goes through a grove of red pine before entering relatively dense woods to a sign (waypoint 11) that informs us we are about to enter private land and please keep on the trail. As we pass the sign Judy points out the dramatic change in the forest—from cutover, with new small trees, to larger, old-growth trees including some very nice white pines.

Twelve: Top of a Small Hill, a "Wow" Spot

It's a nice stroll through the old-growth forest to the top of a small hill (waypoint 12). The view from here is so unexpected it takes our breath away. Coming over the crest of the hill we look down upon what can only be described as a long boulevard, a green "highway" in the woods. The large trees that once bordered this "highway" have long ago been cut, and the way the stumps line up remind Judy of the "Alice in Wonderland" statement "Off with their heads!" The silver-gray stumps now serve to guide our view down the boulevard, to the open woods beyond, woods dominated by large old trees. It is an enchanted forest if ever there was one. Turns out the trees were cut by the Encampment Forest Association to delineate their property boundary.

"Wow!" Judy exclaims. "And amazingly enough you fit right in here. White pines, white spruce, white cedar; all these old-growth trees, and you wearing that old, white sweater."

"This sweater," I inform her, "came from Edinburgh 14 years ago and has lasted through lots of field seasons. So it's an old friend. Also, it would be nice if you recognized what these trees and I really have in common."

"Which is?"

"We're tall and stately."

14

"And here I was sure you were going to say silver and gray!"

Thirteen: White Pine Zoos

A beautiful, long stroll through the old forest, which has virtually no undergrowth, to what I call a "white pine zoo"–small white pine trees completely enclosed by fencing. This is at waypoint 13, where there is a large "no trespassing" sign.

Judy explains the fencing is to protect the young trees from moose and deer who love the tops or terminal buds. They snip them off and this stops the trees from growing any taller. The droopy yellow flowers around the "zoo" enclosures are wild oats, sessile *bellwort*, called that because of their bell shape. Ojibwe hunters chewed the root of the plant believing it would help attract deer and moose.

Fourteen: Start of Steep Downhill Section

A short distance from waypoint 13 we walk up a diabase outcrop then follow a rocky trail bordered by nice red and white pines to the start of a steep downhill section (waypoint 14). There is also lots of moose browse on the mountain maples. Mountain maples are tall shrubs and called "moose maples" because their leaves look like large maple leaves and moose just love to nibble on them. Perhaps that's why the Ojibwe gave the name "twig eaters" to moose.

Fifteen: Encampment River

It's steep, rocky, and downhill over diabase outcrops and boulders, followed by a long, flat, wet stretch through cedar, spruce, and white pines to the sign that ends the private land section. From here we can hear the Encampment River and, as we head toward it, we will be walking on slippery, sticky red clay.

The red clay bank seen from the bridge over the Encampment River (waypoint 15) contains very few *boulders*, *cobbles*, or *pebbles* and is thus different from the red bank of glacial till at Wilson's Creek. The red clay here is the good ole sticky stuff that covers a large portion of the North Shore, clay that once formed the bottom of *Glacial Lake Duluth* and now forms part of the Superior Hiking Trail. This smaller, but much deeper, lake immediately preceded Lake Superior. These clay deposits overlie the Wilson's Creek Till and are called the Knife River Formation. In the last year this bank has been undercut by the river, and has undergone major *slumping*. In fact the small *meander* that was here last year is gone; the river has cut a new, straight channel!

The numerous boulders and cobbles in the Encampment River come from the erosion and slumping of the Wilson's Creek Till. These round to sub-angular rocks are dominantly basalt, both massive and amygdaloidal. Other than basalt, which has weathered to a pale red color due to the oxidation of the iron in it, you may find a few layered or bedded rocks here. These are *sandstones* and *siltstones* that formed from sediment deposited by ancient streams flowing over the lavas when there was no active volcanism.

The old *flood plain* of the river is clearly visible as a flat terrace just ahead and uphill from the current river. It's easy to see how the river has cut down through the flood plain to its present position. The old flood plain is covered in *cow parsnip,* which by midsummer will be 4-10 feet tall. The "maple-like" leaves can be over a foot long, and the umbrella-like flower clusters are wooly and rank smelling.

Sixteen: Ridge Top, View to Northwest

From the river it's a nice walk through an old-growth forest with lovely white pines, cedars, and balsam fir, a forest Judy calls "enchanting." Part of this walk has another "off with their heads" section–cut stumps lining both sides of the trail. There is lots of *coltsfoot* here, a member of the daisy family that has reddish scales on its stalk and bristly yellow flowers that look something like dandelions. There are also more "white pine zoos," or forest study areas, which occur just before an uphill section that takes us past a moss-covered outcrop of diabase to waypoint 16. This is at the top of the ridge and provides great views of the Encampment River and Silver Creek valleys and the landscape beyond.

As we walk along the ridge we pass pieces of six-sided *cooling joints* in the diabase. These boulder-size pieces have smooth, planar surfaces at 60 degrees to each other, separated by narrow sharp ridges. The rocks may be partially hidden by plants, such as *Sarsaparilla* (Ginseng Family), a tall plant that is prolific here. Sarsaparilla has white, round, umbrella-like flower clusters with leaves that start off a burgundy color then slowly turn green. Its blue-black berries ripen in mid-July. This is a close cousin to wild ginseng and, supposedly, was the root used in the original root beer or the drink called sarsaparilla.

Seventeen: Lumpy Diabase and a Panoramic View

The trail follows the ridge of lumpy diabase outcrop with sections of kibbles and bits to waypoint 17, a beautiful view of Two Harbors to the south and of the Encampment River and Silver Creek valleys to the west.

The outcrop of Silver Creek Diabase is lumpy with hard, round, raised lumps dominated by the black mineral *pyroxene* (gives the rock a heavy "pepper" look), separated by grayer areas composed of the mineral *plagioclase feldspar* (gives these sections of the rock a heavy "salt" look). The finer-grained feldspar-rich areas weather more easily than the pyroxene-rich areas, and this gives the rock its lumpy appearance. This lumpy look is an intermediate step between hard, fresh rock and old crumbly rock.

Eighteen: Red Pine Overlook

Continue along the ridge, with nice views of the Encampment River and the Silver Creek Valley and farms to the west, through an old-growth forest with two of Judy's favorite evergreen plants–*pipsissewa* (terminal cluster of waxy white and pinkish flowers) and *bearberry* (paddle-shaped evergreen leaves and egg-shaped white or pink flowers, Native Americans used the leaves for tobacco). After a fairly long walk along the diabase ridge, with nice red and white pines, there is a ninety-degree bend in the trail (waypoint 18). From here there is a view back to the high part of the ridge we just walked over, and through a small grove of red pines there is a good view of farms along County Road 106, the road the hiking trail parking lot is on. The diabase outcrop at this waypoint exhibits "lumpy" weathering, and there are some nice hexagonal cooling joints.

Nineteen: Ssh!

Leaving the red pine overlook the trail turns and heads downhill passing some large white pines to waypoint 19.

"Don't say anything nasty, mean or critical here," I tell Judy, pointing toward the sign.

"Sensitive area," she reads. Then with a smile, she says, "I'll try and be good but it will be hard to do with all this *"wild" lettuce* around."

There is a wide ATV trail here which crosses the walking path along which *rose-twisted stalk* grows. Rose-twisted stalk is also known as "scootberry" because if you eat its berries you tend to "scoot" to the bathroom a lot.

Twenty: Wet Meadow

It's flat and boggy to waypoint 20, a small creek that drains a wide, wet marsh. Just past waypoint 20 there is a nice view down the marsh. There is a lot of coltsfoot here.

Twenty-One: Crow Creek Valley

From waypoint 20 we proceed along a flat, dry trail for 0.2 miles to an old logging road. The trail then turns to parallel the road for a short distance before heading northeast along a hillside that looks down into an open "meadow-like" area. In this section the trail goes over lumpy Silver Creek Diabase with some kibbles and bits.

Passing a "private property" sign and crossing an old logging road it's a short walk to waypoint 21, which is marked by a wooden bench. This is a great place to enjoy a snack or lunch while taking in the marvelous view of the Crow Creek Valley, Highway 61, Wolf Rock (across the valley and at the east end of the high ridge), and Lake Superior. From waypoint 20 to 21 the trail remains relatively flat as it crosses the Silver Creek Diabase. Now begins the descent into Crow Creek, a descent that takes us through the Silver Creek Diabase into the underlying basalt lava flows. The rock outcrop at this waypoint is lumpy Silver Creek Diabase.

Twenty-Two: Start of Steep Trail Section Down To Crow Creek

From waypoint 21 the trail descends downhill, followed by a long, flat plateau before another short downhill, which is followed by yet another short flat section to waypoint 22. The flat areas represent flood plain surfaces or terraces of ancient Crow Creek, and the downhill sections are old creek channels. At waypoint 22, the start of the final descent to Crow Creek, there is an outcrop of basalt.

Twenty-Three: Crow Creek

It's awesome from start to finish. The start is the final steep descent to Crow Creek. The hiking trail is narrow, rocky, and has a wall of basalt on one side and a precipitous drop on the other. Though relatively short, this is a section of trail worthy of the Grand Tetons or Big Horn Mountains. The finish is the forty-foot bridge across Crow Creek (waypoint 23). Standing on its wooden surface the world becomes a fascinating collage of rock, sky, and water. It's simply awesome and beautiful. On the way down Judy notes elderberry bushes along the creek bank.

It's rock world–from the pale red basalt cliffs that tower above us, to the rocky bottom of the stream channel, and the boulders, cobbles, and pebbles of amygdaloidal basalt, massive basalt, and diabase that cover the stream banks and form intricate patterns for the water to surge around.

The cliffs are steep, barren, and composed of numerous basalt lava flows (see *Crow Creek Lava Flows*). At their base and along the hiking trail are numerous angular pieces of frost-wedged basalt; these provide a perfect habitat for *trilliums, columbine,* and wild ginger. There are also large red and white pines that look impressive as they rise up from the cliff tops.

Twenty-Four: Top of Crow Creek Valley and Poison Ivy

It is a steep climb over a barren, rocky hillside out of the Crow Creek Valley. As we climb we pass a sign warning us of poison ivy. Turns out there is none here because the poison ivy has itself been poisoned to make the trail less itchy. Waypoint 24 is at the top of the Crow Creek Valley.

Twenty-Five: Parking Lot, West Castle Danger Road (Silver Creek Township Road 617)

From the top of the creek it's a short walk to highway 106 followed by a very wet section, replete with morel mushrooms, before the trail bends around the base of a steep, rocky hill (more Silver Creek Diabase) to arrive at the parking lot on Township Road 617.

Our two dogs, Charlie, a standard wire-haired dachshund, and Sammy, a part Lab mix, are muddy, tired, and want only to climb into the back of my Explorer and go to sleep. I feel the same way but have to drive back to Duluth. Fortunately, there are the memories of this first good hike–the changing landscape; different flowers, trees, and habitats; the varied geology, and awesome Crow Creek to keep me awake.

Superior Hiking Trail
Walk 2: Gooseberry River, The Nestor Grade, and Wolf's Rock

Walk Logistics

Start: Silver Creek Township Road 617 (West Castle Danger Road)

Getting There: Take Highway 61 north past the Encampment River and Crow Creek to Castle Danger. At Castle Danger turn left onto Lake County Road 106 (West Castle Danger Road). This becomes township road 617 about 0.6 miles from Highway 61. The parking lot is 2.4 miles from the Highway 61-Lake County 106 intersection and is on the right.

End: Gooseberry Falls State Park Visitor's Center

Getting There: The park entrance is off Highway 61 about 2 miles north of Castle Danger. Follow signs for visitor's center parking. To access the Superior Hiking Trail walk past the visitor's center and follow the paved trail that goes under the highway, crosses the Gooseberry River, and passes the old visitor's center. The start of the hiking trail is about 50 feet past the old visitor's center.

Walk Distance: 8.8 miles   **Date Walked:** May 28th, 2004

Worth a Longer Look:

Wolf Rock: 3	Gravel Bar: 19
Black Ash Swamp: 7	River Pavement: 23
Ephemeral Pond: 8	Oxbows: 24, 25, 26
Cattail Marsh: 9	Split Tree (if still there): 28
Yellow Birch: 10	Unconformity and Falls: 32
Nestor Grade: 15	Pot Holes: 33
Slumps on the Gooseberry River: 18	

Waypoint-to-Waypoint

One: Parking Lot off West Castle Danger Road (County Road 617)

It's a bright and cheerful morning though the air seems reluctant to give up its heavy aroma of damp earth and wet grass from the previous evening's rain. Rain, and a stiff northeast breeze off Lake Superior, is about all the weather has offered us over the past three days. Even so, with May coming to an end, the temperature away from Superior's shore has managed to crawl into the low sixties. This gradual warming has given trees a chance to perform their yearly magic. Over the three days since our Crow Creek hike,

20

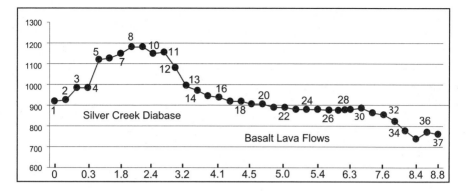

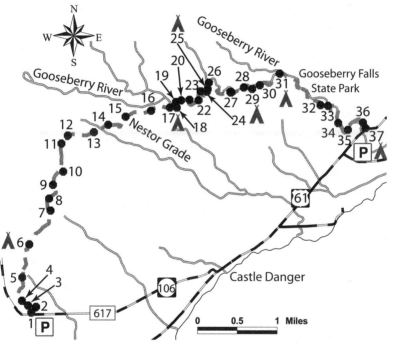

leaves have sprouted about as fast as the dandelions in my backyard, and the forest canopy has become denser and greener. This morning the breeze comes from the southwest, soft and light and filled to all its corners by singing birds. There are chickadees, finches, wrens, flickers, ovenbirds, and other warblers. What a difference sunshine, warmth, and the first bug hatchlings of the spring make.

Two: The Ridge

It's a short hike from the parking lot to the base of a high rock ridge. The ridge is part of the *Silver Creek Diabase* (also see *diabase*), the rock that made the 1400 foot long tunnel at Silver Cliff on Highway 61 an expensive necessity. Dark and ominous in the morning's shadows, the Silver Creek Diabase is *massive* and nondescript which, geologically speaking, makes it about as exciting as reading "War and Peace." What gives this diabase, and other similar rocks along the Superior Hiking Trail, character are the different looks they give hikers as they weather or break apart; there is: "smooth and even," "lumpy," and finally "crumbles" along with crumbles friends "kibbles and bits" (see *diabase weathering*). The *outcrop* here, at the start of the climb to Wolf Rock is–well, I'm letting Judy make up her own mind.

Three: Wolf Rock

The climb to Wolf Rock begins with a steep ascent up the side of the diabase followed by a relatively flat section that ends at what Judy and I call "the diabase staircase." The "staircase" is composed of angular and smooth slabs of Silver Creek Diabase that have been fashioned into makeshift steps. These are supposed to make the short climb to Wolf Rock easier. However, with all the May rain, rivulets of water flow over and around the steps turning them into slippery obstacles; climbing them is like climbing up a greased sheet of plastic.

Even though the climb to the ridge crest offers nice views of Lake Superior, it's Wolf Rock that really provides what we would call the first "wow" spot of the day. Judy and I both find it hard to drag our eyes (and minds) away from the great lake–open, blue, and sparkling all the way to the horizon.

From Wolf Rock it's easy to see Highway 61, the beautiful Crow Creek Valley we hiked into and out of on Monday, and, in the distance, the Silver Cliff Tunnel. Looking at the tunnel, it's easy to follow two high ridges of Silver Creek Diabase inland with the valleys seperating them formed by the Encampment River and Crow Creek. Wolf Rock is also composed of Silver Creek Diabase and represents part of a third and final ridge formed by that intrusive body.

Wolf Rock is just the kind of place to look for to see turkey vultures: a rocky escarpment that causes large updrafts of wind. On this particular morning twelve turkey vultures circle below us, their red, featherless heads constantly move, back and forth like pendulums to windup clocks. They seem to float, nearly perfect in their ability to glide and adjust to the smallest changes in the wind. They circle slowly, around and around, rising, then falling on the swirling currents of air before deciding to follow the wind west toward the Encampment River. No other birds seem to have mastered the art of soaring as have these magnificent scavengers.

Four: Log Bench

Just past Wolf Rock the hiking trail makes a sharp turn to follow the diabase ridge, which now parallels the Crow Creek Valley. There are nice white pines through here and the trail goes over lumpy diabase to waypoint 4, a cut log bench (in memory of Pat Detweiler) from which there is a view similar to that seen from Wolf Rock.

Five: Aspen Circle

After some great views of the Crow Creek Valley, the rocky trail cuts across the diabase to follow the northeastern edge of the ridge. Waypoint 5 is in the center of a circular grove of young aspen trees. These small trees no doubt sprouted at the same time and are most likely all sharing the same root base underground. Their smooth tan to greenish bark contains chlorophyll, aiding in photosynthesis.

Six: Spur Trail to the Crow Creek Valley Campsite

Descending quickly to the bottom of the ridge, the trail becomes relatively flat and wet as it passes through a forest of balsam poplar, maple, spruce, cedar and some yellow birch. A lot of the larger balsam and birch trees have been broken off half-way up due to high winds and disease. The cedars have an understory of alder, willow, and dogwood, all plants that thrive in damp soils. Just before waypoint 6, at the spur trail to the Crow Valley campsite, we come to a small creek and a spur trail that leads to a nice overlook of the Crow Creek Valley. The creek is full of *marsh marigolds*.

Seven: Black Ash Swamp

From waypoint 6 the trail passes through a dense cedar forest followed by a walk through a more mixed forest dominated by maple and birch with some yellow birch and pockets of closely spaced cedar trees.

Waypoint 7 is at the edge of a black ash swamp (right of trail), and this marks the beginning of a long trail section that goes through several different classifications of wetlands, the first being a hiker's all-time favorite–swamp. Generally speaking, a swamp is a wetland with trees. Many trees die when their roots are flooded, while others tolerate having their feet wet for a good part of the year. One of the trees in our region that doesn't mind having wet feet is the black ash, which is abundant along this section of the trail.

Eight: Ephemeral Pond with Black Ash

From waypoint 7 to 8 we walk through an open forest of paper birch and maple with maple becoming dominant just before the waypoint. Waypoint 8 is another wet area where spotted *jewelweed* abounds below black ash. The word ephemeral in this wetland description means the standing water in this pond is here for only a short time, a few weeks to months at most except in an unusually wet year. Soils in these areas tend to be rich and fertile.

In early spring it's hard not to notice tiny, heart-shaped succulent-looking leaves close to the wet ground. These first leaves look nothing like what will be found on the plant later in the summer, when it reaches a height of several feet. Spotted jewelweed has small orange and yellow flowers that give way to a seed pod that gives the plant its other name: "touch-me-not." The pods *can* be touched, in fact, it can be downright fun! This plant spreads its seed by exploding them everywhere!

Nine: Cattail Marsh

Leaving the forested area, the trail follows the western edge of a large cattail marsh. We take some time to look around this type of wetland–cattails along with lots of standing dead trees. Over time the water table has risen (thanks to the beaver?), and the tree roots have been flooded long enough so the trees have died. Now, in the large pockets of standing water, cattails have taken hold, much to the pleasure of two species of animals that make their homes here. Male red-winged blackbirds arrive in spring and stake out their territories in these marshes. A few weeks later they will try to impress the returning females with the real estate they have established. Muskrats make lodges using cattail stems and leaves along with mud from the wetland and survive here year-round.

Ten: Yellow Birch Grove

Heading north from the cattail marsh the trail crosses an outcrop of lumpy diabase, and passes through a muddy, wet section to Waypoint 10, a grove of lovely yellow birch. To the left of the trail the forest is pretty much gone; it has been recently cut and logged.

Eleven: Mike's Rock

As the trail continues north towards Mike's Rock, maple and ash trees give way to paper birch and aspen. There are numerous *pebble, cobble*, and *boulder* covered trail sections. These rocks come from the *glacial till* and in places have been concentrated by weathering with the finer grained material having been washed away. The rocks are dominantly parts of old lava flows with some diabase and pink *monzonite* mixed in.

After crossing a new logging road and walking through a forest dominated by paper birch we make the final climb to Mike's Rock. Mike's rock is at an elevation of 1155 feet. and is composed of lumpy Silver Creek Diabase, which provides great views north and east to the Gooseberry River Valley and Lake Superior. The lumpy weathering of the diabase represents an intermediate step between smooth and old crumbly, and is due to a rock texture referred to as *ophitic*.

Twelve: Bottom of a Steep Hill

Leaving the overlook, the trail heads downhill, gently at first, followed by a

24

final steep descent. The steep section uses what can loosely be called diabase "steps" to help get to the bottom. These are large, angular blocks of rock that go down the side of a diabase outcrop to the bottom of the ridge (waypoint 12). Charlie, my wire-haired dachshund, did not appreciate these. I carried him over one steep section, and he gingerly picked his way down and around the rest of the large blocks.

Thirteen: Alder Thicket

With Charlie safe, sound, and happy we walk along a relatively flat and wet section of trail. This takes us through an aspen forest where some of the larger (40+ year-old) trees have been snapped off at various heights. This is due to a combination of strong winds and disease, such as heart-rot.

A sure sign one is hiking through a wet area is the presence of speckled alder. This shrubby plant has whitish speckles (lenticels) on its bark. These clumps in dense thickets (waypoint 13) are usually clones, sprouting both male and female catkins on the slender branches, the male of which gives the shrub another one of its names-tag alder. This refers to the elongated 'tags' or catkins. The female catkin is cone-like, and many people ask just what kind of tree *is* it with the miniature "pine cones?" But alder shrubs produce alder cones, cedar trees produce cedar cones, and only pine trees make pine cones! Alder needs oxygenated water, and so the swamps they occur in usually have some water flowage. This is the case here. In heading down the wet, muddy trail we come to a small creek which drains from the swamp (lots of marsh marigolds here).

Fourteen: Cinquefoil Carpet

After the creek, the trail passes through a relatively dry aspen forest before entering another alder swamp. At the edge of this swamp, which is waypoint 14, there is yellow or dwarf *cinquefoil*. This plant blooms in early summer and at this spot the ground is carpeted with it! This five-petaled flower spreads by runners and prefers drier soils, and, on this side of the alder swamp, the habitat is definitely much drier.

Fifteen: Nestor Grade

It's pretty much flat and wet all the way to the Nestor Grade. This grassy open road bed is all that remains of one of the short railroad lines built in the late 1800's to get at the white pines that were far from the lake shore and fairly inaccessible. Logs were taken down this rail line to the Gooseberry River where they were dumped into a holding pond, made into "rafts" of logs, and then towed across the lake to Ashland, Wisconsin or to Baraga, Michigan. The record log raft for the entire North Shore came out of here, six million feet of logs towed over to Baraga. It took eight days to get them there. Imagine where they might have floated to if a Lake Superior nor'easter had blown up!

So the white pine went. But not without a fight. Trying to operate a railroad in white pine country was challenging to say the least. Tracks would simply disappear in thawing swamps, locomotives and cars would get lost in the soupy muck, and rails would actually move or slide down the red clay hills when a train was loaded. Imagine that sensation, a Disney ride at its best. However, even with all the problems, these railroads were efficient, and by 1920 there was virtually no large white pine left on the North Shore.

The name "Nestor Grade" has two parts to it. First, Nestor referred to the logging company. They called themselves "Estate of Thomas Nestor" and were a Michigan logging firm that cut white and red pines in this area from 1900 to 1909. Grade refers to the railroad tracks and the degree to which they sloped toward the lake.

Imagine being able to see a whole forest, hillside to hillside, covered by magnificent white pines. Grand trees, immense, so large at the base it would take three of Judy to reach completely around them. Up they would rise, great cloud catchers and, in the shade beneath them, would be soft green mosses, spotted ferns, and the skeletons of fallen branches. Three and four hundred-year old trees of history that are now history themselves.

Sixteen: Marsh and Creek

Crossing the Nestor Grade and several ATV trails, we walk through a mixed forest to a small creek (waypoint 16) which drains an open, grassy marsh that is surrounded by spruce trees.

Seventeen: Spur Trail to the West Gooseberry Campsite

After a fairly long walk along a muddy trail through a mixed forest with some nice, large balsam poplars we cross a small creek before coming to the spur trail leading to the West Gooseberry campsite (waypoint 17). At the spur trail there is a large clump of gooseberries. In fact, gooseberries are prevalent all along the Gooseberry River. These shrubs, which grow up to three feet in height, have pale, palm-shaped green leaves and thin, woody stems covered in thorns. The name "Gooseberry River" began to appear on maps as early as 1670 with the name coming from either the "Anglicized" version of the name of the French explorer Sieur des Groseilliers, or from the translation of the berries Ojibwe name, Shab-on-im-i-kan-i-sibi. The campsite is perched on a small rise that overlooks the river.

Eighteen: Large Slump Area

Don't buy a summer home here, or even route a hiking trail through this area, for this is a place where geology is hard at work. The river bank and hiking trail are actively *slumping* away to slip, slide, and splash into the river. The river has a nice *meander* bend and the outside ot this is where the slumping occurs.

There are relatively recent beaver chewed trees here but no sign of beaver or lodge. This is also a good spot to look for cliff swallows and bank swallows. Black ash continues to be the dominant tree along the river's edge.

Nineteen: Gravel Bars and Lunch

Great lunch spot–sunny, open, *strawberries* in bloom, and the Gooseberry River, pale red in color, slowly flowing by. The color of the water is due to the clay and silt particles it carries. Derived from the red glacial till, these are light enough to be suspended throughout the water column giving the river its reddish color. On the opposite side of the river a bank of glacial till is exposed showing us just how jam-packed the till is with rocks of various sizes.

Upstream from this waypoint there is a slumped bank. This is where the gravel bar we are standing on came from. As the bank is eroded, sand and different sized rocks are rolled and pushed by fast moving water to this spot which, today, represents the inside bend of a meander, the place where water flows the slowest. In the case of this gravel bar, stream velocity was such that the river was actually able to try and size-sort the material it was carrying; sand grains moved the furthest and were mostly deposited at the downstream end of the gravel bar, and cobbles moved the shortest distance being deposited at the upstream end. Later in the summer this will be a good place to look for Michigan Lilies. Year around this is a good place to look for Lake Superior *agates*.

Twenty: Giant Spruce

Following an old river terrace we come to waypoint 20, a giant white spruce, one at least four feet in diameter. Judy doubts she has ever seen a spruce this large or old. It has big, full branches from getting lots of sunlight. Simply put it's beautiful and elegant even to the distinctive scar marking where the tree was struck by lightning.

Twenty-One: Beaver Lodge

Continuing along the river there is another area of active slumping before the trail comes to an old beaver lodge. The lodge is no longer occupied by beaver as it sits high above the waterline. However, it may provide a refuge for an otter or mink.

There are leeks (also known as *wild onions* or ramps) everywhere in this along-the-river section of the trail. They have huge, oblate leaves at this time of year. The leaf's main function is to capture the sun's energy for the bulbs beneath the ground, from where the flower stalk will emerge. The leafless flower stalks have purplish bud heads resembling garden chives, and they usually appear after the leaves have disappeared. When the bud opens, tiny white flowers will be present. And, of course, being an onion, the bulbs are the source of a wonderful, delicious food.

Walking along Judy and I talk about how the Gooseberry River is typical of most North Shore streams. In the lower reaches, most of them are like most of us–in a big rush to get where they are going. In the upper reaches, however, these streams are reflective of another time and age. They are slow, deliberate, meandering: kind of like they're taking their time, investigating the landscape around them, enjoying their trip to the lake. In this way the Gooseberry, up here, is more my kind of river, a river to dream by. Standing here I almost expect Huck Finn and Jim to come drifting around the bend, fishing lines strung out behind a makeshift raft.

Twenty-Two: Ash Trees and Meadow Rue

After the beaver lodge it's a short uphill climb to an old *flood plain*. The trail wanders along this, passing more areas of active undercutting and slumping, before heading back to the river's edge. Waypoint 22 is at an old, hollowed-out ash tree and a large meander in the river.

Ash trees and *early meadow rue* are abundant all along this section of the trail. Rue and its cousin, *tall meadow rue*, are common in bottom land environs of streams and rivers. Both are members of the buttercup family, have whitish or greenish, nondescript flowers, with early meadow rue growing 1-2 feet tall and tall meadow rue 3-8 feet tall.

Twenty-Three: River Pavement and Strawberries

Continuing along the river's edge we pass by the "leaning spruce" and a nicely sorted gravel bar before coming to a wide, flat area composed dominantly of boulders and cobbles. In fact there are so many rocks it is almost like walking on a cobblestone street, and reminds me of something called desert pavement.

Desert pavement may be found in Death Valley or the Kalahari Desert and is composed of a layer of cobbles, boulders, and pebbles that are too large to be moved by the wind. The desert wind blows away the finer material, the silt and sand, and, as it does so, the boulders, cobbles, and pebbles become more and more concentrated until they eventually form an almost uniform surface cover.

The "Gooseberry River pavement" looks like an old river channel. Over the years water flowing over this area removed the silt, clay, and sand leaving behind larger pebbles, boulders, and cobbles it couldn't move. Eventually a river pavement formed, lots of cobbles and boulders forming the surface we are now walking on.

This area is also a good spot to come back to in late June or early July, for strawberry plants are prolific through here. Their small white flowers remind

28

Judy of the first light coating of snow on winter's ground. The other ground-hugging leaves Judy notices in this dry, sunny area are rosettes of reddish-green leaves. These basal leaves are those of *evening primrose* whose life cycle happens over a two-year span. Evening primrose has four gorgeous lemon-colored petals, and its flower stalk may be six feet tall! Like the wild onions, the leaf's job is to store the sun's energy, but in the case of this plant, it takes two years to send up its flower stalk (but then it has a long way to go).

There are two fire rings located here.

Twenty-Four: Oxbows and Swamps

Leaving the river pavement, the trail unexpectedly turns away from the river, bending inland to avoid a large alder swamp. This detour in the trail represents an old *oxbow* or cut-off meander. There are *nodding trilliums* all along here with *wood anemones*, yellow and purple *violets*, and some *bloodroot*.

The trail bends around the oxbow back to the river (waypoint 24), but the river isn't where it should be! According to the topographic map on my Garmin GPS unit, the river "should" be some 160 feet to the north. Instead, we stand right on the bank. The topographic map was made in 1976, so, even with the accuracy of the GPS (currently at only 20 ft.) over those 30 years the river has migrated or meandered some 130 feet to the south. This is really neat because right here we see the power of erosion and how fast a river can change course or migrate, a phenomenal speed on the scale of geological time, but barely perceptible to those who hike along its banks.

Twenty-Five and Twenty-Six: Oxbows, Spring Plants, and the East Gooseberry Campsite

There are more slumps to waypoint 25, the spur trail to the East Gooseberry campsite. There are grape vines growing here, and I am more than surprised when Judy tells me they are a native plant: wild riverbank grapes. This is also a good place to watch for water fowl and shorebirds such as yellowlegs and sandpipers. We also see recent beaver chews but no sign of a lodge or the beavers themselves.

From here the trail continues along the river, turning inland to wind around another alder swamp, another partly filled oxbow. Waypoint 26 is at the other side of the oxbow, back at the river. Arriving there all Judy can say is "holy wow!"

"Holy wow," for the spring flowers are everywhere: *wild ginger*, sessile *bellwort*, *wild onion* (leek), *cow parsnip*, rue*, Mertensia*, *Jack-in-the-pulpit*, wood anemones and bloodroot (with flowers)! Mertensia is the plant with the "nodding" trumpet-like bluish flowers whereas the "wild oats" or sessile bellwort have drooping bell-like yellow flowers. Bloodroot has 8 to 12 white-petaled flowers, and the broken stem oozes reddish-orange "juice," used by the Ojibwe as a dye.

The ash buds are worth an extra loud "wow," for the trees are about to leaf out. Ash trees are slow to turn green in the spring. They are so slow-growing Judy thinks of them as the last to leaf out and the first to drop their leaves in the fall (I think of them as the "ten month dead trees" in my woods back home). But the tiny, inconspicuous flowers are emerging as they do during May and into June. Seeds produced by ashes are winged, with a single seed called a samara. The samaras can be seen hanging in clusters on a good seed year and usually fall by October or November. The seeds typically are dormant until they are two years old and can remain viable for about eight years.

Twenty-Seven: Snowmobile Bridge

Passing more bloodroot and nodding trilliums we follow another oxbow back to the river and waypoint 27, a snowmobile bridge across the Gooseberry River.

Twenty-Eight: The River in Action

Continuing along the river we pass more meanders, more gravel bars, and more beaver sign. After walking by a large cedar tree we come to waypoint 28, a good place to see the river in action. On the opposite side, the red clay and silt that make up the steep bank are being washed away. As this happens, the large boulders embedded in this material, as well as smaller cobbles and pebbles, become less and less secure until, one fine day, they fall, roll, or tumble into the water. The smaller rocks will be moved slowly down stream, but the larger stones, like those now on the edge of the river, remain where they come to rest. Even in a large flood, I doubt those bigger rocks would move further than a frog's hair.

Also, at this waypoint, the change in the river is noticeable. It's becoming straighter, and there is a lot more noise. We can feel its wind–the river breeze as it flows past.

Turns out most rivers have multiple personalities. We think the Gooseberry has three: slow and meandering; faster, straighter, and noisier; and finally roaring and raging as it crashes over rocky falls in its sudden rush to the finish line, Lake Superior.

Twenty-Nine: Split Tree

Following the river, the trail parallels a large, long gravel bar (agates here) and passes the Gooseberry multi-use campsite before coming to yet another area of recent slumping. This particular slump is fascinating because of the split tree: a good size spruce tree with a large crack up the center of its trunk.

The tree is located right on the detachment line of a currently growing slump. Half of the tree wants to stay, and half wants to go and visit Lake Superior. Pretty incredible, for here you can see what is meant by the domino effect. One slump leads to more instability upslope, and this, in turn, leads to another slump, which leads to more instability, and on it goes. So next year there may be half a tree, no tree, or–standing tall and tough–a split tree.

Thirty: State Park Boundary

Just before we reach waypoint 30 we pass a large glacial erratic right at the edge of the river. Did this come from the melting glacial ice or was it eroded by the river out of the glacial till? Waypoint 30 is at the park boundary which coincides with a large cedar tree that is growing almost horizontally over the river. How it hangs on I don't know, but obviously it doesn't want to go. For now life wins out.

Thirty-One: Camping Shelter

The trail follows the river a short distance before turning inland and heading uphill. There is a sign for the new visitor's center (1.8 miles away) before the trail makes a right angle turn to come back to, and again follow, the river to a small, three-sided camping shelter (waypoint 31). The forest in this section is mostly black ash. The cow parsnip is now, in early spring, about 10-15 inches high. Later in the summer these will obscure views of the river as they grow to about six or seven feet tall with leaves over a foot wide.

Thirty-Two: Fenced area
From the camping shelter it's a long walk along a straight section of the river through a black ash forest to a meander bend and more slumping. From here we continue to follow the river with an old flood plain to our right. Climbing up, onto the flood plain we turn inland and pass a swamp full of marsh marigolds before heading uphill to intersect a wide ski/hiking trail. There is a map of the Gooseberry State Park ski/hiking trails here. *Swamp saxifrage* is in the wet areas all along the ski/hiking trail. The plant has big, toothless leaves, small buds, and white, green, or purple flowers. The hiking trail then follows the ski trail passing the "elbow birch" and more bloodroot and Mertensia before coming to a large fenced-in area.

"I guess "deer away" doesn't work," is my comment when I see the fencing.

"Not nearly as well as a 16 foot-high fence" is Judy's. "In walking through the forest this morning I'm sure you noticed the absence of small cedar trees?"

"Of course," I lied. "But there were lots of big old ones."

"Right. The small trees have almost no chance of growing large and old because the deer love to chomp on their tops and branches. This is such a large fenced-in area, it can be used to study how a deer and hare-free forest would grow."

Thirty-Three: Across the Gooseberry

Leaving the "rabbit proof fence," we walk along the ski trail until it splits away from the Superior Hiking Trail. The hiking trail then passes a junction with a park trail to 5th falls, before coming to the bridge across the Gooseberry River.

Standing in the center of the bridge (waypoint 33), looking upstream, a nice meander is visible. There is also a well-exposed contact between red glacial till and a *basalt* lava flow. The contact looks knife-sharp, making it even harder to imagine this thin line represents over a billion years of time! The lava flow is part of the *North Shore Volcanic Group* and is 1.1 billion years old, whereas the glacial till may be all of 10,000 years old. Here the till rests *unconformably* on the glacially abraded and scoured lava flow.

The nice water fall on the downstream side of the bridge is due, not to glaciers, but to the nature of the lava flows themselves (see *Gooseberry waterfalls*). From here there is also a nice view of the balsam, spruce, and cedar lining the river bank and hillside.

Standing here, watching the water rush past, we get the impression the river we have just walked down is smaller and quieter. Here it seems noisier and bigger, though it is essentially the same size. As the advertisement goes, "perception is everything." Upstream the river flows through and over glacial till, leading to slumps, meanders, and river pavement. Here, where it cuts through the till into the underlying bedrock, there are waterfalls, cataracts, rapids, and roaring water. Falls and raging water make this part of the river very popular, much more so than the quiet, meandering upper reaches.

Thirty-Four: Potholes

Crossing the bridge over the Gooseberry River, the trail goes gently downhill following the river, at times along its side and then moving above it. There are several nice views from the trail looking back up the river of lava flows and falls. Waypoint 34 is at the river's edge on a large outcrop of basalt. This *outcrop* is neat because the rock has small to large, circular or bowl-shaped holes in it. Some are such perfect circles they look like some ambitious person has drilled out a series of holes.

Humans had nothing to do with these; the river did it with the help of the sand, pebbles, and cobbles it carries. These holes are called *potholes*, and here they vary in shape from circles to ovals and in size from donuts to wedding cakes.

Thirty-Five: Signs and Bridges

Continuing down the river we pass a nice set of rapids and some large white pines and paper birch before arriving at a sign marking the Superior Hiking Trail route.

I study the sign, then head for the bridge across the Gooseberry. "Where are you going," Judy asks?

"Home."

"Not that way. You just spent two minutes reading this sign and telling me which way we had to go and then you head the wrong way, across the snowmobile bridge."

Feeling stupid all I could think to say was "Following my dog," which would not be a smart thing to do either for he always goes the wrong way!

Thirty-Six: Trail Splits

From waypoint 34 the planked trail descends with the river, which is wider here and full of boulders. There are nice views upriver of tree-lined banks and rocky water. The trail then turns away from the river, crossing two small creeks and a not very attractive power line before coming to a trail junction: the Superior Hiking Trail goes to the left and on to the Split Rock River Wayside, and a park trail continues to follow the river on toward the lake (waypoint 36). There is lots of balsam poplar in this area, a typical tree that is found in wet soils.

Thirty-Seven: Old Visitor's Center

About 50 feet from waypoint 36 is the old park visitor's center (waypoint 37). From here there is a paved trail leading under the highway bridge, passing the upper and middle falls, to the beautiful new visitor's center and, just beyond, the parking lot.

The old visitor's center has cedar shakes on its roof and beautiful red and black rocks for the walls–black *gabbro* from a quarry near Beaver Bay and red granite from a quarry on Kenwood Avenue in Duluth near the College of St. Scholastica. The red sand and clay for the mortar came from Flood Bay, just south of the park. Most of the other structures in the park, except for the new visitor's center, are built with these materials as well. This includes the 300-foot stone concourse we will travel en route to the parking lot. On the way back to the new visitor center it is interesting to stop and read the information on the construction of the park's stone buildings and walls.

Superior Hiking Trail

Walk 3: Bread Loaf Hill and the Split Rock River

Walk Logistics

Start: Gooseberry Falls State Park Visitor's Center

Getting There: The start of walk 3 is just past the old visitor's center on the northeast side of Highway 61. To get there from the parking lot, walk past the new visitor's center and take the trail to "Upper Falls." Cross over the river on the paved pathway, which you follow to the old visitor's center. The hiking trail begins about 50 feet northeast of the old visitor's center.

End: Split Rock River State Wayside

Getting There: The wayside is located 5 miles north of the entrance to Gooseberry Falls State Park. It is on the left hand side of the road just before crossing the Split Rock River.

Walk Distance: 5.2 miles (to spur trail) **Date Walked:** June 1ˢᵗ, 2004

Worth a Longer Look:

Upper Falls: 1
Nelson's Creek: 2
White Pine: 12

Bread Loaf Ridge: 15, 16
Split Rock River: 23
Split Rock Estuary: 24

Waypoint-to-Waypoint

One: Upper Falls, Gooseberry Falls State Park

Thunderous, that's the only way to describe the Gooseberry River on this gray, rainy morning. We can hear the river booming from the parking lot, feel its ground-shaking power as we walk past the new visitor's center; but even that doesn't prepare us for the real thing. Roaring like a lion where three days ago it meowed like a kitten, water filled the gorge. Hurtling over the upper falls, brown and angry, the river literally tore itself apart; foam, spray, and strings of ragged droplets are flung in all directions, each part of, yet separate from, the crazy river. At the bottom of the falls the river manages to gather all these different parts together to form a wall of churning, brown fury that speeds over the lava flows and down the gorge heading for the lake with the same mad determination a bull has when it charges an armed matador.

What a difference three days and 2.5 inches of rain makes–turning a river you can wade across into one that will carry a SUV to the lake like a child

34

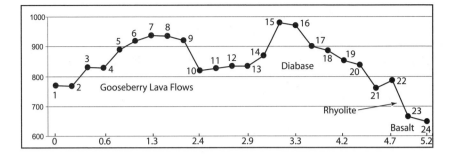

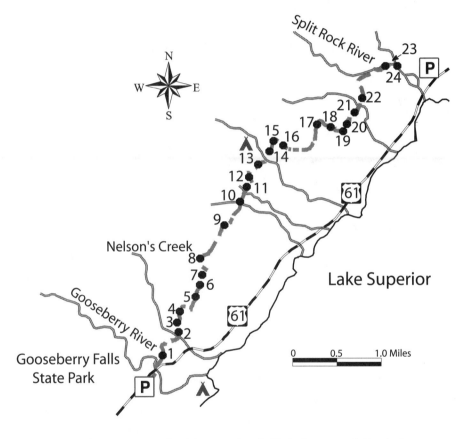

carries a toy boat to a pond. This morning is little improved. Dark dense clouds, the lowest looking like shreds of gray cloth caught on a barbwire fence, dash over us, pushed inland by a cold, relentless wind tuned perfectly to a somber, slate-colored sky. The rain they carry comes and goes, mostly light, horizontal, and stinging.

Judy and I feel and think cold, shivering even though dressed in gortex rain jackets with heavy wool sweaters and long-sleeve shirts beneath. Our two traveling companions, Sammy and Charlie, seem not to notice the rain, wind, or cold. They are off, up the trail, poking in and out of the *horsetails*,

35

wood anemones, dewberries, Mertensia, and *Canadian mayflowers* as well as what could be Minnesota's state flower–dandelions. Embarrassed by their enthusiasm, we think warm and follow their lead.

Two: Nelson's Creek

From the old visitor's center, the hiking trail heads gently uphill following a wide, grassy ski trail that passes under a power line before skirting the edge of a large rocky hill. The hill is composed of *basalt* lava flows that are locally referred to as the Gooseberry Flows, the same that form the many waterfalls in this park. These 1.1 billion-year old lavas also form the prominent road cut just north of the bridge on Highway 61.

The forest is dominated by paper birch, many of which are dead or dying. This appears to be the norm for paper birch trees in northeastern Minnesota. After a junction with a park ski trail, we arrive at Nelson's Creek (waypoint 2). Two branches of the creek merge here, and the new bridge across the creek may be indicative of the creek's power when in flood stage. Now, however, the creek is but a shadow of its former self, for there is a new beaver dam just downstream from the bridge (this was broken in spring of 2006) and what was a vigorous, noisy creek is now a muddy pond.

Wetland plants are abundant along the creek and throughout the adjacent area: *marsh marigold, blue flag iris,* yellow *violet, coltsfoot,* and *ostrich fern* along with alder and ash trees.

Three: Hilltop

Leaving the creek, we continue along the wet, muddy ski trail through an open area with more dead and dying birch, past a small tributary to Nelson's Creek. This is followed by a walk up a gentle slope over a trail composed of *glacial till* to the hilltop, which is waypoint 3. Today, so far, it's been all ski trails, which are better suited for skiing than walking on. Seems like wherever hiking trails follow cross-country ski-trails there is always a certain amount of mud, wetness, and swamp. Enough snow, however, and these trails would be fantastic.

The hilltop is flat and open, mimicking a small plateau, one covered by many dead and dying paper birch. However, here there are also lots of young birch trees coming up, both from seeds and suckering from adult plants.

Four: A Small Creek

After crossing the hilltop "plateau," the trail descends down a gentle slope to a small creek lined by marsh marigolds (waypoint 4). The rain has stopped, at least for the moment, but the wind charges on, cold and biting. Even the birds are affected by it. I'm certain I can hear the ravens calling "cold, cold, cold."

Five: Junction of the Ski Trail with the Superior Hiking Trail

From "cold raven" creek, the trail heads north through an open birch forest, passing junctions with other park ski trails and going through a cedar grove before a final uphill section brings us to, in Judy's words, "finally and thankfully" the junction where the hiking trail leaves the ski trail and once again becomes a real footpath (waypoint 5). There is also a sign at this point telling us we are 4.8 miles from the Split Rock River Wayside.

There are areas in this section where the trail is rock-covered. The rocks are mostly basalt, but there is also some pinkish *rhyolite (Split Rock Rhyolite)* and *monzonite* with dark *diabase* that have weathered out of the glacial till.

Even though many of the birch trees are dead or dying, they continue to support and nurture life. The many small, round holes are homes for small birds; larger holes may house flying squirrels, and downy and hairy woodpeckers are busy as beavers on the sides of the trees. Judy watches a chickadee go into and out of a hole, the size of a half-dollar, in a dead birch tree. The bark of the birch doesn't decay nearly as rapidly as the wood inside, and so it is easily excavated to make a cozy nest.

Six: Canadian Carpet and Start of an Uphill Section

With the Superior Hiking Trail back to "footpath" status, meaning it's narrow, crossed by tree roots, and littered with all sorts and shapes of rocks, head uphill through a forest that contains cedar, balsam poplar, and spruce trees along with the ubiquitous birch and a few white pine. The purple *clematis* is almost open, the *starflowers* have buds, and the *Juneberries* have flowers. Mostly, however, what we walk through is a rich, never-ending sea of green stalks, leaves, shrubs, and ferns. This so-called *Canadian carpet* is typical of northern forests.

Waypoint 6 is at the top of the hill with a nice view to the southwest of the valleys of the Gooseberry River and Nelson's Creek. There is also an outcrop of lichen covered, *massive* basalt (Gooseberry Lava) in the hillside.

Seven: Private Land Sign

The hiking trail follows the hilltop through a forest of spruce, balsam poplar, and birch before heading gently downhill to waypoint 7, a sign noting the trail is about to enter private land. Roughly ten percent of the Superior Hiking Trail goes through private land, and the Superior Hiking Trail Association has worked diligently to ensure on going use through trail easements.

Coltsfoot is common here, as the soil is damp. There are also foot-high broad beech ferns and purple clematis.

Eight: Donated Land Sign

From waypoint 7 to waypoint 8, some 0.4 miles, the trail is mostly muddy and wet with one planked section. This is definitely one of those "just walk and get it over with" sections. The forest is made up of spruce, cedar, birch, and balsam fir trees with some balsam poplar. There is one cedar grove which is dark and foreboding and could be woods right out of "Lord of the Rings;" a good place for Orcs to hide. Judy's comment about this entire section is "Even though there isn't anything that really stands out, I'm still enjoying the forest and just being able to be out here."

When I think about it, the feeling she expresses is true. The wind is enjoying the loud music it brings to the trees, there are constant showers of spray from the tree leaves, the coltsfoot and *springbeauties* are in flower, and all this is set against a sky that looks like folded slate. Standing here, just being is like WOW!

Waypoint 8 is at a memorial sign for Philip P. Economon. According to the sign his family donated 330 acres of land in this area to the DNR in his name. The sign is attached to a birch stump and aging aspen, so we both hope someone considers reposting it before it falls down and is forgotten.

Nine: Moss-Covered Outcrop

We now have a long, easy walk along a drier trail that follows the edge of a high hill through a birch dominated forest with cedar groves and lots of hazel and mountain or moose maple. As we hike along, Judy points out *oak fern*s, *bracken fern* fiddle heads, *naked miterwort* with its small greenish flowers, *Solomon's seal*, and northern white and yellow violets, which are just about done flowering. Her favorite this time of year are the three-parted oak ferns–lime green in color as they emerge. They are the smallest of our three-parted ferns, bracken ferns are the tallest. Waypoint 9 is at a moss-covered *outcrop* (right of the trail) of very fine-grained, massive basalt that is reddish-brown in color (more Gooseberry Lava).

Ten: Marigold Creek

Just past waypoint 9, the hill ends and the hiking trail descends into a low swampy area. It then crosses a small creek and an ATV trail, which marks the start of private property. Here the forest has an "open" feeling and is dominated by paper birch.

Waypoint 10 is on a bridge over a small creek with lots of marsh marigolds and full of cobbles and boulders that have been weathered out of the glacial till. There are also *sessile bellworts,* and *Mertensia* flowering.

Eleven: Angular Float and End of Logged Area

From "Marigold Creek" the trail crosses "Marigold Creek II" and an ATV trail before entering the "split woods." To the west and northwest (left) the forest has been recently logged. From the size of the new birch and aspen trees, Judy thinks it was about ten to fifteen years ago. To the southeast and east of the trail the forest is older, more mature, and mixed.

Though the weather is finally changing for the better, we remain in water world crossing two more creeks. The wind has dropped to a steady moan, and the slate grey sky has given way to puffy white clouds that Judy describes as "warm quilts."

Through this trail section there are lots of *columbine, honeysuckle, pussytoes,* sessile bellwort, *strawberries,* and gooseberries. These plants are expected in the abundant sunshine–so very different than damp forests full of Canadian carpet plants.

Nearing the end of the logged area, and just past a large birch stump, the trail becomes littered with angular pieces of massive and *amygdaloidal* basalt. This is "frost-heaved" material–rocks broken and heaved upward by the freezing and thawing of water that fills in pore spaces and fractures in the rock. This is the subsurface equivalent of *frost wedging* and indicates outcrop is close to the surface.

Waypoint 11 is in a grove of large spruce trees with a sign marking the end of private land.

Twelve: Large White Pines

It's a short hike through a spruce, aspen, and alder forest to waypoint 12, a grove of big, beautiful white pines. Unfortunately, these trees will all too soon be part of history because they have blister rust.

Thirteen: Blueberry Hill Campsite

Leaving the grove of dying white pines the trail is wet and muddy as it passes by a large spruce tree and a nice white pine tree to cross the Blueberry Hill Road to waypoint 13, the spur trail to the Blueberry Hill campsite and Split Rock Creek.

The forest is dominated by birch with white spruce scattered throughout. Juneberries are everywhere and blooming like crazy, and there are lots of SBM's, Judy's term for small brown mushrooms. You can also find orange "witch's" butter in this area.

Fourteen: Split Rock Creek and Large Spruce Trees

Just past the spur trail cross Split Rock Creek, which is flowing fast and furious today. The creek banks and adjacent small *flood plain* are full of *Jack-in-the-pulpit,* sessile bellwort, and *wild ginger,* marsh marigolds, Mertensia, and yellow violets. After the creek, the trail climbs a small hill and passes through a grove of cedars, birch, and large spruce trees to a small creek and waypoint 14.

Fifteen: Top of Bread Loaf Ridge

The trail crosses yet another muddy section before heading uphill. Climbing up a steep, rocky slope through a spruce, birch, and balsam poplar forest, the trail eventually emerges onto a long ridge of solid rock that is referred to as Bread Loaf Ridge. The ridge top (waypoint 15) provides the best views of the day. It's open and clear to the southeast, northeast, and north; after being on low, wet ground most of the day and feeling closed in, this openness seems really expansive. The blueness of the lake, with small white caps moving across its surface, and the wind-driven motion of the green landscape is mesmerizing.

The rock, of which the ridge is made, is fine-grained and massive: nondescript is the best term I can think of and, in my book, this makes it diabase. Since we left the *Sliver Creek Diabase* behind when we entered the Gooseberry River Valley, this is one of its close relatives. It's a *sill*, part of a related group of *gabbro* and diabase intrusions which, as a whole, are referred to as the *Beaver Bay Igneous Complex*. This particular sill forms part of the *Beaver River Diabase*. The only interesting aspects of this rock, and this is grasping for geological straws, are the pink feldspar (*orthoclase*) and *quartz* veins that cut across it.

Sixteen: Lunch on Bread Loaf Ridge

It's a short hike along the ridge to waypoint 16 and lunch. This point not only provides spectacular views (we vote it the "Wow" spot of the day), but it is also heaven for a plant lover. Here there are reindeer and xanthoria lichen, pink and white *wild roses*, pale pink *corydalis*, Juneberries, *cinquefoil, bearberry, sheep sorrel*, and, in Judy's own words "Tons of *Blueberries*. A must-come-back-to spot for later in the summer."

Uphill from here, just before reaching the trees, there is a fire ring made out of blocks of diabase.

Seventeen: Outcrop Along the Edge of a Steep Hillside

After lunch, which I spend admiring the view and Judy spends in amongst the "green stuff" checking out plants, we continue along the diabase ridge.

In walking along, admiring the view, it was a surprise to find a "rock" bridge spanning a small creek. The water is running out from under the vegetation, flowing across the rocks, and over and down the slope. Judy wants to know just how there could be so much water "On Top" of all this rock! There is pink corydalis here.

It is then a long ridge walk to waypoint 17, the place where the "almost" continuous diabase outcrop ends.

Blueberries continue to be abundant and occur with clematis vines. The maple trees are setting seed, while sumac are trying to grow but have been extensively browsed by deer. We wonder how much browsing these plants can sustain before simply giving up.

Eighteen: Lumpy Beaver River Diabase

The trail heads up hill, and as it does there are partial views of the lake through the spruce, balsam, and big-tooth aspen trees. Clematis vines are abundant, and there are a few honeysuckle vines to go with them. Crossing the top of a small knoll the trail heads gently down toward a steep cliff with a row of spruce trees along its edge with white pine along the top. The trail then follows the cliff edge a short distance to an outcrop of lumpy (see *diabase weathering*) Beaver River Diabase (waypoint 18).

The *sarsaparilla* is blooming here, and Judy thinks the flowers, overall, are a bit ahead of others probably because the cliff is south-facing and thus warmer.

Nineteen: State Park Sign

Walking along the hillside we pass several small outcrops of lumpy diabase to arrive at a sign telling us we are now back in Split Rock State Park (waypoint 19).

Twenty: Bottom of the Ridge

Leaving the cliff and state park sign, the trail starts downhill through a birch dominated forest with clumps of mountain maple, "big huge clumps" according to Judy. Naked miterwort is abundant, and Judy points out this plant definitely goes along with the birch forest. Waypoint 20 is at an outcrop of diabase that weathers reddish-brown.

Twenty-One: Fernhenge

Continuing gently downhill over a muddy, wet slope littered with pieces of diabase, the trail passes through a birch forest and crosses another small creek to reach what we call Fernhenge.

This is an area about 20 yards in diameter that is a complete circle of ferns that grow over the grass underneath; there are no other plants and the circle is almost perfect. "Tis the little people," I tell Judy, "so speak softly and kindly or druids on ATV's will come and take you away."

"Go away," she laughs, "you might be contagious."

Twenty-Two: Rhyolite Outcrop

Saying good-bye to Fernhenge, the trail crosses a small stream and passes through a flat, muddy area to another stream with a nice meander and flowering bellwort and marsh marigolds along its banks. The trail then heads up a small hill and through a birch forest, to waypoint 22–an outcrop of rhyolite lava called the *Split Rock Rhyolite*. Just before the outcrop the trail is covered with sharp, angular pieces of frost-heaved rhyolite.

Twenty-Three: Strand Creek, Nice Waterfalls

Continuing down the rhyolite-covered trail it's a 0.5 mile walk to Strand Creek. Waypoint 23 is at the creek and a beautiful waterfall with a nice, deep emerald pool at it's base. In watching the water cascade over the lip of the falls we think of hidden grottos, summer picnics, and quick, refreshing swims. With enough water, a small pool forms behind the falls which, in summer, makes for a nice place to sit beside, dip our feet in, and read a book. The falls are here because a resistant diabase *dike* (part of the Beaver Bay Igneous Complex) has intruded the more easily eroded basalt.

Twenty-Four: Superior Hiking Trail Sign

From the falls its a really short walk to the junction (waypoint 24) between the Superior Hiking Trail, which continues to the left and the 0.5 mile spur trail to the parking lot at the Split Rock River wayside on Highway 61. We take the spur trail. The most noticeable feature of the river as we walk down the trail to the parking lot is the alder-filled *estuary*, or drowned river mouth.

Superior Hiking Trail
Walk 4: Split Rock River Loop

Walk Logistics

Start and End: Split Rock River Wayside

Getting There: The wayside is 2.5 miles south of the Split Rock State Park entrance on the right side of Highway 61. If coming from Two Harbors the wayside is 5 miles north of the entrance to Gooseberry Falls State Park, and on the left just before crossing the Split Rock River.

Walk Distance: 4.6 miles, 5 miles return to parking lot on Highway 61

Date Walked: June 25th, 2004

Worth a Longer Look:

Split Rock River Estuary: 2	Contact Point: 18
Glacial Till: 3	Pinhead Pahoehoe: 19
Aa Lava Flow and Grotto: 5	Pot Holes: 20
Unconformity: 9	Picnic Place: 21
Unloading: 12	Forest Glade: 23
Rose Garden: 13	Lady Slippers: 28
Beehive: 15	Lake View: 29
Two Towers: 16	

Waypoint-to-Waypoint

One: Sign at South Edge of Split Rock River Wayside

It's early morning at the Split Rock River Wayside; a gentle breeze blows in off Lake Superior as we stand by the hiking trail sign watching a large orange ball break free of the horizon to float above the quietness of the blue water. As the ball rises, the ground fog, clinging to the rocky shore and covering the highway in feathery patches, lifts upward like smoke from a dying campfire. In eddies and ragged wisps, the fog rises and is gone, vanishing in the glow of the orange sun. This was a special moment in time, and Judy and I both recognize, somewhat sadly, that the moment and the vanishing mist have much in common.

Two: The Estuary

After leaving the parking lot it's a short walk uphill to a prominent sign offering various explanations for the origin of the name "Split Rock." Unfortunately, there is no mention of the possibility the name refers to the "shingle-like" way the *Split Rock Rhyolite*, which forms the spectacular river

43

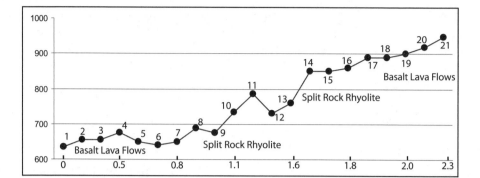

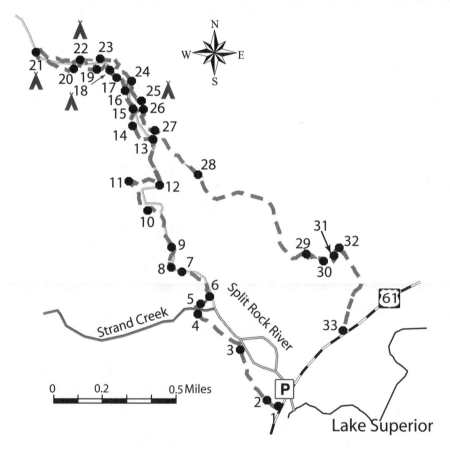

gorge further upstream, breaks or splits apart. From the sign there is a wonderful view of the Split Rock River *estuary*, a great feeding and nesting place for waterfowl and other birds, and for animals who might prey upon their eggs, like mink and otter.

Three: Glacial Till

Leaving the "Split Rock" sign, the wide, graveled spur trail continues uphill offering numerous views of the estuary, before passing an *outcrop* of dark grey *basalt* to reach a nice exposure of *glacial till* that forms the hillside to the left of the trail (waypoint 3). The valley is filled with alder, fir, and cedar. The plants along the trail include *bunchberry, twinflower, strawberry,* and *blue bead lily* (*Clintonia*).

Four: Junction With the Superior Hiking Trail

As it continues uphill, the trail passes through a stand of aspen trees, many of which are missing their upper portions due to a combination of disease (heart rot) and stiff winds. The woods are filled with the lovely pinkish-bluish flower *Mertensia*. It has such a wonderful color for a flower and is so different from the blue bead lily or the white *dewberry*. The trail is partly gravel, courtesy of park personnel, and partly glacial till.

Waypoint 4 is at the junction of the spur trail and the Superior Hiking Trail. The left branch of the Superior Hiking Trail, in about a hundred feet, reaches the top of a beautiful waterfall. When the creek is high enough a small pool forms in the rocky basin behind the falls. This provides a shady place to sit and read or simply watch curtains of water cascade over the falls.

For the Split Rock River Loop take the right branch of the Superior Hiking Trail.

Five: Waterfalls, Grotto, and Aa Lava

From the trail junction we descend a long flight of wooden steps (slippery when wet) to the bridge across Strand Creek (waypoint 5). To the right is a nice grove of cedar trees, and to the left is the waterfall, whose top can be explored just above waypoint 4. From the bridge it is fascinating to watch water tumble some 40 feet over a *diabase* ledge and crash into a rock-surrounded pool. To explore this scenic grotto it's an easy walk up the river bank. Judy thinks "grotto" is the perfect word to describe this spot because "It could be a mini version of some remote South Seas Island waterfall. It's so lush and green–the rocks are filled with mosses, liverworts, and algae and other plants, with so many shades of green I can close my eyes and easily insert a few palm trees into the picture."

There is also a "happy" book here provided by the Superior Hiking Trail Association in which you can record your impression of this special place. Last time I was here the book was completely full, so this is obviously a popular place.

To cap off this spectacular spot there is a section through an *Aa lava flow*. This 1.1 billion year old flow is exposed on the rock wall immediately across the river from the cedar grove. The once rubbly flow top, pieces and/ or angular chunks of *amygdaloidal* and *massive* basalt "stuck" together by more massive basalt, gives way downwards to a dark, fine-grained basalt that represents the flow center.

Waterfall, grotto, rock wall, and cedar grove, all make for a great place to have a picnic, or just sit and enjoy the view and music of the falling water (a blowdown in the fall of 2005 has temporarily made this a somewhat less pretty place).

Six: Split Rock River

It is difficult to leave this idyllic place but, when we do we follow the trail uphill and cross the narrow ridge separating Strand Creek from the Split Rock River. The trail then descends to an outcrop of dark, massive basalt exposed at the river's edge (waypoint 6). The forest remains unchanged with an understory of mountain maple.

Seven: River View

The trail, now composed of glacial till, rises above the river and crosses a small, rocky stream that flows over pieces of amygdaloidal basalt. From here it's a short walk to waypoint 7, an open view up the Split Rock River flowing over reddish-colored Split Rock Rhyolite. There is also a small waterfall and rapids here caused by erosion of the rhyolite along vertical *cooling joints* and horizontal fractures.

Eight: Split Rock Rhyolite and Creeping Cedars

From waypoint 7 it's back to the river and a grove of large cedar trees (waypoint 8) that appear to be having a tough time staying in place. *Creep*, the imperceptible downslope movement of soil under the pull of gravity (measured in fractions of inches a year), is slowly taking the trees to the river. The "snake-like" curve in the lower part of the trunks represents the cedars attempt to offset this motion and grow straight upward.

The outcrop of rock along the river is the Split Rock Rhyolite. Here it has a "knobby" weathered top, numerous criss-crossing fractures, and breaks into angular, and/or "flagstone" like pieces. Growing in amongst the rocks is *sweet cicely*, a favorite flower of Judy's as it smells faintly of licorice.

Nine: Waterfall and a Billion Years of Time

It's a short hike from the "creeping" cedars to a small bench and restful view of the river, rhyolite, and tall white pines. From here we can see prominent, closely spaced horizontal fractures in the rhyolite giving the rock, in Judy's opinion, the look of saucers or pancakes stacked on top of one another. On the ground there is a tiny, easily passed over plant with a tiny greenish flower–*naked miterwort*.

Leaving the bench it's a short hike to waypoint 9, a grand view upriver of a small waterfall which, at the present level of the river, has "lace-like" fingers of frothy water flowing lazily over the slick red rock.

The rock outcrop at waypoint 9 is knobby, fractured Split Rock Rhyolite and, directly across the river, is an *unconformity*, a well-exposed contact between 10,000 year-old glacial till and 1.1 billion year-old rhyolite. A billion years of time and just an inch or two of soil to show for it! We thought about all the comings and goings, all the geological history that thin line represents. There was the coming and going of the dinosaurs, the several different oceans that have covered the Lake Superior Hiking trail, the wooly mammoths and giant beavers who walked along it, and the somber fact that the last tenth-of-an-inch represents most of the history of the human race!

Ten: Flint and More Creeping Cedars

Just past waypoint 9 keep an eye out for a large boulder of a black "glassy-looking" rock embedded in the till composing the trail (tree root growing across it). This is *flint,* a fine-grained, dark variety of *quartz* that was used by Native Americans for arrowheads and tools. Waypoint 10 is in a grove of cedar trees that, like their kin at waypoint 8, are slowly "creeping" downhill. Nice view of the river from here. *Coltsfoot* leaves grow all through this section along with some *wild roses* and *rose-twisted stalk*.

Eleven: Two Bridges and Jack-in-the-Pulpit

The trail, still above and away from the river, crosses two rock-filled creeks (no water in either at this time of the year). There are lots of *Jack-in-the-pulpit* along the banks of the second creek, which is waypoint 11. These are coming up through the *thimbleberry* and *columbine*.

Twelve: Frost Wedging and Unloading

It's back to the river's edge and a series of stone steps that lead to the water, which is waypoint 12. On the opposite side of the river is a large, vertical wall of rhyolite with small fan-shaped piles of rock talus at its base. The *talus* forms due to a process called *frost wedging*.

The top of the rhyolite exhibits closely spaced horizontal fractures that grow wider apart from the top of the "wall" to river level. These horizontal fractures form by a process called *unloading* or *exfoliation*. This process gives the rhyolite its "split rock" look in the upper portions. The forest is dominated by birch, and there are lots of *bunchberry, clematis,* and *pyrola* here.

Thirteen: The Rose Garden

The trail continues along, then climbs above the river with nice river views, before heading back to the water, and a large outcrop of knobby, fractured rhyolite. Here the Split Rock Rhyolite contains small, tabular white feldspar crystals and tiny gas cavities lined with quartz crystals. From the rhyolite outcrop it's a short walk along the river to a nice waterfall and rapids. The rhyolite here has nice cooling joints and a "swirled" look which may represent poorly developed *flow banding*. *Golden Alexander's* grow here.

Head steeply uphill (this section may be rerouted in the future) over rough, broken rhyolite and a set of steep, wooden steps to the top where we literally step into another world. This quieter place (waypoint 13) is dominated by the sight and smell of hundreds of pink and white wild roses that line both sides of the trail. The smell is intoxicating, and the number of blooming roses is amazing. Lots of blue bead lily beneath the roses.

Fourteen: State Park Sign

Leaving "the Rose Garden" the trail heads away from the river but, as we walk along, there are nice views of the steep gorge the river has managed to cut into the fractured and jointed rhyolite. Waypoint 14 is at the "leaving the state park" sign.

Fifteen: Thimbleberries, Glacial Erratics, and the Beehive

Passing through a "forest" of thimbleberries come back to the river where a short path leads down to a large outcrop of knobby, fractured rhyolite and a small waterfall. A large boulder of *Beaver River Diabase*–a *glacial erratic*– sits on top of the rhyolite outcrop. The erratic has probably been in this spot for hundreds of years, simply moving downward as the water slowly eroded and lowered the landscape.

From here the trail heads uphill to an opening (waypoint 15) where there is a nice view of a waterfall and rapids as well as an outcrop that has the shape of a large "beehive." It's a conical mass of fractured rhyolite that has been weathered and eroded along unloading fractures into a beehive shape, this is a small example of the process that forms the "domes" in Yosemite National Park. The "beehive" outcrop is covered by rock talus formed by frost wedging along horizontal fractures.

Sixteen: The Two Towers

From waypoint 15 it's uphill and along the edge of the river to waypoint 16; two 15 foot-high pillars composed of Split Rock Rhyolite. These represent two large columnar cooling joints that also have numerous, closely spaced horizontal (unloading) fractures. To the right of the Two Towers is the back side of the "beehive," which has nice columnar joints. Weathering along some of these joints shows definite signs of one day producing twins to the Two Towers, and illustrates how they formed. There is abundant *polypody* fern here–a six-inch tall fern that grows on rocky places such as this.

Seventeen: "Wow" Spot

Leaving the Two Towers the trail is made up mostly of angular pieces of rhyolite all the way to waypoint 17, a large opening in the forest that provides a spectacular view of a waterfall that has several nice steps that curtains of water cascade over and down. There is also a distinct color change in the rocks from one side of the river to the other. Reddish rhyolite outcrops to the right of the falls, while dark grey basalt outcrops to the left. The river has "split" around this outcrop, with the basalt/rhyolite contact along the far fork, the one with the small *meander*-like bend.

Eighteen: Contact Point

It's a short hike to waypoint 18, an outcrop of dark grey basalt to the left of the trail and, to the right, a path down to the river. This leads to an outcrop of basalt, and a nice view up and down the river. This basalt outcrop is similar to the one seen on the trail, but has been polished smooth and shiny by flowing water. The contact between rhyolite, which you can see across the river, and the basalt is in the middle of the river. The Southwest Split Rock River Campsite is located at this waypoint.

Nineteen: Pinhead and Pahoehoe Basalt

Continuing along the river we come to an outcrop of "pinhead" basalt (waypoint 19). The rock is called this because the dark basalt is speckled with white pinhead-to dime-size *amygdules* that are composed of a fine-grained variety of quartz called *chert*. You can also see small, lath-shaped crystals of *plagioclase feldspar* between the amygdules. This outcrop, with its rolling, billowy upper surface, may represent the top of a *pahoehoe lava* flow.

Twenty: Old Bridge and Potholes

It's not far from the "pinhead" basalt to the site of the old bridge across the Split Rock River. The basalt outcrop in the river is what we call "holey" basalt, a rock full of gas cavities (vesicles) that were once filled in by minerals (most likely *calcite*, chert, and *zeolites*) but these have now been mostly weathered out. There are also beautiful *potholes* in the rock. Some of these are so round they look like someone has spent time here with a rock drill. Some of the potholes contain round and/or oblate, polished rocks that represent, in part, the "drills" that helped make the potholes. One-flowered *wintergreen* and *raspberry* are blooming here.

We both laugh as Sammy slides down a smooth, steep rock face straight into the rushing river. A bit frightened and frantic, she manages to swim to the opposite side and pull herself out. She then sits there for a few minutes giving Judy a very befuddled look.

Twenty-One: New Bridge and Picnic Spot

A thousand feet up the trail from waypoint 20 is the "new" bridge across the Split Rock River (waypoint 21) and the Northwest Split Rock River campsite. Crossing the bridge we hike a few feet upriver to find a lovely picnic spot. Spreading our lunch out over an outcrop of "pinhead" basalt, we

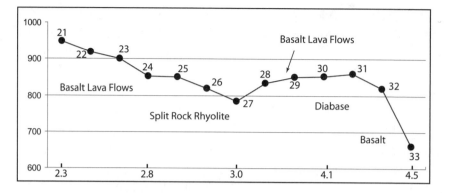

sit amongst wild roses beneath a large white pine watching the river glide by. There are potholes in this outcrop and the "pinheads" are difficult to see because of green lichen growing on them.

Twenty-Two: Northeast Split Rock River Campsite and the Old Bridge

From the bridge the trail heads downriver and downhill passing an amygdaloidal and pothole filled basalt outcrop, before arriving at the site of the old bridge (waypoint 22). This is directly across from waypoint 20. The Northeast Split Rock River campsite is located at this waypoint.

Twenty-Three: Pahoehoe Lava and Forest Glade

Continuing down river we pass another amygdaloidal basalt outcrop. The top surface of the outcrop has "billowy" shapes representing the top of a pahoehoe lava flow. Four hundred feet further on there is a fire ring located in a small opening surrounded by birch and balsam trees. Glacial till is exposed in the bank at the back of the opening, and the outcrop along the river is amygdaloidal basalt. The amygdules vary from pinhead-size to more than two inches in diameter. These are filled by chert, calcite, and zeolites. There are more potholes plus a small waterfall and rapids. The water flowing over the rapids outlines the top to a "billowy" pahoehoe lava flow. The massive basalt seen on the opposite bank represents the base of the flow that overlies the "billowy" lava.

Twenty-Four: Cooling Joint

The trail moves away from the river, crosses a dry creek bed, passes a lot of amanita mushrooms, and continues gently downhill providing nice views of "contact" point and the "split" river which marks the rhyolite/basalt contact. This contact was described at waypoints 17 and 18. Continue downhill crossing a second creek, with rhyolite forming the stream banks, to a large outcrop of rhyolite on the river side of the trail (waypoint 24). This is a large cooling joint, and, given its precarious position, it will soon be river bound! There is also a spectacular, but somewhat scary drop straight to the rushing river some 100 feet below.

Twenty-Five: State Park Sign and Campsite

From waypoint 24 it's a short distance downhill to the Southeast Split Rock River campsite, which is right across the river from the Two Towers. Nice view of the Two Towers and back of the beehive from the campsite. From waypoint 25 continue downward, along and above the river gorge with its rhyolite walls, passing the "beehive" outcrop and crossing a small creek with rhyolite forming the banks and bottom. Waypoint 25 is at a state park sign.

Twenty-Six: Flagstone Rhyolite and White Pine

Not far from waypoint 25 there is a nice view of the river gorge as well as a sharp, steep drop straight to the river. A few feet past this spot is waypoint 26, a great view upriver of the rhyolite-walled gorge. There are nice white pines along the trail and broken "flagstone-like" rhyolite litters the pathway.

Judy makes the observation here that many of the rocky outcrops on this hike have had white pines attached to them. She wonders if this made them too hard to cut and so aided in their preservation during the westward migration of logging early in the last century.

Twenty-Seven: Split Rock Junior and a Talus Slope

We continue to walk downhill along and above the river with great views of the "divided" or "split" river along with a small waterfall, rapids, and pool. We also pass a small "split rock" in the making, one with a balsam fir growing out of the "split." The trail passes by some nice six-sided cooling joints in the Split Rock Rhyolite. Waypoint 27 is at a large talus slope formed by frost wedging. The rhyolite is grayish-green in color due to lichen growth, so it's easy to tell which rocks have been newly turned over by passing critters because the lichens are missing.

Twenty-Eight: Lady Slippers

From the talus slope the trail crosses a small creek and turns inland, passing first through a mixed forest then into one dominated by aspen trees. Waypoint 28 is at the end of a wet section that has cut logs laid over part of it and, along the edges of these and continuing a short distance beyond, are yellow lady slippers (see *orchids*).

Twenty-Nine: Tortured Basalt, Lake View, and Gabbro

The trail continues away from the river heading gently downhill over more "corduroy" or log-covered sections. Just before crossing a small creek with ash trees along it we pass through an area carpeted with Mertensia. From the creek we climb gently upwards to a high, wide opening that affords a great view of the Split Rock River Valley, Lake Superior, and the small bay into which the Split Rock River empties. The rock outcropping in the trail just before the opening looks like knobby, fractured rhyolite, but turns out to be its much darker, similarly weathered and fractured cousin, *Tortured Basalt*.

The rock outcrop at waypoint 29 is Beaver River Diabase. The diabase is smooth and massive and weathers a rusty-brown color. There are nice red and white pines all along this section of the trail as well as some white spruce along the ridge. H*oneysuckle,* columbine, and *wild geranium* are also found along this section.

Thirty: Shelter and White Pines

The trail follows the open ridge with diabase outcrops along it, and white pine add an elegance to the view which remains spectacular. Waypoint 30 is at a shelter that is meant for day use only. The shelter is surrounded by red pine trees.

Thirty-One: Split Rock Lighthouse

Leaving the shelter, the trail is wide and covered with pine needles to waypoint 31, an opening to the northeast that provides a view of the Split Rock Lighthouse and, to the right, Day Hill, a *whaleback* formed by glacial ice.

Thirty-Two: Junction with the Superior Hiking Trail to Beaver Bay

From waypoint 31 it is a short distance to waypoint 32, a trail intersection with the Superior Hiking Trail continuing to the left to Agate Flow Ridge and Beaver Bay, and a spur trail to the right (Split Rock River Loop) that takes us downhill toward the highway.

Thirty-Three: Sign and Highway

Heading down the spur trail, we go by two grassy (at this time of year) ski trails to the left and cross more Beaver River Diabase, and an outcrop of Tortured Basalt with pale-pink *corydalis* and *blue-eyed grass* around it, before reaching the hiking trail sign at Highway 61. From here it's a 0.35 mile walk along a grassy path that parallels the highway, crosses the bridge over the Split Rock River (we stay on the river side of the guard rail), and ends at the wayside parking lot and our vehicle. Another option is to cross the highway, follow the new Gitchi Gami bicycle trail across the new bridge over the river. Doing this gives us the opportunity to stop at the shoreline and "skip" rocks across the water (Judy is much more proficient than I) and cool our feet in icy Lake Superior. We then cross the highway to the parking lot.

Superior Hiking Trail
Walk 5: Agate Flow Ridge

Walk Logistics

Start: Split Rock River State Wayside

Getting There: The wayside is 2.5 miles south of the Split Rock State Park entrance on the right side of Highway 61. If coming from Two Harbors the wayside is 5 miles north of the entrance to Gooseberry Falls State Park, and on the left just before crossing the Split Rock River.

End: Lake County Road 4 (Lax Lake Road)

Getting There: Take Highway 61 to Beaver Bay and just before the bridge across the Beaver River turn left onto Lake County Road 4. The hiking trail parking lot is on the right about 0.8 miles from the junction.

Walk Distance: 9.9 miles (not including the 0.35 mile walk from wayside to start of the hiking trail)

Date Walked: June 4th, 2004

Worth a Longer Look:

Whale Back: 2
Purple Clematis: 5
Pahoehoe Lava Flows: 6
Split Rock Creek: 7
Merrill Grade: 8, 9
Agate Flow Ridge: 11, 12
Orchids: 13
Rough Agates: 14

Bird Droppings Basalt: 15
Jack Pines: 17
White Pines: 20
Anorthosite and Red Pines: 23
Fault Line Creek: 27
Odd Birch: 29
Sawtooth Mountains: 31
Beaver River Valley: 33

Waypoint-to-Waypoint

One: Split Rock River Wayside

A warm cloudy day. In fact it is the warmest morning we have had for walking, and Judy, dressed in shorts, t-shirt, and sandals, is determined to take full advantage of it. I think she's crazy for the warm weather brings bugs, and wearing sandals on the rocky and root-crossed Superior Hiking Trail is asking for bruised, bloody toes! She, on the other hand, claims to have never stubbed a toe. Ha! Of course, being a northern Minnesotan, she is hedging her bets about the weather: in her backpack are a fleece, long pants, raincoat, and shoes. I have no such optimism and am dressed in long pants, hiking boots, and a long-sleeved shirt.

53

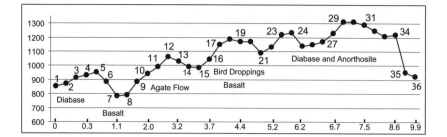

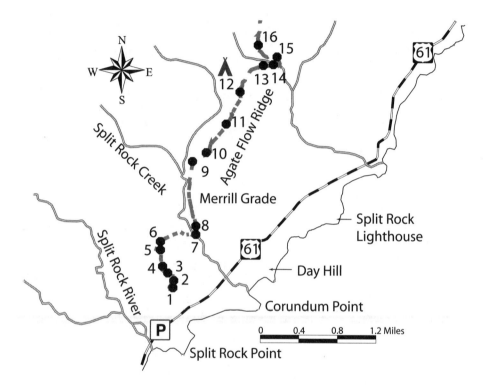

From the Split Rock River wayside it's a noisy, traffic-filled 0.35 mile walk north along Highway 61 (please stay on the river side of the guardrail or use the Gitchie Gami Bike Trail on the other side of the highway) to a sign post for the Superior Hiking Trail, which is located at the start of a spur trail.

Following the spur trail uphill we pass two ski trails that head to the right, and cross one *outcrop* of *Tortured Basalt* and one of *Beaver River Diabase* (also see *diabase*) before reaching the Superior Hiking Trail. The left branch of the trail takes you on the Split Rock River Loop, and on to Gooseberry Falls State Park. The right branch (waypoint 1) goes to *Agate Flow* Ridge and Beaver Bay.

Two: Whalebacks, Song Birds, and Blooms

Leaving waypoint 1, it's a short uphill walk to an open ridge with marvelous views of Split Rock Lighthouse, Day Hill, and the hill above Corundum Point (both to the right of the lighthouse). Both represent geological features called *whalebacks*, tapered, blunt-nosed hills formed by glacial erosion of rocks that are intensely fractured. They are called whalebacks because, in profile, they look like the backs of whales heading out to sea.

The rock exposed along the open ridge is Beaver River Diabase and here, as in most places, it is *massive* and fine-grained. The broken surface of the rock may have a reddish color due to oxidation of iron in the minerals that make up the rock.

We continue along the ridge to waypoint 2, which is just inside the edge of a spruce forest. In walking along the open ridge Judy finds lots of *Juneberries, wood anemones,* red clover, and choke cherries, all of which are in full bloom. The *strawberries* have flowers, the dandelions are puffy white, and the air is filled by the music of the hermit thrush (Judy loves their song), white-throated sparrow, black-capped chickadee, blue jay, song sparrow, and black-throated-green warbler. It's surround sound with a great view.

Three: Beaver River Diabase, Spruce Budworm

Hiking through the spruce forest it's sad to see all the dead and dying trees, their demise due largely to the spruce budworm and its happy helper–the red squirrel. As we walk along Judy points out currants and purplish *hairy rock cress* growing on outcrops of the Beaver River Diabase. The pink and white minerals filling cracks in the diabase are *orthoclase* and *quartz.*

The trail moves back into the open with more great views to the east and northeast before making a right turn to parallel the side of a small valley. After the turn there is a dramatic change in the forest with maple and paper birch replacing the spruce. Descending from the diabase ridge, the trail crosses the valley to waypoint 3, the start of an uphill section.

Four: Top of the Hill

At the hilltop (a large outcrop of diabase) there is a nice view of Lake Superior. A black manganese mineral (pyrolusite) coats cracks in the rock. Birds continue to serenade us, prompting Judy to proclaim this a fantastic day for bird watching. And it is, so much so I have to force her along by pointing out that at the rate we are moving we will also be here to enjoy the sight of the rising moon!

Five: Kibbles, Bits, and Purple Clematis

Continuing along the trail there is a noticeable change in the character of the diabase: massive and fractured to kibbles and bits (see *diabase weathering*). The "kibble and bit" texture indicates the character of the rock has changed from massive to *ophitic.* Views of the lake come and go, and the trail is lined

55

with blooming *yarrow*, *nodding trillium*, and blue *violet*; the purplish hairy rock cress continues to cover the rocks. Turning to follow a steep hillside, the trail arrives at an outcrop of diabase with purple *clematis* growing around it (waypoint 5).

Six: Lava Flows and Amygdaloidal Basalt

Heading downhill the rock material that covers the trail undergoes a dramatic change. The kibbles and bits of diabase give way to flat, angular, and/or "slab-like" pieces of *basalt* lava. After passing a small outcrop of *amygdaloidal* basalt, the rock material on the trail becomes amygdaloidal, then noticeably changes to massive lava, before becoming amygdaloidal again. In going downhill we have walked over the amygdaloidal top of a *pahoehoe* lava flow into the massive base of the next flow, and then up toward its flow top (which is not seen here). In continuing downhill the rock material becomes massive and remains that way to a small creek at the bottom of the hill (waypoint 6). The forest from waypoint 5 to 6 is dominantly paper birch and balsam poplar–hazel and mountain maple dominate the understory. *Mertensia* and clematis are in bloom, and there is abundant *baneberry, coltsfoot, starflower, blue bead lily*, and *Canadian mayflower*.

Seven: Old Poplar Trees and a Flooded Stream

After crossing the creek, the trail is low, wet, and swampy all the way to waypoint 7. This part of the trail is what Judy and I refer to as a "just walk and get it over with section." In doing this we pass by a few large, old-growth poplar trees mixed in with cedar, spruce, paper birch, maple, and ash. The ash trees have yet to leaf-out, so they continue to look dead. Judy figures if they were in my yard I would have cut them down by now!

Crossing two small creeks, with *Dutchman's breeches* flowering along the trail between them, we pass through an alder thicket and cedar grove (lost satellite reception here) to a state park sign and a bridge over "flooding" Split Rock Creek (waypoint 7). The flooding is on the upstream side and is caused by a new beaver dam. With all the alder here these busy beavers have to be happy campers indeed. There is a ski trail to the right of the bridge, while the Superior Hiking Trail continues across it.

Eight: Merrill Grade and Spur Trail to Split Rock

Beyond the bridge the trail is wide and open to waypoint 8, the junction of the Superior Hiking Trail with the "Merrill Grade" railroad bed. There is a sign with historical information on this old logging railroad that the hiking trail will follow for about 0.75 miles. Also, from this point there is a spur trail that goes down to the Split Rock State Park campground.

Nine: On the Merrill Grade

The old railroad bed is lined with large aspen trees, and a few older birch and spruce, making for a pleasant walk; it's almost like walking through an arboretum. These large trees most likely grew in soon after the area was logged for its white pine in the early 1900's. Small *cobbles* and *pebbles* line the side of the rail bed and represent part of the gravel brought in during its construction.

Judy considers the forest here to be "quite rich," for there is abundant *wild ginger*, gooseberries, nodding trillium, *rue, cow parsnip, blue bead lily, Mertensia,* and yellow *violets*–all blooming and tall. The ferns are nearly unfolded from their fiddleheads and help complete the dense greenery that covers the forest floor. All through this section we hear the drumming of a pileated woodpecker. The bird is most likely working on one of the large aspen trees, which make excellent "drums" as well as homebuilding sites. The reason for this is that many aspens have the start of heart rot (aspen fungus) by the age of 40. Waypoint 9 is where the Superior Hiking Trail leaves the Merrill Grade and heads to the right (east).

Ten: Agate Flow Ridge

Heading uphill, past *blueberries*, white *violets*, and a small outcrop of sparsely amygdaloidal basalt, the trail emerges onto a large, flat outcrop that marks the beginning of Agate Flow Ridge (waypoint 10). *Pussytoes* and pale *corydalis* are blooming here.

Eleven: Moss Carpet and Lake Superior Agates

This part of the ridge consists of amygdaloidal basalt that weathers to knobby and/or round and irregular gravel-like pieces. The *amygdules*, which make up 5-20% of the rock, are filled by *chert* (very fine grained quartz) and chert with a variety of color bands (both can be referred to as agates). The amygdules vary from pea-or bean-size up to 2.5 inches in length but are difficult to see due to all the lichen on the rocks. As we walk along we have fun searching through the "gravel" on the trail, for some of it is weathered out *agates*.

Much like the rocks, the forest on the ridge is special. It's dominantly spruce and balsam fir–thick, dark green, and filling the air with a wonderful aroma of fresh pine making Judy think it's Christmas in June with gifts (agates) included.

"So how do you tell a balsam from a spruce, or which kind of Christmas tree will you end up with?" Judy asks me.

"Does it matter?" I said. "They're both pines." This was not only the wrong reply, but meant I had to make up for it by being formally introduced to each of the trees. This included shaking "hands" with Mr. Spruce and Miss Balsam Fir for, as I learned, this is one way to tell them apart. "Balsam,"

Judy explains, "has soft, flat, smooth needles that are easy to grasp unlike the sharp and stiff spruce. It's no wonder Native Americans chose balsam fir boughs for their bedding."

Through this section the pathway varies from solid rock to a soft carpet of green moss. False morels, *bunchberries*, and Canadian mayflowers can be found along the way; reindeer lichen covers the rocks.

Waypoint 11 is a large open area with really nice, large agates and a view of the Split Rock Creek Valley to the west.

Twelve: Black Flies and Jasper Agates

Agate Flow Ridge continues with chert and/or banded chert-filled amygdules making up 5-15% of the lava flow. The balsam-spruce forest remains fragrant and beautiful, and the trail is lined by blooming *wood sorrel* and *bearberry*. Spring azure butterflies are out and about, and Judy finds a sphinx moth that is 2 inches long. In turn the mosquitoes find us, and the first black flies of the year are out. But the bugs are hardly noticeable on this enchanting ridge (unless you're wearing shorts!).

Waypoint 12 is a large outcrop area that's especially notable because it marks the first appearance of *jasper* (red chert) bands in the agates. Also some of the amygdules have hollow centers and edges lined by tiny quartz crystals. These are quite pretty and make a nice contrast to the solid chert amygdules. The amygdules make up 25-40% of the rock giving it a distinct "pock-marked" look. The flow and its agates are weathering to kibble-and bit-like material, so mining the gravel might well pay off!

Thirteen: Meadows and Orchids

From waypoint 12 to 13, outcrops of agate flow come and go, and the trail continues its Christmas tree look with some white pine mixed in. At waypoint 13, there is both jewelry and flowers: beautiful *pink lady slippers* stand out amongst the many shades of green and there is an outcrop of agate flow. From this waypoint we can hear the water in Chapin Creek below us.

Fourteen: Chapin Ridge Campsite and "Rough" Agates

It's a short hike downhill to the spur trail to the Chapin Ridge campsite. The outcrop here is agate flow, and this is a good place to examine the "loose" agates, those weathered out of the lava flow. They are rough, angular, and not at all shiny or polished like those found along Lake Superior's shores. The agates of Agate Flow Ridge have yet to be washed to the lake to be tumbled, smoothed, and polished by Superior's ocean-like waves. The agates here are up to 2 inches in diameter, and some are nicely banded, making this a good "agate picking" spot.

Fifteen: Bird Droppings Basalt, Beaver Pond, and Flooded Valley

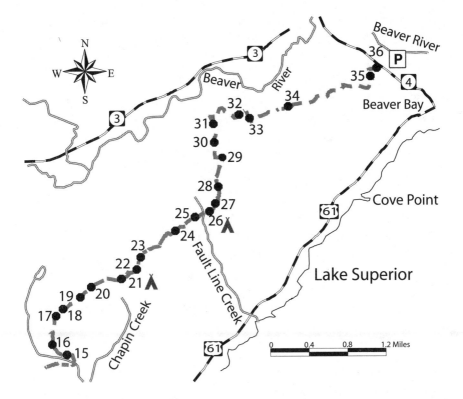

A few feet beyond waypoint 14 there is a dramatic change in the appearance of the basalt lava flow. Crystals of *plagioclase feldspar*, up to an inch long and tabular to lath-shaped, make a sudden and spectacular appearance. They compose 25-40% of the rock. In places, the crystals have been weathered out leaving only lath-like or tabular holes in the lava flow. This new kind of lava flow continues to have agate-filled amygdules–some of these are a pretty blue color. Because the flow reminds me of a basalt lava flow I once saw in a penguin rookery we decide to name it *Bird Droppings Basalt*.

The trail heads downhill to an opening in the forest that provides a dramatic view of a large beaver pond, dam, and beaver lodge in the valley below. There is also a dramatic change in the forest from the "Christmas trees" on the ridge above, to paper birch, aspen, and alder we are now amongst.

Continuing on, we cross "flooded" Chapin Creek and get a close-up view of the beaver dam before the trail crosses a relatively new road/ATV trail then heads uphill over Bird Droppings Basalt to waypoint 15, an open area with a panoramic view back to Agate Flow Ridge and the Christmas tree forest. From here nice white pines are visible in amongst the balsam and spruce on the ridge.

Sixteen: More Christmas Trees

From waypoint 15, we head uphill over more Bird Droppings Basalt with lots of kibble-and bit-size material on the trail. In places this material has been size-sorted by water that runs down the trail during heavy rains.

In heading uphill the forest is again dominated by balsam fir and spruce with some white pine, and this continues to waypoint 16, the hilltop that affords a nice view of the beaver pond, Agate Flow Ridge, and Lake Superior to the east. There is a large outcrop of Bird Droppings Basalt here.

Seventeen: Pegmatite and Jack Pines

On this section of the trail jack pines, along with white pines, make a nice addition to the balsam and spruce forest. The rocks the trail passes over range from Bird Droppings Basalt to massive lava flow material. These lava flows are intruded by small *dikes* of the Beaver River Diabase. At waypoint 17 the trail turns away from the ridge, and at this point there is a *glacial erratic* of *granite pegmatite* (meaning individual crystals are greater than 5 inches in size). The pegmatite is composed of "glassy" quartz along with pink and cream-colored feldspar crystals. As the trail leaves the ridge, the forest changes from balsam and spruce to one dominated by aspen and birch.

Eighteen: White Pine Remains

From the glacial erratic it's a short walk to the start of a large cleared area. This is a strange place. An open, grassy area with dark, rotten tree stumps. "An old white pine cemetery?" Judy asks. Waypoint 18 is beside some of these old stumps. We wonder when they were cut, and were they taken out over the Merrill grade?

Nineteen: Moose Country

From waypoint 18 to 19 the trail passes through a dense second-growth forest. The entire area along here appears to be actively managed as a logging site with recently cut, open areas mixed in amongst sections of larger, older trees. There is abundant hazel and mountain or moose maple in the understory and, with all this moose "browse" about, there is also abundant evidence of the real McCoy. Moose tracks and poop are everywhere, though with two dogs it's unlikely we will ever see a moose. Waypoint 19 is at a small clearing with white pine.

Twenty: White Pines

Leaving "moose heaven," the trail passes into an old-growth forest with large white pine and sugar maple to waypoint 20, a small outcrop of agate flow.

Twenty-One: Beaver Dam and Beaver Pond Campsite

The old-growth forest continues to the "attached" twin white pines. We then head downhill into woods dominated by balsam poplar and paper birch with some maple. Now flat, the trail crosses three small creeks and an old beaver dam. The pond behind the beaver dam is largely dried up. From this spot we count five separate dams and two beaver lodges (one old and one new), and Judy believes the clear cut area on the opposite side of the pond is the work of beavers.

From the dam the trail continues along the edge of the pond to waypoint 21, the spur trail to the Beaver Pond campsite. It's a short hike to the campsite, which is located right next to the pond. This is one of those "not in my lifetime" campsites, a low, buggy place where Judy manages to find three wood ticks!

Twenty-Two: Anorthosite Knob

Past the spur trail the hiking trail crosses an outcrop of diabase and passes over a wooden bridge spanning an old railroad bed before heading uphill to a rock knob that is waypoint 22. The hill begins in Beaver River Diabase, but the knob is composed of *anorthosite* with the contact between the two just below the rock knob. The anorthosite appears to be a miniature version of the roads in Duluth at winter's end; it's full of pits, holes, and cracks, places the plagioclase feldspar has weathered out. From the knob there is a nice view of Lake Superior, and the hilly terrain to the northeast and southeast.

Twenty-Three: Red Pines

We continue uphill over the anorthosite to the top, which is covered by red pine trees. The anorthosite at the top of the hill is more massive and finer-grained than that at waypoint 22. Waypoint 23 is the start of a downhill section .

Twenty-Four: More Anorthosite and More Red Pine

It's downhill, through a mixed forest, before walking up over diabase outcrops, to another knob of anorthosite which is weathering to pea-size gravel. From this outcrop we continue downhill, through a birch-dominated forest that, with balsam and spruce, hems the trail in on both sides. We go up and down over diabase to waypoint 24, a large red pine tree at a small anorthosite outcrop.

Twenty-Five: Bowling Ball Anorthosite and Talus

Hiking up and over the Bowling Ball Anorthosite (this smooth, round weathering shape is characteristic of anorthosite all along the hiking trail), we pass alongside an anorthosite outcrop shaped like a small whale (all we need is a painted eye), before crossing an outcrop of diabase to enter a low, wet, muddy area dominated by *thimbleberries*. The trail then heads uphill, over more diabase, before descending steeply to a small brook, which is waypoint 25. Across the stream there is a high cliff of diabase with a large pile of *frost-wedged talus* at its base.

Twenty-Six: Fault Line Creek Campsite and Giant Beaver

The trail follows the edge of the creek and eventually crosses it to bend around the base of the cliff, boulders from which now form part of the trail. Waypoint 26 is at the spur trail to the Fault Line Creek campsite with a diabase outcrop to the right. The campsite is on the shore of a small beaver pond of which there are several here. The beaver that once lived in these ponds may well have been "giant" beaver, for they sure cut down some very large trees! There is Mertensia, blue bead lily, and Canadian mayflower all through here.

Twenty-Seven: Fault Line Creek and Beaver Dams

It's a short hike to Fault Line Creek, which, on the down stream side, has a beaver dam across it. Upstream there is a large pond, which is held in place by yet another dam. From Fault Line Creek the trail goes gently uphill, then descends back to the pond and waypoint 27, which is directly across the pond from a large beaver lodge.

Twenty-Eight: Fault or Contact Line Ridge

The trail curves around the beaver pond, crosses a rough, jagged pile of diabase talus, before heading uphill, over diabase outcrops, along with cobbles and pebbles of anorthosite and basalt, to the top which is waypoint 28. From this spot there is a nice view of the beaver pond and a steep talus slope. The valley floor is some 200 feet below us.

This hilltop marks the start of what has been named Fault Line Ridge, which the trail now follows for 0.8 miles. A geological *fault* is a break or rupture in the earth's crust along which there has been displacement of one side relative to the other. It's not clear whether the edge of this ridge actually represents such a break, or simply marks an intrusive contact between the diabase and more easily eroded basalt lava. Faults, as well as contacts, are typically zones of weakness and thus tend to form depressions that are occupied by lakes, ponds, or wetlands; these tend to be aligned along the surface trace of the fault or contact.

Twenty-Nine: Odd Birch and Cove Point Lodge Spur Trail

Walking along Fault Line Ridge there are numerous overlooks of the beaver pond, beaver lodge, and some rather odd-looking paper birch trees. These have been so severely bent and tilted, they lean precariously over the pond. This bowed shape may be due to the dual effect of the weight of heavy snow and/or ice, and the downhill *creep* of the hillside. The trail passes through a grove of red pines, with views across the valley, to arrive at a large pile of diabase talus, and the junction with the Cove Point Lodge spur trail (waypoint 29).

Thirty: Mile Post 7 Tailings and Wintergreen

The Superior Hiking Trail continues to the left, going over diabase talus before heading uphill to yet another overlook into the beaver flooded valley. Lake Superior can be seen in the distance, and *wintergreen* and blueberries grow in profusion around a small diabase outcrop. From here we follow a rocky diabase trail, passing numerous red pines, to waypoint 30, a great view of the Beaver River Valley, and the Milepost 7 tailings pond. The milky-looking pond is the place where the tailings, fine waste material (mainly iron silicate minerals and chert) from the *taconite* process, is stored. The tailings used to be dumped into Lake Superior, but fears of contaminating the drinking water of Duluth and other cities, mainly from asbestosform iron silicate minerals, led to a landmark court case and the end of dumping into the lake. This lawsuit was the start of an environmental movement that culminated in the passage of the Clean Water Act.

Thirty-One: The Wind

We continue along the edge of Fault Line Ridge, which has a steep drop-off into the valley to the west. The ridge is composed of diabase that has nice six-sided *cooling joints*; there are piles of frost-wedged talus at the cliff base. Waypoint 31 is where the trail turns to the right. There is a signpost here letting us know we are 2.5 miles from Beaver Bay.

The wind in the red pines is making a low, muted sound, one that blends well with the soft crunch of pine needles underfoot. The gentleness and wilderness-like quality of these sounds is rudely broken by the whistle of an iron ore train as it rounds a bend on the tracks below us.

Thirty-Two: Mosquito Creek and Cinnamon Ferns

The trail winds across the ridge through a mixed "scrubby" upland forest with a sharp turn to the southeast before crossing a creek blessed with tons of mosquitoes and cinnamon ferns. From here it's gently uphill over lots of loose rock and diabase outcrops to waypoint 32, another outcrop of anorthosite.

Thirty-Three: Dark Green Landscape and the 1870 Forest

From the anorthosite we head downhill, crossing a small creek from which we can hear the low, muted rumble of the Glen Avon waterfalls on the Beaver River about 0.5 miles to the north. Blue bead lily is blooming along the creek, and there are some nice paper birch trees here. After crossing the creek, the trail is relatively flat to waypoint 33, yet one more anorthosite outcrop that provides nice views of the Beaver River Valley. From this spot we look out over a dark green landscape composed of spruce, fir, and cedar. This makes a nice contrast to the more typical birch-aspen second-growth forest. This is a good place to imagine what the forest might have looked like in 1870 with its towering white pines, huge spruce trees, and gigantic cedars.

Thirty-Four: West Loop to Cove Point Lodge

Twisting and turning, the trail follows the edge of the diabase ridge, lined with red pine and offering views into the river valley and of the Beaver River. We can also see Lax Lake Road and the red topped water towers in Silver Bay. The forest along the ridge is paper birch, spruce, balsam fir, and maple, and the trail is relatively flat to waypoint 34, the western loop of the spur trail to Cove Point Lodge

Thirty-Five: Spruce, White Pines, and Cedar

The trail now includes gentle ups and downs through a paper birch and maple forest with a few large spruce, balsam fir, and ash trees. After following a long diabase outcrop, the trail starts gently downhill, passing through a wet, swampy area, and a mixed forest with some nice spruce trees. An outcrop of Bowling Ball Anorthosite is located in a grove of cedar trees (waypoint 35). There is a weird paper birch here, one with "long legs" that straddle an old stump.

Thirty-Six: Ash Trees and the Trailhead

Staying in the cedar grove, the trail passes back into diabase and crosses a small creek lined by black ash trees. This is followed by a long section of newly boardwalked trail to the highway (Lake County Road 4) and parking lot.

Judy and I are both glad to be done, but the dogs are even more so. They are not used to this kind of humidity or heat, and both are tired, hot, and wanting nothing more than to curl up and go to sleep.

This walk abounds with interesting rocks, flowers, old-growth trees, and scenic views along with a dash or two of history. It's a long walk (about 10 miles total), but with an early start on a nice day well worth the time. The photographs taken and the agates collected will provide great memories of this section for years to come.

Superior Hiking Trail
Walk 6: Cove Point Loop

Walk Logistics

Start and End: Cove Point Lodge Parking Lot

Getting There: Highway 61 to Beaver Bay. As you enter the town look for two large white deck chairs on right. These mark the entrance to the lodge. Follow road to parking lot.

Walk Distance: 5.3 miles   **Date Walked:** June 11th, 2004

Worth a Longer Look:

Waterfall and Green Garden: 2   Beaver River Valley: 14
Cove Point Gabbro: 2, 3, 4   Odd Birch: 15
Picturesque Creek: 4   Orchids: 17
Wild Flowers: 6   Grotto: 20

Waypoint-to-Waypoint

One: Cove Point Lodge and Spur Trail Sign

Driving down the road to the Cove Point Lodge I wonder if I am a Lilliputian about to enter Gulliver's world. The entrance to the lodge greets visitors with two extremely large white Adirondack chairs. They are so large that the Jolly Green Giant could occupy one and Paul Bunyan the other.

Today is another one of those iffy days: grey sky, cold wind blowing in off a lake festooned with white caps, and rain threatening. Judy wants to know if the April-like weather will ever end! So hi ho, off once again we go, but at least we can expect it not to snow!

From the parking lot walk up the lodge road to the spur trail sign for the Superior Hiking Trail, which is waypoint 1.

Two: Cove Point Gabbro and a Waterfall

It's a short uphill walk along a small, unnamed stream to a nice waterfall. The waterfall and stream, with its rocky course and all the green plants along it, is a picture-perfect, garden-like place and probably a favorite with lodge guests.

The rock exposed in the trail marks waypoint 2. It's a medium-grained, reddish-brown *gabbro* made up of dark, elongate *pyroxene* and grey weathering *plagioclase feldspar*. On a fresh surface the pyroxene may exhibit a pronounced parallel alignment of crystals. With no official name

Walk 6

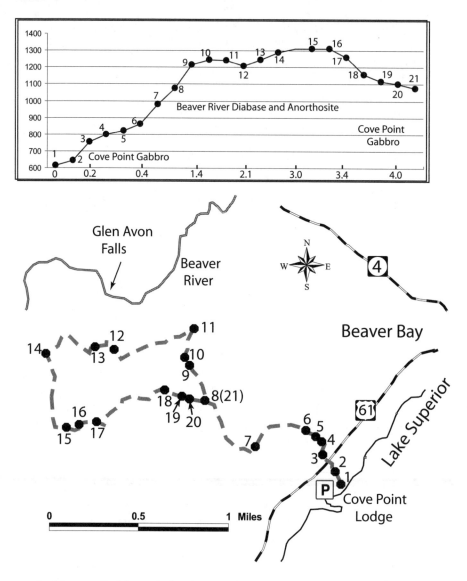

we decide to call this rock the Cove Point Gabbro. It forms part of the *Beaver Bay Igneous Complex.*

Vegetation is kept low in this area due to the power line, but that doesn't stop the *strawberries* and *wood anemones* from blooming. Common buckthorn is abundant through here.

Three: Gitchi Gami Bike Trail

Continuing uphill there is more Cove Point Gabbro before crossing the Gitchie Gami Bike Trail and Highway 61. There is a large *outcrop* of Cove Point Gabbro along the edge of the highway. On a weathered surface the gray feldspar is obvious, but on the fresh surface the rock is dark looking

66

with the plagioclase a dark gray. From the highway we head up a gravel road to waypoint 3, the spur trail that leads to the Superior Hiking Trail (to the right). Elderberry is blooming all along here.

Four: Trilliums

The trail is level and grassy as it passes through an alder thicket and young aspen forest to again follow the edge of the small stream that flowed past waypoint 2. Nodding *trilliums* are large and pretty and are joined by *clematis*, *Canadian mayflower*, and more buckthorn.

Passing a small waterfall we continue to the stream crossing, which is waypoint 4. The stream continues to be picturesque with its crystal clear water gliding and bubbling over and around large *boulders* and outcrops of Cove Point Gabbro.

Five: Mink Farm and Traps

It's a short, uphill walk along the opposite side of the stream past some nice size birch trees to an old clearing with mink traps stacked along side of the trail (waypoint 5). This, once upon a time, was the location of a mink farm.

Six: Cell Phone Road and Wildflowers

Another short walk along the stream to another crossing. Cove Point Gabbro outcrops in the creek bed and along the trail. There is lots of *tansy* growing in the open areas. On the opposite side of the creek the trail heads gently uphill to a wide gravel road (waypoint 6), which eventually leads to a cell phone tower.

Judy thinks this section would be a good place to see a lot of different wildflowers in the early spring such as large flowered *bellwort*, *wood anemone*, *Mertensia*, trilliums and *violets*, . The plants are now knee-high, which means way over Charlie's head, but the *starflowers* can be seen amongst the sea of green.

Seven: Road Walk and Twinflowers

The walk uphill along the gravel road is 0.3 miles. Along this stretch we cross four creeks and several outcrops of Cove Point Gabbro before reaching the Superior Hiking Trail spur at waypoint 7. Other than the gabbroic rocks we see *twinflower*, *honeysuckle*, *blueberries,* and *bunchberries* blooming.

Eight: Cove Point Loop Junction

The trail goes over and along rusty weathering Cove Point Gabbro then through a balsam fir-spruce forest with some red pine and large, nice white pine, which soon gives way to an ash-alder swamp. From the swamp we walk up a gentle slope through a birch-aspen forest with a lot of dead and dying birch trees. *Columbine,* gooseberries, cream vetch, yellow and purple violets, *dewberries*, and *baneberries* are blooming all through this trail

67

section, and wood anemone, Mertensia, and large flowered bellwort would be abundant in the early spring.

Walk over a fine-grained diabase *dike* (*Beaver River Diabase*), and cross a small creek. The wild ginger still has lots of flowers, *rose-twisted stalk* is in bloom, but the bellwort is finished blooming and the *marsh marigolds* are long gone. After crossing the creek, it's up a gentle slope through a thick mixed forest with *blue bead lily* in full bloom. It's then an easy walk to the "Y" junction for the east and west branches of the Cove Point Trail. This is waypoint 8.

Nine: East Branch, Rock Contacts, Lost Gardens, and Toilet Paper Aster

Taking the east loop (right fork) we head uphill though the pathway is now more like the Superior Hiking Trail proper, crossed by tree roots, rocky, and, in places, muddy. The forest is dominated by paper birch with a moose maple and hazel understory. The large leaved *aster* is "toilet paper" size as are the *thimbleberry* leaves.

The trail gets much steeper as it passes over outcrops of Beaver River Diabase. With the diabase exposed here it means the trail has passed over the contact between the Cove Point Gabbro and this finer-grained rock, which is one of the more common rock types found along the length of the hiking trail. Here the diabase can be described as "lumpy" (see *diabase weathering*).

We continue uphill over and along lumpy diabase, crossing an ATV trail in a short, relatively flat section before continuing steeply uphill over more "lumpy" diabase to the hilltop (waypoint 9) and the reward for the climb: a nice view of Lake Superior with the Wisconsin shore in the distance. Closer is the cell phone tower on Cell Phone Road.

Judy, rather sadly, informs me that the "garden" effect we have experienced for the past couple of weeks on the trail is near an end. The *Juneberries* have consistently lined the trail and surrounded the rock outcrops in sunny open places. With their abundant, drooping clusters of white flowers, they have given the trail the pleasant aspect of walking through a "natural" garden but now they appear to be done flowering, and so the natural gardens of the northwoods will be gone until next season.

Ten: In About An Hour

Continue gently uphill over lumpy diabase, which is now joined by its friends, kibbles and bits. This "dog food" size material covers the trail to waypoint 10, where there is a nice view to the west and northwest into a steep valley (no name) and, above this, a large ridge of Beaver River Diabase which, with easy walking, we will be on top of in about one hour.

Eleven: Superior Hiking Trail and Blueberries

It's a gentle up and down walk over Beaver River Diabase through a spruce, balsam fir, and white pine forest with occasional openings that give views to the west and northwest. The trail then levels out over smooth diabase with a final short, steep descent to the main branch of the Superior Hiking Trail, which is waypoint 11. There are oodles of blueberries through this section.

Twelve: Dark Green Landscape, Anorthosite, and Fault Line Ridge

At the junction we take the left branch of the Superior Hiking Trail. The trail is relatively flat through here as it twists and turns through a birch-balsam fir forest passing outcrops of Beaver River Diabase. There is one uphill section over boulders and *cobbles* of *glacial till* before the trail turns to follow the edge of a diabase ridge. The ridge is lined with red pine and offers nice views into the Beaver River Valley to Waypoint 12, an outcrop of *anorthosite*. From the anorthosite we look out over a dark green landscape composed of spruce, balsam fir, and cedar. This makes a nice contrast to the more typical birch-aspen second-growth forest. This is a good place to imagine what the forest might have looked like in 1870 with its towering white pines, huge spruce trees, and gigantic cedars.

The anorthosite is a *xenolith* or inclusion in the Beaver River Diabase; the rock that forms this ridge. The ridge has been called Fault Line Ridge. In geology a *fault* is a break or rupture in the earth's crust along which there has been displacement of one side relative to the other. It's not clear whether the edge of this ridge actually represents such a break, or simply marks an intrusive contact between the diabase and more easily eroded basalt lava. Faults, as well as contacts, are typically zones of weakness and thus tend to form depressions that are occupied by lakes, ponds, or wetlands; these tend to be aligned along the surface trace of the fault or contact.

Thirteen: Glen Avon Waterfall and Blue Bead Lily

The trail is relatively flat to a small stream from which we can hear the low, muted rumble of the Glen Avon waterfalls on the Beaver River about 0.5 miles to the north. Blue bead lily is blooming along the creek, and there are some nice paper birch trees here. After crossing the creek it's uphill to waypoint 13, another outcrop of the relatively rare and unusual rock anorthosite.

Fourteen: Red Pines, Milepost 7, and the Wind

From the anorthosite we head gently downslope, over lots of loose rock, to a small stream blessed with a ton of biting mosquitoes and lined with cinnamon ferns. After crossing the stream the trail winds across Fault Line Ridge passing through a mixed, scrubby, upland forest as it goes gently up and down over outcrops of Beaver River Diabase to waypoint 14, a signpost letting us know we are 2.5 miles from Beaver Bay.

Waypoint 14 is in a lovely grove of red pines located at the edge of a steep cliff with frost-wedged talus at its base.

The opening provides a great view of the Beaver River Valley and the Milepost 7 tailings pond. The milky-looking pond is the place where the tailings, fine waste material (mainly iron silicate minerals and chert) from the *taconite* process, is stored. The tailings used to be dumped into Lake Superior, but fears of contaminating the drinking water of Duluth and other cities, mainly from asbestiform iron silicate minerals, led to a landmark court case and the end of dumping into the lake. This lawsuit was the start of an environmental movement that culminated in the passage of the Clean Water Act.

Fifteen: Odd Birch, Wintergreen, and the Cove Point Lodge Loop Trail

Continue along the edge of Fault Line Ridge, which has a steep drop-off into the Beaver River Valley to the west. The ridge is composed of diabase that has nice six-sided *cooling joints;* there are piles of frost-wedged talus at the cliff base. The trail continues along the rocky ridge, passing over numerous diabase outcrops with one steep downhill section before coming to an overlook at a small diabase outcrop that has *wintergreen* and blueberries growing around it. The overlook gives us a nice view into a beaver flooded valley with some rather odd-looking paper birch trees. These have been so severely bent and tilted, they lean precariously over the pond. This bowed shape may be due to the dual effect of the weight of heavy snow and/or ice, and the downhill *creep* of the hillside. Lake Superior can be seen in the distance.

From the overlook it's downhill, over diabase talus, to the junction with the Cove Point loop trail. This is waypoint 15.

Sixteen: Diabase Talus

Take the Cove Point Trail (to the left) which winds along the edge of a boulder field of smooth and lumpy weathering diabase that represents an old talus deposit. There is a short uphill section over diabase before a walk along a ridge of rusty weathering, smooth and lumpy diabase. The trail then turns away from the ridge passing through a mixed forest to waypoint 16, an outcrop of lumpy diabase.

Seventeen: Chiseled Joints and Orchids

The trail is relatively level as it winds over lumpy diabase that exhibits nice six-sided cooling joints. These cooling joints look like someone has come along and hand-chiseled them. There is a lot of new growth on the *clubmosses.*

Remaining level as it continues over lumpy diabase the trail winds its way through a forest of balsam fir, birch, and maple. At waypoint 17 Judy finds spotted and northern coralroot *orchids* growing along the trail.

Eighteen: Creek and Boulder Steps

Continuing gently up and down over smooth to lumpy diabase the trail passes through a forest with abundant oak trees. It's then gently downhill, with flatter sections, through a birch, spruce, balsam fir, and maple forest; there are some really nice birch trees just before a small creek. The understory is moose maple and hazel.

The trail flattens out as it reaches the creek, which is waypoint 18. The creek is full of *basalt* and gabbro boulders, and pieces of this material have been used as steps to help walkers climb up and out of the creek.

Though it is rather late in the walk, Judy officially names the white flower for today's walk: it's the starflower. Trilliums would have won, she says, except they do too good a job hiding themselves. Third place goes to Canadian mayflowers or false lily of the valley. Their three-parted white flowers hide under an umbrella of leaves.

Nineteen: Glacial Erratics and the Murmuring Brook

We follow the creek downhill over a bouldery surface, possibly an old stream channel. The lumpy diabase boulders come from the hillside to the left. The trail passes through a birch-maple forest (one birch has mistletoe growing on it) to a large glacial erratic of Cove Point Gabbro at waypoint 19; the erratic is in the stream bed. There are also lots of boulders of grey *granite* and pink *monzonite*, basalt, and diabase. The creek at this point is definitely a murmuring brook. There are lots of wildflowers through this section in early to late spring.

Twenty: Grotto and Cove Point Gabbro

The trail parallels the creek to an outcrop of Cove Point Gabbro. Here the creek flows smoothly over the slime-covered rock (waypoint 20) before descending into a small grotto, one that is definitely elf-size. Just past here it's downhill as the creek flows over several small ledges of gabbro through this mini-canyon.

Twenty-One (Eight): Junction with the East Branch of the Cove Point Trail

Turning away from the creek we walk through a birch-aspen forest to waypoint 21, which is the same as waypoint 8, the junction between the east and west branches of the Cove Point Trail. After that it is a leisurely walk back to the parking lot and/or the lodge. Overall this is a nice, easy walk with lots of nice views and interesting flowers and rocks to see and explore.

Superior Hiking Trail
Walk 7: Beaver River, Blueberry Ridge, and the Agate Flow

Walk Logistics

Start: Lake County Road 4 (Lax Lake Road)

Getting There: Take Highway 61 to Beaver Bay and just before the bridge that crosses the Beaver River turn right onto Lake County Road 4. The hiking trail parking lot is on the right about 0.8 miles from the junction.

End: Lake County Road 5 (Penn Boulevard and Outer Loop Road)

Getting There: There are two ways to reach this parking lot:
1) Take the Lax Lake Road (Lake County Road 4) to Lake County Road 5 (Penn Boulevard). Travel toward Silver Bay and the large parking lot is on the left about 1.3 miles from the junction of county roads 4 and 5.

2) Take Highway 61 to Silver Bay. Turn left at the traffic light onto Penn Boulevard (Outer Drive), pass the Visitors Center, old High School, and the sign for Mariner Mountain to the parking lot on the right (this is about 2.4 miles past the Highway 61 and Penn Boulevard Junction).

Walk Distance: 4.7 miles   **Dates Walked:** June 5th, 2004, April 26th, 2005

Worth a Longer Look:

Orchids: 2	Anorthosite and Lake Superior: 12
River Campsite: 4	Beaver Pond: 17
Cliffs and Rapids: 5	Blueberry Ridge: 18
Potholes: 7	Bird Droppings Basalt: 20
White Pines: 11	Agate Gravel: 21
Sulheims Lookout: 12	Different Flows: 22

Waypoint-to-Waypoint

One: Parking Lot on Lake County Road 4 (Lax Lake Road)

What a difference a day makes. The first time Judy and I walked this section it was cold, bone-chilling cold for the 5th of June. The temperature was 47 degrees with rain falling steadily out of a lead grey sky. The second time was on April 26th the following year, and it was sunny and 60 degrees–a glorious day for a really nice walk.

Two: Orchids and the Beaver River

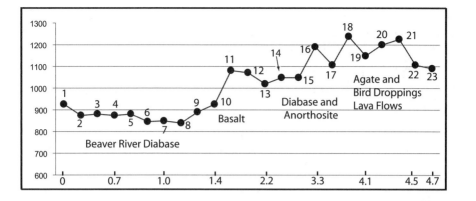

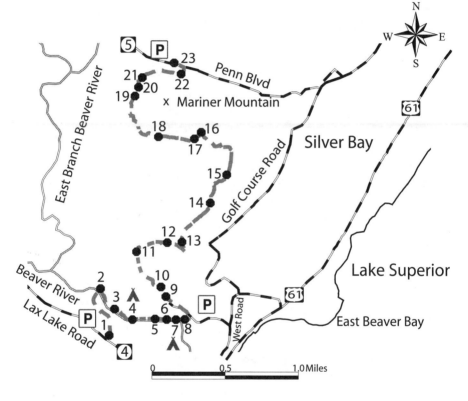

The first section of the trail follows the North Shore State Trail which sets the mood for the June walk. It is raining, I'm on a muddy, wet snowmobile trail with the immediate view to the left an expanse of sewage settling ponds the smell from which reminds me of a stockyard! Judy's mood is much different, for within the first 100 yards she finds a number of *orchids* (trifida) and is in seventh heaven. On the second hike the trail is dry, and though the sewage ponds are still there, the smell from them is barely noticeable. On the downside there are no orchids or any sign they had ever been here.

The trail heads gently downhill from the parking lot, passing a fenced area that encloses small cedar trees, to a wide snowmobile bridge over the Beaver River (waypoint 2). In late May and early June along with orchids, this section has lots of *wood anemone* or windflowers.

Three: Beaver River and Red Clay

After the bridge the trail immediately takes a sharp turn to the right to follow the river to waypoint 3, a large outcrop of *Beaver River Diabase* with a small white pine growing out of the *outcrop*. At this waypoint there are large boulders of *diabase* in the river, and these form a small rapids.

The trail from the bridge to waypoint 3 is composed of red clay, which can become very sticky when it's raining. The clay represents deposits left behind by *Glacial Lake Duluth*, the smaller but deeper lake that preceded Lake Superior.

Four: North Beaver River Campsite

The red clay trail continues through thick, dark balsam woods, passing a small grass and alder covered island around which the river has split, to the North Beaver River campsite (waypoint 4). The campsite looks like a delightful place to spend an afternoon and evening. It is set in amongst large cedar and balsam trees with some white pine, and the sound and sight of rushing white water is just a stone's throw away. At the river's edge, during times of low water, large diabase boulders are available for sitting or rock-hopping. *Solomon's seal* is abundant all through this area.

Five: Rapids, Cliffs, and Ostrich Ferns

The trail continues along the river, which flows over and around large diabase boulders. The boulders come from the cliff on the opposite side of the river, having been broken loose by a process called *frost wedging*. At waypoint 5 these form a nice set of rapids; there are also diabase outcrops on both sides of the river.

Ostrich ferns are the dominant foliage along this particular part of the trail, and there is one short corduroyed section over a wet area.

Six: Large Cedar Tree

Heading uphill, over diabase outcrops and through a spruce and balsam fir forest with white pine, the trail offers views of river and rapids. Descending through cedar and red pine, it's back to the river and another set of rapids, along with more outcrops of Beaver River Diabase. Waypoint 6 is at a large, old cedar tree that leans precariously out over the river.

It is along this section Judy decides to sample the tastiness of the local plant material: blue bead lily. Even though the leaves taste not too bad, kind of like a peppery cucumber, I'm sticking to my Snickers bar, thank you.

Seven: South Beaver River Campsite, Potholes, and Water Shoots

The trail continues along the river and rapids. The water has now become mesmerizing as it hustles down and through little v's in the rocks or "soft" pillow-like shapes in the diabase to spill over a small waterfall in a fierce avalanche of white froth. Waypoint 7 is at the South Beaver River campsite, a good place to listen to the falls and venture out onto the rocks for an impressive view of large *potholes* the river has cut into the bedrock. Here the water races through a narrow chute it has carved into the diabase by eroding and connecting numerous potholes. It does this by eroding through their sides. There are also six-sided *cooling joints* in the diabase, and there is a lone *glacial erratic* of amphibolite (metamorphosed basalt), sitting forlornly amongst the diabase outcrops.

In hiking from the bridge to this waypoint it's difficult not to appreciate the change in the river: from quiet and gently gliding over a rocky bed at the bridge, to the rush, roar, and violence here.

Eight: Diabase Boulders

Mimicking the river the trail weaves its way through a large field of diabase outcrops and boulders to waypoint 8, a small creek that marks the place the hiking trail turns away from the river and heads uphill.

Nine: Betzler Road, Railroad Tracks, and Taconite

Gently rising through a forest of spruce, cedar, and birch the trail crosses the hilltop and turns left onto the Betzler Road. Temporarily following the road the walking path crosses a gas pipeline and the mainline tracks of the railroad that brings *taconite* ore from a mine near Babbitt, Minnesota, to the Northshore Mining processing plant located on the shore of Lake Superior south of the town of Silver Bay. From the railroad tracks it's a football field walk to a curve in the road from which point the hiking trail turns due north to head off into a balsam thicket (waypoint 9).

Ten: Amygdaloidal Basalt

Muddy and flat, the trail passes through a forest of closely spaced balsam, spruce, and birch trees before coming to the base of a small hill and an outcrop of *amygdaloidal basalt* (waypoint 10). *Amygdules* compose 10-15% of the rock and are filled by fine-grained *quartz* (*chert*), gray and pink *zeolite* minerals, and soft, green *chlorite*. In places the amygdules are zoned with pink zeolite centers and clear quartz or grey zeolite edges. Where these are weathered out they leave round holes in the rock. The fine-grained basalt has a reddish-brown weathered surface, and is friable and soft due to intense weathering.

Eleven: White Pines

The trail heads uphill through some nice red and white pines over more basalt that varies from massive to amygdaloidal. This change in the basalt may represent different lava flows, with the amygdaloidal zones representing flow tops and the more massive material flow centers. *Boulders* and *cobbles* of *glacial till* locally cover the trail making for short rocky sections.

Waypoint 11 is at the top of the hill. There are nice white pines here and an open view back toward Beaver Bay, the parking lot where the hike began, and the blue, sparkling waters of Lake Superior in the distance. The outcrop here is fine-grained, sparsely amygdaloidal basalt.

Twelve: Northshore Mining and Sulheim's Lookout

Following the hillside the trail passes over and by small outcrops of massive to amygdaloidal basalt with views of a tailings pond for waste rock from Northshore Mining's taconite processing plant, a pumping station that pumps this waste sludge uphill to the huge tailings pond referred to as Milepost 7, the paved Silver Bay Golf Course Road, and, behind all of these, a long rocky ridge of rugged-looking diabase. The tailings pond is a pretty milky blue color and reminds me of glacial meltwater. Sulheim's lookout is waypoint 12.

Thirteen: Steep Hillside and Talus

From Sulheim's Lookout the trail follows the edge of the hill, passing a set of old, slippery wooden steps that descend down a steep hillside following a natural break in the rock outcrop. These stairs represent the old route of the Superior Hiking Trail, and I, for one, am very glad the trail was rerouted! Past the steps the trail soon heads down a steep and rocky hillside to the edge of a dirt road or snowmobile/ATV trail. At the bottom the trail turns and follows the base of the hill over piles of *talus* with outcrops of basalt in the adjacent hillside. These exhibit nice hexagonal cooling joints. Weathering is enhanced along these features and this, along with frost wedging, is responsible for most of the talus on the trail. The basalt is amygdaloidal and heavily stained by the iron oxide mineral *hematite* (red-colored material). Waypoint 13 is at the end of the talus and start of an open forest.

Fourteen: Paved Road, Powerline, and Anorthosite

Traveling through the open forest of red pine, spruce, balsam fir, and paper birch the trail crosses the dirt road/ATV trail then, almost immediately, the Silver Bay Golf Course Road. Passing the tailings pond and pump station the trail goes under a power line before heading gently uphill over small outcrops of massive, smooth-weathering diabase. Waypoint 15 is at the top of a smooth knob of *anorthosite*, a large *xenolith* or inclusion in the Beaver

River Diabase, that can be likened to a bowling ball. Large *plagioclase feldspar* crystals, which make up the anorthosite, sparkle in the sun, and some crystals have fine parallel lines through them (twin planes), which are typical of this mineral. There is a great view of the lake from here along with a nice stand of large white pine.

Fifteen: Small Creek and Red and White Pines

From the "bowling ball" it's downhill and back into the Beaver River Diabase, passing by nice red and white pines to a small creek. On the other side of the creek the trail is covered by round to subround cobbles and boulders of glacial till, some of which contain layers and veins of red *jasper*. The trail, as it heads gently uphill, passes a small diabase outcrop and more red and white pine. There is also a crumbly rock composed of pink feldspar crystals in a fine-grained, brownish-grey matrix. This rock is surrounded by diabase and may represent another type of xenolith or inclusion in the Beaver River Diabase.

Waypoint 15 is at the top of the hill in a very nice stand of red pine. There are burned out tree stumps, each about 3 feet high, all through this section. A round "bowling ball" glacial erratic (diabase) and the mysterious ladder tree occur at the very top of the hill, which is about 50 feet to the right of the trail at this waypoint. The ladder tree has wooden rungs nailed to it, and these go part way up the trunk before coming to an abrupt end. We guess this must have something to do with the hunting of deer.

Sixteen: Steep Ascent and Great Views

From waypoint 15 the trail winds through a red pine forest, along a pathway covered by pine needles and/or composed of diabase outcrops and boulders. Crossing a well-used ATV trail the hiking trail is flat and muddy to a steep ascent up and over large diabase outcrops. These vary from smooth and massive to lumpy with kibbles and bits (see *diabase weathering*) locally covering the trail.

Waypoint 16 is at the hilltop, which affords views to the northeast and east of Silver Bay, Northshore Mining's Taconite Processing plant, and the natural "gap" in the rocks Highway 61 was routed through. This gap may represent the contact zone between the Beaver River Diabase and the *North Shore Volcanic Group*: a natural zone of weakness that would have been susceptible to erosion. You can also see two red-topped water towers along with the ridges and hills of resistant diabase to the north and northeast. Palisade Head, the high knob-like hill (composed of *rhyolite*) with the radio tower on top, is clearly visible to the northeast. The blue painted arrows on the rocks along the trail mark the route, as it is easy to get lost on this heavily used hill top. At waypoint 16 there is a short spur (to right at iron post with Superior Hiking Trail logos) that provides nice views of the Silver Bay area.

Seventeen: Beaver Pond and Juniper

Waypoint 17 is a short walk across the hilltop from waypoint 16 and is located on a high bluff overlooking a beaver pond and large beaver lodge. The outcrop is lumpy diabase that weathers to kibbles and bits. The views are to the northwest and west, over the Beaver River Valley. From here can be seen the pumping station and tailings pond of waypoint 14, which provide quite the contrast in both natural, environmental, and economic terms to the beaver pond. From the pump house it is easy to follow the discharge pipe along the road and uphill until it disappears over the ridge to the north; behind this is the Milepost 7 tailings pond. Mariner Mountain, at an elevation of 1,212 feet, is visible straight ahead, and the hiking trail passes near its top.

Juniper bushes and low, leafy *bearberry* seem to be everywhere.

Eighteen: Mariner Mountain and Blueberry Ridge

From the bluff, which has a large pile of talus at its base, it's a steep descent past red pines and over massive diabase to a short flat section where the trail is composed of glacial till. Then it's up a steep hillside, over diabase outcrops, with continuing views west and northwest to the top, which is the start of Blueberry Ridge. At the right time of the year there will be no trouble figuring out where that name came from! On the ascent the trail is lined by *evening primrose*, juniper, and bearberry. Near the top of Mariner Mountain the nice views to the west and northwest continue. The Lax Lake Road can also be seen from here (to left).

Nineteen: Leaning Birch

The trail follows blueberry ridge, and the diabase rock it is composed of, with overlooks to the west and northwest before bending around the mountain to the opposite side. Here there are views of the red-topped water towers of Silver Bay and rolling topography to the north and northeast. From here the trail heads downhill, crosses a small stream, then passes over lumpy diabase with lots of kibbles and bits to waypoint 19, a birch forest with many of the trees leaning precariously to the east (wind storm?). There are also large rotting stumps of white pine, which were most likely cut over 100 years ago!

Twenty: Bird Droppings Basalt

From waypoint 19 we have a short walk to the base of a small hill and an outcrop of A*gate Flow* with some feldspar crystals. From here the trail heads uphill to outcrops of *Bird Droppings Basalt* (waypoint 20). The flow is called this because the large, tabular to lath-shaped, plagioclase feldspar crystals give the rock a similar appearance to a basalt lava flow I once saw in a penguin rookery! The feldspar crystals compose 30-50% of the rock, but may be difficult to see due to weathering and/or lichen growth. The pea-size gravel along the trail forms from the weathering of the feldspar crystals. The flow contains sparse amygdules.

This is the same lava flow that forms the last part of the prominent ridge of walk 5; Split Rock to Beaver Bay. Once upon a time the rocks were connected, but they have been separated or broken apart by the intrusion of *dikes* and *sills* of the Beaver River Diabase. Here the separation is about 5 miles with diabase found between these two exposures of Bird Droppings Basalt.

Twenty-One: Agate Gravel

From the outcrop of waypoint 20 we cross a small gully followed by a short uphill section. The rock outcropping in the gully and along the hilltop is amygdaloidal basalt, what we would call Agate Flow because the feldspar crystals have decreased in both abundance and size. Amygdules, up to an inch in diameter, compose 20-40% of the rock and, in places, give the rock a frothy appearance. The amygdules are more visible when the outcrop is wet; they tend to fade into the background on dry sunny rocks. If this outcrop were scoured pristine clean, this whole hill top would be absolutely spectacular. The amygdules are filled by fine-grained quartz (chert) as well as pink and gray zeolites and *calcite*. In a few places the quartz is banded with jasper or blue quartz alternating with the normal milky white or clear quartz. These *agates* weather out to form part of the pea-size gravel at the trail's edge.

Twenty-Two: Many Flows and the Giant Feldspar Crystal

Continuing along the almost continuous outcrop, the more freshly exposed surfaces exhibit a noticeable change from amygdaloidal material back into Bird Droppings Basalt. Walking toward waypoint 22 we pass over two more amygdaloidal-rich areas followed by crystal-rich material. This progression, amygdaloidal followed by more massive, crystal-rich material, suggests we are walking across different lava flows; possibly the amygdaloidal material represents flow tops, and the crystal-rich material the more massive centers. Waypoint 22 is located at a truly impressive feldspar crystal, one that is 2.25 inches long and 1.5 inches wide. This occurs just before the descent to White Rock Creek.

Twenty-Three: White Rock Creek and Parking Lot

It's a gentle walk downhill over one last outcrop of Bird Droppings Basalt, across White Rock Creek and Penn Boulevard, to the wide snowmobile trail that leads to the parking lot.

Walk 7

The April hike was our first of the year, and it turned out to be a wonderful day. It also served to show how much more observant and interested one is in rocks, plants, scenery, and history when the sun is shining. We missed a few things that first foggy, wet hike.

The dogs, after a long winter of not hiking, are completely exhausted! In fact they were flat out, on the ground, resting every chance they got from Mariner Mountain to the end of the walk.

Superior Hiking Trail

Walk 8: Bean and Bear Lakes, Mount Trudee, and Palisade Creek

Walk Logistics

Start: Lake County Road 5 (Penn Boulevard and Outer Drive)

Getting There: There are two ways to reach this parking lot:
1) Take the Lax Lake Road (Lake County Road 4) to Lake County Road 5 (Penn Boulevard). Travel toward Silver Bay, and the large parking lot is on the left 1.3 miles from the junction of County Roads 4 and 5.

2) Take Highway 61 to Silver Bay. Turn left at the traffic light onto Penn Boulevard (Outer Drive) pass Visitor's Center, old High School, and sign for Mariner Mountain to parking lot on the right (this is 2.4 miles past the Highway 61 and Penn Boulevard Junction).

End: Highway 1 to Finland, 0.8 miles past intersection with Highway 61

Getting There: Take Highway 61 north past Tettegouche State Park to Highway 1 (0.5 miles past park entrance). Turn left and travel 0.8 miles to small hiking trail parking lot on the left (easy to miss).

Walk Distance: 10.5 miles   **Date Walked:** June 7th, 2004

Worth a Longer Look:

Bird Droppings Basalt: 2, 3

Tortured Basalt: 8

Forest Walk and Pond: 10, 11

Bean Lake Overlook: 12, 13

Bear Lake and Talus: 14

Bear Lake Overlook: 16

Whaleback Anorthosite: 19

The Lunch Spot: 26

Mt. Trudee: 27, 28

Sugar Maple Forest: 29, 30

Paul Bunyan White Pine: 32

Drainpipe: 33

High Falls: 36

Bridge Across Baptism River: 37

3M and Anorthosite: 41

Waypoint-to-Waypoint

One: Parking Lot off Penn Boulevard

Sunny, clear, and eighty degrees! At least that was the weather forecast. However, in the real world where Lake Superior is a major factor in determining the local weather conditions, it is windy, 48 degrees, and the fog is beginning to roll in off the great lake. Judy took the local weather forecast to heart and arrived at the parking lot in shorts, t-shirt and goosebumps; she is now busy adding layers: pants, fleece, and gloves. I am one step ahead of

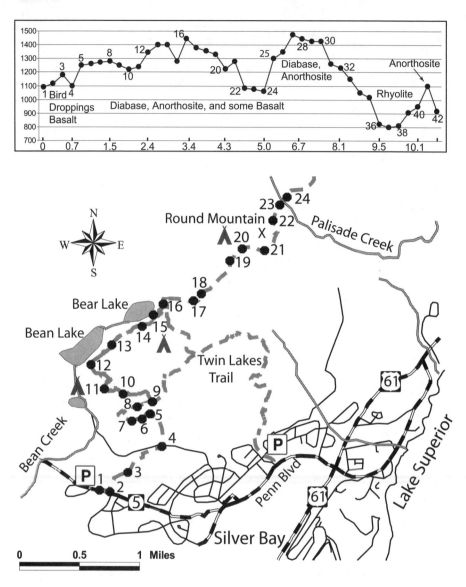

her and am already wearing my "Superior" survival gear!

Sammy is out and about and ready to go. This is a good thing because she smells like she rolled in something that has been very dead for a very long time. Charlie is not with us, he bruised a pad on his paw on the last hike so is "sitting this one out."

Two: Bird Droppings Basalt and the Superior Hiking Trail

A wide, gravel road serves as a short spur trail to the start of the Superior Hiking Trail (waypoint 2). The *outcrop* here is a *basalt* lava flow, part of the *North Shore Volcanic Group* that formed 1.1 billion years ago as a result of the *Mid-continent Rift*. This particular flow is called the *Bird Droppings Basalt* because it looks much like a basalt lava flow I saw a few years ago in a long established penguin rookery! The bird droppings are large tabular-shaped, grey to white *plagioclase feldspar* crystals that vary from 15-50% in abundance. The flow also contains *chert*-filled *amygdules* that range from pinhead-to quarter-size. This same flow occurs across Penn Boulevard at waypoints 19 to 21 on Hike 6; it is also found at the end of *Agate Flow* Ridge on Hike 5. See waypoints 19 to 21, Hike 6, for a further explanation and description of this distinctive and very interesting lava flow.

Three: More Bird Droppings, Some Kibbles, and a Nice View

We walk uphill, going by a cell phone tower and crossing more outcrops of Bird Droppings Basalt. All along here the gray-weathering plagioclase crystals vary greatly in abundance and, in places, weathering has reduced the "bird droppings" to kibble-and bit-size pieces (see *diabase weathering*).

Every outcrop of Bird Droppings Basalt along this section has, as Judy laments, the same darn plants; *pussytoes, dewberries*, gooseberries, *starflowers, wood anemones*, and fruit trees. Later in the summer there will be orange and yellow *hawkweed, mullein, yarrow, buttercups* and *daisies*. The forest along this section is a mix of balsam poplar and cedar, with lots of white flowering shrubs (*Juneberries*). *Violets* (wooly) are blooming all along the trail, and the *blueberries* are flowering. Periodically there are openings through the trees that provide views of the Silver Bay area to the east and northeast.

Waypoint 3 is at a dirt road and, just beyond this, there is a large outcrop of Bird Droppings Basalt that contains amygdules filled with chert and a pink *zeolite* mineral (laumantite).

Four: Power Line, Views, and Glacial Erratics

Continuing gently uphill over the feldspar-rich lava flow we come to a power line from which there is a great view of Silver Bay, the Northshore Mining Taconite processing plant, and the red-topped water towers that are visible over a large portion of this hike.

From the power line we continue gently up and down over a different kind of basalt lava flow. This flow lacks the distinctive feldspar crystals but does have amygdules filled by chert and a pink zeolite mineral (laumantite). The trail turns northeast to follow the Bean Creek Valley (actually this valley has no name so we unofficially called it this because the creek flowing along the valley bottom gets it start in Bean Lake). There are purple *clematis* vines in this section.

Heading down the valley side the trail passes over outcrops of Bird Droppings Basalt as well as *cobbles* and *boulders* of pink and white *granite*, and black and white *banded gneiss.* These are *glacial erratics,* with the gneiss possibly coming from the Voyageurs National Park area, and the granites either from the Giants Range or the Finland area. *Mertensia* (nodding trumpet-like blue flowers) is profuse through this section.

Passing through a typical mixed upland forest with a few white pine, the trail reaches the valley bottom where it becomes flat, muddy, and swampy with some planked sections as it passes large spruce trees to arrive at a gravel road that is waypoint 4. Nodding *trilliums* and yellow violets are blooming here.

Five: Diabase, Old Stream Beds, Clematis, and Anorthosite

Remaining flat and muddy the trail passes over outcrops of a basalt lava flow that contain small tabular feldspar crystals. This outcrop is followed by a rocky uphill section with the trail passing over more basalt before returning to flat and muddy as it passes by an area that is chock-a-block full of round cobbles and boulders that once formed the bed of a now dried-up stream. After the stream bed we come to an outcrop of medium-grained *Beaver River Diabase* (also see *diabase*). Clematis is abundant at this outcrop, and this seems to support Judy's claim that this plant has an affinity for the diabase. Starflowers and *oak ferns* are common, and mountain maple forms the forest understory.

After this we head uphill passing over and between outcrops of medium-grained diabase to waypoint 5, a small knob of *anorthosite*. The anorthosite occurs near the top of the hill with red oak and *jewelweed*.

Six: Diabase and Views

Continuing gently uphill, over and past more medium-grained diabase we come to a nice overlook at waypoint 6. From here there is a nice view of the red-topped water towers, Northshore Minings Processing plant, the town of Silver Bay, Lake Superior, and the Bean Creek Valley. There is an outcrop here of rusty weathering, lumpy (see *diabase weathering*), medium-grained diabase.

Seven: Basalt-Gabbro Contact, River Pond, and Tortured Basalt

Leaving the diabase outcrop the trail crosses a flat area as it goes through a maple and birch forest before heading up a rocky slope to another overlook. Starflowers are prolific through here. From this point it is a short walk to a great view of the hilly topography to the south and southeast. There is also a nice contact here between massive basalt lava (to the right) and medium-grained Beaver River Diabase (to the left). The contact is knife sharp, and the basalt contains chert-filled amygdules and small feldspar crystals. It turns out this basalt outcrop is completely surrounded by the diabase and thus represents a large *xenolith* or inclusion in that rock body.

Waypoint 7 is at an overlook into the Bean Creek Valley. The rock outcrop here is what we call *Tortured Basalt* because it looks like planet earth has given this rock a really hard time. This gray weathering lava flow contains numerous chert amygdules, and exhibits a rectangular fracture pattern along which it breaks, producing its trademark "tortured" look. The cracks or fractures that parallel the hillside represent the edges of six-sided *cooling joints,* while the fractures at right angles to these are most likely the result of stresses the rock underwent long after it hardened.

Eight: Anorthosite Bowling Balls

From the lava flow we pass medium-grained diabase to follow the side of a small valley and its poplar, birch, and spruce forest. The Juneberries through here have mistletoe on them. Crossing the head of a small gully the trail then turns back to follow the opposite side to waypoint 9, a series of small anorthosite "knobs" or bowling ball-shaped outcrops. The forest through here is dominantly birch and maple. Yellow hawkweed will be prolific later in the summer.

Nine: Twin Lakes Trail and a Nice Forest Walk

From the anorthosite "bowling balls" we head downhill into a flat, dry area with nice old-growth maple, birch, and ash trees. The ash is beginning to "come to life," there are now leaves on the branches while all the other tree species have been fully leafed-out for weeks. It's a nice walk through this forest past outcrops of Beaver River Diabase to the junction with the Twin Lakes Spur Trail (waypoint 9). This is a 7.5 mile long loop trail (walk 9) that begins at the Silver Bay Visitor's Center/Historical Society parking lot in Silver Bay. It joins the Superior Hiking Trail here for a scenic walk past the twin lakes of Bean and Bear, before leaving the Superior Hiking Trail for the return walk to Silver Bay.

Ten: Penn Creek, Maples, and Birch Forest

Heading downhill, the trail, composed of *glacial till*, passes an anorthosite outcrop to the left before crossing a small creek. Cinnamon and *ostrich ferns* are notable through here along with *swamp saxifrage.* The trail then winds through a maple and birch forest with *bellwort* and *rose-twisted stalk* covering the forest floor to a small pond. I think the pond is the perfect home for some hideous swamp monster, but Judy thinks it's a beautiful spot with lots of interesting plants. There is an outcrop of anorthosite on the far side of the pond whose shape suggests either the "pond monster" crawling out of the swamp, or a sand worm from the planet Dune! Red oak trees are abundant here and have joined maple, birch, and ash to make a nice open forest.

Continuing past an outcrop of Beaver River Diabase and lots of *thimbleberries*, we walk through a nice forest to an outcrop of dark, massive-looking Tortured Basalt. The basalt, which in places looks "twisted," is breaking along crossing fractures and vertical cooling joints into small angular pieces with sharp edges. From this outcrop there is a nice view of the rolling hills and forest to the south. Lots of red oak grows here along with swamp saxifrage, mullein, *blue bell* and hedge *bindweed* (a morning glory-like flower). The green flecks of color seen on the rocks is paint used "long ago" to mark the trail. From the basalt outcrop the trail remains flat, with glacial till sections, until reaching the rock steps that lead down to Penn Creek (waypoint 10). Along the creek there are lots of ferns, *meadow rue*, and *honeysuckle*. The *marsh marigolds* are done blooming and have set their round fruits.

Eleven: Penn Creek Campsite, Tortured Basalt, and Beaver Pond

A set of rock steps leads out of Penn Creek to the spur trail to the Penn Creek campsite. Just past the spur trail there is a large outcrop of Tortured Basalt that forms a rock ridge with an overlook (waypoint 11) to the southwest. There is a beaver pond (formed by the Penn Creek Beavers?) down in the Bean Creek Valley. We also have nice views back toward Silver Bay and the red-topped water towers. Pale pink *corydalis* is flowering here, and the choke cherries have buds.

The wind has suddenly found new energy and decides to blow the lake fog inland. Dark clouds are starting to roll over the horizon to the northeast, and we both agree there's a storm coming.

Twelve: Bean Lake

Tortured Basalt continues as the trail passes through a mixed birch, maple, red oak, balsam poplar, and balsam fir forest. Passing an access trail to Bean Lake, and a sign pointing ahead toward Bean and Bear lakes, it's uphill over wooden steps and small outcrops of massive basalt lava. Crossing a small stream, we walk up to an open area where there is an outcrop of Beaver River Diabase. In looking at a geology map of this area there is an interconnected network of diabase *dikes* and *sills* that have intruded the North Shore Volcanic Group and, in places, have completely enclosed or surrounded parts of these lava flows. The diabase tends to be finer-grained close to the flows and coarser-grained further away.

Continuing along the hillside there are views of the Bean Creek Valley and a beaver pond as we walk over outcrops of what we call painted diabase because of all the red hematite through the rock. It is then uphill to waypoint 12, an overlook directly above Bean Lake, the first "wow" spot of the day. There is a fantastic view over a steep rocky cliff with a sheer drop of 120 feet to the small, rock-bound lake below. Today, with the strong wind, there are white caps on the lake! To the south is the Beaver River Valley and, in the distance a high, shimmering cloud-like feature that is not a mirage or a high mountain lake but part of the huge tailings pond for the Northshore Mining taconite processing plant located in Silver Bay. This feature is called Milepost 7 tailings pond, the place where the fine waste material (mainly iron silicate minerals and chert) from the taconite process is stored.

Bean Lake is ringed by cedar trees, an almost continuous line, with birch and aspen behind them. The diabase that outcrops here and along the trail to this waypoint looks like someone came along with a can of red paint and painted lines, swirls, bands, and circles on the rock. Throughout this area, brick red *hematite* (iron oxide) forms veins and intricate patterns through the rock. In fact the light-colored "dots or splotches" seen on some outcrop surfaces represent the original rock; the rest has been converted to red hematite.

Looking again at the geology map of this area, Bean and Bear lakes sit in a narrow wedge of basalt lava that is completely enclosed by the diabase. The cliffs on either side of the two lakes are composed of Painted Diabase. The basalt lava is easier to erode than the diabase, and this, along with the help of the glacial ice (*glacial plucking)* led to the formation of the deep valley in which the lakes now sit.

Thirteen: Scary Cliff, Stunted Trees, and a Jasper Vein

The trail turns northeast to follow the steep cliff that rises 120 feet above Bean Lake. The rock exposed along the cliff is Painted Diabase. On the cliff wall across the lake prominent cooling joints stand out due to the preferential weathering that occurs along them.

The trail turns into the trees, and those closest to the cliff–the ones exposed to the cold and wind–are pretty sad looking and stunted. They look like Paul Bunyan made it a point to sit on each and every one. These are, however, hearty trees, that are able to hold their own against the fierce wind and snow that constantly pummels and piles on them. Their tenacity is a good lesson for us all. The forest beyond these front line warriors is dominated by maple and birch with more and more large white pine the deeper you travel into it; the low vegetation is dominantly *pipsissewa, pyrola,* and *club moss.* The trail passes through the forest and up a set of stone steps over Painted Diabase before turning back toward the cliff and a steep drop-off. Waypoint 13 is at an outcrop of lumpy diabase that has a large vein of *jasper* through it (just beyond the overlook). At first glance the vein looks like a thick tree root that has wedged its way into and through the rock. The outcrop is also crossed by veins of quartz and *orthoclase* (pink feldspar). There is a nice view down the length of Bean Lake and, in the distance, the shimmering Milepost 7 tailings pond.

Fourteen: Bear Lake and an Old Cabin

The trail follows the cliff edge over Painted Diabase with great views of Bear Lake and all the rock *talus* that's been *frost-wedged* from the surrounding diabase cliffs. The woods are a mix of maple and birch with some large spruce. Waypoint 14 is at the remains of an old cabin or shelter, which is now just a pile of cut logs and wood. This small cabin was built by a group of kids from Silver Bay in the 1960s.

Fifteen: Bear Lake Campsite Spur Trail

From the wood pile we head downhill over Painted Diabase to the northeast end of Bear Lake and a spur trail (waypoint 15) down to the lake and the Bear Lake campsite (4 tent pads). The woods continue as before but now have some nice, old-growth maples. *Bunchberry* and blue bead lily are common along this trail section.

Sixteen: Cliff and Talus, Bear Lake, and Twin Lakes Trail Loop

The hiking trail heads east into the woods to follow the bottom of a steep cliff with lots of talus before climbing up the cliff. In fact the trail consists mostly of diabase boulders and diabase steps. The Beaver River Diabase exposed here has lost its painted look. At the cliff top there is a spectacular view down Bear Lake; the diabase outcrop here is intensely weathered with lots of kibbles and bits along the trail. There is *large flowered bellwort* and clematis along the trail up to the overlook, and, at the top, *yellow vetchling*.

From this overlook it is a short distance over Beaver River Diabase to waypoint 16, the junction with the northeast loop of the Twin Lakes Trail. At the waypoint Judy and I find what we call a "happy" book. This is a log book placed here by the Superior Hiking Trail Association for hikers to write their thoughts in, good or bad, though most are good, which is why we call these "happy" books. A stone path leads down to the cliff edge and a nice overlook of Bear Lake. Oak trees along with *Canadian mayflowers, asters*, and clubmoss are common here.

Seventeen: Steep Descent, Chocolate Chips, and Vanilla Ice Cream

Turning away from the cliff the trail heads east through a maple-birch forest with outcrops of lumpy diabase before heading steeply down to the bottom of the hill which is waypoint 17. The diabase at the base of the cliff is composed of large *pyroxene* crystals, which stand out like chocolate chips in vanilla ice cream giving the rock a kind of texture called *ophitic*.

Eighteen: Georges Gorge Snowmobile Trail and Giant Trilliums

Just past waypoint 17 there is an ATV trail where the hiking trail enters a maple forest with giant nodding trilliums lining the pathway. These continue all the way to the Georges Gorge snowmobile trail (waypoint 18). Here rose-twisted stalk is blooming.

Nineteen: Whaleback Anorthosite and the Palisade Creek Valley

The trail is relatively flat through a maple, birch, and balsam poplar forest as it passes a long outcrop of anorthosite that has been glacially sculpted into what I see as a whale's back: a whale plowing through deep green water to get out to sea. Judy, however, thinks the outcrop looks more like the Duluth Public Library building. The process that formed this *whaleback* is called glacial plucking.

From the whaleback we travel through a maple and birch forest with some oak, passing outcrops of lumpy diabase to waypoint 19, a large black and grey diabase outcrop with rusty weathering spots. There are great views from here into the upper part of the Palisade Creek Valley (northwest and north). To the west and southwest we can see the Cedar Creek Valley; Cedar Creek drains into the Beaver River. The ground is thick with green vegetation; bellwort is profuse, and the understory is dominated by hazel.

Twenty: Beaver Pond Creek and Round Mountain Campsite

From the overlook it's a steep descent down the diabase (be careful, for the rock is slippery when wet), followed by a nice walk through a maple-birch forest to Beaver Pond Creek (waypoint 20). Upstream from the trail are numerous beaver dams. The Round Mountain campsite is located here, and only one night's stay is allowed. I tell Judy the reason for this is obvious–anymore and you would need a blood transfusion. This is one low, swampy, buggy place–especially in mid-summer. The place is loaded with different kinds of ferns along with *cow parsnip*.

Twenty-One: Round Mountain

Walking through a nice maple-birch forest we find the hiking trail routed for a short distance along an ATV trail. To the left of us is Round Mountain, a knob of anorthosite with the top at an elevation of 1312 feet (the hiking trail through here varies from 1180 to 1280 feet). The hiking trail bends around the base of the mountain to a spur trail (waypoint 21) that takes us to the top.

The 0.25 mile spur trail is lined with yellow corydalis and thimbleberries. The anorthosite at Round Mountain is coarse-grained with plagioclase feldspar crystals over 5 inches across.

Twenty-Two: Old Stream Bed and West Palisade Creek

The trail continues around the base of Round Mountain through a nice forest of maple, birch, and balsam poplar trees past a moss-covered anorthosite outcrop to a long set of wooden steps. The steps are really slimy and slippery when wet so care is needed as we descend to an ATV trail. From this point the hiking trail is covered with cobbles and boulders of various colors and compositions; these mark an old stream bed. Passing a circular area to the right of the trail, one where all the balsam poplar trees have been

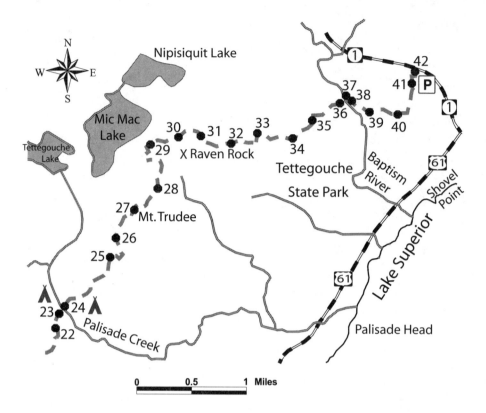

cut down, the trail becomes wet and muddy before a series of stone steps and wooden planks brings us to the West Branch of Palisade Creek (waypoint 22). Amongst the abundant coltsfoot and ferns are bellworts and *Jack-in-the pulpits*, whose three parted leaves resemble nodding trillium.

Twenty-Three: West Palisade Campsite, Circle Tree, and Bewitched Forest

After crossing the creek it's uphill along a trail lined with nodding trilliums, bunchberries, and currents, to the spur trail to the West Palisade campsite. From here there is a flat, muddy section with several planked and corduroyed areas before arriving at the Bewitched Forest. This is a really neat cedar grove with weird, twisted, and spooky-looking trees. One tree has a trunk that looks like it made a complete, twisted circle in order to get the opportunity to grow upwards. This tree marks waypoint 23, a scary place when shadows are long and the day is drawing to a close.

Twenty-Four: Palisade Creek and the East Palisade Campsite

It's a short walk from the cedar grove along a muddy trail to the spur trail for the East Palisade campsite. From here it is down wooden stairs to a footbridge over Palisade Creek (waypoint 24). The creek is dotted with large glacial erratics of different compositions. *Blue flag iris* emerges from the water and along the shore *wild lettuce* is abundant.

Twenty-Five: Lumpy Diabase and Palisade Creek Valley

From Palisade Creek we climb a set of wooden stairs and continue gently uphill over a muddy, planked trail section to the Georges Gorge snowmobile trail. This is the second time we have crossed this trail and Judy wants to know if my GPS is working!

Crossing the snowmobile trail we continue uphill over glacial till through a forest dominated by sugar maples. The rocks are lumpy diabase with kibbles and bits. Waypoint 25 is at an overlook with a view of the Palisade Creek Valley and a beaver pond. There are nice red and white pine trees all along here.

Twenty-Six: Palisade Head and a Great Lunch Spot

From waypoint 25 we turn east going up a steep section via rock and wooden steps and boulders of lumpy diabase to an anorthosite outcrop. The outcrop provides a nice view of Palisade Head, composed of *Palisade Rhyolite*, and its tall radio tower. From here it's over lumpy diabase to a junction with a short unmarked trail that leads to a nice overlook and a great lunch spot.

The view from the overlook is of the headwaters of Palisade Creek, which has its start in Tettegouche Lake. The lake to the northeast of Tettegouche is called Mic Mac, and this lake drains into Nipisiquit Lake. From here you can also see Round Mountain and the diabase ridge and hills that border Bear and Bean Lakes to the southwest; the valleys are composed of basalt. Below us the frogs are in full song as the males try to lure the females into their territories.

Twenty-Seven: Mount Trudee

From waypoint 26 there is a short downhill, followed by a flat section past two outcrops of lumpy diabase and two large white pine trees before arriving at an opening that provides a nice view of the Palisade Creek Valley and Mic Mac and Tettegouche lakes. The forest through this section is dominantly balsam poplar, birch, and sugar maple with some spruce and white pines.

We then head uphill, over lumpy diabase, to the top of Mt. Trudee at waypoint 27. Mount Trudee, at an elevation of 1500 feet, is an anorthosite knob with bowling ball weathering and *plagioclase feldspar* crystals up to 3 inches long. Just below the top of the anorthosite knob there is a nice grove of red pines, which make for a beautiful sheltered picnic spot with wonderful views of Raven Rock to the northeast and the Palisade Creek Valley to the northwest.

Twenty-Eight: Large Yellow Birch

From the red pine grove the trail continues along the top of Mt. Trudee with elevations ranging from 1480 to 1540 feet; there are nice views to the west and northeast.

Heading downhill, over and between anorthosite outcrops, we enter a forest dominated by large yellow birch, white pine, sugar maples, and paper birch. Passing a small creek the trail flattens out as it goes through an old-growth forest with nice sugar maples to waypoint 28, a series of bowling ball-shaped anorthosite outcrops. The outcrops are small, round, and covered by lichen and moss. *Columbine, Dutchman's breeches,* and *wild ginger* flowers are prevalent along here. Bloodroot leaves are abundant but the flowers are long gone.

Twenty-Nine: Anorthosite Sharks

From the anorthosite "bowling balls" it's a gentle walk downhill, passing more anorthosite, and a small pond with blue flag iris, through a forest dominated by sugar maple and paper birch with some balsam poplar. The trail is mostly flat as it passes an anorthosite outcrop that is shaped like a shark (no argument from Judy on this one). Continue through the open maple forest with short uphill and downhill sections to a state park trail junction; the hiking trail continues to the right (waypoint 29).

Thirty: Raven Rock and Maple Forest

The Superior Hiking Trail continues through an open maple forest with some spruce trees. After passing a small swamp marked by wooden planks, it's a nice walk through open maple and birch woods to the spur trail leading up to Ravens Rock (waypoint 30), another anorthosite knob.

Thirty-One: A Place To Rest and Yellow Birch

Beyond the spur trail it's gently downhill to a state park ski trail. The Superior Hiking Trail continues behind the wooden bench; the outcrop to the south (right) of the trail is anorthosite. From the bench the hiking trail continues downhill through a yellow birch and cedar forest to waypoint 31, another anorthosite outcrop, but one with a yellow birch growing on top of it. The tree's root system is draped over the outcrop like a bull rider atop a big bull. There is a small creek to the northeast.

Thirty-Two: Giant White Pine

The trail continues gently up and down through an open, rolling forest of yellow and paper birch and maples. Passing a small swampy area with cedar trees, continue through the forest to the Paul Bunyan White Pine at waypoint 32. This tree must be 80-100 feet tall and at least 5 feet in diameter. This has to be the Empire State Building of the forest, for up it goes–straight, beautiful, and majestic all the way to the nearest star.

Thirty-Three: Drainpipe

It's a nice walk through open woods with yellow and paper birch, maple, cedar, and spruce before heading uphill to an outcrop of lumpy diabase that is weathering to kibbles and bits. Continue on past a small rock pile composed of basalt and diabase (exposed due to a tree tipping over) then along the edge of the hill before starting down into the Baptism River Valley. Passing outcrops of lumpy and crumbly diabase, and nice overlooks of the valley, we come to a 150-foot-long descent through a steep rock crevice. A wooden railing and stone steps help in getting down part of the crevice, but otherwise we are on our own as we climb over large, angular boulders of diabase to the bottom. This crevice has been named the "drainpipe," and Judy and I decide this is a good name because, if you happen to be here in a rainstorm, you will be sucked like a spaghetti noodle straight down the steep rock face. Waypoint 33 is at the bottom of the drainpipe amongst large boulders of lumpy diabase that have been derived from the cliff by frost wedging. There is a nice grove of cedars at this point.

Thirty-Four: Mighty Tree

The trail is level through cedar and yellow birch woods to a cutover area with second-growth aspen, birch, and mountain maple. Crossing an old road the trail passes through a cedar grove then back into a paper and yellow birch forest.

The ridge to the right is composed of lumpy diabase. Judy and I decide the tree growing from the diabase at waypoint 34 was there before the boulder. The boulder rolled into it, and the tree split it apart.

Thirty-Five: Spur Trail To Tettegouche

The hiking trail passes over outcrops of lumpy diabase as it goes through an older birch-balsam poplar forest to a Tettegouche State Park spur trail (waypoint 35). Tettegouche State Park Headquarters is 2.1 miles to the east, and High Falls, the highest waterfall entirely in Minnesota, is 0.5 miles to the northeast.

Thirty-Six: Palisade Rhyolite and High Falls

From waypoint 35 the Superior Hiking Trail follows a winding, wide gravel state park trail with balsam, paper birch, and large cedar trees to the junction with the Two Step and High Falls trails. Taking the High Falls Trail we come to wooden steps that lead to viewing platforms of the falls. Waypoint 36 is on the second platform, the one directly over the falls. There is an outcrop of the Palisade Rhyolite here. This resistant rock forms the high cliffs associated with Palisade Head and Shovel Point which are on the shoreline of Lake Superior. As this large flow cooled, columnar joints formed. These evenly spaced cooling fractures allowed running water, probably helped by glacial plucking, to form the waterfalls seen here.

Thirty-Seven: Bridge Across the Baptism River

Walking along the wooden boardwalk we cross a small creek to the suspension bridge across the river. The bridge, built with the help of Minnesota Power, has a unique single cable design and is really springy and bouncy. Waypoint 37 is in the middle of the bridge. There are nice upriver views of the rapids and the falls speak for themselves.

Thirty-Eight: Flow Banding and Hanging Joints

At the end of the bridge is a large outcrop of rhyolite that contains small, square crystals of orthoclase feldspar and irregularly shaped grey quartz. From the bridge the trail follows the river, passing an outcrop of intensely weathered rhyolite that has parallel wavy lines through it that may represent *flow banding*. The rock is intensely fractured and breaks across the flow bands.

Waypoint 38 provides a nice view of the falls and the deep pool at the base. The cliff is impressive, and there are lots of logs piled up on the river bank below the falls. At this waypoint the rhyolite outcrop contains feldspar crystals and exhibits nice columnar cooling joints. There is one large joint hanging over the river, and we decide this is a small demonstration of how the falls may have formed. Judy and I both wonder how long it will be before the rhyolite rock joint is river rock debris? Below, on the northeast side of the river, there is a gravel bar formed from deposition of sand-to cobble-size material left stranded when water velocity dramatically decreases (and thus the river's carrying capacity) after the long fall into the rocky pool.

Thirty-Nine: Gravel Bar

Not far down the river there is a junction with a short side trail that goes down to the gravel bar at the bottom of High Falls. The hiking trail continues on, paralleling the river before turning inland toward Highway 1. Waypoint 39 is at the junction between the Superior Hiking Trail and a Tettegouche State Park trail.

Forty: White Pines and That Closed-In Feeling

The walking path is level with nice white pines along it, before suddenly becoming dark and close, seemingly crowded out by a dense growth of small spruce, balsam fir, and cedar. Waypoint 40 is in a small cedar grove.

Forty-One: Anorthosite and the 3M Company

Past the cedar grove the trail becomes more open, the forest dominated by spruce and paper birch. After a 0.35 mile walk the trail heads uphill over massive basalt and diabase outcrops to an anorthosite outcrop that forms the hilltop. We both figure this last ascent a cruel joke. Tired, hot, and hungry after the long hike, all we want is to get to the parking lot and our vehicle. This last steep climb is not appreciated; a friend called it a "real sting in the tail!"

From the top of the anorthosite outcrop (waypoint 41) there is a nice view back to Palisade Head and the Baptism River Valley. The anorthosite has a pitted appearance, possibly due to the presence of mafic minerals, like *ilmenite* and *magnetite*, that have weathered out. On the west side of this anorthosite knob there is a small quarry that was started by the 3M company in the early 1900s. At that time they mistakenly believed the relatively soft, calcium-rich plagioclase in the anorthosite to be the hard and durable mineral corundum (Al_2O_3), which is extensively used as an abrasive. This mining venture took place before there was a highway, so the company constructed a tramway that carried the "corundum" down to Crystal Bay for crushing and shipping. Needless to say this business venture was not long for the North Shore, yet in real Minnesota fashion 3M survived and prospered.

Forty-Two: Parking Lot

Crossing the knob, it's down off the anorthosite, and back into diabase to the spur trail leading to the parking lot (waypoint 42). The black sky, which has been threatening rain for the past hour, decides the time is right and the ensuing torrential downpour is accompanied by really nasty thunder and lightning. This all begins at the moment we reach the car–perfect timing which, for us, is most unusual!

This has been a long but great day. Bean and Bear lakes, Mt. Trudee, High Falls, Pual Bunyan Pine, and long, beautiful walks through maple and birch forests are well worth all the effort. So pick a nice day, bring a camera, start early, and enjoy a really special adventure on the Superior Hiking Trail.

Superior Hiking Trail
Walk 9: Twin Lakes Loop

Walk Logistics

Start and End: Silver Bay Visitor's/Historical Center

Getting There: Take Highway 61 to Outer Drive (Penn Boulevard). Turn left at traffic light onto Outer Drive and go about 0.5 miles. Visitor's Center is on the right.

Walk Distance: 7.5 miles   **Date Walked:** April 30th, 2005

Worth a Longer Look:

Lombardy Poplar Trees: 2	Forest Walk and Pond: 13, 14
Blow Down: 5	Bean Lake Overlook: 15, 16
Drop Pools: 8	Bear Lake and Talus: 17
Anorthosite and View: 9	Bear Lake Overlook: 19
Elam's Knob: 11	Amazing Forest: 21

Waypoint-to-Waypoint

One: Visitor's Center in Silver Bay

It's clear, sunny, and warm for our second hike of 2005. Both Sammy and Charlie are keen to be out and about, and this summer-like April weather can last all the way into November as far as I'm concerned. We are at the north end of the parking lot for the Silver Bay Visitor's/Historical Center. This is the start of the Twin Lakes loop trail, which is an official spur trail to the Superior Hiking Trail. This trail, which winds its way up to Bean and Bear Lakes, was laid out and built largely by Toivo Savonen of Silver Bay. He was one of the laid off miners at the then Reserve Mining Company (now Northshore Mining) who were hired to help build the Superior Hiking Trail.

Two: Spur and Snowmobile Trails

Leaving the parking lot it's a short downhill walk to the wide, graveled Silver Bay ATV/snowmobile trail, which parallels a small creek and cuts through a Silver Bay neighborhood. As we walk along Judy points out a row of tall, spindly Lombardy poplars. These aspen cousins are all males, and all clones. In the poplar and willow family, plants are either male or female, each with male or female flowering parts. This makes for a tough time getting together and means their relationship really does blow in the wind. The term botanists use is dioecious, having male and female flowers on different plants of the same species. The counterpart to this is monoecious, having male and female flowers on the same plant. Hazel is a good example

96

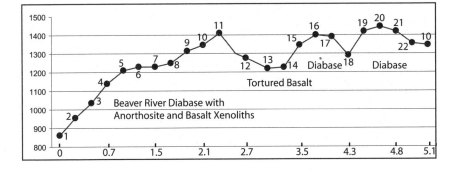

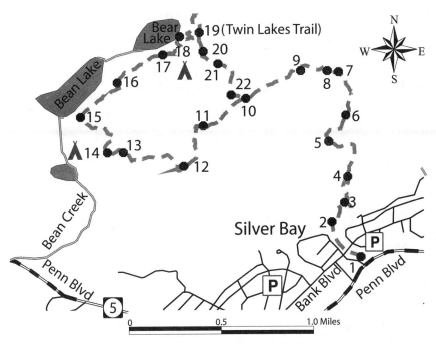

of this with tiny, barely able to be seen red female flowers and larger male catkins. The red female flowers hang around waiting for the catkins to release the pollen which hopefully will fertilize them and produce our familiar beaked hazelnuts.

Crossing Bank Boulevard and passing by a large, round *glacial erratic* of *Beaver River Diabase* (also see *diabase*) we come to a trail junction with the spur trail that leads up to the Superior Hiking Trail going to the right (waypoint 2).

Three: Three Diabase Maidens

Entering the woods we cross the creek on a trail composed of *glacial till*, which forms deposits called *ground moraine*. Glacial erratics are strewn through the woods, and just past the creek there are three *boulders* of Beaver

River Diabase that are grouped together and remind me of the three maidens of the pipestone quarries at Pipestone National Monument. There are many different Native American stories about these three erratics of *granite*, but all refer to the belief they were placed there to guard the quarries. What the three diabase maidens are guarding here is a question to ponder.

The hiking trail heads uphill over a sinewy ridge of gravel-size till to a junction with a side trail that used to go to an overlook, however, this trail is now no longer maintained.

Four: Overlook and the East Spur

From the trail junction we continue uphill over lumpy (see *diabase weathering*) Beaver River Diabase with some kibbles and bits past an ATV trail to a large outcrop of smooth, lichen-covered Beaver River Diabase. From here there is a nice view of Silver Bay, the Northshore Mining taconite processing plant, Lake Superior, and the Bayfield Peninsula on the other side of the lake. The red-topped Silver Bay water towers are to the right.

From the overlook the spur trail takes a left turn to a junction with what is called the "East Spur." This goes to an overlook that is no longer used because of local road construction.

Five: Blow Down

We stay on the trail to the left, which flattens out as it goes over lumpy, lichen-covered diabase with patchy areas made up of kibbles and bits. Kibbles and bits weathering is most pronounced on south-facing slopes because of more sunshine and thus more warmth. During winter and spring this leads to many more freeze–thaw cycles than occur on north-facing slopes and thus more rapid weathering and disintegration of the rocks.

A profusion of spruce cones litters the walking path as it crosses a ATV trail, followed by a well used snowmobile trail before heading up, into a birch forest with abundant mountain maple and balsam fir. The walking path is composed of glacial till with *cobbles* and boulders of *basalt*, diabase, granite, and bedded sedimentary rocks. The sedimentary rocks are the same age as the basalt lavas (1.1 billion years old) and formed from the erosion of the lava flows. Reaching the rounded hilltop, we get to walk through an area where there is a thick maze of fallen, twisted, and dead aspen trees; many have been broken half-way up and stand like wounded soldiers guarding their fallen comrades. This mess is the result of the infamous July 4th, 1999 blow down that destroyed so many trees in the Boundary Waters Canoe area. Weather conditions were such that a 'straight line wind' or derichio at the front of a severe thunderstorm line attained speeds over 100 mph. Aspens, being brittle and sometimes hollow trees, are susceptible to such high winds and break and snap like a piece of asparagus being cleaned for dinner.

Waypoint 5 is a curve in the trail just at the edge of the blow down. There is an outcrop of massive, lichen-covered Beaver River Diabase here.

Six: Beaver Pond and Forest Change

Walking along the hilltop there are views of a beaver pond in an unnamed valley to the left (southwest) as we go through a dominantly birch forest to waypoint 6. This waypoint represents a dramatic change in the forest. Maples become dominant, and the forest is no longer white with birch, but dark and green with maple.

Seven: Green Paint and Dogwoods

This section of the trail provides a very nice walk through the maple forest. The trail passes several moss covered mounds; these are *outcrops* of diabase emerging from the glacial till and not the work of ancient Native Americans or gravediggers. In walking this section we notice greenish flecks on the rocks in the trail. These don't mark the route of a St. Patrick's Day parade but were originally used as trail markings; over time the trail has become obvious and the paint is nearly worn away.

The trail passes from the maple forest to a nice birch forest with a lot of hazel and dogwood. If this walk is done during leaf-off time, it will be a treat to see the subtle reds and oranges of the dogwood bark and the speckled brown of the hazel set against a backdrop of white birch bark. From this point we can hear the creek below. Waypoint 7 is located where the trail intersects the creek.

Eight: Drop Pools and Tortured Basalt

The creek winds its way around large, angular boulders of Beaver River Diabase that represent an old *talus* deposit. The creek has a nice "drop pool" effect as it flows down a fairly steep little valley. The water tumbles over rocky ledges (2 to 3 feet high) to then rest in a shallow pool before falling over the next low, rocky ledge to rest in the next drop pool.

From the creek the trail climbs out of the ravine to waypoint 8, an outcrop of *Tortured Basalt* to the right, to the left aspen trees are piled one onto another looking very much as though they came tumbling down like a row of dominos. The basalt is massive and grey and breaks into angular pieces along numerous fractures.

Nine: Bowling Ball Anorthosite and a Barred Owl

The walk continues through a birch forest over a trail composed of angular basalt and glacial till, which includes cobbles and boulders of diabase, basalt, and granite, before heading uphill to a large, rounded outcrop of *anorthosite* (waypoint 9). The anorthosite is moss-covered and dark and exhibits the typical smooth bowling ball weathering seen in many of the anorthosite *xenoliths*. The outcrop is ringed by maples, oaks, and *Juneberries*.

Overhead two broad-winged hawks call and fly about, landing in nearby trees, then diving down into the brush, then back up onto a branch. There is a barred owl calling its "who cooks for you all" question, and the robins are singing like crazy. One could sit for a long, long time on top of this ancient bowling ball breathing in the fresh spring air and contemplating the spiritual completeness of this little patch of ground in the north woods. The view is about 270 degrees, and, without leaves, the rolling hills, beaver pond, and great lake beyond are prominent. The *honeysuckle* is already blooming with bright yellow flowers!

Ten: Twin Lake Trail Loop and Amygdaloidal Basalt

Immediately past the anorthosite bowling ball there is an outcrop of *amygdaloidal basalt* with 10-15% raised *quartz*-filled *amygdules*. These may be hard to see because of the lichen growth. Just past the basalt, to the right, is an outcrop of Beaver River Diabase, possibly indicating that both the anorthosite and basalt are xenoliths or inclusions in the diabase.

From the diabase outcrop it is a nice walk through an open maple, birch, and oak forest to the Georges Gorge Snowmobile trail. Apparently the trail has been eroding here due to water seepage, and rocks (diabase) have been brought in to try and stabilize the soil. The rocks give this part of the trail a "cobbled street" look. From the snowmobile trail the pleasant walk through open woods continues with gentle ups and downs past a small stream full of *marsh marigolds* and tiny naked *miterwort* leaves. This is probably a great area for wildflowers; unfortunately on this early April day, with snow showers threatening, there isn't much to be seen.

The trail heads uphill along an intermittent stream to the junction with the Twin Lakes Loop trail and waypoint 10.

Eleven: Elam's Knob

Taking the left trail to Bean Lake we continue through an aspen-birch forest with some maple, passing by an ash swamp with large aspen trees. Crossing a corduroy trail section, the foot path heads uphill through an open birch-maple forest with the green whorled leaves of *shinleaf pyrola* covering much of the ground. Passing an anorthosite outcrop we arrive at the junction with the Twin Lakes Trail and a spur trail to Elam's knob. This knob is a high anorthosite hill from whose top there is a nice view of Silver Bay.

Twelve: Ephemeral Pond and the Superior Hiking Trail

Just past the spur trail there is a small *ephemeral* pond with ash trees. From here it's across and down lumpy Beaver River Diabase (medium-grained variety) that contains "clots" of the black mineral augite (a pyroxene); on the weathered surface this gives the rock a "salt and pepper" look. We then descend, over rocky steps, into a valley filled with maple, birch, and oak with some ash trees. Passing another ephemeral pond we come to the junction with the Superior Hiking Trail which is waypoint 12.

Thirteen: Penn Creek, Maples, and Birch Forest

Heading downhill, the Superior Hiking Trail, composed of glacial till, passes an anorthosite outcrop to the left before crossing a small creek. Cinnamon and *ostrich ferns* are notable through here along with *swamp saxifrage*. The trail then winds through a maple and birch forest with *bellwort* and *rose-twisted stalk* covering the forest floor to a small pond. I think the pond is the perfect home for some hideous swamp monster, but Judy thinks it's a beautiful spot with lots of interesting plants. There is an outcrop of anorthosite on the far side of the pond whose shape suggests either the "pond monster" crawling out of the swamp, or a sand worm from the planet Dune! Red oak trees are abundant here and have joined maple, birch, and ash to make a nice open forest.

Continuing past an outcrop of Beaver River Diabase and lots of *thimbleberries* we walk through a nice forest, to an outcrop of dark, massive-looking Tortured Basalt. The basalt, which in places looks "twisted," is breaking along crossing fractures and vertical cooling joints into small angular pieces with sharp edges. From this outcrop there is a nice view of the rolling hills and forest to the south. Lots of red oak grows here along with swamp saxifrage, *mullein*, *blue bell* and hedge *bindweed*, (a morning glory-like flower). The green flecks of color seen on the rocks is paint used "long ago" to mark the trail. From the basalt outcrop the trail remains flat, with glacial till sections, until reaching the rock steps that lead down to Penn Creek (waypoint 13). Along the creek there are lots of ferns, *meadow rue*, and *honeysuckle*. The marsh marigolds are done blooming and have set their round fruits.

Fourteen: Penn Creek Camp Site, Tortured Basalt, and Beaver Pond

A set of rock steps leads out of Penn Creek to the spur trail to the Penn Creek campsite. Just past the spur trail there is a large outcrop of Tortured Basalt that forms a rock ridge with an overlook (waypoint 14) to the southwest. There is a beaver pond (formed by the Penn Creek Beavers?) down in the Bean Creek Valley. We also have nice views back toward Silver Bay and the red-topped water towers. Pale pink *corydalis* is flowering here, and the choke cherries have buds.

The wind has suddenly found new energy and decides to blow the lake fog inland. Dark clouds are starting to roll over the horizon to the northeast, and we both agree there's a storm coming

Fifteen: Bean Lake

Tortured Basalt continues as the trail passes through a mixed birch, maple, red oak, balsam poplar, and balsam fir forest. Passing an access trail to Bean Lake and a sign pointing ahead toward Bean and Bear Lakes it's uphill over wooden steps and small outcrops of massive basalt. Crossing a small stream, we walk up to an open area where there is an outcrop of Beaver River Diabase. In looking at a geology map of this area there is an interconnected network of diabase *dikes* and *sills* that have intruded the North Shore Volcanic Group and, in places, have completely enclosed or surrounded parts of these lava flows. The diabase tends to be finer grained close to the flows and coarser gained further away.

Continuing along the hillside views of the Bean Creek Valley and a beaver pond remain prominent as we walk over outcrops of "painted diabase." It is then uphill to waypoint 15, an overlook directly above Bean Lake, the first "wow" spot of the day. There is a fantastic view over a steep rocky cliff with a sheer drop of 120 feet to the small, rock bound lake below. Today, with the strong wind, there are white caps on the lake! To the south is the Beaver River Valley and, in the distance, a high, shimmering cloud-like feature that is not a mirage or a high mountain lake but part of the huge tailings pond for the North Shore Taconite Processing Plant located in Silver Bay. This feature is called Mile Post 7 Tailings Pond, the place where the fine waste material (mainly iron silicate minerals and *chert*) from the *taconite* process is stored.

Bean Lake is ringed by cedar trees, an almost constant line with birch and aspen behind them. The diabase that outcrops here and along the trail to this waypoint, looks like someone came along with a can of red paint and painted lines, swirls, bands, and circles on the rock. Throughout this area brick red *hematite* (iron oxide) forms veins and intricate patterns through the rock. In fact the light colored "dots or splotches" seen on some outcrop surfaces represent the original rock, the rest has been converted to red hematite.

The geology map of this area shows that Bean and Bear Lakes sit in a narrow wedge or raft of basalt lava that is completely enclosed by the diabase. The cliffs on either side of the two lakes are composed of "painted" diabase. The basalt lava is easier to erode than the diabase, and this, along with the help of the glacial ice (*plucking)* led to the formation of the deep valley in which the lakes now sit.

Sixteen: Scary Cliff, Stunted Trees, and a Jasper Vein

The trail turns northeast to follow the steep cliff that rises 120 feet above Bean Lake. The rock exposed along the cliff is Painted Diabase. On the cliff wall across the lake prominent cooling joints stand out due to the preferential weathering that occurs along them.

The trail turns into the trees, and those closest to the cliff–the ones exposed to the cold and wind–are pretty sad looking and stunted. They look like Paul Bunyan made it a point to sit on each and every one. These are, however, hearty trees, that are able to hold their own against the fierce wind and snow that constantly pummels and piles on them. Their tenacity is a good lesson for us all. The forest beyond these front line warriors is dominated by maple and birch with more and more large white pine the deeper you travel into it; the low vegetation is dominantly *pipsissewa*, pyrola, and *club moss*. The trail passes through the forest and up a set of stone steps over Painted Diabase before turning back toward the cliff and a steep drop-off. Waypoint 16 is at an outcrop of lumpy diabase that has a large vein of *jasper* through it (just beyond the overlook). At first glance the vein looks like a thick tree root that has wedged its way into and through the rock. The outcrop is also crossed by veins of quartz and *orthoclase* (pink feldspar). There is a nice view down the length of Bean Lake and, in the distance, the shimmering Milepost 7 tailings pond.

Seventeen: Bear Lake and an Old Cabin

The trail follows the cliff edge over Painted Diabase with great views of Bear Lake and all the rock talus that's been *frost-wedged* from the surrounding diabase cliffs. The woods are a mix of maple and birch with some large spruce. Waypoint 17 is at the remains of an old cabin or shelter, which is now just a pile of cut logs and wood. This small cabin was built by a group of kids from Silver Bay in the 1960s.

Eighteen: Bear Lake Campsite Spur Trail

From the wood pile we head downhill over Painted Diabase to the northeast end of Bear Lake and a spur trail (waypoint 18) down to the lake and the Bear Lake campsite (4 tent pads). The woods continue as before but now have some nice, old-growth maples. *Bunchberry* and *blue bead lily* are common along this trail section.

Nineteen: Cliff and Talus, Bear Lake, and Twin Lakes Trail Loop

Walking east into the woods we follow the bottom of a steep cliff with lots of talus before climbing up the cliff. In fact the trail consists mostly of diabase boulders and diabase steps. The Beaver River Diabase exposed here has lost its painted look. At the cliff top there is a spectacular view down Bear Lake; the diabase outcrop here is intensely weathered with lots of kibbles and bits along the trail. There is large flowered bellwort and *clematis* along the trail up to the overlook, and, at the top, *yellow vetchling*.

From this overlook it is a short distance over Beaver River Diabase to waypoint 19, the junction with the northeast loop of the Twin Lakes Trail. At the waypoint Judy and I find what we call a "happy" book. This is a log book placed here by the Superior Hiking Trail Association for hikers to write their thoughts in, good or bad, though most are good, which is why we call these "happy" books. A stone path leads down to the cliff edge and a nice overlook of Bear Lake. Oak trees along with *Canadian mayflowers, asters,* and club moss are common here.

Twenty: Talus Pile and Overlook

From the Superior Hiking Trail the Twin Lakes Trail heads southeast, uphill over Beaver River Diabase, to a large, open grass-and-lichen-covered basalt outcrop with an impressive talus pile at its base. The basalt contains small amygdules and feldspar crystals. There is a nice view from here to the southwest and south of an aspen-birch forest, Bear Lake, Silver Bay and its red-topped water towers, and the hilly landscape carved out by glaciers and running water. Diabase dikes and sills tend to form the hills, and basalt lava flows form the valleys. There are currents blooming on the outcrop.

It was here I made a one in a million shot. Breaking off a piece of basalt at the edge of the outcrop I tossed it toward Judy so she could look at it. Would you believe it? The rock landed smack on top of my GPS unit! Not if I tried 100 times would I be able to do that again. Needless to say the GPS didn't like being smacked by a three-pound piece of rock, so it decided not to work. Fortunately it came back to life long enough to finish the hike, but I fear it is permanently out of whack.

Twenty-One: The Amazing Forest

We follow the hillside with nice views of "no name valley" and the Milepost 7 tailings pond; red pines put in an appearance along the ridge crest. Passing over an outcrop of Beaver River Diabase, the trail descends into a low area with large aspens. Judy gets all excited here telling me what an amazing place this is because of the forest mix. There are maple, ash, oak, birch, aspen, and red pine all in one place. The maples are flowering like crazy and really stand out on this grey day. Waypoint 21 is in the wonderful mixed forest down in a small valley between two ridges.

Twenty-Two: Swamp and Ash Forest

From here it is a really nice walk over a hard-packed, relatively smooth trail through an open maple, birch, and oak forest. As we walk along Judy notices the increasing number of maple trees, and the corresponding decrease in the number of oak trees. Waypoint 22 is at a wet, swampy area with an ash forest. The swamp is filled with marsh marigolds, naked miterwort, and ferns. There is a corduroy boardwalk here.

Ten: Junction of Twin Lakes Loop

It's a short walk from the swamp to the junction for the loop trail which was waypoint 10 on the way up. From here follow the trail back to waypoint 1 and the parking lot in Silver Bay.

"A very nice walk," Judy says. "I wonder how many people get to visit Elam's Knob and see the Lombardy pines, blow down, as well as beautiful Bean and Bear lakes. A easy walk for those not inclined to do the long walk from Silver Bay to Tettegouche."

Superior Hiking Trail

Walk 10: Kennedy Cliffs and Sawmill Dome

Walk Logistics

Start: State Highway 1 to Finland

Getting There: Just past the Tettegouche State Park Visitor's Center turn left onto State Highway 1. The parking lot for the hiking trail is on the left 0.8 miles past the turn off (it's small and easy to miss).

End: Lake County Road 6 (Little Marais Road)

Getting There: Take Highway 61 to Little Marais. Turn left onto Lake County Road 6 and go 2.1 miles to the parking lot in a gravel pit located on the right side of the road.

Walk Distance: 6.8 miles   **Dates Walked:** June 14th, 2004, August 6th, 2005

Worth a Longer Look:

Crystal Creek: 2	Crack In The Rock: 16
Pink Anorthosite: 7	Maple-Birch Forest: 18
Wolf Lake Overlook: 8	Sawmill Dome: 19
Spotted Rocks: 9	Anorthosite Steps: 20
Great Cliff: 11	Old Maples: 21
Superior View: 14	Sawmill Creek Valley: 22

Waypoint-to-Waypoint

One: Parking Lot off Highway 1

The small parking lot off Highway 1 IS hard to find. Judy and I missed it the first time, but creeping along the highway like army worms searching for birch trees, we are successful on the second attempt. I think part of the problem is not paying attention (us); the other part is that we didn't expect it to be so close to Highway 61.

As it turns out the army worms beat us here. Leaves have been eaten on a few of the trees, but the damage is not too bad considering the havoc these voracious caterpillars caused two years ago. I remember highways oily black and slick as ice from the thousands of tire-flattened bodies, not to mention worm-covered houses and cabins. Worse was hiking through the woods when they were hatching out or on the move to a new food source. They

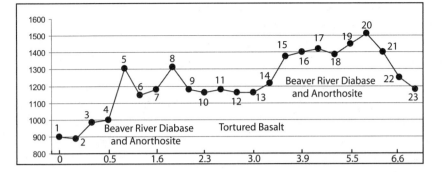

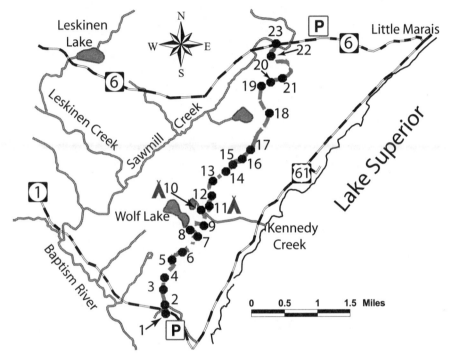

descended from trees on long silk threads filling the forest with a constant pitter-patter that sounded like raindrops on dry leaves as they fell the final few feet to the ground. They drop on anything that is in their path, and walking into the nearly invisible silk parachutes is about as much fun as walking through a giant spider web or being covered in wood ticks. Fortunately, they are now on the down cycle, and it should be another 8 years before they return in force. The "friendly flies" are also on the way out. These large, slow, flies eat the larva of the army worms (hence they are called friendly), but when you have a few hundred crawling on you that's not exactly what you're thinking.

Two: Crystal Creek

Leaving the parking lot we cross Highway 1 and walk about 100 feet along the north side of the road toward Finland to the sign marking the start of the Superior Hiking Trail. There are *boulders* of medium-grained *Beaver River Diabase* here.

Following the flat and muddy footpath, lined with *coltsfoot* leaves we come to Crystal Creek, which is waypoint 2. The creek is small and peppy here but it grows larger as it nears Lake Superior. On this section of the trail there are purple and yellow *violets*, M*ertensia*, and *blue bead lily; marsh marigolds* are blooming in Crystal Creek. The second time we walked this section, in August of 2005, the creek is dry as an old bone.

Three: Overlook, Snow White, and the Five Diabase Brothers

From Crystal Creek the trail passes through a cedar grove into an area burned in a 1990 forest fire. The first trees to reclaim such areas are sun loving birch and aspen, which explains why they are all about the same height and size. There are lots and lots of *strawberries* as well as *raspberries*, bracken and interrupted ferns, and alders.

After a short, planked section there is a gentle uphill followed by more flat, muddy trail. It is here Judy proclaims the wildflower of the day to be the *Canadian mayflower* (wild lily of the valley); its white, four-parted flowers are everywhere. The mayflowers are joined by abundant strawberries and *baneberries* to give a speckled white color to the woodland vegetation.

There is another gentle uphill over a trail partly covered by *cobbles* and boulders of *basalt, diabase, rhyolite*, pink *monzonite*, and *granite* which have all been weathered out of the *glacial till.* Crossing a grassy road, Judy names it White Tail Deer Ridge Road, because of all the deer tracks. From here it is uphill to waypoint 3, an overlook to the south and east. There is a nice view of the *anorthosite* knob just south of Highway 1, which ended Hike 8. Standing there, admiring the view, Judy scares the —— out of me by suddenly yelling "Zap!" in reference to the intense lightning storm that immediately followed our descent off that particular rock hill.

The *outcrop* at this waypoint is lumpy diabase (see *diabase weathering*), and because we were singing "whistle while you work" on the way up the hill, this particular rock texture started a train of rather strange thoughts that led me to Snow White and the five kinds of diabase we have so far encountered along the Superior Hiking Trail. For sure there are four that are common: smooth, lumpy, crumbly, and kibbles and bits. Then there is painted which we saw on walk 8. Without doubt Snow White has to be the anorthosite, the small to very large inclusions or *xenoliths* that are imprisoned by the five diabase brothers! When I explain all this to Judy she is kind enough not to groan too loudly!

There are lots of rose buds here but as yet few flowers, and the *Juneberry* is all but gone. Pale or common vetch is in bloom, and *starflowers*, yet another small white flower, are all over the place.

Four: Nodding Trilliums, Mountain Maples, and the Rock Birch

The trail is relatively level over lumpy diabase as it passes through an older birch forest with lots of dogwood before arriving at a diabase outcrop with a large birch tree growing right up out of the rock. Actually, that's not quite true, but that's what it looks like. The tree has managed to find a secure place between the rocks to establish itself. From here the trail turns muddy and is partly covered by cobbles as it enters an area of small birch trees and lots of mountain or moose maples. Coltsfoot leaves continue to be prominent, a good indicator of the wet condition of the soil. The new white flower of the moment is nodding *trillium*.

The vegetation through this section is far taller than Charlie, and he completely vanishes when he wanders off the trail. Though, according to Judy, that doesn't really say much for the height of the vegetation!

Waypoint 4 is a small creek just before an uphill section.

Five: Schist, Diabase, and Fantasia

From the creek it's steadily uphill, over a rocky trail bounded by a thick understory dominated by bracken fern and large-leafed aster. The forest canopy is dominantly paper birch, maple, and skinny aspen. About halfway to the hilltop the trail crosses a small "plateau" before continuing upward over two large, gray angular slabs of basalt and a large, dark glacial erratic of a metamorphic rock called *schist*. There are numerous diabase boulders along this section; these come from the hill to the west. They are mixed with glacial erratics of a composition similar to those of waypoint 3. As the trail takes us closer to the hilltop the forest changes to one dominated by maples.

Waypoint 5 is located at the junction with the spur trail to Fantasia Overlook, a 0.5 mile walk that leads to a high, rocky point from which can be seen Palisade Head, Mount Trudee, and the harbor at Silver Bay.

Six: Funnel Spiders and Glacial Erratics

The main trail, which heads down the hillside, becomes difficult to walk on not only because it's muddy and slick (in August it is so dry we kick up dust walking on it) but also because it's been sloped in the wrong direction. Crossing a small stream filled with boulders and cobbles of pink and grey granitic rocks, along with diabase and basalt, Judy points out another change in the forest. The lower we descend, the less maple and more birch there are which is exactly the reverse of what we observed on the way up the hill.

Continuing downhill there are numerous glacial erratics along the trail: boulders of anorthosite, *Agate Flow*, and pink granite to name a few. At the bottom of the hill (waypoint 6) there is a large glacial erratic of pink granite along with a smaller one of white granite.

Prominent along this section of the trail are the webs of funnel spiders. These are probably a common occurrence all along the hiking trail but are really noticeable in the morning sun after a heavy dew. The water drops outline the funnel-shaped webs, which glisten in the sunshine. Once the web is outlined, it's easy to key in on the spider patiently waiting for a visitor to drop by.

Seven: Pink Anorthosite and One Rose

Walking on we come to an old logging road that offers a grand view of the area logged replete with piles of slash. The forest on the south side of the trail is dominated by closely spaced, scrubby balsam poplar, while the north side still retains large balsam poplar, unfortunately many of these appear to be dead. *Wild geraniums* and *orchids* (trifida) are blooming.

Crossing the logging road the trail passes through an area with old, large balsam poplars and large birch trees with outstretched, spreading branches. We then head uphill to a small hillside creek with *Jack-in-the-pulpit, columbine,* and *wild ginger* in bloom. There are numerous boulders and cobbles in the creek (from the glacial till), and the creek flows around and under many of these rocks making interesting sounds that vary from low, gentle murmurs to impatient gurgles .

Continuing uphill over lumpy diabase we reach the hilltop passing through what has become a dominantly birch forest with lots of *honeysuckle* and *bunchberries*. Just beyond the hilltop a large glacial erratic of pink anorthosite is resting comfortably on an outcrop of lumpy diabase. The pink color of the anorthosite is due to trace amounts of either iron or manganese in the *plagioclase feldspar* crystals, and, fittingly, there is a lone pink rose blooming beside the anorthosite boulder. Plump, red rose hips remain where the flowers have faded, and the purple of the *fireweed* flowers adds extra color to the scene.

At the hilltop there is a view east to Lake Superior. *Yarrow* and choke cherries are blooming while the Juneberry still has its white flowers. There is also another "dang it flower," one Judy can't immediately identify (this one turned out to be *hairy rock cress*). Directly below us is another cutover area, which we decide would be perfect for one of those new North Shore subdivisions. In the tradition of developers naming subdivisions for plants or trees that don't grow anywhere near their development, or which have all been cut down to make room for the development, we figure this could be called Royal Oak Estates or White Pines Retirement Community.

Eight: Wolf Lake, Kennedy Cliffs, and Wolf Ridge

Still going uphill, we pass a large spruce tree and come to a wooden signpost with "entering Wolf Ridge property" on one side and "leaving Wolf Ridge property" on the other. This reminds me of the "enter" and "leave" signs for a very small town, both on the same post. From the property boundary it's a short walk over lumpy diabase with kibbles and bits to the first "wow" spot of the day, the overlook above Wolf (Johnson) Lake. Standing high above the lake and directly across from us is Kennedy Cliffs. Composed of anorthosite, the most prominent part of the cliffs looks like the back of a large bison. There is a peregrine falcon nesting box on the cliffs, and this is also a favorite spot for rock climbers (though I'm not sure what the falcons think of this). In Wolf Lake there is a loon nesting platform. To the left is Fantasia Overlook and to the right Marshall Mountain, another anorthosite knob. Also, from here, we can clearly see some of the buildings and the windmill at Wolf Ridge Environmental Learning Center (WRLEC). Wolf Lake occupies the contact between the anorthosite of Kennedy Cliffs and the diabase, on which we stand. The contact is defined by a geological *fault*.

Nine: Spotted Rocks

Walking along the edge of the cliff over lumpy diabase we turn east into a birch and balsam poplar forest. Passing by some big birch trees the trail goes downhill to waypoint 9, an overlook of Lake Superior and a large outcrop of diabase that is chock-full of small xenoliths of anorthosite. Here, in one outcrop, is a snapshot of the entire Beaver River Diabase and its relationship to the anorthosite inclusions it contains, inclusions like those at Mt. Trudee, Carlton Peak, and Kennedy Cliffs. The knife-sharp contacts between the cream and greenish-gray anorthosite and the lumpy brown to reddish-grey diabase are easy to follow. The sharpness of the contacts indicates the diabase *magma*, when it dislodged and incorporated the many anorthosite xenoliths, was at a temperature far below that of the melting point of the anorthosite (there is absolutely no reaction between the two).

Ten: Kennedy Creek and West Kennedy Creek Campsite

Crossing over the inclusion-rich diabase to the opposite side of the ridge there is a large knob of Bowling Ball Anorthosite and a wonderful view of Lake Superior and the rocky, rugged topography to the east and northeast; the Kennedy Creek Valley is directly below. The round or knob-shaped hills in the distance represent large anorthosite xenoliths in the Beaver River Diabase, the elongate hills are diabase, the valleys in-between are carved into the basalt.

The trail, framed by pale pink *corydalis* and white baneberry, heads downward through a birch forest with some nice spruce trees over more anorthosite (there is one large outcrop with nice ferns growing out of it) and

111

lumpy diabase to Kennedy Creek (waypoint 10) and the West Kennedy Creek campsite. On this particular morning the weathered white bones of a dead moose grace the edge of the campsite.

Eleven: East Kennedy Creek Campsite, Large Anthills, and a Great Cliff (30)

From Kennedy Creek it's a short walk to a triple junction in the trail. The trail heading west goes to the WRELC, the one going east leads to the East Kennedy Creek campsite, and the main trail continues ahead.

From the junction onward large anthills can be found along the trail, and these may represent fast food for a wandering bear or a nice winter home for snakes. The trail then goes uphill over lumpy gabbro to the hilltop and more anorthosite. A short walk along the hilltop brings us to Great Cliff or what Judy calls a "magical little place." The cliff is almost level with the tops of young birch trees whose white bark provides a dramatic backdrop that enhances the bunchberries marking the cliff edge, the spotted diabase that provides the geology, and the Kennedy Creek Valley that provides the view.

Twelve: Hazelnuts, Black Bear, and Basalt

Departing Great Cliff it's back into pure diabase with the trail leveling out and becoming partly covered by roundish rocks weathered from the glacial till. These add an element of excitement to the hike, for walking over them is like walking on a road covered in oil coated marbles. There is a giant anthill in this section (made by giant ants?), and the forest is dominantly birch with a hazel understory.

Black bears actually migrate into this area each fall, from as far north as Tower and Ely, to feast on the hazelnuts. If hiking this section in the fall, be prepared for lots of bear signs (but hopefully, with enough noise, no bears).

Continuing through the birch-hazel forest, come to an area where the trial is littered with pieces of basalt lava (waypoint 12), which geologists call "float". The basalt, frost-heaved from an outcrop just below the surface, contains small feldspar crystals along with vesicles (gas cavities) that are lined by tiny *quartz* crystals and partly filled by calcite and a pink *zeolite* (laumantite). The *sarsaparilla* is blooming all long here.

Thirteen: Johnson Road, Spittle Bugs, and Large Aspens

After the basalt float the trail enters a wide, grassy area with dead and/or dying birch trees. With all the tall grass to wade through Judy thinks this place would be the closest thing to heaven for a tick. Having no interest in finding out we hurry on passing between some very large, old aspens (70-80 years?) to arrive at the junction with a ski trail to Wolf Ridge (waypoint 13). This trail, in part, follows an old road called the Johnson Lake Road. It is through this trail section that Judy sees her first spittle bugs of the year.

These winged insects are best known for the unusual way they protect themselves. They produce a liquid that they whip up into a mass of bubbles, and then they hide inside it. This mass is called "spittle" and that's where the bugs name comes from. The "spittle" also helps insulate them from heat and cold, they also use it as a moisturizing agent.

Fourteen: Superior View and Tortured Basalt

Following the ski trail we come to a power line and small creek, both of which are crossed by the hiking trail. The Superior Hiking Trail now follows the route used by classes from the WRELC to reach a spectacular overlook called Superior View. Along this route there are big spruce trees, and the trail is partly covered with rocks (diabase, basalt, anorthosite) weathered out of the till. There is a steep hill to the left with *frost-wedged talus* at its base; the forest is dominantly spruce, aspen, birch, and balsam. Judy calls this a SABB forest; I guess that's for small, abundant and blatantly boring!

Part of this section follows a well maintained boardwalk which ends at a massive basalt cliff. The trail goes up the steep cliff, passing lots of blueberry plants and a few old white pine stumps.

At the top is waypoint 14 and the second wow spot of the day–Superior View indeed! Looking east it's a sea of green all the way to the wide, sparkling blue waters of Gitchi Gummi. The low green hills slope toward the lake because they are formed from basalts of the *North Shore Volcanic Group*, all of which dip or are tilted in that direction. To the south and southeast are Fantasia Overlook, Kennedy Cliffs, and Marshall Mountain. The high hill immediately to our left is composed of diabase.

The basalt outcropping here is *Tortured B*asalt. The rock has irregular, sharp to step-like surfaces formed by weathering and breaking along numerous fractures or cracks that criss-cross the rock. All-in-all it would appear this rock has been given a rough time by Mother Earth.

The shrubs and small trees around the overlook have been extensively browsed by deer (apparently they appreciate the view too); there is abundant orange *hawkweed* and, the first time we were here, there were zillions of "friendly" flies." The pipe you see cemented into the outcrop is used for a spotting scope by WRELC classes.

Fifteen: Glacial Striations and Snow Storms

Continuing upslope to the opposite side of the hill over lumpy diabase with lots of kibbles and bits, we come to an overlook with a view of the Kennedy Creek Valley (the birch in the valley are noticeable because they are mostly dead), Kennedy Cliffs, and the hill we stood on at waypoint 8. This hill has the classic shape of a *cuesta*, and these shaped hills form the so-named *Sawtooth Mountains* seen further north. Canadian mayflower remains dominant through here, and the thick maple-birch woods make a nice contrast to the thinner look of the SABB forest.

Walking along the hillside there are steep drop-offs and more massive diabase, along with lots of kibbles and bits, before entering into a birch-maple forest. Passing a small pond with alder we arrive at Chatter Mark Creek and waypoint 15. The creek bed is partly composed of a *massive* outcrop of diabase that has been worn and polished by the running water; in fact it looks like the perfect water slide. The polished look emphasizes the *glacial striations* and *chatter marks* on the outcrop. When the creek is dry the outcrop may be covered in moss making the striations difficult to see, but the triangular chatter marks remain prominent.

Rose-twisted stalk is blooming, and the big aspens are in full seed. In fact, the wind blowing through the big trees is creating a mini-snowstorm as it brings the seeds to the ground, each tiny seed is attached to a dandelion-like parachute.

Sixteen: Crack in the Rock

Leaving the creek the trail goes gently uphill past a talus pile of diabase boulders and over diabase outcrops to a nice view of Lake Superior. Today the wind blowing over the surface of the lake, combined with the reflection of the sun off the popcorn-shaped clouds, gives the lake a delicious variety of blue, green, and gray colors, as well as an array of rapidly changing patterns and textures.

Continuing uphill, over steps of diabase, we come to waypoint 16, the famous Crack In The Rock. At this place the trail is routed between a large, smooth outcrop of diabase and a large chunk of rock that was once part of that outcrop. Frost wedging along fractures and *cooling joints*, caused the chunk to break off and fall to where we now see it. Just before reaching Crack In The Rock, there is a smaller example of the same process. The columbine is really large through here.

Seventeen: Trembling Leaves and Crack in Rock In Progress

The trail winds along the hillside passing a Crack In Rock in progress and through a forest of nice older spruce and aspen with some maple. The wind is making soft music with the trembling leaves, and with no other sounds in the forest or from the outside modern world, this makes a wonderful backdrop to the great variety of bird songs. Waypoint 17 is a smooth outcrop of diabase with a large, angular diabase boulder balanced on the outcrop. The boulder is in the process of splitting in two and thus forming another Crack In The Rock.

Eighteen Garden Smells and a Nice Walk

The trail, with gentle ups and downs, winds through the maple-birch forest, providing a lovely 0.5 mile walk. The sun gives the forest floor a speckled appearance, and the only sounds are the wind in the trees and the songs of many different birds. There are lots of flowers through here: wild roses and rose-twisted stalk, *Dutchman's breeches*, Canadian mayflowers, and pin cherries. The mixture of sweet and earthy smells is delightful. Blue bead lily, with its blue berries, and baneberry, with its white berries, will make a dramatic appearance in August.

Waypoint 18 is at a small pond with dark brown water (the brown color is due to tannic acid which comes from swamps and/or dead leaves and other organic material); there are some ash trees on the north side and lots and lots of ferns around the pond. Judy refers to it as a "grove of fern trees;" perhaps it's one of the imaginary forests of Lilliput. There is a small glacial erratic of white granite to the right of the trail.

Nineteen: Sawmill Dome

From the pond we continue through the maple-birch forest, passing an overlook with views of Lake Superior and the forest east, to the Chocolate Milkshake Bog. The water here is thick, slimy, and chocolaty brown; neither dog wants anything to do with it. Elderberry is in flower, and *false Solomon seal* is abundant. There are a few very large birch mixed in with the maple, and we know the moose like this forest because their tracks are everywhere.

The long walk through the nice maple woods continues with kidney-leaved *buttercups*, blue bead lily, *dewberries*, purple violets, and Mertensia in bloom; the *bedstraw* has buds. We walk over lumpy and smooth diabase outcrops, and go by two large white pine on the ridge to the left.

The trail traverses a flat diabase outcrop in a muddy section before heading uphill over anorthosite to waypoint 19, Sawmill Dome. The dome is a knob of anorthosite that overlooks the Sawmill Creek Valley. Descend down from waypoint 19, via a series of steps made from cut logs, to the open edge of the Dome. This spot offers great views to the north, northwest (old Finland airbase), and of the Sawbill Creek Valley and Highway 6 below us.

Twenty: Right Angle White Pine and Anorthosite Steps

After soaking up the great view for a while, we walk down off the dome, and along its edge over anorthosite steps; this is one of the only places in the world where there are steps of this rare rock type. Continuing on past a moss-covered bank and a hummocky outcrop of anorthosite with cedars growing on it we come to one amazing white pine that grows horizontally out, away from the rock, before taking a right turn to grow straight upward. The parallel cracks in the large anorthosite outcrop are due to *exfoliation* or unloading, and this process leads to the formation of the ledges seen in the rock. There are a few large maple and yellow birch here.

Twenty-One: Picnic Rock and Old Maples

We continue downhill past the junction with the spur trail to Picnic Rock (a wonderful, cool, open place on a hot summer day) and on through a forest of large old maples, their branches and leaves high above the forest floor. There are also cedars here and really big yellow birch, though most of these are dead and on the ground. Juneberries, elderberries, currents, and *blueberries* are common through here along with some old choke cherry trees. Waypoint 21 is at an outcrop of Tortured Basalt, and this rock forms a small ridge that parallels the trail.

Twenty-Two: Steep Drop-Off and More Anorthosite

The long, but nice forest walk continues through large maple and yellow birch to the edge of the diabase ridge with a steep 200-foot drop into the Sawmill Creek Valley. From here we follow the ridge with views of the gravel pit and parking lot off Highway 6. After passing a large white pine there is a short downhill section over lumpy diabase with lots of kibbles and bits. This is followed by a short walk up and over crumbly anorthosite, via some wooden steps, to waypoint 22, another anorthosite knob. There are nice views back to Sawmill Dome and down into the Sawmill Creek Valley. The forest is no longer filled with beautiful maples, it's now a much younger SABB forest (spruce, aspen, balsam popular, and birch).

Twenty-Three: Highway 6 and Sawmill Creek Flood Plain

The trail heads steeply down over anorthosite and diabase to the valley floor. This is followed by a short walk across the logged off flood plain of Sawmill Creek to the Superior Hiking Trail sign at Highway 6 (waypoint 23). From here there is a 0.4 mile walk along the highway, crossing over Sawmill Creek, to the parking lot in a gravel pit on the left side of the road.

Yet another great walk on a superb foot path. Kennedy Cliffs and the Wolf Lake Overlook, pink anorthosite, Crack In The Rock, Sawmill Dome, old maple forests, Great Cliff, Superior View, Tortured Basalt, and the anorthosite steps were all, in their unique way, worth long extra looks!

Superior Hiking Trail
Walk 11: Giant Erratic, Lady Slippers, and Sawmill Creek

Walk Logistics

Start: Lake County Road 6 (Little Marais Road)

Getting There: Take Highway 61 to Little Marais. Turn left onto Lake County Road 6 and go 2.1 miles to the parking lot in a gravel pit located on the right side of the road.

End: Finland Recreation Center

Getting There: Take Highway 61 to Highway 1. Turn left and follow Highway 1 for 7.4 miles to the junction with County Road 7 (Cramer Road). Turn right on to County Road 7, and go 1.3 miles to the parking lot on the right just past the baseball field at the recreation center.

Walk Distance: 7.3 miles   **Date Walked:** June 21st, 2004

Worth a Longer Look:

Wetlands: 1	Beaver Dam Crossing: 12
Wild Flowers: 2	Sawmill Creek Valley: 13
Turtle Pond: 4	Giant Erratic and Orchids: 15
Twin Flowers: 5	Lady Slippers: 17
Judy's Canyon: 6, 8	Magical Bog: 18
Anorthosite Whale: 9	Pink Anorthosite: 21
Anorthosite Creek: 10	Tortured Basalt: 25
Orchids: 11, 23	

Waypoint-to-Waypoint

One: Spruce Budworm and Wildflowers

Leaving the small parking lot next to the gravel pit we walk 0.25 miles north along Highway 6, crossing Sawmill Creek to the Superior Hiking Trail sign at waypoint 1. Sawmill Creek crosses under the road in a large culvert, and the result is a wonderful wetland environment on both sides of the road. Take time to note birds and seasonal flowers in bloom.

It's a warm and humid morning with a pale orange sun trying its best to burn off the patchy grey scum that separates its heat from us. It's officially the first day of summer, and, in honor of this, Judy is dressed in shorts, a t-shirt, and sandals. If nothing else I figure she will keep the black flies and mosquitoes happy and away from me.

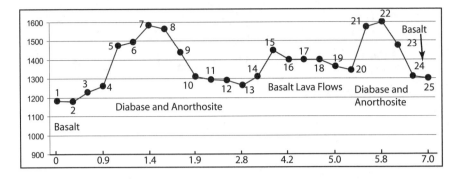

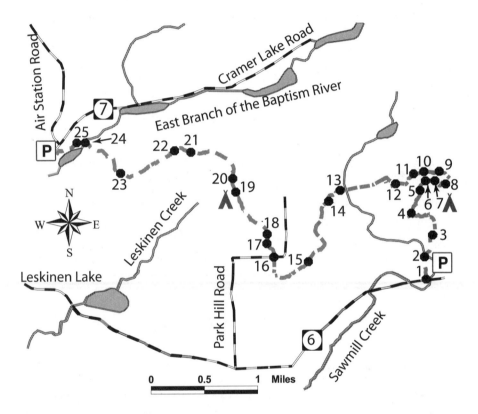

At the trail sign there are *starflowers*, *Mertensia, blue bead lily, bunchberry*, and *nodding trilliums* along with lots of *wild ginger*. Many of the spruce trees have a sticky, white substance on the ends of their branches, the start of spruce budworm and probably the demise of the tree.

Two: Sawmill Creek

Moving into the woods the trail passes through a boggy lowland with some cut and logged sections. Meadow *rue* is hip high, the elderberry is blooming, and, at long last, the ash trees are almost leafed out. Elderberry is one of the early-blooming shrubs; its buds are first cradled by green bracts and soon after, smallish white flowers appear. Late in the season, look for tiny red berries in clusters at the ends of twigs. Waypoint 2 is at Sawmill Creek; the creek water looks like brewed tea: it's tannic brown from having drained through bogs and swamps as it heads toward Superior.

Close to the creek there are *Canadian mayflowers* (wild lily of the valley), yellow and purple *violets*, white *baneberry, strawberries, false Solomon seal, rose-twisted stalk,* and *sarsaparilla.* The woods appear as two colors, green and white. According to Judy this is a good section to hike with all the different habitats giving rise to a variety of flowering plants.

Three: Ground Moraine and a Small Bog

It's a short hike up and out of the creek valley over a dry trail to a small bog (waypoint 3) and a view back (south) into the Sawmill Creek Valley. The rock material on and along the trail comes from weathering of the *glacial till* which, in this area, forms deposits called *ground moraine.*

What with the dogwoods, blue bead lily, strawberries, and purple *clematis* in bloom, Judy tells me it officially smells like summer. I'm not sure about that, but it definitely sounds like summer with the buzz of mosquitoes and the busy hum of tiny black flies.

Four: Glacial Boulders and Aspen Fluff

The trail is dry and level as it passes through a mixed forest of birch, spruce, aspen, and balsam poplar to a small *boulder*-filled creek. The boulders consist of *basalt*, pink *granite, rhyolite, Bird Droppings Basalt*, and the universal *Beaver River Diabase*. All this rock material comes from the erosion and removal by running water of the finer-grained silt, sand, and clay in the glacial till. The larger rocks are left behind and slowly become concentrated.

Ostrich and cinnamon *ferns* are common along the creek. *Dewberry* is done blooming and aspen fluff coats the trail and green vegetation giving this first day of summer a definite winter look. Aspen fluff, tiny white, hair-like structures, enable the seeds to float great distances from the parent tree.

From the creek the trail heads gently uphill passing a dry creek bed to a small pond full of *chickweed; pussytoes* and *wild roses* seem to ring the pond. According to Judy this is a good place to look for turtles, so we do and actually find several painted turtles sunning themselves. The forest at this point contains a lot more maple with birch and spruce mixed in. Canadian mayflowers are everywhere, and Judy proclaims them the white flower of the day. "Pretty amazing," I tell her, "Mayflowers at their height on the first day of summer; seems like we're behind in everything." Large-leaved *aster* and baneberry (doll's eye) leaves are just emerging.

Past Turtle Pond the trail continues uphill, gently at first then more steeply to the top where there is an *outcrop* of Beaver River Diabase (waypoint 4). To the southwest there is a nice view of the Sawmill Creek Valley (with numerous dead trees, thanks to the energetic beaver), and of Sawmill Dome (Walk 10). To the west, 4 miles away, is the old Finland airbase. There are pussytoes and wild roses here along with *blueberries* and *Juneberries*. Judy is having a whale of a time kicking old puffballs to get them to emit a cloud of fine, brown spores.

Five: Twinflowers

The trail follows the ridgeline over outcrops of Beaver River Diabase through a mixed forest of maple, birch, aspen, and balsam fir. Watch for *twinflowers,* pink *corydalis,* and northern white violets.

Passing a small seep we come to a spur trail (waypoint 5) that leads to an overlook of the Sawmill Creek Valley, and a small beaver pond with lodge. To the south Sawmill Dome remains visible as does the airbase to the west. There are piles of drowned birch and maple in and around the beaver pond. The rock outcrop here is smooth diabase that is in the early stages of going to pot, or turning lumpy (see *diabase weathering*).

Six: Bowling Ball Anorthosite and Judy's Canyon

It's a short walk through a nice maple-birch forest past moss-covered diabase and Bowling Ball *Anorthosite* to an anorthosite outcrop and overlook at waypoint 6. Here *spheroidal weathering* and *unloading* gives the anorthosite its bowling ball shape, and weathering also provides deep "finger holes" in the rock so giants can actually use this anorthosite for one of their thunderous bowling matches. At waypoint 6 the sharp contact between this grey anorthosite *xenolith* and the rusty brown *diabase* is clearly visible.

There is a nice view of the Sawmill Creek Valley and, directly across from the overlook is a small, steep canyon with prominent anorthosite knobs and ledges. I decide to name this Judy's Canyon because she is fascinated and intrigued by it. The canyon, reminiscent of those out west, is the result of a *fault* along the contact between the Beaver River Diabase and the anorthosite xenolith. *Columbine* and three-toothed *cinquefoil* are common here.

Seven: Anorthosite Sand and Section 13 Campsite

It's a short uphill walk to yet another overlook on more anorthosite. Here the anorthosite xenolith has been deeply and intensely weathered; it is pitted and, in places, has broken along crystal boundaries into lumps, which then weather to sand-size material.

From the overlook the trail heads down, off the anorthosite into Beaver River Diabase, through a maple-birch forest to the spur trail for the Section 13 campsite and another, more *massive* anorthosite outcrop (waypoint 7). Section 13 is a reference to topographic maps with each section a one-mile square or 640 acres.

Eight: Chicken Track Diabase and the Canyon

Off the anorthosite over a wide trail then uphill, passing outcrops of Bowling Ball Anorthosite, to a brand new (hooray) kind of diabase. This one Judy and I call Chicken Track Diabase because of the way the lath-like *plagioclase feldspar* crystals are oriented. They look like a chicken has walked randomly through the cooling magma leaving its "footprints" behind, much like a person does after walking through wet cement. The "chicken tracks" occur in a fine-grained dark diabase that represents a *dike* that intruded the Beaver River Diabase. The dike is part of the *Beaver Bay Igneous Complex* and therefore probably represents a feeder to lava flows of the *North Shore Volcanic Group*.

Waypoint 8 is yet another anorthosite knob, which provides a beautiful view of Judy's Canyon. There are lots of acorns on the trail, and though oak trees are present the forest is dominantly maple and birch with a hazel understory.

Nine: Section 13 Loop and the Anorthosite Whale

A steep descent into Judy's Canyon takes us past zillions of *naked miterwort* plants over a trail covered by boulders and *cobbles* of anorthosite, diabase, and basalt. We pass by numerous small Bowling Ball Anorthosite outcrops as we walk through a forest of maple and birch. Cedar trees become more abundant and larger the closer we get to the canyon floor. As we move deeper into the canyon, the darker and more secluded it seems. *Oak ferns* and naked miterwort are common; and the understory is predominantly mountain maple and hazel. All that is needed now is the sound of a canyon wren bouncing off the rock walls.

We pass a small creek with pink granite boulders (glacially derived) then walk over a muddy, planked area with lots of violets along with *bloodroot* leaves and *columbine*. Reaching the canyon bottom, there are large anorthosite boulders everywhere. These represent *frost-wedged* material from canyon walls. Waypoint 9 is at the spur trail for the 0.8 mile loop walk called Section 13. There is also a large anorthosite outcrop here that is shaped like a whale, one that appears to be coming straight at us. There are wild ginger and violets at the spur trail, which is well worth the side trip.

Ten: Canyon Wall and Anorthosite Creek

We walk along the narrow, steep canyon bottom with anorthosite outcrops, and a great view straight up a 200 foot high rock wall to the canyon top.

Past here, the trail follows a boulder-filled creek lined by cedars and one large white pine. Because the boulders in the creek are anorthosite, Judy and I decide to call this Anorthosite Creek. In places, small cedar trees are growing on top of the anorthosite boulders.

Walk over an outcrop of diabase to a long set of wooden steps that lead down to where Anorthosite Creek crosses the hiking trail (waypoint 10). The rocks in the creek are dark grey basalt; some of them exhibit nice six-sided *cooling joints*. Yellow birch trees grow near the creek along with one-sided *pyrola*. This little plant is unusual for pyrola plants for the flowers are on one side of the stalk. In the rest of the pyrolas they are spirally arranged.

Immediately past and above the creek are outcrops of Beaver River Diabase. A change in grain size from medium to very fine is noticeable as we walk down the trail. This size change is most likely due to the diabase magma having been "chilled" or "quenched" against the old, cold basalt when it intruded into this material. This would lead to a fine-grained rock close to the basalt contact, and a coarser-grained rock (more slowly cooled) in the interior portions of the diabase.

Eleven: Orchids

Passing out of the canyon we enter a more open forest of aspen, birch, spruce, and balsam fir. Judy thinks the flowers in her canyon are 2 to 3 weeks behind similar species seen on the canyon rim and here in the open forest.

Waypoint 11 is located in the midst of abundant white and pink coral root *orchids* (Corallorhiza trifida). Coltsfoot leaves are also common through here. *Coltsfoot* is another odd plant that sends up its flowers first, like the bloodroot does. When the flowers die back the leaves take over making food to store in the root system for next spring's flower stalks.

Twelve: Hazardous Crossing

From the orchid patch the trail is gently up and down passing through one muddy area followed by a flat, dry section with more orchids all the way to an ash, cedar, and alder swamp with an active beaver population. The busy beaver have used the planked trail across the swamp as the anchor for their brand new dam. The dam is constructed of sticks and mud that now cover most of the planked section making for an adventuresome and rather hazardous crossing. At the end of the planked section there is a view back to the ridge of anorthosite we recently walked along. The dragonflies are huge here (or are they extra large mosquitoes?), and there are tons of moose tracks. The waxwings are feeding all around us, and mink frogs are sunning themselves on the banks of the swamp.

Halfway across the dam, Sammy tries to rush past me, almost sending both of us into the murky, tannic water. Fortunately I keep my balance and stay dry, but Sammy does not! And with a splash, followed by a loud sucking noise, she is in the muck. Half swimming and half "slushing" Sammy forges her way to the shore and when we arrive on the opposite side there is one wet, muck-covered, stinking dog happily waiting for us.

Thirteen: Cobra Tree and Sawmill Creek Boardwalk

Leaving the swamp, but not the dog, the trail is level but rocky as it passes the Cobra Maple, a tree so twisted it actually looks like a cobra ready to strike. There are large ash trees mixed in with the maple and birch. The forest is so thick through here I ask Judy where the sun went? The trail through this sunless place is lined with rattlesnake ferns (what else when you have a cobra tree). Passing into a more open, sunny section which, in forest talk, says "cutover," Judy tells me this gives the forest a very different feel. What with the small aspens and open, sunny areas, they have a "dried out" feel, "shriveled like a prune," she says. "What a difference," she went on, "compared to the lush, moist dark woods we just walked through." *Wild lettuce, hairy cress,* and dragonflies abound in the "shriveled prune" section.

The trail continues through a small cedar grove dotted with stumps of large white pine and/or cedar, before returning to the young aspen woods that contain chokecherries, orange *hawkweed,* and *sheep sorrel.*

Arriving at Sawmill Creek there is a long boardwalk that follows a beaver dam allowing us to cross this wide waterway. As we walk over the boardwalk there is a deep pond to the right with a beaver lodge and a wet grassy marsh to the left. The dogwood is in bloom along with *blue flag iris* and meadow rue. Fish are jumping out in the pond, geese and mallards are in the grassy marsh, and four turkey vultures soar overhead. Serenity and beauty definitely come together in this one place, and, from the things written in the Superior Hiking Trail Association's "happy" book at waypoint 13 (at the end of the boardwalk and a nice rest-lunch area), we are not the only folks who think this way.

From the rest area there is a great view back to the anorthosite cliff. We have now come to refer to this feature as half-dome because its steep, sheer, and impressive cliff is reminiscent of one of the *exfoliation* domes in Yosemite National Park. *Labrador tea*, what Judy refers to as "a large, friendly flower," is blooming, and *marsh marigolds* and *goldthread* are setting seeds.

Fourteen: Half-Dome

Crossing a planked, boggy section we enter a cutover area. Waypoint 14 is where lots of birch trees are down or hanging over the trail and there is a spectacular view back to half-dome. *Daisies* and chickweed are blooming across the cutover, sedges have puffy seed pods, and tall *buttercups* are in bloom.

Fifteen: Giant Erratic

Heading gently uphill over pieces of *amygdaloidal* to massive basalt and till boulders of banded black and white *gneiss*, the trail takes us past a large wood pile and lots of stumps of maple and birch. Lots of yellow buttercups along here, both tall and tiny.

Passing a large birch stump we enter a thick, dark older forest of maple and birch with some oak, ash, and cedar. Through this really nice section the trail crosses a dry, rocky creek, with *Jack-in-the-pulpit* growing along its banks, then crosses an old logging road.

After the road, which is lined by early primrose, there is a small outcrop of amygdaloidal basalt, followed by a giant *glacial erratic* of anorthosite. The anorthosite boulder is 15 feet high with plagioclase feldspar crystals up to 4 ½ inches long that are greenish to bluish-grey in color. Standing here, staring up at this monster from another time and place it is difficult to imagine that only 13,000 years ago there was more than a mile of ice above this spot. Around the boulder are small white, pink, and brown orchids along with lots of mint (*hemp nettle*) and polypody ferns.

Sixteen: Park Hill Road and Lupines

After leaving our "erratic" lunch spot we walk into an area of young birch and balsam poplar trees with older red pines; tiny purplish-whitish mint occurs along the trail. Red clover, daisies, blue-eyed grass, yellow hawkweed, and *pearly everlasting* are common alongside the trail, especially in sunny areas. Passing through a clearing and crossing an ATV trail the walking path turns right (north) and enters an area with large maple trees. There are rose bushes through here along with *Dutchman's breeches* and bloodroot leaves. The small mountain maple alongside the trail gives one a definite closed in feeling.

Waypoint 16 is at the Park Hill Road. The ditches are lined with the exotic plant *lupine*. There are large aspen here along with alternate-leaved dogwood.

Seventeen: Lady Slippers

From the road the trail enters a nice forest of aspen, maple, and birch. We then cross a wooden bridge over a ditch before coming to a muddy, planked section with noticeable (even I see them) moccasin flowers (lady slipper orchids) and bog orchids (waypoint 17). There are lots of moose tracks in this area, and just past the waypoint, there is a sign proclaiming this "Lady Slipper" area. Large cedars and black spruce occur through here, and the *horsetails* are soft and feathery.

Eighteen: Magical Bog

Walking over the planked bog area with its numerous lady slippers and Jack-in-the-pulpit, Judy also sees *Sphagnum moss* and goldthread along with abundant ash trees. Waypoint 18 is at the bog's end. I never thought I would come to call a bog beautiful but this one really is. With its gorgeous flowers, bright green moss, and large trees it's a special kind of place, one that Judy calls magical. I think of it as a place for fairies and unicorns.

Nineteen: Leskinen Creek Campsite and Bears

The trail, now dry and level, passes through a nice maple-birch forest, crosses a small bog with abundant jewelweed, then a small road to the Leskinen Creek campsite, which is waypoint 19. A bear cable stretches between two trees, so if you want to give the bears a treat other than hazelnuts, ants, acorns, and *raspberries*, don't use it.

Twenty: Leskinen Creek and the Otters

A short walk from the campsite brings us down into a bog with large cedar trees and out onto a boardwalk across Leskinen Creek, which is more of a swamp drainage than an actual flowing body of water. The creek is named for Jacob and Emma Leskinen who homesteaded 160 acres here in 1913. An old beaver lodge sits just up from the creek crossing, and beyond this is a wet, grassy area. Last winter, while hiking here on snowshoes, Judy saw otters sliding down the snow banks out onto the ice-covered creek; they may have been temporary residents of the beaver lodge.

Twenty-One: Oaks and Pink Anorthosite

Heading steadily, but gently, uphill we find the trail rocky in places as it goes over cobbles and *pebbles* weathered from the glacial till. Passing through a dense maple-birch forest and over outcrops of lumpy Beaver River Diabase, the trail continues to wind uphill and, as it does, oak trees become mixed in with the maple and birch. Waypoint 21 is at a glacial erratic of pink anorthosite. The pink color is due to trace amounts of iron in the plagioclase feldspar.

Twenty-Two: Fool's Gold and Thimbleberries

We continue gently uphill over smooth, massive diabase to an outcrop of basalt that has fine, disseminated pyrite (fool's gold) distributed through it, along with small, white plagioclase feldspar laths. *Thimbleberries* are prolific here and occur with sarsaparilla, blue bead lily, and columbine.

Twenty-Three: Nickerson Road, Large Birch, and More Orchids

The trail goes gently downhill, over more basalt, through a maple-birch forest to an outcrop of diabase with nice hexagonal cooling joints. There are more coralroot orchids in this section, along with rose-twisted stalk.

The trail winds gently up and down over numerous small diabase outcrops. Along here the partial views are southwest toward the Leskinen Creek Valley and adjacent hillside. The trail then crosses a small, dry creek with lots and lots of bear signs. From the creek it's a nice walk through a birch-maple forest to the junction with the Finland cross-country ski trail and the Nickerson Road. There is a large, flat outcrop of massive basalt in the open area.

Twenty-Four: East Branch of the Baptism River

The hiking trail turns right and follows the road/ski trail to a posted Superior Hiking Trail sign. There are lots of angular pieces of basalt on the road (frost-heaved). The trail then goes right with maple-birch woods to the south and a cutover area to the north. Heading gently downhill the trail passes over a large boulder field to arrive at the East Branch of the Baptism River (waypoint 24). The dominantly basalt boulders have come from the glacial till and were concentrated by the river; in fact, this large area may represent an old river channel. There are cedar and black ash trees lining the river with Jack-in-the-pulpit, chokecherries, and wild lettuce.

Twenty-Five: Tortured Basalt, Tower Creek, and Trail Junction

From the river crossing the hiking trail follows Tower Creek to "steps" of basalt. The basalt is what Judy and I call *Tortured Basalt*; here it is dark gray and has been broken into angular flagstone-like pieces. Cross Tower Creek and its fish ramp and, just beyond this, is a trail junction. The spur trail takes you to the parking lot at the Finland Recreation Center while the Superior Hiking Trail continues to Crosby Manitou State Park. Tired and satisfied with our day we choose the spur trail, 0.3 miles, over tortured basalt and fields of *bunchberries* to the parking lot.

This is an absolutely great hike; it has a bit of everything–cliffs, canyons, bogs, giant glacial erratics, orchids and more orchids, beautiful old forest, interesting geology, wildflowers, large trees, and a glacially carved landscape. This is northern Minnesota at its beautiful best.

Superior Hiking Trail
Walk 12: Egge Lake, Rock Island, and the Baptism River

Walk Logistics

Start: Finland Recreation Center

Getting There: Take Highway 61 to Highway 1. Turn left and follow Highway 1 for 7.4 miles to the junction with County Road 7 (Cramer Road). Turn right on to County Road 7, and go 1.3 miles to the parking lot on the right just past the baseball field at the Finland recreation center.

End: Crosby Manitou State Park (State Park sticker needed)

Getting There: Take Highway 61 to Highway 1. Turn left and follow Highway 1 for 7.4 miles to the junction with County Road 7 (Cramer Road). Turn right on to County Road 7, and go 7 miles (passing the Finland Recreation Center and the Sonju Lake Road) to the park entrance. Turn right, and the parking lot is 0.6 miles up the dirt road.

Walk Distance: 10.5 miles to park entrance, 11.1 miles to parking lot

Date Walked: June 29th , 2004

Worth a Longer Look

Tortured Basalt and Wildflowers: 2	Oxide Gabbro: 14
Spring Wildflowers: 3	Microhabitat: 15
Unconformity: 4	Contacts and Wildflowers: 16
Orchids: 5, 6	Yellow Birch: 17
Egge Lake: 6	Rock Island: 19
Pink Rocks: 11	Bearing Tree: 23
Egg-Shaped Erratic: 12	Falls and Rapids: 24

Waypoint-to-Waypoint

One: Trail Junction

Waypoint 1 and the beginning of the hike are at the junction where one branch of the Superior Hiking Trail heads east to half-dome and Highway 6 (Hike 11), and the other branch goes north to Egge and Sonju lakes then on to Crosby Manitou State Park. The junction is about 0.3 miles from the parking lot at the Finland Recreation Center and is reached via a well-marked spur trail.

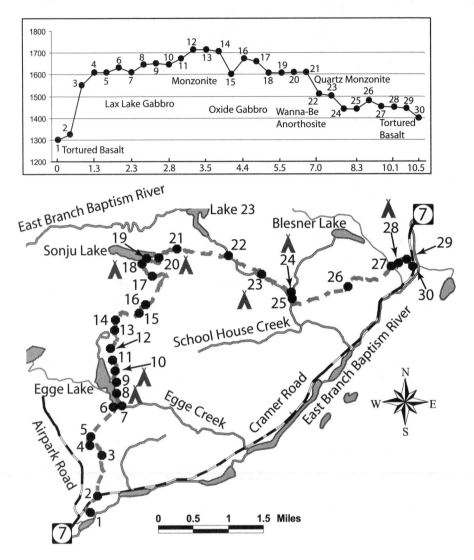

Today's walk to Crosby Manitou State Park is going to be a warm one; there is not a cloud in the sky, and at 8 am it is already 62 degrees. The sun is blazing orange instead of its usual yellow color; an indication of just how much moisture is in the air. Charlie takes no notice of this; he's excited and ready to go. In fact he has already vanished up the spur trail, but the poor guy has no idea of how long a hike this will be. Sammy is not hiking; she tore a nail on her paw and is home sulking until she recovers.

Two: Tortured Basalt and Wildflowers

Heading toward the Crammer Road the trail starts off in a mixed forest. There are numerous small *outcrops* of *Tortured Basalt*. This distinctive lava flow gets this name because it breaks into angular or blocky pieces with sharp edges or rough ridge-like weathering surfaces; all-in-all this lava flow looks like it's been treated rather badly by planet earth. Plants blooming through this section are *strawberries*, *hawkweed*, *Canadian mayflowers*, *blueberries*, *pussy toes*, and *pyrola*.

At the Cramer Road turn right and walk about 0.3 miles down the road to the Superior Hiking Trail sign (waypoint 2) on the left side just before a gravel road. The East Branch of the Baptism River runs parallel to the road. Look for waterfowl and muskrats in the river.

Three: Spring Wildflowers and North Shore State Trail

From the Cramer Road it is steadily but gently uphill over a walking path that is composed of *glacial till* and bounded by a lot of chokecherries, mountain maples, and *wild roses*; all of which are beautiful. Mixed amongst these are *columbine, bluebells, bloodroot* leaves (with spittle bugs), *cow parsnip, starflower, trillium, Jack-in-the-pulpit*, and *sarsaparilla*. If one wanted to see a whole slew of spring wildflowers all at once, this would be a section of trail to do it on!

After crossing a snowmobile trail continue uphill over glacial till and pieces of Tortured Basalt through a young aspen, birch, and maple forest to waypoint 3, the North Shore State Trail. The *bracken ferns* are knee high, and the *thimbleberry* is blooming.

Four: The Billion Year Line

We continue uphill to a small clearing in a mostly maple forest with the forest floor covered by large leaf *aster*. There are big, ancient-looking stumps, mostly of yellow birch all through here. The trail goes gently up and down to a dry creek bed filled with large boulders of moss-covered *gabbro* (waypoint 4). Just off the trail and down the creek is an outcrop of medium-grained gabbro. The gabbro has a layer of boulder till resting on top of it. The contact between the till and the gabbro represents a geological *unconformity*; the thin contact zone separates rocks that are 1.1 billion years old from glacial deposits (*ground moraine*) that are about 10,000 years old! Mountain (or moose) maples appear to grow right out of the billion year old boulders. The twigs show signs of moose browse with jagged, torn branches where there was once a bud.

Stepping off the trail Judy points out the plant diversity and shows me the shapes and textures of the tree trunks. The cedars are twisted with stringy, dark brown bark, and the maples have many black knobs on their smoother gray bark.

Five: Orchids and a Bear Den

Continuing over gabbro boulders we come to a long boardwalked section across a swampy area. There are numerous coral root *orchids* growing here, and they extend along the trail as it heads gently uphill to an outcrop of coarse-grained gabbro that weathers to a mottled salt and pepper color. This rock, as well as the one at waypoint 4, is part of what has been named the Lax Lake Gabbro, which extends from just north of Tettegouche State Park to the old Finland Air Station. The gabbro is part of the *Beaver Bay Igneous Complex,* but it is older than the *Beaver River Diabase.*

We continue over gabbro as the trail parallels a small creek full of angular gabbro boulders to waypoint 5, an old bear den and a sign informing us of that fact. If not for the sign, we would never know this rather small hole in the ground was a winter home for a bear.

Six: Egge Lake, Glacial Erratic, and More Orchids

The trail heads generally uphill through a sun-deprived maple forest with big birch trees and rattlesnake ferns as it passes over mottled Lax Lake Gabbro before coming to a large *glacial erratic* of an igneous rock called diorite. Diorite is the intrusive equivalent of what we call *Half-Way Rock* because, in composition and mineralogy, it is half-way between the intrusive rocks *granite* and gabbro. This particular erratic may not have traveled far in the glacial ice, for rocks of similar composition are found to the north and east of here.

Continuing on through dark maple-birch woods, with large, majestic trees and glacial erratics of gabbro, we come to a cutover area dominated by alder and mountain or moose maple. Two large, beautiful yellow birch trees remain standing, and close to these Judy finds more orchids. Walk through the cutover and down a small hill to return to an older maple-birch forest with balsam fir.

Leveling out the trail passes through a more mixed forest with large yellow birch and spruce; cedar trees become more common as we get closer to Egge Lake (waypoint 6).

Egge Lake is surrounded by a grassy marsh, and at waypoint 6 there is a small concrete dam that controls water flow out of the lake into Egge Creek. There is also a bench that provides the opportunity to sit and gaze out over the quiet waters.

Seven: Egge Creek, Yew, and Ping-Pong Ron

The trail parallels Egge Creek to waypoint 7, which is a rope bridge across the creek. There is a large outcrop of Lax Lake Gabbro in the creek bottom. Going down to check it out I slip on the wet, mossy rock, lose my balance, and do a frantic ping-pong ball dance from one side of the creek to the other, one rock to the next. I manage not to fall, either in the creek or on the rocks, but in so doing I give Judy several seconds of hilarious laughter. Charlie merely stares at me though I must admit I was waiting for him to sadly shake his head and walk away. The birch and cedar trees along the banks of the creek have a definite lean to them; they appear to be headed down slope thanks to the ever present geological process of soil *creep*.

There is yew growing here, which is unusual these days because it is disappearing due partly to overgrazing by deer. Yew looks like low, creeping balsam without the racing stripes on the underside of the needles.

Eight: South Egge Lake Campsite

We head away from the creek with the trail paralleling the lakeshore (at a distance) through a birch forest with some white pine, balsam fir, and maple. Waypoint 8 is at the spur trail to the South Egge Lake campsite.

Nine: Branded Pine and the North Egge Lake Campsite

Turning away from the lake the trail heads northeast for a short distance before jogging back to again parallel the shoreline as it passes over and past outcrops of mottled gabbro. Passing what Judy calls the "branded" white pine, a large tree with a long, dark lightning scar down its side, the trail continues through a dominantly maple-birch forest to the spur trail (waypoint 9) to the North Egge Lake campsite.

Ten: Maple Archway and the Trapper's Cabin

It's a very nice walk through a beautiful old forest of yellow birch with maples and some large spruce and cedar to the Maple Archway. Then it's on to Art Griffin's cabin which is referred to as an "old trapper's" cabin: it's a pile of plywood and windows lying beside the trail. The plywood and windows indicate the cabin is not really that old, and the shape it's in verifies it was never meant to get that way. The cabin marks waypoint 10.

Eleven: Pyroxene Monzonite

A short distance past the cabin is a cedar grove with boulders of a medium-to-coarse grained pink and black rock; the rock outcrops just past here (waypoint 11). The rock is composed of long, black crystals of *pyroxene*, and these can be randomly distributed or aligned which gives the rock a banded or laminated look. Other minerals in the rock are pink potassium feldspar (*orthoclase*) and cream to grey *plagioclase feldspar*. The pale green glassy mineral that occurs in small amounts is *olivine*. This rock, unlike most "granitic" rocks on our planet, contains no *quartz* and, because of this, is called an "alkalic" rock, one rich in alkalis like potassium, calcium, and sodium. This particular alkalic rock, based on mineral composition, is called a pyroxene *monzonite*. The monzonite represents the uppermost and most "felsic" unit of a layered igneous intrusive body called the *Sonju Lake Intrusion,* which we will see more of further down the trail.

Twelve: Egg-Shaped Erratic

From waypoint 11 there are lots of outcrops and boulders of monzonite which, in places, weathers to a crumbly mess that simply disintegrates when hit by a hammer. This section of the trail passes through a maple-birch forest with a balsam understory to waypoint 12, an egg-shaped glacial erratic. The day we went by this fossilized egg, obviously left by the mega Ice Age Easter Bunny, a rock person had been built on top of it, and one of the cobbles used to construct this rock person was pure red *jasper*, The glacial erratic is composed of diorite, the Half-Way Rock, similar to the one at waypoint 6.

Thirteen: Coarse-Grained Gabbro

Leaving the egg-shaped erratic, the trail heads steeply downhill into a narrow gorge with a dry, rocky creek bed. The walls of the gorge are composed of pyroxene monzonite, and here the alignment of the pyroxene crystals is more distinct than in the previous rocks.

The trail continues over and past outcrops of monzonite and boulders of black and white gabbro. Pass another diorite erratic to waypoint 13, which is an outcrop of a coarse-grained gabbro containing crystals of black pyroxene and chalky plagioclase. This is a *sill* or *dike* related to the Beaver Bay Igneous Complex, and it appears to mark the contact between the monzonite, and the next rock unit of the Sonju Lake Intrusion.

Fourteen: Oxide Gabbro and the Sonju Lake Intrusion

The trail enters a low area, and the rock outcropping here is medium-grained Oxide-Rich Gabbro. It is called this because it contains abundant *magnetite* and *ilmenite* crystals. This rock forms the second unit of the Sonju Lake Intrusion, a sheet-like body composed dominantly of layered gabbroic rocks. The monzonite seen earlier represents the youngest and uppermost layer of this intrusion.

Fifteen: Microhabitat and Beaver Lodges

Walking through a maple, birch, cedar, and balsam fir forest with a few nice yellow birch we come to the edge of the valley the trail has been following since waypoint 14. We continue along the steep hillside (a 75 foot drop to the bottom); the rocks exposed along the edge are Oxide-Rich Gabbro.

According to Judy the area along the cliff has its own little microhabitat. The forest we have been walking through suddenly changed into this enchanted world of dark spruce and leathery looking plants with abundant *Labrador tea*, *sphagnum moss*, blueberries, and *cranberries*. "Wow, really neat and amazing," are Judy's words.

The trail then heads downhill past outcrops of Oxide-Rich Gabbro into more mixed woods followed by a cedar forest with some large cedar trees. A boardwalk takes us over a small creek and bog before the trail heads uphill along the edge of a beaver meadow and pond. An old beaver lodge marks waypoint 15. Lots of moose and beaver sign, but we see neither of these animals.

Sixteen: Contacts, Corydalis, and Sunshine

It's a short walk to an outcrop that has both Oxide-Rich Gabbro and pink pyroxene monzonite in it; a boulder to the right of the trail shows the knife-sharp contact between the two. The monzonite most likely represents a pocket of felsic magma trapped in the largely crystalline gabbroic body. Being completely surrounded by the crystallized gabbro, the magma had no place to go so it sat there and crystallized in place to form this small mass of monzonite scattered in the Oxide-Rich Gabbro.

The trail heads uphill through a grove of large cedars to a small opening with an outcrop of Oxide-Rich Gabbro and lots of *corydalis*. "There is sunshine here," are Judy's first words. The forest walk to this place has been dark because of the thick canopy of leaves overhead. To suddenly emerge onto an open outcrop represents a stark contrast. Today we are also aware of the massive, heavy, thick feeling of heat and humidity when out in the sun!

Seventeen: Large Yellow Birch and Goldthread

Continuing on we walk through a cedar, yellow birch, and spruce forest over mixed outcrops of gabbro and monzonite with lots and lots of violets. Cross a dry creek bed and continue on through what is now a maple-birch forest to waypoint 17, a large yellow birch tree with a huge root growing across the trail. Hazel shrubs and large patches of *goldthread*, along with princess pine (see *clubmoss, running*) and *ground cedar* are common along this trail section. The latter two are species of clubmoss. One looks like a small white pine seedling (princess pine) and the other appears to have scale-like leaves similar to cedar trees.

Eighteen: South Sonju Lake Campsite

From the large yellow birch we walk over a planked area along the edge of a large swamp through a yellow birch and cedar forest. This is followed by a short downhill over outcrops of coarse-grained gabbro, and one outcrop of the same coarse-grained dike seen at waypoint 13, to the spur trail for the South Sonju Lake campsite (waypoint 18).

In the sunny areas there are blueberries, woodsia ferns, spreading *dogbane,* and *honeysuckle.*

Nineteen: Rock Island, BWCA , and Wanna-Be Anorthosite

Waypoint 19 is one of Ken Oelker's favorite places. He built the boardwalk out to the small, rocky island in Sonju Lake. A perfect lunch spot the island is covered in *sweet gale* and Labrador tea, and there are loons calling across the lake. A merlin (medium-sized falcon) zips past us in pursuit of a songbird. There is another "happy" book here to record impressions, and Judy writes "feels like being in the boundary waters but without a canoe."

The island is composed of medium-to coarse-grained gabbro that has a laminated or banded appearance on the broken surface. On the weathered surface the rock could be mistaken for anorthosite because of its color, tan to grey, which enhances the plagioclase but makes the pyroxene crystals difficult to see. After some "humorous" discussions we decide to call this particular rock a Wanna-Be *Anorthosite*. This kind of rock makes up the third unit of the Sonju Lake Intrusion.

Twenty: North Sonju Lake Campsite

The trail parallels Sonju Lake through a forest of cedar and birch before heading uphill over outcrops of gabbro that are a bit finer-grained than the Wanna-Be Anorthosite, to the hilltop, where there are high bush cranberries. From here it's gently up and down to the junction with the spur trail to the North Sonju Lake campsite and waypoint 20.

Twenty-One: Rock Cedars

Crossing Sonju Creek with *blue flag iris* blooming we walk through two groves of "rock" cedars: cedar trees clutching and growing over and around outcrops of Wanna-Be Anorthosite. Entering into an old clear cut area filled with hawkweed and wild roses, we head gently downhill into a wet, boggy section with waypoint 21 at the end of a planked over area.

Twenty-Two: Mosquito Point, Bogs, and the East Branch of the Baptism River

Continuing past the bog we arrive at what is called Mosquito Point; a place full of buzzing, biting, and annoying little creatures. Unfortunately we stopped here to look at an outcrop of diorite (dike?), and the nasty things take full advantage. From here it's through an open area with a view of the Sonju Lake Valley and bog.

The trail heads downhill through an old clear cut with more boggy areas, crosses an old road, and then passes through a small grove of red pines. We cross another logging road then walk through more boggy and muddy areas to the East Branch of the Baptism River and waypoint 22. There is a spur trail here leading to a small parking lot on the Sonju Lake Forest Road. The boulders are similar to the pyroxene monzonite seen at waypoints 11 to 13; however they are not related to it. When looked at in detail this rock contains 5-15% quartz along with potassium and plagioclase feldspar and pyroxene enclosed by a fine-grained pink groundmass. The rock is not layered, not magnetic, and contains no olivine. With quartz present this rock is not "alkalic," and so is called a *quartz monzonite*. This unit also forms part of the Beaver Bay Igneous Complex, and appears to be of similar age to the Lax Lake Gabbro, possibly representing a more granitic part of this intrusive body.

Twenty-Three: Bearing Tree and East Baptism River Campsite

Leaving the river, pass a large cedar tree that is also a "bearing" tree. From here it is a "just walk and get it over with" section through clear cut and an alder swamp. All of the loose rock on and around the trail is quartz monzonite. Waypoint 23 is at the East Baptism River campsite.

Twenty-Four: Falls and Rapids, Blesner Creek Campsite

Walking along and above the East Branch of the Baptism River we pass numerous outcrops, ledges, and rock walls of pink quartz monzonite, which here weathers into angular slabs or column-like pieces. This weathering pattern leads to the series of small falls and rapids seen in the river. The quartz monzonite outcrops all the way to the Blesner Creek campsite, which is waypoint 24.

Twenty-Five: Bridge and Snowmobile Trail

It's a short walk to the bridge across the East Branch of the Baptism River (waypoint 25) and the North Shore State Trail. There is blue-eyed grass here, a tiny blue iris with grass-like leaves that thrives in sunny places.

Twenty-Six: Sonju Lake Road and Red Pines

The trail becomes root-crossed and rocky as it passes an outcrop of Beaver River Diabase. The diabase is a dike or sill because quartz monzonite outcrops in the river below it, and just up a small hill above it. The trail turns away from the river and crosses a small creek near a huge downed cedar, and heads through yet another clear cut with groves of planted red pine before entering a low, boggy area with cedar trees.

From here the forest is yellow birch, maple, and ash with more cedar trees as we cross a dry creek bed and come to the Sonju Lake Forestry Access Road, which is waypoint 26.

Twenty-Seven: Alder Swamp and Blesner Lake Road

From the road we continue through a maple-birch forest over glacial till to an open clear cut area. Making our way through the clear cut we cross a small creek in an alder swamp with ash trees and more cedars, to reach waypoint 27, the Blesner Lake Road.

Twenty-Eight Aspen Knob Campsite

It's a short walk to the Aspen Knob campsite. There is no knob and only a few aspen; the trees are dominantly white pine, balsam, and birch. This is waypoint 28.

Twenty-Nine: Charlie Flop Creek and Tortured Basalt

At the next small creek Charlie does a belly flop and then just lies there slowly lapping the water–he is dead tired. From here it is uphill with outcrops of Beaver River Diabase, and partial views of the Cramer Road and hillside above it. Once the hilltop is reached, the trail immediately heads downhill over more diabase with nice views of the green hillside across the Cramer Road. Continue downhill to an outcrop of Tortured Basalt, the same kind of rock the hike began in. This is waypoint 29.

Thirty: Cramer Road and the State Park

From waypoint 29 it's downhill to the Cramer Road. After crossing it there is a 0.6 mile walk up the Crosby Manitou State Park access road to the parking lot and the end of a long, hot, tiring day. This was also a day dominated by a variety of igneous intrusive rocks. Though all belong to the Beaver Bay Igneous Complex and are part of the *Mid-Continent Rift,* they represent three separate intrusive events, each of a slightly different age. This "multiple" intrusion phenomenon is common in volcanic areas, and is characteristic of magmas that feed lava flows at the surface. "Don't forget the wildflowers," Judy tells me, "they were pretty darn neat too!"

Superior Hiking Trail

Walk 13: Manitou and Caribou Rivers

Walk Logistics

Start: Crosby Manitou State Park (State Park sticker required)

Getting There: Take Highway 61 to Highway 1. Turn left and follow Highway 1 for 7.4 miles to the junction with County Road 7 (Cramer Road). Turn right on to County Road 7, and go 7 miles (passing the Finland Recreation Center and the Sonju Lake Road) to the park entrance. Turn right, and the parking lot is 0.6 miles up the dirt road.

End: Caribou River State Wayside on Highway 61

Getting There: Take Highway 61 to the Caribou River. The wayside is immediately past the river on the left side of the highway. The parking lot is small, and there is no overnight parking.

Walk Distance: 7.6 miles

Date Walked: July 7th, 2004

Worth a Longer Look:

Minnesota Biomes: 1
Magnetic Rock and Yew: 5
Manitou River: 8
Twinflowers: 10
Layered Rocks: 11
Beaver Valley: 12
Lilies and Frogs: 13
Ferns: 17
Lady Slippers: 19
Caribou River Gorge: 22
Vesicle Cylinders: 22
Potholes, Water Chutes: 23
Volcanic Debris Flow: 25
Slumping: 26

Waypoint-to-Waypoint

One: George Crosby and Minnesota Biomes

This hike begins in the parking lot at George H. Crosby Manitou State Park. The park is named, in part, for the man who is best known for developing the iron ore deposits on the Mesabi and Cuyuna Iron Ranges. The other part of the name, Manitou, which is Ojibwe for Great Spirit, is the name of the river that cuts through the park. The Great Spirit is the center of everything, and the river is certainly the center of this park. The park now includes over 8,500 acres of gorgeous woodlands, and in much of it there are old-growth hardwoods and cedars. The ages of some trees within the park have been determined; yellow birch are as much as 400 years old, cedars up to 300, and

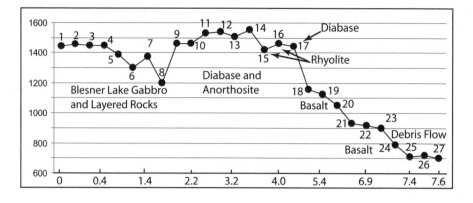

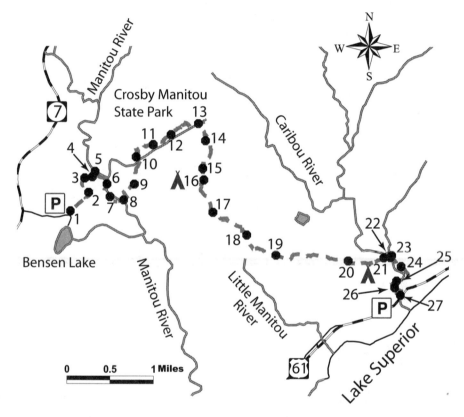

maples over 200! On the hike today we will see many of these truly ancient wonders.

Getting ready to set out on this cloudy, drizzly, 55 degree morning we are serenaded by the flute-like song of the Swainson's Thrush. On the drive over here from the Caribou River Wayside (where we left one car) Judy made the observation that all the plants seem to be behind by about two weeks in their flowering or fruiting; shows what a nice, warm summer we have not enjoyed so far!

Waypoint 1 is at a sign in the parking area that shows an outline of Minnesota and depicts the state's three distinct biomes. Other than more mountainous states, where plant communities change with elevation, it is unusual to have such a diversity of species and three distinct ecological communities in one state. Generally the western part of Minnesota is referred to as "prairie grasslands," the central part as "deciduous woods," and the region the hiking trail passes through as "boreal forest." This latter area easily occupies two-fifths of the state.

Two: Wide Trails and Glacial Erratics

The trail starts out going slightly uphill on a wide footpath that is more akin to a four lane highway. The trail has been constructed this way because this is an extremely popular section with many walkers coming here to view the cascades of the Manitou River. This wide trail size is typical of the Superior Hiking Trail where it goes through state parks.

Pass a large *glacial erratic* of the *Beaver River Diabase* (also see *diabase*) along with numerous smaller boulders of *gabbro* and one gabbro *outcrop* in a dry creek bed. The forest is dominantly maple and birch, with cedar, spruce, and balsam. There are lots of tiny broad beech ferns and *thimbleberries* along this section.

After going by another outcrop of gabbro come to the junction with an unmarked park trail (to the right), which is waypoint 2. The gabbro outcrop is medium-grained, smooth-weathering and forms part of the Blesner Lake Intrusion. The song of the Swainson's thrush has serenaded us to this waypoint.

Three: Huge Cedars, White Flower of the Day, Clubmoss, and Anorthosite

The trail slopes gently upward to the top of a small hill as it crosses over numerous boulders (*basalt*, gabbro, *granite* and *rhyolite* to name a few), which come from the weathering of *glacial till* deposits. Even with the boulders causing us to watch where we put our feet it's difficult not to see the new growth at the tips of the twigs of the balsam firs. Each one of the fir trees we pass has new 3-4 inch additions of bright green color and each is soft and beautiful. Even though we are only at waypoint 3, Judy declares the white flower of the day to be thimbleberry. However, she adds, when one looks beneath the bigger plants there is an abundance of one-flowered *wintergreen* blooming.

There is now a short downhill section past a moss-covered glacial erratic of *anorthosite*. The anorthosite has a birch tree growing over and on it, "life clinging to a poor bare rock, just like it must have all those billions of years ago," is Judy's comment. By billions of years I assume she is referring to stromatolites that grew in large colonies along rocky shorelines; some of which were right where we are now walking! There are also large cedar trees and, as the trail continues downhill, it passes enormous standing and fallen cedars. There is a thick carpet of *clubmoss* and *bunchberry* clinging to the ground everywhere you look, which, according to Judy, represents typical groundcover in boreal forests.

The trail levels out but remains bouldery with anorthosite glacial erratics to waypoint 3, a picnic shelter with fire pit. The rock outcropping by the shelter is Blesner Lake Gabbro. This intrusion is older than the Beaver River Diabase, and may be similar in age to the *Sonju Lake Intrusion*. From this spot we can hear the constant sound of water crashing over rocks in the river, which is not far below us.

Four: Crosby Hill Trail

A short walk over a bouldery trail takes us to the junction between the Superior Hiking Trail and the Crosby Hill Trail which is waypoint 4. Though not an official spur of the hiking trail it leads to an overlook of the Manitou River Valley.

Five: Magnetic Rocks and the Manitou River Trail

The trail, bordered by young cedars, goes downhill, as it winds its way over and around piles of rock. These are *talus* deposits derived by *frost wedging* from the hillside to the left. Some of the rocks making up the talus are unusual and rare. They are composed of 50-75% *magnetite,* with green glassy apatite and silver-colored arsenopyrite along with some *plagioclase feldspar*, *pyroxene,* and *ilmenite*. This would be described as a type of *iron formation*, one formed by crystallization and settling of heavy minerals to accumulate at the bottom of a basaltic magma chamber, much like snow accumulates on a window sill. These heavy minerals end up forming distinct layers or beds in the magma chamber; often they alternate with layers of lighter minerals like plagioclase feldspar. Other rocks found amongst the talus are gabbro and oxide-rich gabbro. These all form part of the well-layered, dominantly gabbroic Blesner Lake Intrusion, which outcrops on the hillside above us. Also occurring on the trail are subround *boulders* of basalt and *quartz monzonite* from the glacial till.

Waypoint 5 is at the junction between the Superior Hiking Trail and the Manitou River park trail. The river trail heads upstream (to the left), and it's only a short distance to a great view of the Manitou River Cascades. The hiking trail continues to the right, and all along this section we see the shrubby, low-growing evergreen called yew. Yews are commonly found in forests that are cool, damp, and shaded, such as occur on north facing slopes like this one. One warbler seen here, the black-throated blue, is known to nest in yew thickets.

The scientific name for yew is interesting. Its first name, Taxus, is a Greek word meaning bow, and apparently this North American species was used extensively by Native Americans for hunting bows. Taxol is a compound derived from yews that has shown beneficial effects in the fight against certain cancers. The second part of its name, Canadensis, is a bit more obvious; it means "of Canada" or in a more general sense "northern."

Six: Campsites and the Manitou River

The rocky trail follows the hillside with nice views of the river to "campsite #3," a nice open site, one Judy would love to spend a lot more time at. This is a state park fee campsite. George Crosby initially donated 3,320 acres that included the river and its waterfalls to the state for a wilderness park. Keeping with this mandate there are many campsites like this scattered throughout the park–the only way to access them is by foot.

The trail heads downhill to the river's edge over more rock talus. Waypoint 6 is at campsite #4, another nice spot with large rocks that provide a place to sit and contemplate the moody river as it flows by. The water is the color of root beer– root beer with a big head of foam–for there is a large amount of frothy stuff slowly circling on eddies in the stream. This is truly hypnotic, the foam going around and around and around.

Shaking off the spell I begin to look at the boulders that jam-pack the river, while Judy investigates what she calls "indicators" of the moist, shaded, cool microclimate we are now in. One she points out is the green stain of the fungus *Chlorociboria,* which is busy attacking stumps and logs–it feeds on the decaying wood. The green color staining the wood is actually the mycelium. Mushrooms are the fruiting bodies (spores) of fungus emerging from the mycelia. In a wet, warm summer and fall the green stains tiny turquoise and seldom seen mushrooms can be found on the underside of sticks.

Seven: More Large Cedars and Spring Peepers

Continue along the river over a small creek through a thick boreal forest of aspen, birch, cedar, spruce, balsam fir, and balsam poplar. Outcrops along the trail are gabbro; boulders from the glacial till include pieces of an intrusive rock with numerous large plagioclase feldspar crystals. This particular intrusion outcrops much further along the hiking trail.

The trail heads uphill to a small pond with large cedar trees. Today the pond is dry, and Judy thinks it is only really full and/or wet soon after snowmelt, or after a large rainfall. This environment would be the perfect place for spring peepers, little tree frogs, to hatch their eggs in early spring.

141

Continuing uphill over a knob of gabbro we walk down to waypoint 7, a cedar grove with large trees.

Eight: River Crossing

The trail crosses outcrops of smooth-weathering diabase to a junction with the continuation of the Manitou River trail. The hiking trail goes to the left, passing more diabase. Heading down to the river pine trees, both standing and fallen, become dominant, and the vegetation looks thick and lush. More yew plants cover the ground.

There is a short, steep descent to waypoint 8, which is on the bridge over the Manitou River. There is a small waterfall, and the rock outcropping along the river is gabbro. A large gabbro outcrop in the river has subparallel fractures which cause it to break into "chunks." Judy says she could sit on the bridge and stare at the river for the rest of the day, before, of course, returning to campsite 3 for the night!

Nine: River Views

Crossing the hypnotic river the trail climbs steeply through soft pines, old birch, and tall spruce past outcrops of gabbro. The trail, as we climb, has less material from the till and more pine needles which make for "softer" walking. Continuing up we come to an opening with a view of the river valley and Lake Superior. From here the trail is a bit more rocky to waypoint 9, an outcrop of gabbro from which there is a great view of the Manitou River Valley and Lake Superior. Judy tells me there is something strange about the quality of the air today, for Wisconsin seems VERY close to us.

As usual, on this rocky outcrop, there are *Juneberries* and other sun-loving species. There are also lots of tiny red *strawberries*.

Ten: Twinflowers, Moose Maple, and a Beaver Marsh

Walking across the hillside over more gabbro we enter a maple forest that all too soon changes into mixed woods. *Twinflower,* normally an early June flower, carpets the ground with its pink blooms. Judy tells the story of the first time she encountered this tiny pink flower. She was on a portage trail in the Boundary Waters Canoe Area and noticed a plant she had not seen before. The plant was about 4 inches tall with paired pink drooping bells. Not knowing its name she called it "pink showerheads." Later she learned it was twinflower, or *Linnaea Borealis*. The first name is connected to biologist Carl Linnaeus who developed the modern taxonomic system in 1757. Legend has it that this was one of his favorite flowers, thus its name. Linneaus wrote that this flower was much like he: "lowly, insignificant, and flowering for a brief space."

Continuing on we cross a small creek (that empties into a rather large swamp) before we head up over gabbro talus to a lichen-covered outcrop of

142

gabbro with views of the stream and swamp just passed. The stream turns into a small pond–thanks to the engineering capabilities of the beaver. There is a little path to an overlook of the marsh/pond with waypoint 10 at the path junction.

Eleven: More Layered Rock

Walking downhill we cross a small valley, then head uphill over fractured gabbro which affords views of the Manitou River Valley and, in the distance, the Finland Air Station. The trail continues over gabbro outcrops crossing a boulder-filled creek; no bridge here but lots of rocks to hop across. The forest is full of maple trees and gives us a nice, cool feel on this hot day.

We cross over more gabbro and, as we do, there appears to be a change in both color and grain-size of the rocks. The color varies from pinkish or tan with black specks on a weathered surface to a much darker-looking rock. There is also an accompanying grain-size change from coarse to fine, which leads to different weathering characteristics. These changes reflect mineral layering in the Blesner Lake Intrusion; the pinkish and tan rock contains more feldspar, and the darker rock more pyroxene and olivine.

Waypoint 11 is an outcrop of coarse-grained, pinkish weathering gabbro with a great view of Lake Superior, the surrounding hills, and of course the Finland Air Station.

Twelve: Strawberries, Kibbles and Bits, and Beaver Valley

The trail parallels the Manitou River, and there is a noticeable change in rock type. Lumpy (see *diabase weathering*) Beaver River Diabase makes an appearance with its friends, kibbles and bits. Strawberries are in bloom and fruiting, and Judy points out two different kinds. On one the seeds appear to be deep inside the roundish fruit (*Fragaria virginiana*), and on the other (*Fragaria vesca*) the seeds appear to be on the outer surface of a more triangular-shaped fruit. Both, however, taste delicious.

Continue over lichen-covered Beaver River Diabase, which is locally lumpy and broken into kibbles and bits. As usual the kibbles and bits are most common on south-facing slopes. Waypoint 12 provides a great view into a narrow, steep valley with numerous marshes and ponds formed by active beaver. For this reason we dubbed this branch of the Manitou River, Beaver Valley.

Thirteen: Calla Lilies, Singing Frogs, and Maple Woods

It's a short walk over more massive diabase through dark maple woods to a small creek with a large slab of diabase in the creek bed. From here the trail follows the hillside of Beaver Valley over more diabase, crossing a dry creek bed full of pink *monzonite* boulders. This is followed by a nice walk through a maple-birch forest with some large spruce trees before heading downhill toward the bottom of Beaver Valley.

As we walk down into the valley wood frogs, chorus frogs, and mink frogs are singing, along with one lone spring peeper. The overall effect sounds like quacking ducks, banjo strings being plucked, someone zipping their fingers along a comb, and one lonely, rising Peep.

At the bottom of the valley beautiful white *calla lilies* are blooming in the wet areas, and more clucking of wood frogs can be heard. Waypoint 13 is on a mud-packed beaver dam that we cross to reach the opposite side of the valley. Overall, it seems this entire valley is simply a series of beaver ponds, marshes, and dams; it's hardly a branch of the river any longer.

Fourteen: Anorthosite and Corpse Plants

The climb out of Beaver Valley is relatively steep with the trail going past outcrops and talus of diabase to an outcrop of anorthosite, which is a xenolith or inclusion in the Beaver River Diabase. The anorthosite appears darker than normal due to lichens growing on it, but it does have the typical "bowling ball" weathering The forest is maple and birch with some spruce trees chock-a-block full of cones.

From the anorthosite it's a nice walk through maple-birch woods over small outcrops of anorthosite to waypoint 14, an outcrop of pinkish-tan gabbro with black pyroxene spots. This is the same rock type seen at waypoint 11 and represents part of the layered Blesner Lake Intrusion; here it is a xenolith or inclusion in the Beaver River Diabase. There is a nice view of the lake from here as well as the ever present Finland Air Station.

White "corpse plants" (*Indian pipes*) are beginning to emerge in the coniferous duff layers. The official name of this plant is *Monotropa uniflora*, which means one color, one flower. The flowering plant feeds off decaying matter in the forest floor and has no chlorophyll.

Fifteen: Rock in Tree and Rhyolite

A long easy walk through a maple-birch forest over diabase outcrops takes us to the "rock in the tree" outcrop and a great view of the Manitou River Valley and Lake Superior. Waypoint 15 is at a large outcrop of pink to pinkish-grey rhyolite. The rhyolite is intensely fractured, and these subparallel to criss-crossing cracks are filled by earthy red *hematite* (iron oxide) with some pale green *epidote*. The filled fractures give the rock a "ribbony" look: in places it looks like someone has splattered the rock with a brush full of reddish-brown paint to create a random pattern of droplets. *Blueberries* and strawberries are abundant through this section.

Sixteen: Horse Shoe Ridge Campsite

It's downhill over Ribbon Rhyolite to the Horseshoe Ridge campsite, which is waypoint 16. This campsite was officially added to the state park in 2004 through a complicated series of land swap agreements. It's pretty obvious why people wanted this to be part of the park: the thick black spruce and soft carpet of wildflowers, not to mention the views from the ridge, all of which make this spot quite enchanting.

Seventeen: Magical Places and Morning Glories

We continue downhill over broken and fractured Ribbon Rhyolite to a small stream; the area around the stream is full of *ostrich* and *sensitive ferns* as well as large cedars. This spot, according to Judy, is best thought of as one of those "woodsy" magical places.

From the creek it's a long walk through a maple-birch forest. The trail is uphill at first, then relatively level with *cobbles* and boulders of basalt and monzonite as it passes a spur trail before coming to waypoint 17, an overlook with views to the south and east. The outcrop here is crumbly diabase with kibbles and bits. Along with the kibbles and bits are morning glories! Well, not really. Actually they are a low, creeping white *bindweed* that is a member of the morning glory family. Many of the open and sunny outcrop areas (south-facing slopes) have this perky plant.

Eighteen: Grape Vines

Another long walk (0.5 miles) over crumbly diabase with kibbles and bits through a maple-birch forest. Old grape vines grow here and there amongst the diabase outcrops. The last stretch is a downhill section that takes us into a flat, marshy area and a cedar grove, which is waypoint 18.

Nineteen: Lady Slippers

We continue on through a flat, muddy, and boggy area with bog orchids alongside the trail to a boardwalked section that the moose obviously have no use for. Their tracks are scattered all through the muck beside the boardwalk, and boy is their stride huge.

From here we enter an old logged off area that is mostly low and damp, a "just walk and get it over with" section. However, the end of this has its special reward. Just before a small creek with planks across it, Judy discovers beautiful pink lady slippers *(see orchids)*. These mark waypoint 19. Lady slippers are also called moccasin flowers (Cypripedium acaule). This area is so green and lush we have to look carefully for the flash of pink that suddenly catches the eye.

We take some time to look closely as we venture along this section. The orchids are here, and they are beautiful. In fact this area is moist and lush with many wildflowers–*wood sorrel*, twinflower*, goldthread, Canadian* *mayflower*, one-flowered wintergreen to name a few–and the entire stretch is a delight in spite of the wet footing.

Twenty: Large Cedars and the Pork Bay Trail

Crossing the creek we continue through the cutover where there are large cedar and spruce trees along with lots of mountain maple and alder. Crossing an old logging road we continue to walk through the buggy, damp cutover to the Pork Bay Trail, which is waypoint 20. There is a sign here with the trail name on it, and I guess that's a good thing for without it one would never known there was ever a pathway in that direction. The Pork Bay Trail was an old Native American trail that was also used by the voyageurs (thus "pork" bay for pork eaters) to get to Nine Mile Lake (nine miles from the bay).

Twenty-One: West Caribou River Campsite

Emerging from the swamp and cutover area we find ourselves on higher and drier ground. The trail has kibbles and bits along it, and there are outcrops and boulders of crumbly and lumpy diabase. As the trail heads downhill we see pieces of *amygdaloidal basalt* before reaching the junction with the West Caribou Trail (waypoint 21) leading to the West Caribou River campsite.

Twenty-Two: Vesicle Cylinders and the Caribou River Gorge

The trail follows the Caribou River; piles of rocks along the river were deposited during spring run off. These continue all the way to a junction with a park trail, which is waypoint 22. The Superior Hiking Trail continues to the left.

There is a large outcrop of basalt, which contains small cream-colored *amygdules* concentrated in distinct oval zones. These zones represent *vesicle cylinders*. A nice view here of the river gorge with its steep rock walls.

Twenty-Three: Water Chute, Potholes, and Trail Junction

It is a short walk to the bridge across the Caribou River (waypoint 23, the bridge may be moved in the summer of 2006). There is a beautiful water chute here with white water racing down the steep, rocky gorge. A large kidney-shaped *pothole* can be seen under the bridge, and just upstream two branches of the river merge. This is a very pretty and rather noisy place, and it comes with a Superior Hiking Trail Association "happy" book for recording impressions. This is also the junction of the Superior Hiking Trail, which continues to the left to Cook County Road 1, and the spur trail that takes us to the Caribou River State Wayside.

Twenty-Four: Caribou Falls and River Views

We head down the spur trail which follows along and above the river gorge with great views all the way to waypoint 24, the junction with a park trail that leads to Caribou Falls. The outcrops along the trail are weathered amygdaloidal basalt.

Twenty-Five: Caribou River Debris Flow

The trail continues downhill to the river. The rocks outcropping in the river are a classic and beautiful example of a *debris flow*. The debris flow contains numerous fragments of different kinds of volcanic rocks from amygdaloidal and massive basalt to massive and amygdaloidal rhyolite. The fragments are poorly sorted, matrix-supported (meaning they don't touch), and vary in size from fingernail to "longer than your foot." The matrix material is fine-grained and composed of calcite, chlorite, quartz, and red-colored clay minerals.

Judy wants to know how I think this deposit formed. Thinking a long moment I tell her to let her mind drift back about a billion years, back to the *Mid-Continent Rift* and a hazy, barren land; a land without vegetation, dark and forbidding with basalt lava flows from horizon to horizon. Here and there the lava has been intruded by gabbro dikes and sills and topped by thick rhyolite lava flows. A stream has cut down through the rhyolite and into the underlying basalt to form a long, narrow, winding valley that opens into a broad basin dotted by ponds and small lakes. The horizon glows an eerie red, and occasionally the moan of the lonely wind and the cracks and pops of still cooling rocks are drowned out by what sounds like thunder, though the sky is cloud free.

The thunder draws closer, it rumbles and crashes off the valley walls, and when the floor of the valley starts to tremble you realize the sound comes not from above but from the ground below. You watch as the sides of the valley ripple, they seem to fold in on themselves like an accordion. Then, with an ear splitting crack, they are on the move. Basalt, gabbro, and rhyolite slide, fall, and bounce into the stream below. When this jumbled mess is mixed with the streams water it becomes fluid and mobile. Picking up speed, this huge mass of rock and water races down the valley and, with the roar of a thousand lions, is spewed out the valleys mouth into the basin. Here it spreads rapidly, forming a fan-shaped deposit of mud, ground up rock, and pieces of basalt, gabbro, and rhyolite that vary from house-size down to Monopoly hotels.

In the coming years this material will be covered by basalt lava flows and hardened to solid, red rock. A billion years later another stream will uncover these deposits allowing us to appreciate their beauty and speculate on just how they came to be. So there you go. That's my version of how this debris flow formed and got to where we see it. How's that for geological "arm waving?"

"It's great," she said. "I can close my eyes and see it happening, just like I was there. Which I really, really wouldn't want to be!"

Twenty-Six: Gravel Bar and Slumped Glacial Till

Continue along the spur trail to a large gravel bar composed dominantly of boulders and cobbles of basalt. The stream bank on the opposite side is slumping into the river due to undercutting. The bank is composed of glacial till that contains numerous boulders and cobbles, including debris flow material. As slumping takes place the fine clay and silt-size material is carried away while the *pebbles* and cobbles are left behind to form another gravel bar; the boulders pretty much stay where they fall.

Twenty-Seven: Parking Lot

Continue down the spur trail to the Caribou River Wayside and the end of a great walk, one worth each and every step. There was the huge cedars and yellow birch, the Manitou River, Beaver Valley and all its lilies, Indian pipes, morning glories, lady slippers, and grape vines as well as magnetic and layered igneous rocks, potholes, vesicle cylinders, and a spectacular red debris flow–a "wow" day for sure.

Superior Hiking Trail
Walk 14: Alfred's Pond

Walk Logistics

Start: Caribou River State Wayside on Highway 61

Getting There: Take Highway 61 north to the Caribou River. The wayside is immediately past the river crossing on the left side of the highway. The parking lot is small, and there is no overnight parking.

End: Cook County Road 1 (Cramer Road)

Getting There: Take Highway 61 past Taconite Harbor to Schroeder. Turn left onto Cook County Road 1, and travel along it for 3.6 miles (first 1.7 miles are paved). The hiking trail parking lot is on the right and is about 200 feet off county road 1.

Walk Distance: 9.0 miles   **Date Walked:** August 19th, 2004

Worth a Longer Look:

Slump: 2, 3   Sugarloaf Creek Bridge: 14
Volcanic Debris Flow: 4   Indian Pipes: 15
Natural Arch: 5   Lava Flow and Unconformity: 16
View of Caribou Falls: 6   Alfred's Pond: 17
Caribou River Crossing: 7   Lilies: 18
Crystal Creek: 10   Four Diabase Brothers: 21

Waypoint-to-Waypoint

One: West Spur Trail

To get from the wayside up to the Superior Hiking Trail there are two choices. Having been down the east side of the river (walk 13) we decide to go up the west side. To do this we cross the bridge over the Caribou River to the Superior Hiking Trail sign, and the west spur leading up to the Superior Hiking Trail. This is waypoint 1 though I'm not sure how accurate this is on the GPS for when plotted on a topographic map the point lies on the opposite side of the river!

The day is picture perfect, which explains the early morning temperature of 42 degrees. It is now 57 degrees and will get a lot warmer. With low humidity, a clear sky, and light wind this should be a grand walking day.

Two: Large Slump and Fall Colors

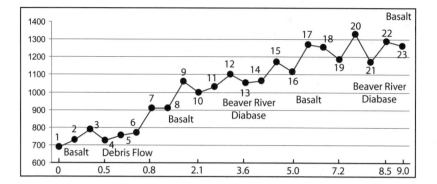

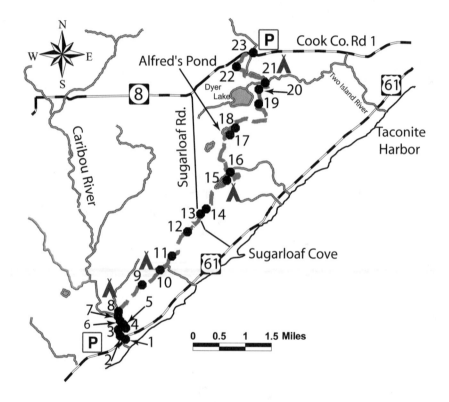

Walking up the river we cross under a power line where the *honeysuckle* is already getting its red fall color. The *bunchberries* are also red, and the *birdfoot trefoil* is no longer bright yellow, but sports fuzzy seeds.

A short distance from the power line is the start of an impressive *slump*, which is waypoint 2. The slumped area extends all the way around a large *meander* bend in the river, some 800 feet. The *glacial till* that makes up the river bank, and the birch and spruce trees growing on it, are slowly sliding into the river because of undercutting by the faster moving water on the outside bend of the meander. However, at this particular spot, it appears to

150

be a slow process, for the tops of the leaning trees have had time to grow straight up. Typical of slumps there is a nice crescent-shaped scarp.

Three: Slump Scarp, Yellow Trees, and Tall Primrose

We continue upriver over lots of exposed tree roots to waypoint 3, the head of the slump scarp and the end of the meander bend seen from waypoint 2. The trees along this section of the trail have a yellowish tinge; so here it is, mid-August, and the trees are already slowing their food production in anticipation of the winter months ahead. A lot of late summer plants are in bloom and setting seed such as white *aster* and *hawkweed*. The *evening primrose* is at its tallest and in full bloom with bright yellow flowers on six foot stalks.

Four: Fireweed, Debris Flow, and Red Basalt Boulders

Leaving the slump scarp, the trail descends steeply to the river over stone steps. Following the river's old *flood plain* the trail goes through an aspen, birch, spruce, and balsam fir forest to waypoint 4, an *outcrop* in the river of a volcanic *debris flow*. This spectacular deposit is described in waypoint 25, walk 13. Also in the river are large *boulders* of reddish *basalt* that were *frost-wedged* from the cliff above. *Fireweed* is abundant through here as are *thimbleberries*.

Five: Natural Arch

Continuing to walk upriver, we pass a small slump on the opposite bank and an outcrop of weathered *Beaver River Diabase* (also see *diabase*) before coming to waypoint 5, an outcrop of intensely weathered debris flow on the trail. To the right is a natural rock arch or chute formed by water running down the hillside and eroding straight through the debris flow. The debris flow is very red in color due to the abundance of the mineral hematite which forms when iron-rich minerals interact with running water. There is a view of Caribou Falls from here, but a much better one awaits just up the trail.

Six: Wow Spot

Just beyond waypoint 5 there is a gorgeous view of Caribou Falls and the water pool below it. The falls are composed of basalt lava and may mark the contact between more easily eroded debris flow material and much more durable basaltic rock.

Seven: "Better Than New Jersey" and Spruce Cones

We continue upriver over *amygdaloidal* and *massive* basalt with some kibble and bit-size basalt pieces (see *diabase weathering*); there are also abundant spruce cones that, in places, carpet the trail. The *zigzag goldenrod* grows all along the pathway; this is a fun plant because of its shape and because of the fact it is different from other goldenrods in that it likes shady places. Purple

151

stemmed aster and *yarrow*, both members of the "composite" family, are common and there are also a lot of small mushrooms.

Waypoint 7 is at the bridge over the Caribou River, and this waypoint is described in Hike 13, waypoint 23. Today the "happy" book the Superior Hiking Trail Association put here so walkers may record their impressions says "better than New Jersey."

Eight: East Caribou Camp Site

From the bridge the trail heads upstream to an outcrop of amygdaloidal basalt that has numerous small *potholes* and is a shiny red color from the water flowing over it. *Harebells*, *wild lettuce*, and sweet *Joe-Pye weed* can be found here.

Just up the trail from this outcrop is the junction with the spur trail to the East Caribou campsite. *Sarsaparilla* and *rose-twisted stalk* are found on this trail section.

Nine: Old Cutover, Ants Nests, and the Dramatic Forest

The trail continues level and dry and partially covered by *cobbles* and boulders as it goes through an old cutover area to the logging road that was used for access. This area was logged between 1900 and 1908 by the "Estate of Thomas Nestor," the rather unusual name of a logging company based in Michigan. They were responsible for building the logging railroad line at Gooseberry Falls State Park called the Nestor Grade.

Meeting, then following the old logging road, the trail is locally covered by kibble-and bit-size pieces of Beaver River Diabase that look just like Charlie's dog food. Along the edges of the road there is *pearly everlasting*, sarsaparilla, and pin cherries. There are also ants nests constructed in, and built out of, kibbles and bits which, with hard work, the ants have managed to turn into sand-size material–pretty darn neat.

Waypoint 9 is under a power line with a view down to Lake Superior. The change in the forest from the barren power line to the green woods opposite is abrupt and dramatic. The forest has large birch and spruce trees that are much older than the trees in the cutover we just walked through. The change makes these woods look darker and closed in.

Ten: Crystal Creek and Crystal Creek Campsite

From the power line it's a nice walk through a birch-spruce forest with partial views of Lake Superior. The crystal blue sky still follows us, and this makes a stark contrast with the white birch bark and green leaves. Kibbles and bits continue to cover the trail, though not as much as before, and once in a while the top of a weathered diabase outcrop peeks up at us from out of the trail. There are white asters, touch-me-nots (*jewelweed*), large plantain, and, in the wetter areas, inky cap mushrooms. These are especially abundant on rotting bits of boardwalk.

Crossing a small, dry creek we arrive at the junction with the spur trail to the Crystal Creek campsite (now called Mine Adit campsite), just past this is Crystal Creek; the pretty covered bridge across it is waypoint 10. Crystal Creek gets its name from the *calcite* crystals that occur in a mining pit just down stream. The crystals are in a wide vein that occupies a *fault* in a basalt lava flow, but just what the prospector who dug the pit was looking for beats the copper/silver/gold out of me.

The many boulders in the creek (which is now dry) are dominantly basalt and diabase; the crumbly outcrop just before the bridge is diabase. There is a ton of fireweed along with *bracken fern* and *dogbane*, both of which are knee-high.

Eleven: Private Land and ATV Trail

The trail follows the hillside as it parallels Crystal Creek through a forest composed dominantly of birch trees that Judy thinks are 25-30 years old. Kibbles and bits continue to cover the trail, and patches of fireweed come and go. As the trail continues along the hillside it bends away from the creek and heads into a dominantly birch forest to waypoint 11, a "private land" sign and ATV trail. From here we can see the power line as it crosses the hilltop to the left.

Twelve: Red Pines and Kibbles and Bits

Crossing another small, dry creek followed by the power line we enter a much wetter area with planked sections. Kibbles and bits continue and, here and there, diabase sticks up out of the trail. It's interesting to note that the closer an outcrop is to the surface, the larger and more abundant the kibbles and bits.

The trail leaves the wet area and is flat and dry to waypoint 12, a nice grove of red pines. There are also a lot of red pine stumps throughout this grove, suggesting the red pines are periodically thinned.

Thirteen: Sugarloaf Road

Walking along a dry trail with some kibbles and bits we cross an old logging road followed by a much newer one with an outcrop of diabase along side. Not far past this is the Sugarloaf Road and a small parking lot for the use of people walking the trail. A sign here indicates it is 5 miles to Cook County Road 1.

The Sugarloaf Road comes out on Highway 61 close to Sugarloaf Cove, a state Scientific and Natural Area that is well worth a visit. There are diabase outcrops along the road, and the mountain ash trees have berries.

Fourteen: Sugarloaf Creek

It's a short distance from here to Sugarloaf Creek and the really neat bridge across it (be sure to look at the bridge railings). This creek is the first one today to actually have water in it, and both dogs really appreciate it.

Fifteen: Marsh, Coltsfoot, Copse Plants, and Sugarloaf Pond Campsite (29)

The trail heads over glacial till through a cutover area of young aspen and birch with several planked and corduroy sections. *Goldthread*, ferns, and tall white aster are abundant.

After crossing a lumpy diabase outcrop the trail comes to, then follows, the edge of a grassy marsh (shown on topographic maps as a small lake). There is an old beaver dam at the marsh's southeastern end that is covered by sweet Joe-Pye weed. *Coltsfoot* is everywhere; in fact Judy claims she has never seen so much in one place. Growing with the coltsfoot are Copse Plants or *Indian pipes*.

Composed of kibbles and bits with larger pieces of diabase and basalt the trail follows the edge of the marsh with the plants typical of a *Canadian carpet* (such as *blue bead lily* and *clubmoss*). The trail moves away from the marsh only to curve back to it and the junction with the Sugarloaf Pond spur trail (waypoint 15), which goes to the campsite of the same name.

The campsite is situated on the edge of a small "pond," which I would describe as a really dismal cutover swamp with lots of dead trees. This appears to be another LBBP (low, boggy, buggy place). There is an old beaver lodge and dam here along with a wood duck house.

Sixteen: Hazel, Scary Descent, and an Unconformity

From the junction with the spur trail we continue on over kibbles and bits, passing two small outcrops of lumpy diabase in a maple, birch, and spruce forest with lots of hazel underbrush. The hazel nuts are ripe and are being actively eaten by squirrels. Passing an unmarked trail we come to an overlook at the edge of a steep valley side. Many seeds are setting this time of year and can be observed here, such as *pyrola* and bunchberry.

Following along the valley edge we soon descend to the bottom through a young maple forest with large aspen and birch. If all goes the way successional plans are supposed to, the birch and aspen will die off and this will one day be a thick maple forest. The trail is kibbles and bits as well as boulders and cobbles derived from the glacial till. The kibbles and bits make the descent interesting, for walking on them is like walking on marbles.

At the bottom we cross a small creek, which is waypoint 16. The creek drains Sugarloaf Pond and has tall purple-stemmed asters growing along it. In the creek bed there is an outcrop of reddish weathering amygdaloidal basalt that sits on top of a more massive, darker basalt. Above both of these are boulders and cobbles of glacial till. The amygdaloidal basalt represents the oxidized top of a lava flow that changes downward into a fresher, more massive flow center. The contact between the flow and the overlying glacial till represents an *unconformity*. This unconformity, the thin contact zone between the two, represents 1 billion years of earth history!

Seventeen: Basalt and Alfred's Pond

From the creek the trail is level and dry without kibbles and bits, possibly indicating a change in the underlying bedrock from diabase to basalt. Coming to a small creek we pick our way across a bridge of rotting timbers with re-bar pipe sticking up out of them. There is abundant coltsfoot along the creek, and the ash trees are fully, and finally, leafed out and gee, it's only August!

The trail goes on through a low, muddy area crossing an old logging road and numerous small, dry creeks to waypoint 17, Alfred's Pond, or as the topographic map calls it, Ruffy Lake.

Alfred's Pond has a bit of everything a bog lover could want. There is a "floating" walkway (rebuilt in 2005) out into the bog giving us the opportunity to fall in! No, not really. It's so we can have the opportunity of seeing an amazing variety of plants without disturbing this sensitive ecosystem. There are two really special plants: *pitcher plants* and *sundew*, both of which eat insects. Associating with these two carnivores are *cranberries*, *bog orchids*, Labrador tea, *calla lilies*, cattails, *sensitive ferns* (what else in a sensitive area*)*, jewelweed, *snowberries*, *blue flag iris*, *sweet gale*, and lots and lots of *sphagnum moss*. Black and white spruce trees grow side-by-side and the tamaracks are simply lovely. This is a special place, and we take time to enjoy it all.

Eighteen: Calla Lilies

After leaving Alfred's Pond the trail goes over planked sections to a grassy marsh with calla lilies and an old, grassed-over beaver dam. Waypoint 18 is at the end of the grassy dam and planked area.

Nineteen: Large Aspen and Clubmoss

It's a long walk (1.2 miles) to the next waypoint, a walk that consists mostly of a "just walk and get it over with" section. The first part is along the grassy marsh with more planked sections; there is a sensitive area here that has abundant clubmoss. Then it's over a rocky trail crossed by numerous tree roots and through an area with large aspen trees, both on the ground and standing. From this point the forest changes into young aspen, birch, and spruce with mountain maple.

We pass two small outcrops of lumpy diabase before heading downhill over more diabase into an open birch forest in a low swampy area; lots of shaggy manes here. The trail is then rocky and crossed by tree roots to waypoint 19, a large slash pile of birch. The *baneberries* are not yet ripe, and wolf scat abounds along with lots of moose tracks.

Twenty: Dyer Hill

The trail continues through a cutover before ascending Dyer Hill, the top of which is at an elevation of 1300 feet and is waypoint 20. Dyer Lake is about 500 feet to the southwest, but due to the thick vegetation it is not visible.

Twenty-One: Four of the Diabase Brothers and Dyer Creek Campsite

Crossing the top of Dyer Hill we descend to a lumpy diabase outcrop. This outcrop is pretty neat for it shows how the Beaver River Diabase weathers from smooth to lumpy followed by crumbly and then kibbles and bits. Four of the diabase brothers at one outcrop–wow! So where in the world is Snow White?

We continue downhill with the descent steep and, in places, rather difficult because once again kibbles and bits make the trail a joy to walk on. There are some rock steps that help in the descent except when it is wet. At the bottom the trail goes through a younger birch-maple forest to Dyer Creek (waypoint 21) and the Dyer Creek campsite just beyond.

Twenty-Two: Slump and Railroad Tracks

After Dyer Creek the trail follows Two Island River with a large slumped area just past the creek. The trail then turns away from the river and climbs steeply uphill over bouldery till to the hilltop at 1250 feet. There is a short walk along the top, which parallels the river, before descending back to the river where there is a nice meander bend.

Moving away from the river the foot path goes through a dominantly birch forest passing an outcrop of lumpy diabase to a set of railroad tracks (waypoint 22) and the Dyer Lake Road. The railroad tracks are used to transport coal to the power plant in Schroeder. Here, in this open sunny area, there are *sunflowers*, evening *primrose*, *goldenrod*, curly dock, and *mullein*.

Twenty-Three: Power Line, Two Island River, and Parking Lot

From the railroad tracks it's a 1000 foot walk to a really wide power line through a birch, balsam, and aspen forest. *Goatsbeard* is blooming. After the power line it's a short walk to Cook County Road 1, which we cross before turning right to follow an old road across Two Island River. From the bridge it's about 350 feet to the parking lot just off Cook County Road 1.

This is a great walk because of Alfred's pond and the floating bog with its large variety of plant life. Add to this the spectacular debris flow on the

Caribou River, Caribou Falls, the mining pit, kibbles and bits ants nests, lilies, and all the other plants and flowers and we have had a special day. A picnic lunch at Sugarloaf Creek provides an added plus.

Superior Hiking Trail
Walk 15: Cross and Temperance Rivers

Walk Logistics

Start: Cook County Road 1

Getting There: Take Highway 61 past Taconite Harbor to Schroeder. Turn left onto Cook County Road 1, and travel along it for 3.6 miles (first 1.7 miles are paved). The hiking trail parking lot is on the right and is about 200 feet off the county road.

End: Either the Temperance River State Wayside on Highway 61 or the Superior Hiking Trail parking lot on Forest Road 343.
Getting There:
1) Highway 61 through Schroeder to the Temperance River. The wayside is immediately past the river.
2) Take Highway 61 through Schroeder. Forest Road 343 is just before the Temperance River. Turn left and the parking lot is 0.9 miles up the dirt road on the left.

Walk Distance: 7.9 miles   **Date Walked:** August 20th, 2004

Worth a Longer Look:

Tortured Basalt: 3	Slump: 15
Cauldron and Grotto: 4	Flow Banding, Spherulites: 17
Rhyolite and Superior: 5	Demolition Ants: 21
Tower Overlook, Agates: 6	Iron Formation: 24
Grassy Marsh: 8	Froth Lava: 26
Cross River: 10	Arches, Pipe Amygdules: 27
Historic Cross River: 11	Pothole Gorge: 28
Meanders: 13	Abandoned Pothole: 29

Waypoint-to-Waypoint

One: Parking Lot

Walk 15 begins in a small parking lot off Cook County Road 1.

After yesterday's walk, from the Caribou River Wayside to here, we spent the night at a National Forest Service campground on Nine Mile Lake. This is a lovely spot with large sites, big trees, and a wooden walkway along the lake; as an extra bonus we were the only ones there! However, this morning it was a brrrr 38 degrees, Charlie wanted in my sleeping bag, and the coffee

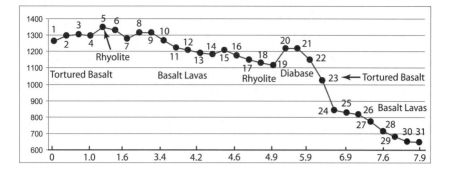

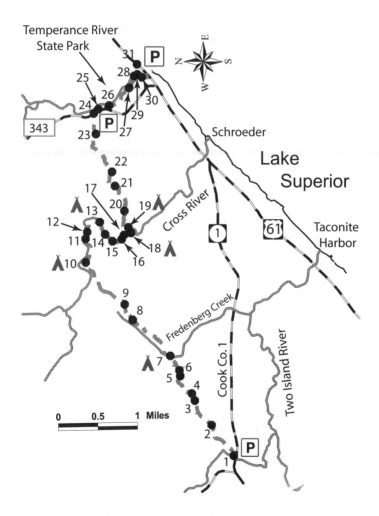

didn't stay warm for long. Even with the cold start the day looks like another of those perfect for hiking; clear, deep blue sky, gentle breeze, and the temperature now at about 55 degrees. Waypoint 1 is in the parking lot and is the same as waypoint 23 from walk 14.

Two: Ground Cover and the Early Morning Light

We start off in *glacial till* with *boulders* and *cobbles* of mixed lithologies. There are several large aspen trees on the ground and this blow down could be the result of the strong wind storm of last week. The *bloodroot* and *coltsfoot* have enormous leaves, and *wild ginger* covers the ground. It's kind of magical, as well as pretty, the way the early morning light streams through the deep summer green of the leaves to highlight the bright red color of the swollen *trillium* fruits.

The trail turns wet and muddy with planked sections; cedar trees become more common, and there are a few yellow birch as the trail comes to a small, dry creek. The area around the creek is full of *horsetails* and *marsh marigolds*. In spring this area would be alive with big green leaves and yellow *buttercup* flowers.

Beyond the creek we pass part of what was once a huge white pine tree. We think of the lovely maple woods that surround us, and what they would be like if they were the understory to a forest of white pine giants. Waypoint 2 is at a large white pine; alas just one of what was once a forest of greats.

Three: Dark Forest, Elbow Maple, and Tortured Basalt

This is a beautiful walk through a dense maple and yellow birch forest with remnants of white pine. Even with the blue sky and sunshine the woods are dark and shadowy due to the forest cover; it's what, as a kid, I used to call "witch" woods. Cross a small creek and come to an opening in the maple woods. After the darkness and smatterings of light through the leaves this bright sunshine is startling Here there are spruce, aspen, and birch. The aspen and birch are pioneer species and come into an area immediately after a disturbance; such as fire or logging. The young maples are about 1.5 to 2 feet tall and fully leafed out. Under the tiny maples are the leaves of spring wildflowers, and a carpet of brown and decaying maple leaves from years past. There is also abundant *jewelweed* along the creek.

After the sunny "opening" it's back into a maple-dominated woods as the trail passes the Elbow Maple and comes to waypoint 3, an area with lots of angular, broken pieces of what we call *Tortured Basalt* on the trail. The basalt is pale red in color and is *amygdaloidal* with the *amygdules* (gas cavities) filled by *calcite, quartz,* and/or *zeolites*. Small quartz crystals form rims around some of the amygdules. Many of the amygdules are empty as the mineral(s) filling them have been weathered out. Some of the flat, angular rock pieces are parts of six-sided *cooling joints*. There are *wild onions* and *starflowers* here.

Four: Cauldron and Rocky Grotto

Tortured Basalt continues along the trail to a small seep where an outcrop of the basalt has amygdules filled by calcite and green *epidote*. Past the seep there is a section of glacial till before Tortured Basalt makes another appearance and remains prominent to waypoint 4, a small dry creek with lots of rock ledges and depressions in the rocky stream channel. In the spring this would be an impressive little cauldron with small waterfalls and roaring chutes. Tortured Basalt outcrops in the stream banks, and as this lava flow breaks apart, it is washed into the creek to add to the stream's rockiness and overall grotto effect. Wood frogs, (small brown frogs with black masks), are common here.

Five: Rhyolite Lava, Wow Spot, and Sun-Loving Flowers

We head uphill over glacial till through a maple-birch forest with cedar and remnants of white pine until we are about two-thirds the height of the maple trees. The trail then flattens out to follow the hillside with a final uphill section to a "wow" spot, which is also waypoint 5. The view to the east is stunning after the closed in feeling and darkness of the maple forest. Stretching before us is a virtual sea of green with the blue of Lake Superior and the Wisconsin shoreline in the distance.

The rock outcropping here is *rhyolite lava* that contains sparse square to ovoid quartz crystals in a reddish-brown quartz-rich matrix. The knobby surface is from weathering. Not only do we have a new rock type but also new plant species due to the south-facing nature of the *outcrop*. The area has abundant *honeysuckle*, gooseberries, and *Juneberries*. Depending on the season there will always be a nice variety of sun-loving species of flowers to admire.

Six: Tower Overlook and Agates

It's a short walk to an official overlook called Tower Overlook, which has the same view as waypoint 5 , which we jokingly call "Not Tower Overlook." The rock outcropping here is amygdaloidal basalt with beautiful banded *agates* as well as clear quartz filling the amygdules. Locally these form raised lumps on the weathered flow surface. The amber-colored crystals in the fractures are an iron carbonate mineral called ankerite.

Seven: Sweet Cicely, Painted Basalt, and Fredenberg Creek

We find *sweet cicely*, with its crazy long seed pods, along the trail from waypoint 6 to an outcrop of massive rhyolite. The fern-shaped leaves of this plant look like a million other plants, but the long pointed pods give it away. This plant's roots are supposed to have a licorice smell, but neither Judy nor I can detect it. There is also *columbine, mullein*, and mountain ash here.

Just beyond the rhyolite the trail goes over sparsely amygdaloidal Tortured Basalt that is beginning to break into angular slabs. From here it's almost continuous basalt outcrop to Fredenberg Creek. The basalt varies from Painted Basalt that has bands and wavy swirls of *hematite* through it, to amygdaloidal basalt. At the creek (waypoint 7) the basalt contains hematite bands. The basaltic rocks appear to represent different flows, but there is not enough exposure to determine exact relationships.

Fredenberg Creek is a beautiful spot with a few old cedars and a deep pool that invites the dogs in. Just past the creek is the Fredenberg campsite, also a nice spot.

Eight Booney Meadow

The trail follows Fredenberg Creek through a maple-birch forest with a thick carpet of ginger. It then moves away from the creek along the edge of a marsh with numerous planked sections. The ginger is joined by *goldthread*, *Indian pipe* (Copse plants), *violet*, starflower, patches of *sphagnum moss*, and bog *orchids*.

Where the trail makes a small bend we pass two large cedar trees and continue to walk along the grassy marsh, which is full of cattails and *blue flag iris*; Fredenberg Creek is at the far northwest side of the marsh. We come to a sign on a broken cedar tree proclaiming this spot to be Booney's meadow. The sign marks waypoint 8.

Nine: Gasco Road

We continue along the marsh, which, in places, is more like a pond, with the surrounding forest made up of maple, birch, and cedar. Passing through a balsam thicket (we lose GPS reception here) we emerge into a more mixed forest with some large spruce trees. Waypoint 9 is at an old road called Gasco Road.

Ten: Cross River, Potholes, Waterfalls, and the Falls Campsite

From Gasco road it's a 1.1 mile walk to the next waypoint through a maple, aspen, spruce, and birch forest with planked sections that have lots of mushrooms along side. Arriving above the Cross River, the trail follows the river for a ways before cutting across an active *meander* bend and dropping down close to the water's edge and the junction with the spur trail to the Falls campsite. This junction is waypoint 10.

The river is named for the cross a Jesuit priest by the name of Father Baraga placed at the mouth of the river in 1846 after escaping a terrible storm on Lake Superior by being washed into the quiet waters behind the gravel bar at the mouth of the river. The Ojibwe named the river "Tchibaiatigo zibi" meaning "wood of the soul." The reference may be related to the fact that it is difficult to see into the river from the rim of the gorge (can not see the river for the trees).

Just below the waypoint the river flows over a large outcrop of *basalt* with small lath-to tabular-shaped *plagioclase feldspar* crystals as well as small quartz, calcite, and/or zeolite-filled amygdules. The surface of the flow has been polished smooth by the flowing water. There are numerous *potholes* in the basalt, and these seem to be associated with fractures in the rock. The water must slowly widen the fracture to form a small depression which then, with time and the right river conditions, leads to a pothole. All stages in this process can be seen here.

The Cross River Falls are a series of large potholes that have been connected together by erosion of the sides of the potholes by fast moving water. *"Turtleheads"* and *Joe-Pye weed* are common long the river banks.

Eleven: Old Stream Channels and a River of History

The trail continues along the river passing through a boulder field that represents an old stream channel. Some of the boulders have been moved by park personnel to form the edges of the trail, which is both a nice and clever touch.

Walking along the boulder-filled trail we come to a set of wooden steps that take us up a steep, though short, hill climb. Crossing the hill it's down the other side, via more wooden steps, to the river then on through a dense and dark forest of cedar, birch, spruce, and balsam to another boulder-filled trail section. Waypoint 11 is at the end of this section.

The river is relatively straight through here, and this characteristic makes it a good candidate for canoeing and floating logs down during spring runoff. In fact the Cross River was originally used by Native Americans and then by voyageurs both of whom, with a few short portages, could access a chain of inland lakes that took them to Lake Vermillion. By the early 1900's loggers were using this river to send Minnesota's white pine to Wisconsin and Michigan. Apparently the booming logging business in this area ended in 1905 due, in part, to a smallpox epidemic.

Twelve: The Pirate's Plank

We continue to follow the river, which maintains its gentle gradient and relative straightness. The river banks are lined with boulders, which appear to be tightly packed together by the force of the spring waters.

Waypoint 12 is truly an engineering marvel: a skinny, scary "pirate's plank" of a bridge over a small creek. Balancing upon it I find it easy to imagine alligators in the water below!

Thirteen: Meander Bends, Gravel Bars, and the Ledge Campsite

We survive walking the "pirate's plank" and continue along the river, which now forms a series of meander bends and gravel bars. The gravel bars form in the slack water on the inside of the bends whereas, along the outside of the meander bends, the faster water is actively undercutting the river bank leading to *slumping.*

The trail passes over another boulder-filled area (an old stream channel) to a small creek with marsh marigolds, mint, and beaver signs. Follow the creek through thick balsam woods (we keep losing satellite reception here) to where it enters the river. From here it's a short walk to the Ledges campsite and waypoint 13. The campsite is located on a natural flat area that represents an old *river terrace* (flood plain). Hedge hog fungus, which looks like a sponge, and flowering shinleaf *pyrola* are common through here.

Fourteen Away We Go

This section of the trail has a lot of downed trees as it goes past a gravel bar before heading up a steep set of wooden steps to cross an area where the hillside is slumping into the river. We then make our way down the "ski slope" to the bottom and waypoint 14. The "ski slope" is composed of loose cobbles and boulders, so it is slip-slide and away we go straight to the bottom. Judy thinks this waypoint, if reached alive, would be beautiful with loads of wildflowers in the early spring.

Fifteen: Active Slumps

After surviving the "pirate's plank" and the "ski slope" we have to wonder what waits ahead?

The trail is rocky to a steep set of wooden steps that take us up, over a large slumped area, to waypoint 15, the top of the slump. From here we can see large clumps of earth that have slid part way down the slope with the trees still in them. It's also obvious where the rocks in the river come from, and it's amazing just how many rocks there actually are in the glacial till forming the river banks. As the till slumps into the river the finer material, clay-and silt-size grains, are washed away completely while the *pebbles* and some cobbles are moved a little way downstream to form gravel bars. The larger boulders stay pretty much where they rolled, fell, or bounced into the river.

Sixteen: Lost Trail, Overflow Channel, and Spring Flowers

We head down the hillside past another active slump. In fact there are places along here where the trail has actually vanished into the river, and we have to detour through the woods. The cedar trees are leaning the river's way, and the wooden stairs want desperately to join them.

After the slumped area the trail flattens out, but it is littered with boulders as it follows the river, suggesting this area may be an active river channel in the spring when the water is high and fast. Waypoint 16 is at a dry stream that represents a river overflow channel. This stream fills with water as the river rises in the spring; logs of all sizes are piled up and packed together where the overflow stream meets the river.

This would be a grand spot for spring wild flowers, and is still beautiful now because purple fringed orchids are blooming.

Seventeen: Flow Banded Rhyolite

It's a short walk to a large outcrop that forms a small waterfall and water chute. The rock is a gorgeous *flow banded* rhyolite. The bands consist of alternating pink and grey swirls, bends, and laminations that are 1/8 to more than 1 inch wide; in places these are emphasized by the presence of plagioclase feldspar crystals. The rhyolite also contains small oval areas or larger irregular shaped patches where ovoids have grown together; these are *spherulites*. Small *lithophysae* through the rock are lined with quartz crystals.

Eighteen: The Cascades and North Cross River Campsite

The trail climbs above the river with rhyolite outcrops both in the river channel and along the banks. From above we have a great view of the river as fast white water first rushes over a small waterfall, then noisily dashes down a series of rapids; the rhyolite has been polished smooth by the racing water.

The trail then descends back to the river, passing an outcrop of rhyolite that has elongate cavities (amygdules) filled by quartz, epidote, and calcite. Flow bands are well-exposed just above a small waterfall at the river's edge. This is a picturesque area with the river flowing down a cascade of steps before rushing through a short canyon. Just beyond is the North Cross River campsite and waypoint 18

Nineteen: Bridge and South Cross River Campsite

It's a short walk to the bridge across the Cross River and the South Cross River campsite.The outcrop on the south side of the bridge is pink rhyolite with small feldspar crystals. The mountain ash trees have been eaten to the bare bone by small caterpillars.

Twenty: Height of Land, Parking Lot, and Diabase

After leaving the Cross River, the trail heads up a set of wooden steps to the junction with a spur trail that leads to a picnic shelter and a parking lot off County Road 357 (Skou Road,1.5 miles away). We can see a small waterfall and pool from here.

The trail then heads gently uphill to the "height of land," the drainage divide between the Cross and Temperance rivers. Water on the west side of the hill flows into the Cross River and water on the east side flows into the Temperance River. From the hilltop we have nice views of Lake Superior.

165

Waypoint 20 is at an outcrop of *Beaver River Diabase* (also see diabase) with some kibbles and bits (see *diabase weathering*) on the trail.

Twenty-One: Red Pines and Demolition Ants

The trail heads down into the Temperance River Valley over small outcrops of reddish weathering diabase to a grove of red pines. The diabase varies from smooth and lumpy to crumbly with some kibbles and bits. Some of this rock weathering is "ant induced." We see one ant nest where the ants are actively turning the diabase outcrop into kibbles and bits.

From the pine grove the trail follows an open hillside, which provides nice views of Lake Superior, to a dry creek bed (waypoint 21).

Twenty-Two: Fast Food and Nice Views

The trail remains relatively level as it passes over more diabase outcrops, several of which have ant hills on them. The diabase varies from smooth and lumpy to crumbly with, once again, help from the active ants. Some of the ant hills have the tops ripped off suggesting a passing bear or raccoon dropped by for a fast food lunch.

We arrive at a large diabase outcrop with a great view to the east of Lake Superior, Taconite Harbor, and the rock-walled safe harbor used for shipping. This spot is waypoint 22. The forest along this hill is young aspen and birch, both of which show signs of having been browsed by moose. We know its moose not only from the fact the height of the browsed trees are significantly taller than the height of a deer, but also because of all the moose tracks.

Twenty-Three: Tortured Basalt and Coltsfoot

It's a 0.6 mile walk to the next waypoint with the trail following along the1230 foot elevation contour over Beaver River Diabase in various stages of weathering. A slight downhill section brings us to waypoint 23, which is an outcrop of Tortured Basalt. Lots and lots of coltsfoot grows along this part of the trail.

Twenty-Four: Iron Formation and Forest Road

Continue downhill passing over a beautiful *glacial erratic* of Mesabi Iron Formation, which contains *jasper* (red quartz) fragments cemented by hematite and *magnetite*. Cross a dry creek bed lined by beech ferns and walk a short distance downhill, over several planked areas, to Forest Road 343 with the Temperance River just beyond. There is a small parking area here so a walk could begin or end at this point. The road represents waypoint 24.

Twenty-Five: Swiss Cheese Basalt and Vesicle Cylinders

Crossing the road we walk down to the river where there are large outcrops of amygdaloidal to *massive* basalt (flow tops and bottoms) that are chock-a-

166

block full of *potholes*. The potholes vary from 4 feet in diameter down to donut size and give the surface of the outcrop a "Swiss cheese" look. The waterfalls are formed by: a) the erosion of the sides of potholes which connects them, and b) having the potholes downstream deepened more than the upstream ones.

About 300 feet down the river we see *vesicle cylinders* in the basalt: small round areas crammed full of amygdules surrounded by massive basalt. Potholes seem to form preferentially in these amygdaloidal zones. The area of vesicle cylinders is waypoint 25.

Twenty-Six: Froth Lava and Basalt Steps

It's 800 feet down the river passing more "Swiss cheese" rock (hollowed out vesicle cylinders) to waypoint 26, an outcrop of "frothy" basalt. This is the amygdaloidal top of a *pahoehoe lava flow* with amygdules from pinhead-size to more than 2 inches in diameter. Quartz, calcite, and zeolites (laumantite) fill the amygdules. Just above this outcrop is a rock wall that provides nice views both up and down the river.

Twenty-Seven: Arches, Flow Contacts, and Pipe Amygdules

We now walk 0.4 miles down river to a basalt outcrop and waterfall. At this point we can see 2 lava flows exposed in the outcrop on the opposite side of the river. These are identified by amygdaloidal tops and massive bottoms. "Arch-like" erosion features have formed in the amygdaloidal part of the flows due to erosion by fast flowing water.

Just below the trail, on the river side, there are *pipe amygdules* near the top of a flow that is overlain by the massive base of the next flow. The pipe amygdules are filled by quartz and zeolites; one large amygdule is filled by radiating crystals.

Twenty-Eight Pothole Gorge and Bridge Across River

We continue on with a nice view down into a large fracture in a basalt flow that has been widened by fast flowing water. Within the fracture zone are excellent examples of how potholes erode and become connected to form falls and narrow, steep-walled gorges. The view down into Pothole Gorge continues to waypoint 28, the bridge across the river. There is a trail junction here with the Superior Hiking Trail continuing northwest to Carlton Peak, and two spur trails, one on either side of the river, leading down to the wayside parking lot. Judy and I take the spur trail that goes down the west side of the river.

From the bridge we have a great view of a beautiful water chute with steep walls and lots and lots of potholes. The rock outcropping here is amygdaloidal basalt.

Twenty-Nine: Abandoned Pothole

The trail goes over amygdaloidal basalt with amygdules filled by quartz and a fibrous zeolite mineral (laumantite or thomsonite) to waypoint 29, a large pothole that has been left high and dry by the river. The pothole looks like a small cave whose top has collapsed; it must be 10-12 feet across. We notice agates on top of the basalt, and this would be a great den for a family of bears.

Thirty: Small Creek

It's a short walk over a rough, rocky trail that parallels the river and Highway 61 to waypoint 30, a bridge over a small creek. From here we can see the parking lot.

Thirty-One: Bridge Across River and Wayside

From the creek it's on to Highway 61 where we cross the bridge over the river to arrive at the parking lot bringing an end to a super two rivers walk.

Superior Hiking Trail
Walk 16: Carlton Peak

Walk Logistics

Start: Temperance River State Wayside on Highway 61

Getting There: Highway 61 through Schroeder to the Temperance River. The wayside is immediately past the river.

End: Britton Peak parking lot on Cook County Road 2 (Sawbill Trail)

Getting There: Take Highway 61 to Tofte. Just past the Blue Fin Resort turn left onto the Sawbill Trail (Cook County Road 2). Go 2.7 miles on the Sawbill Trail to the parking area, which is on the right.

Walk Distance: 4.7 miles   **Date Walked:** August 25th, 2004

Worth a Longer Look:

Froth Rock: 2   Doll's Eyes, Wetland Plants: 7
River Gorge: 3   Up the Anorthosite: 11
Water Chutes and Flow Tops: 4   Top of Carlton Peak Via Spur Trail
River Change: 5   Ted Tofte Overlook: 12
River Delta: 6

Waypoint-to-Waypoint

One: Temperance River Wayside

If you are interested in a drink don't stop at the Temperance River because it is purported to be one of the few North Shore streams without a bar. The lack of a gravel bar at its mouth is the reason given for the river's name, which dates back to 1864. However, Judy and I walked down to the river's mouth and there on the east side of the river is a lovely gravel bar! It was not a mirage so was there no bar there in 1864, or is the rivers name but a figment of someone's teetotaler imagination?

It's a gorgeous afternoon at the wayside; a gentle breeze wafts in from the lake, the sun is high and bright, and the sound of the rushing water not only gives us a good feeling, but draws us to it like bears to honey.

Waypoint 1 is in the wayside parking lot which is part of Temperance River State Park.

Two: Froth Rock and Potholes

It's a short walk up the east side of the river to a park sign for the Cauldron Trail. This is waypoint 2.

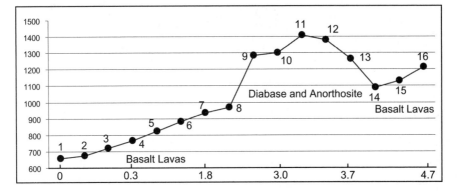

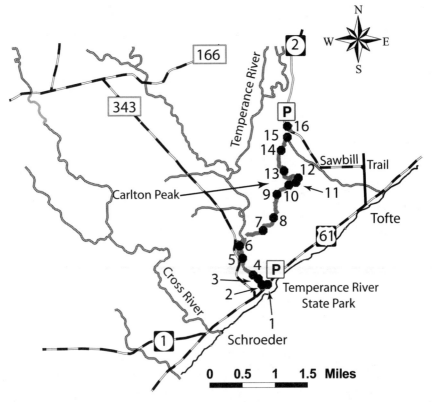

Amygdaloidal basalt outcrops here but we could also call this outcrop "froth" rock. Round *amygdules*, or gas holes, make up 30 to 45% of the lava flow. These vary from pinhead to dime-size and are filled by *chert, calcite,* and/or a cream-colored *zeolite*. This "froth" rock represents the top of a *pahoehoe lava* flow.

Small *potholes* in the rock indicate the river once flowed over this outcrop, probably forming a small waterfall; the river has since cut down through the basalt to form a narrower but deeper channel.

170

Three: Eroded Potholes and the River Gorge

From the park sign the trail goes up and over basalt lava flows to a large outcrop from which Judy and I watch the river race through a narrow gorge (Hidden Falls Gorge) that has been cut into an amygdaloidal basalt lava flow. The gorge owes its existence to 1) a fracture or crack in the rock that the river has slowly widened over time, and 2) the formation of large potholes in the fractured rock and the erosion of the downstream side of each of the potholes. This process is like the cascading fall of a row of dominos; the erosion of the top pothole leads to the erosion of the next one and so on.

Waypoint 3 is at the bridge across the Temperance River.

Four: Water Chutes, White Water, and Billowy Flow Tops

We continue upriver over amygdaloidal lava flows with great views of the river gorge, water chutes, rushing white water, and more potholes to an overlook at a small waterfall (waypoint 4). The waterfall has formed here because the amygdaloidal top of the basalt lava was more easily eroded then the massive lower part; this led to a "terraced" or "stepped" effect in the flow and the creation of the waterfall. On the opposite side of the river the exposed rock ledge has a nice billowy or rolling pahoehoe flow top.

The forest is spruce, balsam fir, birch, and aspen, along with a smattering of bigtooth aspen, willow, and cedar, some of which cling to the sides of the rock ledge. The trail at this point is fairly flat and follows an old *river terrace*.

Five: River Change, Boulder, and Dying Birch

Walking upstream we notice that the river, after the falls and its vigorous lower reaches, becomes a gentler, wider, straighter body of water. Up here the river is dotted with large *boulders* that come from the erosion of *glacial till* deposits that covered the land after the glacial ice melted away. As the river cut down through this material it carried away the finer clay, sand, silt, and *pebble*-size material leaving the heavier *cobbles* and boulders behind.

Passing an area where the river bank is being undercut by the river (there was a green erosion control fence here in 2004) we walk through a forest filled with dead and dying birch, the branches of which abruptly end where the tips have broken away. *Fireweed,* with its pretty purple flowers, is prolific through here. The wide, well-used trail follows along, then above the river to waypoint 5, a well-worn path down to the river where there is a basalt outcrop and a view of a small waterfall.

There are many informal trails where people have attempted to get down to the waterfall. Judy and I are careful to stay on the main hiking trail as some of the side trails are well worn and dangerous.

Six: River Delta

The trail turns away from the river, passing a junction with a state park ski trail. In this section not only are the birch dying but so are the aspen. A sharp bend in the trail represents waypoint 6, and from here there is a nice view of a river *meander*.

Along this section the walking path is of an unusual composition; it is composed of sand instead of glacial till, cobbles, tree roots, gravel, clay, rock outcrop, and/or kibbles and bits. The sand is part of what used to be a large river *delta,* a small version of the ones that have formed at the mouths of the Nile River and the Mississippi River. The Temperance River delta was once a wide, fan-shaped deposit that formed where the river flowed into *Glacial Lake Duluth*; here this roughly corresponds to the nine hundred foot elevation contour. Several sand and gravel pits are located in what remains of the delta deposit between here and the road to Carlton Peak.

The Temperance River delta formed about 10,000 years ago as the river rapidly eroded through the glacial deposits (till). The flowing water sorted the till particles by size into a) clay and silt, which were carried out into the lake, and b) sand and gravel which were deposited as a delta where the river flowed into the lake. This deposition was due to a dramatic decrease in the velocity of the flowing water as it entered the deeper and much larger Glacial Lake. Over time, as water levels in Glacial Lake Duluth fell, the river cut down into, then through the delta largely removing it.

Seven: Honeysuckle, Doll's Eyes, and a Canadian Carpet

The trail, now well above the river, follows the meander to a sign saying it is 2 miles to Carlton Peak. From here the pathway turns east, away from the river, for a long walk (0.4 miles) over a flat, well-packed trail (gravel part of the delta) through a mixed forest with a pretty typical *Canadian carpet*, to a small creek which is waypoint 7. Ferns are abundant along the creek as are numerous other wetland plants giving this area a soft, deep green and full of life feeling. *Baneberry* (with red and white doll's eyes berries) is common here.

Eight: Beaver River Diabase and Dead Trees

Leaving the creek the trail turns rocky with cobbles of basalt and *diabase*, as well as a few larger granitic *glacial erratics*. Following the bottom of a hill, which has outcrops of Beaver River Diabase along it, the trail passes over and past diabase boulders that have, through a process called *frost wedging*, broken free of the hillside and rolled to this position. After passing an outcrop of diabase, it's a short walk to a small rocky creek that is waypoint 8.

Nine: Heinz 57, Rose Hips, and Chokecherries

From the creek we head uphill over a rocky trail with the glacial till providing a Heinz 57 variety of cobbles: *pegmatite, schist, granite, monzonite,* basalt, and diabase. Waypoint 9 is at a spur trail that leads to an outcrop of Beaver River Diabase and a nice view of the Temperance River Valley and Taconite Harbor.

Along this section the rose hips are big and red and fireweed is thick and purple. The chokecherries are falling off the bushes and are incredibly sour–they made my mouth pucker, it was like eating a lemon, lime, and grapefruit all at the same time! Lots of climbing false *buckwheat* can be found along the side of the trail.

Ten: Ash Swamp and the Shadow of Carlton Peak

The relatively flat trail continues over and past numerous small diabase outcrops, through more stands of dead or dying birch with a mountain maple understory. Then it's through an ash swamp with boardwalked sections to waypoint 10, a small clearing with a picnic table and the junction with a state park ski trail/road. At this waypoint we are literally in the shadows of Carlton Peak, with the smooth rock wall rising steeply in front of us.

Eleven: Anorthosite and Jack Pines

The trail heads steeply uphill over *anorthosite* boulders, rocky crevices, and rocky steps as it follows the side of Carlton Peak to the spur trail (here called summit trail) that leads to the top of this large anorthosite *xenolith*. In places we can see where large chunks of anorthosite have broken off (frost wedging and *exfoliation*) from the main mass to form pieces that are now essentially wedged into, or leaning against, the anorthosite outcrop. Many look like "leaners" in the game of horseshoes.

The anorthosite varies from pinkish-gray to greenish-gray (this is the source of the pink anorthosite erratic seen on Hike 10, waypoint 7). The large *plagioclase feldspar* crystals are glassy, and the prominent crystal faces reflect the sunlight in a sparkling array of colors and patterns.

The summit spur trail, which is waypoint 11, heads to the top of Carlton Peak with the hiking trail continuing straight ahead. At the spur trail junction we find a Superior Hiking Trail Association "happy" book to record thoughts or impressions of this hike in. Judy and I refer to it as a "happy" book because most of the entries are just that. Today one person wrote, "climbed here in 1970, nice to see how little it has changed." Carlton Peak is a favorite place for local rock climbers.

This area has some of the biggest fruits on the pin cherry trees that Judy has seen in a long time. This most likely reflects the wet year we have been having.

Spur Trail to the Summit: Views, More Views, Frost Wedging, and More Views

Judy and I take the spur trail to the top of Carlton Peak. In doing so we pay attention to the footpath used to get to the top for there are all kinds of trails that lead down off the bare summit. In fact one of the entries in the "happy" book said "Happy ending–was lost at the top for half an hour, started down the wrong side!"

The top of Carlton Peak is at 1526 feet (waypoint 11 was at 1400 feet), so the views to the east, south, and west are fantastic. Most of the hills visible to the south and west are composed of diabase while the knob-like features are related to Carlton Peak–they are formed by the bowling ball weathering (exfoliation) of anorthosite xenoliths..

The anorthosite is chock full of weathering pits. Rainwater or snow melt gets into cracks or small depressions in the rock and then undergoes numerous freeze and thaw cycles. Slowly these depressions widen and deepen until, eventually, they become joined to form long, irregular channels.

There are a lot of jack pine at the summit along with some red pine; the footings from a fire tower that closed in the 1950's can still be seen.

Twelve: Ted Tofte Overlook

After descending back to the "happy" book the hiking trail continues gently downhill along the edge of this massive block of anorthosite to waypoint 12, the spur trail to the Ted Tofte Overlook. The short walk over a rocky anorthosite trail to the overlook is worth it for this vantage point provides a spectacular 360 degree view. Imposing Carlton Peak, with its jack pine covered top, is immediately behind us, a sheer drop into the anorthosite quarry is straight ahead, and all around are the rolling hills of the North Shore. On a blue sky fall day, it will be red, orange, brown, yellow, green, and blue from north to south and from east to west. This has to be the best overlook on the entire Superior Hiking Trail!

Thirteen: Bowling Ball Anorthosite

The trail continues around Carlton Peak and generally downhill past moss-covered, bowling ball-shaped anorthosite outcrops, to an outcrop of *Beaver River Diabase* with some kibbles and bits. Continuing downhill over a cobble-covered trail we come to waypoint 13, a large outcrop of diabase that is moss-covered and has polypody ferns growing on it.

Fourteen: Cinquefoil and Maple Trees

We continue gently downhill over a smooth trail to a wide bend with expansive views to the east (Carlton Creek Valley and beyond). White cinquefoil grows in abundance over the rocks, and the view, every way we turn, is green, green, and more green. From this viewpoint continue on to waypoint 14, the start of a maple forest and wet area.

Fifteen: Carlton Creek

The maple forest is short-lived for all too soon the trail descends into a generally low, muddy area with waypoint 15 at Carlton Creek, which is merely a trickle of water. The boardwalked sections of trail take us past balsam poplar, willow, and ash, all trees who "like" their feet wet. Waypoint 15 is also close to the headwaters of the creek.

Sixteen: Yellow Birch, Sawbill Trail, and Parking Lot

From the creek it's about 700 feet through a cutover area to the Sawbill Trail. Once across the road it's a short walk, past some nice big yellow birch and red pines, to the parking lot and waypoint 16.

Wow, what a walk! Carlton Peak and Ted Tofte overlook are both great, high places with spectacular views; either would serve as a perfect lunch spot. The Temperance River with its rocks, waterfalls, gorges, and delta is an extra bonus as are all the wetland plants. A short, must-do walk.

Superior Hiking Trail
Walk 17: Britton Peak and Leveaux Mountain

Walk Logistics

Start: Britton Peak parking lot on Cook County Road 2 (Sawbill Trail)

Getting There: Take Highway 61 to Tofte. Just past the Blue Fin Resort, turn left onto the Sawbill Trail (Cook County Road 2). Go 2.7 miles on the Sawbill Trail to the parking area, which is on the right.

End: Oberg Mountain parking lot on Forest Road 336 (Onion River Road)

Getting There: Take Highway 61 through Tofte and past the Chateau Leveaux Lodge to Forest Road 336 (Onion River Road) just beyond the Onion River. Turn left, and travel 2.2 miles to the parking lot on the left.

Walk Distance: 5.3 miles but that does not include the **must** do Leveaux Mountain Loop Hike.

Date Walked: August 26th, 2004

Worth a Longer Look:
Britton Peak: 3
Cedar Overlook: 9
Changing Forest: 12
Slump: 18

Waypoint-to-Waypoint

One: Britton Peak Parking Lot

Early morning, a muffled silence surrounds us as fog quilts the forest, hiding even leaves which have an eerie crinkling sound in the light breeze. There was rain last night, and if we ignore the mist from the fog there is the chance of real showers later on. The thought of having to wear a raincoat on this humid day is already making me sweat.

Waypoint 1 is in the parking lot.

Two: Britton Peak Trail Junction

Right after the hiking trail leaves the parking lot we come to a junction (waypoint 2) with the spur trail to the top of Britton Peak.

Three: Britton Peak

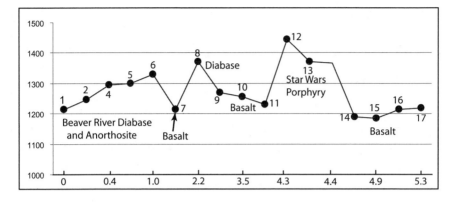

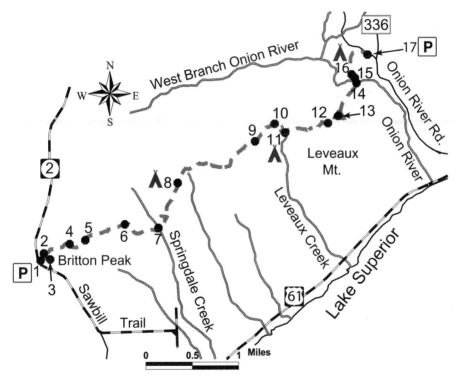

It's about 1000 feet up the wide forest service spur trail to the top of Britton Peak which is at an elevation of 1300 feet. The view from the top is dominated by Carlton Peak to the south and Lake Superior to the east. In the spring these two prominent features must be nicely framed against a garden of white flowers, for the hillsides are covered by *Juneberries* and pincherries.

At the top is a memorial to W.L. Britton, a WW II veteran who worked for the Forest Service and had his ashes scattered here in 1947. The rock his ashes rested on is *anorthosite*, the same material that forms Carlton Peak.

177

Like its larger brother, it is a *xenolith* in the *Beaver River Diabase* (also see *diabase*).

Four: Forest Colors

Descending from Britton Peak we rejoin the hiking trail at waypoint 2, and continue on through a maple-birch forest with leaves starting to turn yellow, orange, and red. The color of the leaves is framed against that of the tree bark and plants. Both the bark and the plants seem to have been enhanced by the leftover moisture of last night's rain, along with the strings of curling fog that continue to swirl through the woods. The dark maple is a vivid contrast to the white birch and, when you add to this the thick green leaves of the *blue bead lily* (Clintonia), the wilting brown of the sharply pointed *starflowers*, the tiny clasping *Canadian mayflower* leaves, and the huge, fuzzy large leaved *asters*, we have a forest scene that would be perfect for Monet to paint.

Through this section the hiking trail passes several ski trails, which are identified by blue markers. This area is a popular place for cross-country skiing as many miles of trails have been carved into the surrounding hills.

After crossing an old logging road we walk through a mature maple forest with a scattering of yellow and paper birch. There are cedar trees in lower areas as well as boardwalked sections edged by *oak* and beech *ferns*.

After a short climb out of the wet area we come to a bend in the trail and a large outcrop of Bowling Ball Anorthosite, which is waypoint 4. The forest here is thick with dogwood, hazel, and elderberry shrubs.

Five: Running Pine and Dwarf Enchanter's Nightshade

The trail continues through the maple forest with anorthosite outcrops in the hillside to the left. Crossing a small, boulder-filled creek we arrive at waypoint 5, a National Forest boundary sign where a lot of running pine (*clubmoss*) carpets the ground. Yellow birch occurs through this section along with *dwarf enchanter's nightshade*–some name for this fragile white-flowered plant that is part of the primrose family. I was certainly expecting something more exotic and significant!

Six: Till Gullies

The walk continues over planked sections and dry, boulder-filled stream beds. Where the streams exit from the hillside they have excavated small, narrow gullies in the *glacial till*. The *cobbles* and *boulders* in the till have slowly become more and more concentrated as the clay, silt, and sand-size material has been washed away.

The trail is littered with cobbles as it continues through the maple forest with lots of young maple saplings; *jewelweed* is all over the place. Waypoint 6 is at an old road with a sign marking a snowshoe trail.

Seven: Springdale Creek

The pleasant walk goes on with the forest full of large, mature maple trees; the woods are so nice we hardly notice the trail is muddy and wet except for the presence of jewelweed, a plant that thrives in damp places. Crossing a mountain bike trail and descending on switchbacks we come to Springdale Creek and waypoint 7. The creek is full of cobbles and boulders that are grey, red, and black in color and dominantly diabase and *basalt* in composition. A few have large *plagioclase feldspar* crystals in them and the rock that is the source of these boulders outcrops further up the trail.

The bridge across the creek has a worn, beaten look and one of its cables is out. This is a good indication the creek may be rather ferocious in the spring.

Eight: Springdale Campsite, Hazelnuts, and the Life of Sugar Maples

Just past the creek is the Springdale campsite; lots of hazel here and, most likely, bears in the fall. From here the trail continues through a forest of maple after maple after maple–a dark, dense woods. These are witches' woods, or so I thought as a kid for they used to scare the heck out of me.

Judy tells me it's not uncommon for sugar maples to spend forty or more years as two to three-foot tall saplings. It is only when a nearby older tree dies or is blown over that the saplings, thanks to the increased sunlight, are able to reach for the sky. The other idea on the subject of maple growth is that the adult maples have a chemical inhibitor that restricts the growth of the younger trees around them. At any rate, this area will be a great place to view fall colors, and a place to be in the spring when the northern hardwoods and their accompanying wildflowers burst into life. This year, with all the rain, it has also become a great place for mushrooms; they are emerging everywhere.

Crossing an old road/ski trail the footpath begins to climb through the maple woods to a moss-covered outcrop of Beaver River Diabase. In continuing uphill we pass two more diabase outcrops and cross another old road to arrive at waypoint 8: a small creek with planks across it. Ash trees are abundant here along with ostrich ferns, *Jack-in-the-pulpit*, and *wild ginger*.

Nine: Cedar Overlook

The maple forest continues, with several low and wet boardwalked areas, to an old road. After the road the maple woods again become dense and dark with some yellow birch and cedar mixed in to waypoint 9, the junction with the spur trail to Cedar Overlook. The spur trail climbs uphill past cedars and a weathered anorthosite outcrop to a great view of Leveaux, Oberg, and

Moose mountains, all part of the *Sawtooth Mountains*. They have been called this because, in profile, these three *cuestas* look like teeth on a wood saw.

Ten: Leveaux Creek

From the overlook it's a 0.7 mile walk through a maple forest to a cross-country ski trail (sign here for the Homestead Loop). We see tons of wetland plants in this section, and near the ski trail the forest undergoes a dramatic change with birch (much of which is dead or dying) becoming the dominant tree with maple and ash mixed in. Moose tracks are all about as are glacial boulders of a red rock type called *monzonite*.

Crossing the ski trail it's a short walk to Leveaux Creek, which is waypoint 10. Here the creek is more like a swamp than a flowing body of water, and the beaver would agree as they have dammed it to make a small pond. There is an old grassed-over beaver house and moose tracks continue to cover the ground.

Eleven: East and West Leveaux Camp Sites

The trail follows a grassy marsh that extends from the pond to a smaller pond (beaver dam between?) and the West Leveaux campsite, which is yet another LBBP (low, buggy, boggy place). Crossing the outflow from the pond we arrive at waypoint 11, the East Leveaux campsite.

Twelve: Changing Forest

Moving on we pass through the low, swampy area, with the trail lined by alders, before emerging for a nice walk through a changing forest. We start off in maples followed by a low area dominated by birch and cedar (perfect beaver food). The trail then crosses through an area of large cedars along with some big yellow birch and maple before coming back into a maple forest just as the uphill climb to Leveaux Mountain begins.

Waypoint 12 is at the junction with the Leveaux Mountain Loop Trail.

Thirteen: Rock Cliff and Mountain Ash

In continuing along the hiking trail we walk past the base of a large cliff with lots of lichen-covered *talus* that comes from the *frost wedging* of rocks exposed along the cliff face. Mountain ash is abundant here.

Mountain ash is actually not an ash; rather it is a member of the sumac family. It is a highly hybridized species from Europe that was cross-pollinated with the North American variety and, because of this, the tree provides a wide variety of berry colors. These range from mustard yellow to fire engine red. The woods around here are moist with lots of wild ginger and ostrich ferns.

Waypoint 13 is at the junction of the hiking trail and the other loop of the Leveaux Mountain Trail.

Fourteen: Onion River

Just past the loop intersection is an ephemeral pond which, at the moment, would be better referred to as a mud hole. The forest surrounding the pond represents a typical Canadian carpet. From the pond proceed over cobbles and boulders of *Star Wars Porphyry*, derived from the hill to the right, through a mixed maple, birch, spruce forest to a huge white spruce on the upper side of the trail.

After the giant spruce it's down to the Onion River (waypoint 14). Just before the river there is a boardwalk constructed out of a single enormous log that has been split in half. A large boulder of Star Wars Porphyry sits in the river, and lots of *Joe-Pye weed* can be found along the river banks.

Fifteen: Slumping

From the river crossing it is uphill to an area where the river bank, composed of glacial till, is *slumping* into the water. Again, as with all the slumps seen along the trail, this one occurs on the outside bend of a river meander. The slump area is waypoint 15.

Sixteen: Onion River Campsite

Just past the slump is the junction with the spur trail to the Onion River campsite (waypoint 16). The campsite is high on the river bank in a mostly spruce forest; definitely not a LBBP (low, boggy, buggy place).

Seventeen: Oberg Mountain Parking Lot

From the spur trail junction the hiking trail is graveled (carried in) as it passes through an old cutover area with several boardwalked sections to the parking lot, which is waypoint 17. Britton Peak, Cedar Overlook, and the lovely, ever-changing maple forest are certainly the highlights of this hike.

Superior Hiking Trail
Walk 18: Leveaux Mountain Loop Hike

Walk Logistics

Start and End: Oberg Mountain parking lot on Forest Road 336 (Onion River Road).

Getting There: Take Highway 61 through Tofte and past the Chateau Leveaux Lodge to Forest Road 336 (Onion River Road) just beyond the Onion River. Turn left and travel 2.2 miles to the parking lot on the left.

Walk Distance: 2.9 miles   **Date Walked:** August 26th, 2004

Worth a Longer Look:
Star Wars Porphyry and Views: 2
Overlooks from the Mountain: 3
Slump: 7

Waypoint-to-Waypoint

One: Oberg Mountain Parking Lot and Start of Loop Trail

Walking to the west end of the parking lot Judy and I take the hiking trial toward Britton Peak. It's a 0.9 mile walk to the junction of the Superior Hiking Trail and the Leveaux Mountain loop trail which goes to the left. This is waypoint one.

Two: Stars Wars Porphyry, Cuestas, and the Sawtooth Mountains

The loop trail ascends steeply via switchbacks through a maple-birch forest over a dark-colored, igneous intrusive rock that contains from 5-15% large plagioclase feldspar crystals. Waypoint 2 is at the junction of the loop trail and a short spur trail to an overlook above a steep cliff. There are nice views from here of what Judy refers to as the "interior"–the vast green forests inland of Lake Superior." A large *talus* deposit occurs at the base of the cliff.

The rock making up the *outcrop* is rather spectacular. It contains 35-50% large white to gray plagioclase feldspar crystals that vary from 1/8 of an inch to 2 inches in diameter. These crystals are enclosed in a fine-grained matrix that, under the microscope, can be seen to be composed of *pyroxene, magnetite, ilmenite,* biotite, and apatite. This is the first place we have seen this kind of intrusive rock in outcrop along the hiking trail.

This rock, along with the sparse plagioclase crystal rock seen on the way up here, are part of what Judy and I call the *Star Wars Porphyry* because some

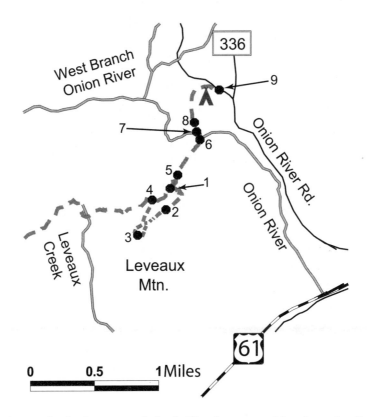

of the large plagioclase crystals look like the space ships from the Star Wars movies. These coarsely *porphyritic* rocks form a near surface, sill-like intrusion that is up to 300 feet thick with a slope of 15-20 degrees towards the lake, this is the same slope as the basalt lava flows. Partly eroded and glacially sculpted, the intrusion now occurs as a series of *cuestas* that include Oberg Mountain, Moose Mountain, the hills north of Lake Agnes, part of Maple Hill above Grand Marais, and Pincushion Mountain. It is believed the *sill* at one time formed a continuous body that extended from just south of Leveaux Mountain to just north of Grand Marais! These cuestas are mostly responsible for the topographic features along the North Shore known as the Sawtooth Mountains.

The sill is part of the *Mid-Continent Rift System* and represents a feeder to lava flows of the *North Shore Volcanic Group*. The Star Wars Porphyry occurs as xenoliths in the Beaver River Diabase so it is older than that rock body.

The sill is distinctly zoned with respect to the feldspar crystals. As we walk up the mountain, from the base to the top of the sill, the percentage of plagioclase crystals changes from 5% at the base, to 10-30% about half-way up, and 30-50% at the top. This increase in crystal content with height is due

183

to the floating of the lighter, or lower density, plagioclase feldspar crystals in the heavier or denser basaltic magma of the sill.

Three: Overlooks

The loop trail continues through maple woods to a junction with a smaller loop trail that goes around the top of the mountain (which is at an elevation of 1550 feet). We continue on this smaller loop to an overlook on the right hand side of the trail. Nice views present themselves to the southeast over Lake Superior toward the Apostle Islands and, to the south, we can see Carlton Peak.

However, the real "wow" spot of the day is at the next overlook, waypoint 3 and a great lunch spot. There is a large outcrop of Star Wars Porphyry here and weathering makes the abundant feldspar crystals really stand out. Lots of dogwood at this spot along with fantastic views to the south and southeast.

Four: Onion River Valley

We continue on the loop trail as it heads northward winding its way back to the starting point. Return to the main Leveaux Mountain Loop trail. The left hand branch takes us back to the Superior Hiking Trail (waypoint 4). On the descent there are nice views of the headwaters to the Onion River and the cliff and talus pile of waypoint 2.

From waypoint 4 we continue northeast (right) on the hiking trail.

Five: Rock Cliff and Mountain Ash

We pass the base of a large cliff with lots of lichen covered talus that comes from the frost wedging of rocks exposed along the cliff face. Waypoint 2 is at the top of this cliff. There is a lot of mountain ash through here and, after Judy made that observation, I just had to say "Well, dah, that's because there is a mountain here!" "Hmm," was her reply.

Mountain ash is actually not an ash; rather it's a member of the sumac family. A highly hybridized species from Europe that was cross-pollinated with the North American variety and, because of this, the tree provides a wide variety of berry colors. These range from mustard yellow to fire engine red. The woods around here are moist with lots of *wild ginger* and *ostrich ferns*.

Go past waypoint 1, the start of the loop. Waypoint 5 is just a short distance ahead and is at an *ephemeral pond* which, right now, could be better described as a mud hole. The forest surrounding the pond represents a typical *Canadian carpet*.

Six: Onion River

The trail proceeds over cobbles and boulders of Star Wars Porphyry, derived from the hill to the right, through a mixed maple, birch, spruce forest to a huge white spruce on the upper side of the trail.

After the giant spruce continue down to the Onion River (waypoint 6). Just before the river we come to a boardwalk that is constructed out of a single enormous log that has been split in half. A large boulder of the Star Wars Porphyry sits in the river, and lots of *Joe-Pye weed* occurs along the river banks.

Seven: Slumping

From the river crossing it is uphill to an area where the river bank, composed of *glacial till*, is *slumping* into the river. Again, as with all the slumps seen along the trail, this one occurs on the outside bend of a river meander. The slump area is waypoint 7.

Eight: Onion River Campsite

Just past the slump is the junction with the spur trail to the Onion River Campsite. The campsite is high on the river bank in a mostly spruce forest; definitely not a LBBP (low, boggy, buggy place).

Nine: Oberg Mountain Parking Lot)

From the spur trail junction the hiking trail is graveled (carried in) as it passes through an old cutover area with several board walked sections to the parking lot, which is waypoint 9.

Superior Hiking Trail
Walk 19: Oberg Mountain Loop

Walk Logistics

Start and End: Oberg Mountain Parking Lot

Getting There: Take Highway 61 through Tofte and past the Chateau Leveaux Lodge to Forest Road 336 (Onion River Road) just beyond the Onion River. Turn left, and travel 2.2 miles to the parking lot on the left.

Walk Distance: 2.3 miles   **Date Walked:** September 7th, 2004

Worth a Longer Look:
Scenic Overlooks: 6-12

Waypoint-to-Waypoint

One: Parking Lot at Oberg Mountain

Oberg Mountain, at 1555 feet elevation, is much like Leveaux Mountain: they are both composed of the same kind of rock and both form *cuestas*. This gives these two mountains, along with Moose Mountain, a profile that looks like teeth on a wood saw. For this reason they are referred to as the *Sawtooth Mountains*. The rock these cuestas are composed of is called the *Star Wars Porphyry* because the large *plagioclase feldspar* crystals in it have shapes suggestive of the space ships seen in the Star Wars movies. The percentage of large feldspar crystals making up this igneous intrusive rock increases dramatically between the lower and upper parts of Oberg Mountain.

It is mid-afternoon and cloudy with a few drops of water being squeezed out of the grayness. The wind is light but gusty and enthusiastically greets the newest addition to our dog family–Rhubarb, or energy plus–a Jack Russell Terrier who will be with us for the next several hikes.

Two: Chaise Lounge Birch

We start off by crossing the Onion River Road to the start of the Superior Hiking Trail and the loop trail to Oberg Mountain. The trail is wide and gravel-covered as it heads gently uphill through a beautiful cedar grove to a large birch tree Judy calls the "chaise lounge" (for obvious reasons). This is waypoint 2.

Three: Oberg Loop Junction
Continue up the wide pathway to the junction with the Oberg Mountain loop trail and waypoint 3.

186

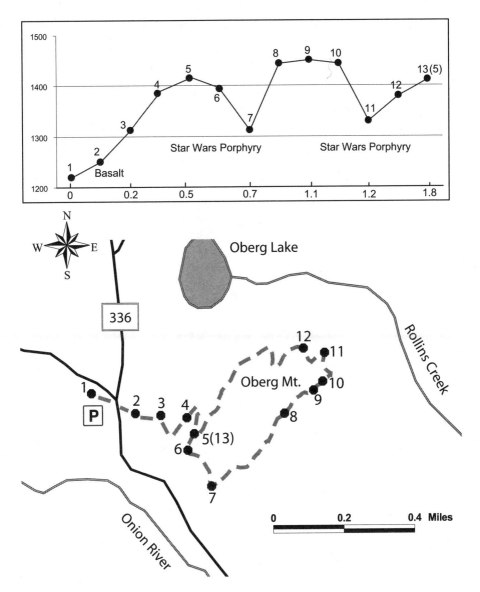

Four: Fall Colors, Canadian Carpet, and the Right Rock

Taking the loop trail (to the right) we climb uphill through a maple forest with some birch and aspen, both of which are near their peak colors. The *boulders* and *cobbles* on the trail are either the same large plagioclase crystal rock seen at Leveaux Mountain or *glacial erratics* of *granite, monzonite,* and *schist*. We cross a dry, planked creek and continue uphill to an *outcrop* of Star Wars Porphyry (waypoint 4). Here this dark intrusive rock contains approximately 5% large gray plagioclase feldspar crystals (*phenocrysts*) and is identical to the rock found near the base of Leveaux Mountain.

187

Judy points out the plants here are those that compose a typical *Canadian carpet* and include *naked miterwort*, white clover, *Canadian mayflower*, *bunchberry,* and *oak ferns*.

Five: Tree Colors and Shapes

We climb more steeply uphill with the trail making a large loop that brings it above and parallel to waypoint 4. We pass an outcrop of Star Wars Porphyry that contains 20-40% feldspar crystals (similar to middle part of Leveaux Mountain). The rock is covered by lichens and is crumbly with the crystals standing up and out of the weathered surface. Nice view from here of Lake Superior, the Onion River Valley, and Leveaux Mountain.

At the junction with the trail that loops around Oberg Mountain (waypoint 5) we take the right branch, which goes in a counter clockwise direction around the mountain.

This is the time of year when it is easy to identify trees by using their shape and color. The spruce trees are needle-like in shape, whereas the pines appear full and puffy in their crowns. The birch and aspens are brilliant yellow and contrast sharply with the deep green of the spruce and the red and orange of the maples.

Six: First Overlook, Maple Red, and Star Wars Porphyry

Continue on the loop trail to the first overlook, which provides views to the south and southwest; visible are Leveaux Mountain and the brilliant red and orange maples on its slopes, Carlton Peak, which looms in the distance, and Lake Superior, more gray than blue on this cloudy afternoon.

The outcrop is Star Wars Porphyry that contains 35-50% plagioclase feldspar crystals, some up to 1.5 inches long. This rock is identical to the rock that forms the top of Leveaux Mountain.

Seven: Bench Overlook and Two Cinquefoils

It's a short walk to the next overlook where a bench invites us to rest and enjoy the view. Here we see the same feldspar-rich intrusive rock as at waypoint 6 and there are similar fantastic views. There are two different kinds of *cinquefoil* plants: three-toothed with its red leaves, and rough-fruited. *Blue bead lily, false Solomon seal,* and *strawberries* are also abundant.

Eight: Picnic Table Overlook

The trail continues over Star Wars Porphyry through a red maple forest with some wet, planked sections. Even though the trail is high up it's wet and swampy because bedrock is just beneath the surface. This means any low areas in the rock have standing water. In fact Judy slips off the boardwalk and gets stuck in the muck, her hiking boot came free with a distinctive "thunk" sound. The dogs were smarter than the two of us, they bypassed the trail and cut through the drier woods.

Walking on we pass the "maple snake" tree, which is horizontal and looks somewhat like a python, and cross another planked section and small creek with lots of boulders to waypoint 8, the Picnic Table Overlook. The overlook provides a wide view of Lake Superior, and today broad-wing hawks are sailing by on their way down the lakeshore to Hawk Ridge and points much further south. A picnic table is provided for lunch or a snack and there is a "happy" book to record your thoughts. Someone wrote "rose hips in full bloom," and Judy agrees.

The rock the picnic table sits on contains 40-50% plagioclase feldspar crystals and has been worn smooth; no lichens have been able to take hold on the popular lunch spot.

Nine: Log Flume Outcrop

Yet another scenic overlook, an open expanse of rock, sky, and lake. There are great views to the northeast of the Rollins Creek Valley and to the southwest of the Onion River Valley. Leaving this outcrop we walk down what we call the "log flume," a rock outcrop with a smooth, u-shaped channel formed over the years by running water during spring melt and summer storms. If wet and slippery this would make a perfect one way ride. The ending, though, would be far from the hoped for "kaploosh." Pearly everlasting, with its pretty white flowers, is blooming.

Ten: Up Shore Overlook

The next overlook provides great views of the beautiful fall forest, Lake Superior, two of the Sawtooth Mountains (Moose and Eagle mountains), and the rolling green forest of the Rollins Creek Valley. Pin cherries, *yarrow*, *raspberries*, and aspens are abundant here.

The plagioclase feldspar crystals in the outcrop are big and easy to see where there is no lichen growing on them. They almost vanish with lichen growth.

Eleven: Railing Overlook

Just past waypoint 10 we come to a bend in the trail, after which there is a short walk through a balsam fir and spruce lined walking path back into maple woods to waypoint 11. A wooden railing at this overlook warns people not to get to close to the steep cliff which has lots of *talus* at its base. This comes mostly from *frost wedging*. We can see Oberg Lake, with a large bog on its northeast side, a red and orange maple forest, with yellow aspen and birch trees along with the green, green, green of the spruce (nice stand near the lake) and cedar trees. We can also see the Rollins Creek Valley, Moose and Eagle mountain (Lutsen Ski area) and, of course, Lake Superior looking gem quality blue in the sunshine that filters through the thinning clouds.

The outcrop here is spectacular with gorgeous feldspar crystals, some over 2 inches long, making up 35-50% of the rock. These are tan to gray in color and have many strange and varied shapes from tadpoles and ameboids to Manta Rays, Stick Bugs, and tablets as well as a whole host of Star Wars Cruisers. This overlook is close to the top of the igneous intrusion.

Twelve: Bog Overlook

This overlook provides much the same view as at waypoint 11, except the bog is more prominent. False *buckwh*eat, mint, plantain, elderberry and blue bead lily are abundant here. Typically these plants favor compacted soil. Here they owe their prolific nature to the heavy foot traffic. So, once again, on this hilltop miles from towns, major highways, and shopping malls human activity has played a role in what grows and what doesn't.

Thirteen: Loop Trail Junction and the Hiking Trail

We continue through the open maple woods to the final overlook on the loop walk. This has views to the west and northwest with Oberg Lake and its bog a prominent feature. As we look at Oberg Lake we see that the spruce trees along the lake shore are different heights. The ones closest to the water are the smallest and they get progressively taller further from the lake shore. Judy says this is indicative of a shrinking lake meaning the shortest ones are the youngest, growing upwards only after the lake water receded away. One day the lake will be gone, and there will be only trees and bog. From this overlook it's a nice walk, through maple woods, back to the junction with the loop trail around the mountain (waypoint 13). Take the trail to the right to get back to the junction with the hiking trail (waypoint 3). From here turn left to get back to the parking lot, or right to continue on the hiking trail to Lutsen (Walk 20).

Rhubarb had a great time but I don't think Charlie and Sammy appreciated it. She was constantly off into the woods after something (mainly squirrels). Sammy and Charlie would naturally be right behind her. By stop 9 they were completely pooped out while "energy" was still running in circles, up and down and around the loop trail. Watching her wears me out!

Superior Hiking Trail
Walk 20: Oberg Mountain, Moose Mountain, and Lutsen

Walk Logistics

Start: Oberg Mountain Parking Lot

Getting There: Take Highway 61 through Tofte and past the Chateau Leveaux Lodge to Forest Road 336 (Onion River Road) just beyond the Onion River. Turn left and travel 2.2 miles to the parking lot on the left.

End: Lutsen Ski Area on Cook County Road 5 (Ski Hill Road)

Getting There: Take Highway 61 through Tofte to the Lutsen Recreation area. Turn left onto Cook County Road 5 (Ski Hill Road), and take this 2.9 miles past the Alpine Slide and Gondola Ride to the end of the road and the parking lot.

Walk Distance: 6.2 miles   **Date Walked:** September 9th, 2004

Worth a Longer Look:
Oberg Cliffs and a Dark Trail: 4   Fire Weed and Maples: 8
Moose Mountain: 7   Gondola Hill: 9

Waypoint-to-Waypoint

One: Parking Lot at Oberg Mountain

Oberg Mountain, at 1555 feet elevation, is much like Leveaux Mountain: they are both composed of the same kind of rock and both form *cuestas*. This gives these two mountains, along with Moose Mountain, a profile that looks like teeth on a wood saw. For this reason they are referred to as the *Sawtooth Mountains*. The rock these cuestas are composed of is called the *Star Wars Porphyry* because the large *plagioclase feldspar* crystals in it have shapes suggestive of the space ships seen in the Star Wars movies. The percentage of large feldspar crystals making up this igneous intrusive rock increases dramatically between the lower and upper parts of Oberg Mountain.

Judy and I camped last night at Nine Mile Lake in the National Forest Service campground. It was a beautiful evening, but on the cool side this morning with the temperature 39 degrees in my tent. Charlie, sleeping in a small dog bed, managed to completely cover himself with the blanket he usually sleeps on; Rhubarb just wiggled her way to the bottom of my sleeping bag and had to be

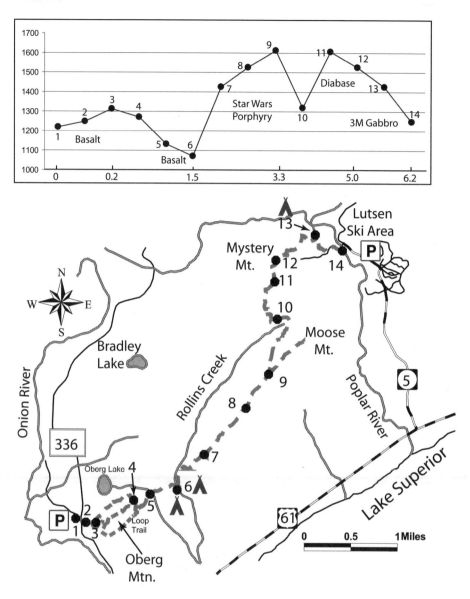

shaken out to get her going. It's now a balmy 50 degrees with blue sky and just a bit of a breeze–a great day for a walk in the woods.

Two: Chaise Lounge Birch

We start off by crossing the Onion River Road to the start of the Superior Hiking Trail and the loop trail to Oberg Mountain. The trail is wide and gravel-covered as it heads gently uphill through a beautiful cedar grove to a large birch tree Judy calls the "chaise lounge" (for obvious reasons). This is waypoint 2.

Three: Oberg Loop Junction

Continue up the wide pathway to the junction with the Oberg Mountain loop trail and waypoint 3.

Four: Dark Trail, Oberg Cliffs and Ginger

Continue on the Superior Hiking Trail, which follows the edge of Oberg Mountain. Through this section the trail is tunnel-like–dark with a heavy closed in feeling due to all the mountain maple and hazel understory that closely guards it. The bigger trees through here are aspen, birch, and cedar. The rocks along the tunnel are pieces of Star Wars Porphyry that have been *frost-wedged* from the high cliffs of Oberg Mountain; there are also some *cobbles* of *basalt* and *diabase* from weathering of the *glacial till*.

Passing two large spruce trees and an *outcrop* of basalt that is partly hidden amongst thick masses of moss and clubmoss the trail descends via switchbacks to a large, old spruce stump. Looking up at the rocky cliff on the side of Oberg Mountain, Judy describes the scene as a "really nice, neck back on the shoulders, jaw-dropping kind of view!"

The trail remains dark and tunnel-like until it reaches a large boulder of Star Wars Porphyry sitting in the middle of a dry stream bed (waypoint 4). This rock contains 35-50% plagioclase feldspar crystals and came from the top of Oberg Mountain. *Wild ginger*, partially hidden by ferns, is abundant through here–both ferns and wild ginger are fans of moist, dark forests.

Five: Creeping Cedars and Mountain Maples

Continuing gently downhill the trail is littered with cedar cones that resemble small, wooden flowers. Walking on we come to a large boulder of Star Wars Porphyry and a *talus* deposit derived from *frost wedging* of the Oberg cliff rocks. The cliff can be seen from here, and if it were leaf off season, it would be a really nice view. The cedars at this point seem to be creeping along the ground with graceful, upward bending trunks.

Continuing on, the trail passes an outcrop of basalt with boulders of Star Wars Porphyry on top of it. The basalt, angular pieces of which litter the trail, is dominantly dark and massive; a few pieces have small plagioclase feldspar crystals and sparse *amygdules*.

It is thick and dark here, so much so that the sunlight doesn't penetrate to the forest floor, and the soil feels perpetually damp. This is a good place to come in the spring, before the leaves are thick, to see the spring wildflowers that take advantage of the early season sunlight. The dominant shrub through this dark section is mountain maple, which has a tan to red-colored bark; its smaller branches are usually red. One of the word plays people often use to distinguish this from another reddish shrub, red-osier dogwood, is "tan pants, red shirt, like the Royal Canadian Mounted Police." The 'mount' is

193

supposed to remind one of the MOUNTain maple. It is also known as moose maple, as it is a favored browse food of the moose.

From the basalt outcrop the rocky trail (glacial till and basalt) crosses two small streams before reaching Oberg Creek and waypoint 5. By the time we reach Oberg Creek the forest is more open being dominated by aspen and birch. The thick mountain maple is disappearing as well.

Six: Rollins Creek and West Rollins Creek Campsite

It's a long walk along a rocky, muddy trail with low, wet sections across two creeks and an old ski trail/road followed by three more small creeks to the West Rollins Creek campsite and Rollins Creek, which is waypoint 6. Near the campsite Judy finds the invasive plant curly dock; a tall plant, with long, thick leaves and a flower stalk full of flattened seeds. This is a low, wet area, with abundant cedar and ash. Also found here are *blueberries*, *thimbleberries*, and *raspberries*.

We have a bit of excitement near the campsite as Sammy rolls (we still wonder why) on a black and white hornet nest. I have to admit she is very stoic about it all, never whining, yelping, or yowling as the hornets swarm around her. However, she does move pretty fast down the trail and into Rollins Creek where she sits, ears back, flopped out and sulking.

Seven: East Rollins Creek Campsite, Moose Mountain, and Broad-Winged Hawks

After crossing Rollins Creek and the East Rollins Creek campsite the trail heads along, then above the creek under a mountain maple canopy that changes to a more open forest of spruce, cedar, and yellow birch. Becoming steeper the trail proceeds over numerous cobbles and *boulders* of Star Wars Porphyry along with basalt to a sharp bend where we find an outcrop of Star Wars Porphyry that continues up Moose Mountain. At this location the porphyry contains about 5% plagioclase feldspar crystals and these increase to 30-40% near the mountain top. This is similar to what we saw during our ascent of Leveaux and Oberg mountains.

We continue uphill to waypoint 7, a nice overlook with views to the east and south over Lake Superior. The wind today is out of the northwest, a perfect direction for the migrating raptors. From our lofty spot we watch the broad-wing hawks floating down the lakeshore as they head south.

Eight: Smoking Fireweed and Thriving Sugar Maples

We continue to walk along the ridge over flat, smooth-to-pitted Star Wars Porphyry. The woods are open and sunny and the *fireweed* is "smoking." These tall, sun-loving plants like open spaces such as those created by forest fires, but that is not why they are said to "smoke." They "smoke" because their long seed pods split open with each seed being carried away from the parent plant on a long wisp of silky material, much like dandelion or milkweed, but longer than either of those. On dry, sunny, breezy days, like today, the wisps rising off the plant make it look like it is "smoking!" There are also pink *corydalis* and raspberries here.

As the trail bends closer to the center of the ridge we see a dramatic change in the forest. In fact the trail seems to be the dividing line between maple forest to the east and a mixed forest to the west. Sugar maples thrive on these eastern slopes, as long as the temperature normally stays above 40 degrees below zero. The lake has a moderating effect on the local landscape keeping the winter temperature milder and the summer temperature cooler. This effect is most pronounced on the eastern, or lake facing slopes. This leads to abundant, thick maple woods on these lake facing slopes, and a general lack of maples on the western facing slopes. The trail at waypoint 8 is in a perfect spot to observe this lake effect! In the fall, the division can be seen by the reds to the east and the yellows of birch and aspen to the west.

Nine: Gondola Hill

It's a long (0.5 mile) easy walk along the ridge through a maple-birch forest to waypoint 9, a marked spur trail that is no longer included as part of the hiking trail.

Deciding to see what is at the top of the spur we follow it upward to a trail marked "trail 33," a Lutsen ski trail. We follow this and shortly arrive at the Lutsen Gondola. This turns out to be a great lunch spot with panoramic views to the east, northeast, and north. The gondola runs from the ski resort in the valley below us up to the top of this ski hill on the side of Moose Mountain. Judy suggests the possibility of one day riding the gondola up to this point then walking down "trail 33" to the spur trail and either back to Lutsen via the Superior Hiking Trail or to the Oberg Parking lot.

Ten: Dwarf Enchanter's Nightshade

Returning to the junction with the Gondola Spur Trail we head downhill, relatively steeply at first, then more gently over a rocky trail littered with lots of Star Wars Porphyry mixed with material weathered out of the glacial till. At the bottom the trail becomes wet and muddy as it goes through an area dominated by mountain maple with patches of *goldthread, violet,* and *bunchberry;* this area must be a delight in the spring with lots of different wildflowers.

This is followed by a flat, muddy section with boardwalked areas and some large yellow birch. Crossing a ski trail we walk through a maple forest to a planked-over dry creek (waypoint 10). Judy finds *dwarf enchanter's nightshade* here along with wild ginger, *Jack-in-the-pulpit*, and *jewelweed*.

Eleven: Empty Rooms at the Yellow Birch

The trail now heads uphill through a maple forest with boulders of Star Wars Porphyry (from Moose Mountain), to a large yellow birch stump with several "empty rooms." These are numerous large holes made by hungry woodpeckers. Continue uphill to waypoint 11, a partial view of Moose Mountain (Gondola Hill) and townhouses in the valley as well as an outcrop of *Beaver River Diabase* that weathers reddish-brown. There are abundant pin cherries and *Juneberries.*

Twelve: Mushrooms and Mountain Bike Trails

It's a short walk over boulders and cobbles of Star Wars Porphyry past a junction with a ski trail after which the hiking trail heads downhill, going by an area crammed with boulders and cobbles followed by an area without boulders into another boulder filled area. The cobbles and boulders are round to subround and of mixed lithologies; these concentrated areas may represent outwash channels, places where streams flowed under, then out of the glacial ice carrying lots of coarse-and fine-grained sediment. Pass an outcrop of Beaver River Diabase to waypoint 12, the junction with mountain bike trail blue 3.

The forest is dominantly maple with birch and spruce making for lots of fall colors. Mushrooms are abundant, especially at the base of birch trees; in fact, you can tell where birches were, even after they have died and rotted, because the mushrooms are there, too, on dead sticks and stumps.

Thirteen: Mystery Mountain Campsite and Gabbro

Continue downhill through the colorful maple forest to an outcrop of *gabbro.* This brown-weathering rock contains lots of *pyroxene* (55%) and greenish-yellow *olivine* (10%) with a lot less plagioclase feldspar than normal gabbro or diabase (more mafic or darker). This rock underlies Mystery Mountain, and since it lacks a name on local geology maps we decide to call it the 3M Gabbro (Mafic Mystery Mountain). Boulders of Star Wars Porphyry are still with us.

Reaching the base of the downhill section the trail flattens out crossing several smooth, brownish-weathering outcrops of 3M Gabbro. Passing a ski trail there are views of Moose Mountain (spring and fall) and the Poplar River Valley before arriving at the Mystery Mountain campsite. Just past the trail junction to the campsite is another spur trail that takes us to an overlook of the Poplar River Valley. In the distance we can see tamarack trees that are changing into their classic "smoky" gold color.

Fourteen: Poplar River and Lutsen Parking Lot

It's downhill, via switchbacks, onto a flat, muddy trail that becomes closed in by alders. Crossing a small creek and a small outcrop of 3M Gabbro we arrive at the junction with a wide ski trail which the hiking trail now follows (to the left).

The ski trail leads us to the bridge over the Poplar River and waypoint 14. There is a rocky gorge on the lower side of the bridge with lots of drop pools and numerous boulders of dark brown 3M Gabbro. The upper side is full of broken rock.

The junction between the Superior Hiking Trail, which continues on to Caribou Lake, and a spur trail that takes us to the Lutsen Parking Lot and the end of the hike is just on the other side of the bridge. We take the spur trail to the parking lot (0.4 miles) bringing an end to this pleasant, scenic walk on a beautiful September day. Other than Sammy and the hornets the best parts of this hike were the long walk along the rocky Moose Mountain ridge, lunch at Gondola Hill, the lovely maple forest, and the 3M gabbro.

Superior Hiking Trail
Walk 21: Lake Agnes and the Poplar River

Walk Logistics

Start: Lutsen Recreational Area on Cook County Road 5 (Ski Hill Road)

Getting There: Take Highway 61 through Tofte past the Onion and Poplar Rivers to the Lutsen Recreational Area. Turn left onto Cook County Road 5 (Ski Hill Road), and take this 2.9 miles past the Alpine Slide and Gondola Ride to the end of the road and the parking lot.

End: Small parking lot above Caribou Lake adjacent to County Road 4

Getting There: Highway 61 past Cook County Road 5 to Lutsen where you turn left onto Cook County Road 4 (Caribou Trail). Drive 4.1 miles up the road to Caribou Lake, and the hiking trail parking lot is on the right.

Walk Distance:
5.3 miles plus a 0.9 mile walk to the parking lot

Date Walked:
September 14th, October 1st, 2004

Worth a Longer Look:

Lutsen: 1	Ginger: 10
Moose Mountain: 3	Poplar River View: 13
Maple Woods: 5, 12	Red Pine Overlook :15
Glove Overlook: 6	Hunter's Rock: 16
Giant White Pine Stump: 9	East Lake Agnes Campsite: 17

Waypoint-to-Waypoint

One: Lutsen Recreational Area

Lutsen has become a popular place winter, summer, and fall. In fact some call it the "Disney World" of the North Shore and I'm not certain if that's a compliment or a rude remark. Winter is obvious for it's difficult to miss the wide "freeways" cut through the woods that cover the surrounding hillsides. Summers have become much more interesting because Lutsen is no longer the sole property of golfers. They are now outnumbered by hikers, mountain bikers, and yes, even horseback riders. Fall is the color season, and both Mystery and Moose Mountains, which form part of the Lutsen recreational area, are ablaze with a wide range of reds, oranges, browns, and yellows. I

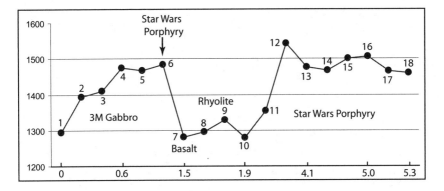

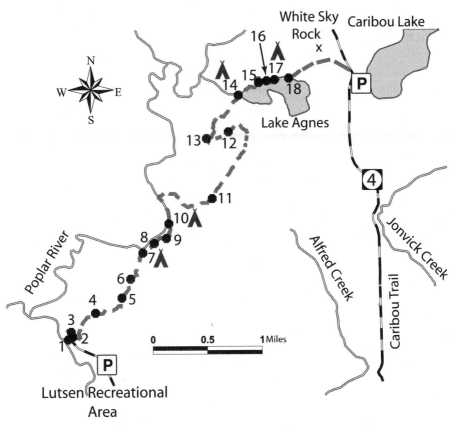

have no idea why Mystery mountain is called this, but to me it is a mystery how a topographic feature with an elevation of 1700 feet can be called a mountain!

Last night we were kept awake by some good, old-fashioned, house rattling thunderstorms. However, the rising sun brought with it a stiff breeze and a bright blue, sunny sky. The woods remain wet and drippy, but the wind and sun will soon change that.

It's a 0.4 mile walk, from the parking lot at the Lutsen ski area up a wide, multi-use road to the trailhead sign for the Superior Hiking Trail; this is waypoint 1.

Two: Hazel Brush and Mystery Mountain Gabbro

The trail to Lake Agnes begins by climbing, via switchbacks, through a forest of aspen, birch, balsam, and spruce. Today, with a gorgeous blue sky for a backdrop, the palette of colors for the eye to take in is glorious indeed. As we climb, we notice how the hazel dominates, and its brown twigs sport golden yellow, toothed leaves that seem to glow in the sunlight. A closer look at the faintly speckled twigs reveals tiny brown bumps that are next year's male catkins, tightly bound now, but they will unfurl to more than an inch in length come next spring.

As we continue upwards we pass two *outcrops* of 3M *Gabbro*. This medium-grained, brown-weathering, gabbro underlies Mystery Mountain and thus the 3M name-Mafic Mystery Mountain. The trail continues upward through a thick balsam and birch forest to a sharp bend where there are two *glacial erratics,* one composed of dark *basalt* and one of pinkish *monzonite*. These *boulders* represent waypoint 2.

Three: The Embarrassed Mountain and Cuestas

The trail continues uphill, past more 3M Gabbro, with kibbles and bits covering the trail on south-facing slopes (see *diabase weathering*) before arriving at a 3M Gabbro outcrop that affords nice views to the east and southeast. Lake Superior can be seen in the distance and, on this day, with a bit of moisture in the air, the line between sky and water, both a brilliant blue, is obscured by a fuzzy, whitish haze. The sounds of the Poplar River crashing over rocks can be heard below, and we have a very nice view across the river valley to Moose Mountain. The mountain appears to be all atremble and slightly embarrassed as the blanket of red, orange, and yellow leaves flutter in the lake breeze. Both Moose and Mystery mountains, one composed of *Star Wars Porphyry*, the other of 3M Gabbro, are *cuestas* and, in profile, look like the teeth on a dull saw. They form part of the *Sawtooth Mountains*.

Four: Clubmoss and Evergreen

Walking uphill we cross more 3M Gabbro from which there are nice views of Eagle Mountain which is directly east of us. At the top of some beautifully crafted stone steps, we find a nice patch of two different kinds of *clubmoss*. One is commonly called "ground cedar" and the other is called "running pine." Both have fruiting stalks that shake out brownish spores when touched.

The trail then levels out, passing a fairly large patch of *thimbleberries* with the large, green maple-shaped leaves starting to take on a fading yellow color. We then head downhill over a variety of boulders derived from erosion of the *glacial till*; these include gabbro, basalt, pink monzonite, *rhyolite*, and Star Wars Porphyry. Passing a large gabbro outcrop the trail again levels out as it winds through a forest dominated by spruce and birch. This section is followed by a short uphill to a gabbro outcrop, then down a gentle slope into a low, swampy area with wooden planks across the muddiest and wettest sections (waypoint 4). *Goldthread*, with its shiny lobed leaves, along with *blueberries* and white *violets* are common in this low area.

Five: Too Much Color

After leaving the swampy area, the boulder-rich trail heads uphill where it levels out as it enters a maple forest. Layer upon layer of red and brown maple leaves cover the trail, and the aroma of wet, decaying organic material fills the air. The colors through the woods are breathtaking; the dark bark of the maple trunks, the soft, green ground cover of large-leaved *aster*, and the splashes of red, fire engine red, salmon red, burnt orange, lemon yellow and the still green of the more stubborn maple leaves. Judy imagines trying to paint this scene and admits she could never reproduce adequately this incredible abundance of color.

The trail then heads downhill, still in the maple forest, to a ski and/or mountain bike trail which is waypoint 5.

Six: Glove Overlook and Sawtooth Mountain Porphyry

From this junction we continue on a boulder strewn and tree root-crossed walking path to Glove Overlook. We have no idea how or why the overlook received this name, but it is impressive to arrive and look over a large, round expanse of rock, full of worm-like holes, to the green valley and hills beyond. Looking north, we can see past the tops of spruce trees, which look dark and green in comparison to the yellowing birch leaves and their white paper bark. To the northeast we can see Lake Superior and tree-covered, tilted lava flows that form the distant hills.

The round expanse of rock is Star Wars Porphyry, and here it contains 30-45 % plagioclase feldspar crystals (*phenocrysts*). In places these are hard to see because of all the lichen covering the tan to grayish-brown rock. Many of the feldspar crystals have been weathered out leading to the rock's distinctive "wormy" look. Star Wars Porphyry makes up Leveaux, Oberg, Moose, and Pincushion mountains.

Seven: Hornets and the West Poplar River Campsite

From the overlook the trail passes by an outcrop of 3M Gabbro and lots of clubmoss before heading downhill past large boulders of 3M Gabbro, Star Wars Porphyry, and a pinkish monzonite, all of which appear to have come from frost wedging of rocks exposed on the upper portions of the hill. We have partial views over the Poplar River Valley from openings in the birch-balsam forest that covers the hillside.

We continue down to the Poplar River and, in so doing, pass a very active hornets nest; active because Rhubarb manages to stir it up and, in return, the hornets stir her up by chasing her into the water. I knew she was fast but zowie does she ever move! How a small dog can run that fast while filling the air with pitiful yelps is a mystery to me.

Waypoint 7 is at the spur trail to the West Poplar River campsite. There are lots of boulders here of *amygdaloidal basalt*; the *amygdules* are round, and many are now empty because the mineral(s) that once filled them have weathered out.

Eight: Rhyolite and Clubmoss

Leaving the river's edge the trail goes uphill, over boulders of basalt, to an outcrop of rhyolite lava (waypoint 8). The rhyolite contains lath-to tabular-shaped pink feldspar (*orthoclase*) crystals (up to a half-inch long) and 15-20% angular amygdules filled by *quartz*, pink feldspar, and *epidote*. As we walk up the cedar-filled hillside to the outcrop we admire dense carpets of green on both sides of the trail; clubmosses, bristly looking plants that are soft to the touch, dominate the groundcover and are joined by yews, a low-to-the-ground evergreen shrub.

Nine: Ents and Caribou

Walking along the hillside, above and parallel to the river, we climb up to a gigantic white pine stump (waypoint 9). Judy thinks it would take three people to encircle this ancient giant, a tree that could have easily walked side by side with the forest "Ents" of Tolkeins "Lord of the Rings." Trying to envision a complete forest of these giants, stretching for miles over the hillsides, towering above everything but the stars and rising moon, is like trying to envision a world full of living, breathing dinosaurs. Judy, imagining what it would have been like to walk through such a forest, pictures herds of caribou, not dinosaurs, moving under the high green canopy that lets little light down to the forest floor and would have provided plenty of room for these large antlered animals.

Ten: Ginger and the East Poplar River Campsite

Leaving the imaginary world of white pine giants we continue over a root-crossed and bouldery trail passing by another rhyolite outcrop before descending to a small creek that is just beyond a snowmobile trail crossing.

We take time at the creek to look for a heart-shaped, soft green leaf close to the ground. This is *wild ginger*, which loves these moist shady spaces. While the entire hardwood forest would be a wonderful place to search for spring wildflowers, Judy likes these low-lying wet areas best, and ginger is one of the reasons because she loves its purplish, cupped flower that is generally hidden under the leaves.

The trail, now along the river, passes by numerous low-lying areas and crosses several small streams. In this wet setting, in and amongst running pine, are patches of *wood sorrel*. Most people, like me, would look at these three-parted heart-shaped leaves and call it clover. And for good reason; it does resemble a clover leaf, even folding up in the approaching darkness. However it is not part of the clover family. In June it has a little pinkish-white flower that would be seen scattered throughout the evergreen clubmosses.

Waypoint 10 is at the spur trail to the East Poplar River campsite.

Eleven: Sprucey and Moosey

The trail continues along the river with lots of asters, *goldenrod,* and *Joe-Pye weed*, along with the leaves of *cow parsnip* and delicate meadow *rue*. Cross over three closely spaced, but separate, wooden planked areas (the planks coming from the old deck of Papa Charlie's restaurant at Lutsen). We then turn away from the river for a long walk, over a root-crossed trail, through a spruce dominated, low, swampy area with planks over the really wet, muddy spots. The muck near these muddy places is a likely spot to find large holes made by wandering moose. Sprucey and moosey, that's what this section seems to be about. Though there is *baneberry* (with its white and red doll's eye berries), and thick carpets of princess pine.

Waypoint 11 is at an elevated boardwalk over a small, but now dry creek.

Twelve: Dewberry and the Ephemeral Pond

The trail continues over more boardwalked areas with wild ginger growing everywhere along with *dewberry*, a cousin of raspberry and strawberry that seems to like these wet spaces. As we wander in this low area, we notice that as the trail goes up a slight rise, the forest changes from spruce to aspen. A depression on the upper side of the trail represents an ephemeral pond which, in the spring, will be filled with water, making it a haven for tree frogs and toads. Today it is as dry as an old dog's bone. We find a nice, big, upwardly spreading paper birch here along with a single, sad ash tree.

The ephemeral pond is followed by a long walk through a gorgeous maple forest–a shady and cool place on a hot summer day, a place to go looking for *springbeauties* and *Dutchman's breeches* in early spring, or a place to ooh and awe at the contrast of the multitude of fall colors. There seem to be all ages of maple trees through here, with many ancient ones dead and on the ground.

The trail heads uphill over a couple of flat outcrops of "wormy" Star Wars Porphyry to waypoint 12, a nice overlook of the valley we just walked across as well as views to the east of rolling hills composed of basalt lava flows. The outcrop at the overlook is Star Wars Porphyry with numerous, oddly shaped plagioclase feldspar crystals that make up 35-40 % of the rock. There is a lot of *Juneberry* here.

Thirteen: Poplar River View

The trail heads downhill, passing through the "giant log" and over flat outcrops of Star Wars Porphyry as it wanders through the maple forest to waypoint 13, the well known and advertised Poplar River view. The view gives us a panoramic look at the gentle S-shaped *meanders* of the Poplar River, the beautiful dark pointed spruces (which we just walked through), and the multicolored maples and birches on the hills beyond.

The lovely outcrop that provides the view is Star Wars Porphyry, which drops off abruptly to a large *talus* pile at its base. Around this overlook are cherries, elderberries, and Juneberries.

Fourteen: Stressed Maples and Fir-Aris (25)

The trail follows the edge of the hill passing outcrops of Star Wars Porphyry with sparsely distributed feldspar crystals (base of the intrusion). The hillside is dominated by trees that seem to be infested with a tangled, snarled mass of heart-shaped leaves and tendrils that lead up nearly every vertical surface. This entangling stuff is climbing false *buckwheat*, which seems to be taking over. The tenacious vine seems to be strangling the younger trees, actually bending them low and down to the ground. The maples thus have to deal with a double whammy: thin soil, which they really don't like, and the false buckwheat.

Heading downhill we come to beautiful Lake Agnes and waypoint 14, the bridge across the creek that drains this small lake. From the bridge, looking toward the lake, we can see a beaver dam stretching across the outlet of the stream. Below the bridge, we take a minute to look again for yew which, this time, can be found near balsam fir trees. So here we have a great opportunity to see the difference between the two. Judy turns over a flat balsam needle and shows me the tiny stripes. She tells me that some people remember this as a fir cause it has racing strips like in a "fir-ari." Turning over a yew needle she shows me how it looks the same on the other side. Deer love to browse the yew, and in some places it has been exterminated.

Just past the bridge is the spur trail to the West Lake Agnes Campsite, and the outcrop here is gabbro.

Fifteen: Juniper and Red Pine Overlook

The trail follows the lakeshore with spruce trees growing close to the lake and maples farther away. There are also tons of blueberry plants; I expect August would be a good, tasty month to be here. Heading uphill we walk away from the lake, before turning back toward an overlook with large, sky-reaching red pine trees. The exposed rock is Star Wars Porphyry with 20-30 % plagioclase feldspar crystals. Just over the crest of the hill one of the pines appears to have been burned, and the local story has it that some kids had a fire at the base of this beautiful tree and it kind of got out of hand. Juniper, with sharply pointed needles protecting the sage-colored hard fruits, grows around the rocky area.

Sixteen: Hunter's Rock

Just past the overlook there is a rocky outcrop that has been named "Hunter's Rock," and this is waypoint 16. A new "happy" book was placed here in September of 2005. In the book can be written impressions of this hike, Lake Agnes, the Superior Hiking Trail or the state of your love life which we have seen recorded in other very "happy" books. At this spot we overlook a floating bog, and a beautiful pine leans far out over the bog. Judy thinks she could sit here and take in this view for hours and hours and be very happy.

Seventeen: East Agnes Campsite

From Hunter's Rock it is downhill over Star Wars Porphyry with the trail paralleling the lakeshore to waypoint 17, the spur trail to the East Lake Agnes campsite. This is one of the most popular campsites on the trail for it is nestled in amongst the spruce, fir, and pines. It also has a great swimming hole–deep and alluring and wonderful on a warm summer day. But beware, there are numerous reports of moose keeping folks up at night in this area.

Eighteen: Trail Junction

From here it's a short walk to the junction of the Superior Hiking Trail. One branch of the trail continues on to Cascade River State Park, and the other is a 0.9 mile long spur trail to the parking lot on the Caribou Lake Road (Cook County Road 4). We take the spur trail, and so this ends the wonderful Lake Agnes Hike with lots of highlights to talk about on our trip home. The trail description from the parking lot to Lake Agnes (this waypoint), including the spur to White Sky Rock, can be found in Hike 22.

Superior Hiking Trail

Walk 22: Lake Agnes, Jonvick Creek, and Lookout Mountain

Walk Logistics

Start: Small parking lot above Caribou Lake adjacent to County Road 4

Getting There: Highway 61 past Cook County Road 5 to Lutsen where you turn left onto Cook County Road 4 (Caribou Trail). Drive 4.1 miles up the road to Caribou Lake, and the small hiking trail parking lot is to the right.

End: Cascade River State Park on Highway 61

Getting There: Highway 61 north from Lutsen passing Jonvick, Spruce and Indian Camp creeks to the Cascade River and the wayside parking lot at the side of the highway.

Walk Distance: 10.2 Miles   **Date Walked:** September 8th, 2004

Worth a Longer Look:

Rock Cedars: 4	Sawtooth Mountains: 13
Lake Agnes: 5	Adoxa: 15
Bazillion Steps and Overlook: 6	Snowmobile Overlook: 18
Maple Forest Walk: 8	Another Overlook: 20
Dam Crossing: 10	Lookout Mountain: 23
Cathedral of Pines Overlook: 12	

Waypoint-to-Waypoint

One: Parking Lot

It's a lovely fall day in northern Minnesota, lending support to the claim this is the state's nicest time of year. The day is partly cloudy, it's a comfortable sixty degrees, and there is no wind. To top this off the fall colors are nearing their peak with the intense red of the maples intimately mixed with more subtle burnt oranges, amber browns, and pale to vivid yellows. Today we get to hike through this blaze of color with the first waypoint being the small parking lot near Caribou Lake.

Two: Wide Trail, Star Wars Porphyry, and White Sky Rock

From the parking lot a wide, gravel spur trail, littered with *boulders* of *Star Wars Porphyry* and *basalt* lava of the *North Shore Volcanic Group,* leads uphill through a blazing red maple forest. This spur trail is more like a driveway than a walking path, and the reason for this is the heavy use it gets

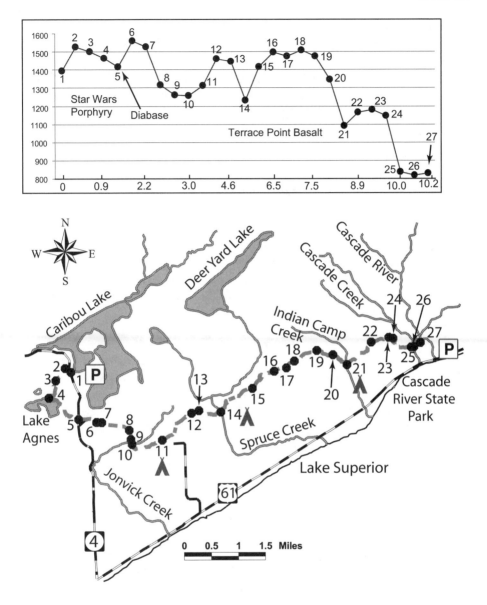

as an access point into the popular Lake Agnes campsites. These camping spots are situated on rocky prominences amongst stately white and red pines on the shoreline of lovely Lake Agnes.

Waypoint two is at the junction of the spur trail and the trail to White Sky Rock. This rocky overlook is composed of Star Wars Porphyry and provides a wonderful view of Caribou Lake.

Three: Running Pine and Talus

At the junction continue toward Lake Agnes with the trail going through a dominantly maple-aspen forest with a balsam understory; there are some large white pines in here along with a few enormous birch and fir trees. The ground is covered by a variety of *clubmoss* that is called running pine because 1) it sends out runners that take root along the ground, and 2) it is evergreen and resembles a small pine tree. White *baneberry* is abundant through here.

The walking path is a web of tree roots and dark boulders composed mostly of Star Wars Porphyry. In places the large *plagioclase feldspar* crystals have weathered out, so the rock looks like it is full of worm holes.

Waypoint 3 is at the base of a steep hillside with a large *talus* pile composed of Star Wars Porphyry.

Four: Log Stairway, Rock Cedars, Crannies, and Nooks

The trail heads steeply uphill over numerous boulders, some of which have steps notched into them. Above the stone steps is a log stairway, and while these carved, wooden steps get us where we are going, they are slippery when wet.

Climbing the staircase we pass many nooks and crannies that have cedar trees growing out of them. Some of these cracks in the rock are wide enough to allow for the growth of some pretty large trees! *Dwarf enchanter's nightshade*, polypody ferns, *oak ferns* and lots of cedar trees make this damp, rocky, mossy place quite enchanting. When you add together rock cedars, the dark rock wall, and all the nooks, crannies, and cracks, you could be in the middle of the woods at Hogswart Castle and might expect to see Hadwig or Harry Potter pop up at any moment.

The rocky trail continues all the way to Lake Agnes (waypoint 4) and a sign for the hiking trail that indicates it is still 8.8 miles to Lookout Mountain.

Five: Lake Agnes, Crunching Leaves, and the Caribou Trail

Following the shoreline of Lake Agnes, a rock-enclosed blue jewel that reminds us of the Boundary Waters Canoe Area, look for *blueberries, blue flag iris, sweet gale, twinflower, bunchberry,* elderberry, and turtles, which sun themselves on partially submerged logs.

Passing an outcrop of lumpy *Beaver River Diabase* (also see *diabase*) the trail turns away from the lake, crosses an old ATV trail and then a snowmobile trail. From here it is a pleasant walk through a maple forest with a traditional *Canadian carpet*. Maple leaves cover the trail–red, orange, and amber brown–making this the first hike where we actually walk on crunchy fall leaves. Waypoint 5 is where the hiking trail crosses the Caribou Trail (County Road 4).

Six: A Bazillion Steps and Dying Maples

From the Caribou Trail the walking path goes by an established exercise course then crosses County Road 39 (Cathedral of the Pines Road) before ascending a steep hill by way of a bazillion wooden steps and 42 tree roots (I counted these). The uphill climb is over a thick section of *glacial till*. From the hilltop it's a short walk to waypoint 6, an overlook with numerous wooden benches that provide a chance to rest after the steep climb. From the overlook we have a nice view of Caribou Lake and Moose Mountain which, with all the bright red of the maple, looks like someone has managed to set it on fire. However, all is not perfect, for Judy points out stands of maples on the mountain that look unhealthy or dying.

Seven: Jack-In-The-Pulpit

Leaving the overlook it is a short walk to a side trail that goes northeast (waypoint 7). *Jack-in-the-pulpit* and baneberry are found throughout this section. The name "Cathedral of the Pines" keeps bothering us because we have not seen a pine tree since we left Lake Agnes; towering maples, yes, but pines, no.

Eight: Maple Forest and Maple Elbows

From the trail junction it is a long walk (0.6 miles) through a nice, old maple forest. The trail is muddy in places and passes over several planked sections and a bridge across a small creek full of large ferns, *jewelweed*, and *marsh marigolds*; this would be a pretty spot in the spring.

Past the creek there is a huge tip up of maple trees (waypoint 8). There are six maples that have tipped over and together they now form a single, massive connected root system. These six trees are leaning on half a dozen other trees. When we come back a few years from now, we might see "elbow' trees," which are U-shaped bends where the branches of these supporting trees grow upward while the dead trees slowly break apart and rot away.

Nine: Changing Woods and Jonvick Creek

After the tip-up the forest undergoes a dramatic change with maple giving way to ash, birch, and spruce as the trail descends to Jonvick Creek, which is waypoint 9. The creek is filled with alder, *buttercups,* bulrush, and sedges. A stump-filled pond nearby has a grassy marsh and an old beaver dam.

Ten: Dam Crossing, Sunflowers, and Rosehips

To continue on this walk we have to cross the beaver dam, and to do this it seems like we have two choices: walk across or take the canoe that has been left here for that purpose. However, as we walk across, it becomes pretty obvious the canoe is but a Don Quixote gesture, for the pond is filled with tangled tree limbs and stumps making a water passage quite impossible.

As we walk across the dam we see lots of small, pretty sunflowers mixed with blue flag iris, *calla lilies*, rosehips, *raspberries*, *fireweed*, and baneberry. Judy thinks June would be a great time of year to be here because all the roses would be in bloom.

Waypoint 10 is at the old canoe dock at the end of the beaver dam.

Eleven: Camping Shelter

After the beaver dam adventure it is a short walk along a rose-hip lined trail to the Beaver Trail Snowmobile Trail. The trees are mostly aspen and birch, and the groundcover is dominantly *sarsaparilla* and *honeysuckle* with some raspberries. With all the tree roots across the trail we really need to watch where we are putting our feet. Crossing an old road called Hall Road we come to a wooden camping shelter built in 1982, which is waypoint 11.

Twelve: Cathedral of Pines Overlook and Goblet Shaped Mushrooms

It's back to a maple-spruce forest as we cross an ATV trail; along this section there are lots of "goblet-shaped" mushrooms (Amanara) as well as "dead man's fingers." The trail then heads gently uphill to a relatively flat area as it passes through a nice maple-birch forest to an overlook that offers views down the hillside. Many of the maples seen from here are dying, possibly because they are at the edge of their comfort zone. However, with their death they are opening the forest floor to sunlight. Sun-loving raspberries are thick through here.

The tree root-crossed trail takes us past a few outcrops of massive basalt and onto the "Cathedral of the Pines" overlook (waypoint 12), with a nice view toward the interior forest. We see lots of white pine trees and running pine here. The ridgeline is thick with plants, and these include *hepatica* (look for its fuzzy stems), *pyrola* (waxy round leaves), *Canadian mayflower* (arrow-shaped leaf), and twinflower.

Thirteen: Spruce Creek Valley

Along the edge of the steep hillside we pass an outcrop of massive basalt before coming to an overlook of the Spruce Creek Valley with the *Sawtooth Mountains* in the distance (this is waypoint 13). The rock *outcrop* here is *amygdaloidal basalt* with the minerals that filled the *amygdules* (gas holes) largely weathered out. Minerals present include *chert, calcite,* and *zeolite* (thomsonite). The basalt has a nice *ophitic texture*. This lava flow is called the Terrace Point Flow and is some 160 feet thick; it can be traced from just west of this waypoint across the Cascade River to Good Harbor Bay, a distance of about 15 miles.

Fourteen: Spruce Creek and Spruce Creek Campsite

Walking along the hillside, over massive basalt, we come to another overlook from which we can see hill after hill after hill all the way to the horizon. The hills slope toward the lake and represent massive basalt lava flows which have had their amygdaloidal tops weathered off. The one flat topped hill represents a diabase intrusion.

The trail heads downhill, over massive basalt, past a lot of goldthread and bunchberries crossing a dry creek before flattening out as it passes through a spruce, cedar, and aspen forest to Spruce Creek (old maps show it as Deer Yard Creek). The last bit of the descent to the creek and waypoint 14 is via wooden steps. There are big pines and cedars here as well as a *massive* basalt outcrop in the creek. Just past the bridge is the Spruce Creek campsite.

Fifteen: Adoxa

From the creek the trail heads uphill, steeply at first then more gently passing through large cedars into a mixed upland forest to an old logging road. The trail continues uphill to a ridge top where maple trees are mixed with cedar and spruce. Walking along the ridge we come to an outcrop of massive basalt followed by outcrops of lumpy (see *diabase weathering*) Beaver River Diabase and angular pieces of basalt with amygdules filled by white thomsonite.

It is just past the basalt that Judy discovers the rare plant *Adoxa*, near some old cedar trees, and this is waypoint 15. Adoxa, also known as muskroot because of its faint musky odor, has 5 greenish-white flowers, four of these point to the 4 cardinal directions and the fifth points straight up. The plant has leaves similar to corydalis and likes shady, moist forests. It is a rare and threatened plant.

Sixteen: Maple Forest and Ridge Walk

From the adoxa plant we have a long (0.6 miles) walk through a maple forest with stands of cedar and spruce as the trail follows the edge of the ridge to an outcrop of amygdaloidal basalt. Just past the rock outcrop there is an overlook into the Spruce Creek Valley which is filled with red maple trees and green spruce. From here the trail continues along the ridge crest to waypoint 16, a junction with a snowmobile trail. *Goldenrod* is abundant along here indicating its love for open, sunny spaces.

Seventeen: Large Basalt Outcrop

The trail follows the snowmobile trail over massive basalt to waypoint 17, a large outcrop area of massive to amygdaloidal basalt with the amygdules filled by a cream to pale pink, fibrous to concentrically zoned zeolite (thomsonite?), along with calcite and *quartz*. The amygdules are up to two

211

inches long and predominantly round. The basalt has an ophitic texture and is weathering to kibbles and bits.

Eighteen: Snowmobile Overlook

We continue along the snowmobile trail over outcrops of ophitic basalt to the junction with a trail to the Indian Camp Creek overlook (waypoint 18); there is a snowmobile pullout and parking lot for this overlook. On the short trail to the overlook Judy finds fireweed, goldenrod, and *pearly everlasting*. The overlook provides views of the interior forest that carpets the hillsides of the Spruce Creek and Indian Camp Creek valleys.

Nineteen: Another Nice Overlook

Continuing downhill on the snowmobile trail we come to the junction with the Superior Hiking Trail proper, which goes to the right. The hiking trail follows the ridge top through a mixed forest dominated by spruce and birch as it passes over flat ophitic basalt outcrops to waypoint 19, an overlook of the Indian Camp Creek Valley and, just through the trees, a slice of blue that is Lake Superior. From the overlook you can see how the maples dominate, their red leaves standing out in contrast to the yellow and gold of the birch and aspen.

Twenty: Grand Marais and More Basalt

The trail heads downhill along the edge of the ridge through a mixed forest with lots of dead and dying birch over flat, massive to sparsely amygdaloidal basalt. There are kibbles and bits on the trail from the weathering of this ophitic basalt. Waypoint 20 is at an overlook with nice views of Grand Marais, Lake Superior, and the distant hills. The basalt outcrop has amygdules filled by a radiating zeolite.

Twenty-One: Indian Camp Creek and Campground

We now head downhill over numerous small ophitic basalt outcrops and lots of kibbles and bits. It is interesting to note that the kibbles and bits are on the downhill trail sections (south-facing) and not on the uphill or north-facing sections. This has to do with the amount of sunlight during spring and fall. The south-facing slopes get more sun and thus are warmer. This leads to more freeze and thaw cycles than on the north-facing slopes and thus more weathering of the basalt. Waypoint 21 is at Indian Camp Creek with the Indian Camp Creek campsite (say that ten times in a row) just on the other side.

Along the creek we find lots of neat, quiet pools of water to explore, and from the bridge the amygdules in the lava flow really stand out, especially on the downstream side. The campsite is in a nice open area with a good water source.

A lot of the aspen and birch through this trail section have been snapped in two, and it's a real possibility this damage was the result of the fierce straight-line winds that caused the destruction in the Boundary Waters Canoe Area during the 1990 July 4th storm.

Twenty-Two: Twin Creeks

The trail crosses a snowmobile trail in a birch, ash, spruce forest with some balsam poplar; a lot of the birch is dead. The outcrop is basalt with ophitic texture and kibbles and bits weathering. Crossing the twin creeks–two small dry creeks next to each other–we come to the junction with a state park "hiking club" trail (waypoint 22) that now joins the Superior Hiking Trail. This entire section is rather flat and marshy.

Twenty-Three: Lookout Mountain and Confusing Trail Junction

We now walk around Lookout Mountain on a wide, smooth footpath to arrive at waypoint 23, a rather confusing trail junction. The Superior Hiking Trail continues straight ahead. Use caution here, don't follow the hiking club signs.

Lookout Mountain is a *cuesta*, but unlike the cuestas formed by Leveaux, Oberg, and Moose Mountains, this one is composed of the Terrace Point basalt lava flow. The steep north-facing slope is due to *glacial plucking* and subsequent *frost wedging* of *cooling joints* in the massive part of the flow, after most of the amygdaloidal flow top was removed by erosion. The south-facing slope dips gently toward the lake and represents the general dip of the lavas along the North Shore. Though composed of an entirely different kind of rock Lookout Mountain joins the others as part of the Sawtooth Mountains because of its shape.

Twenty-Four: Shelter and Overlook

We come to another trail junction, one with a picnic table, shelter and outhouse. The Superior Hiking Trail continues to the left to a bench from which we have nice views of Lake Superior and the Cascade River Valley to the north. There are signs here for Lookout Mountain, and it is 1.3 miles to the Cascade River.

Twenty-Five: Cascade Lodge

The hiking trail widens, which seems typical of the Superior Hiking Trail in state parks, and continues downhill, over kibbles and bits, through a mixed upland forest to a junction with a trail to an overlook. There are state park boundary signs here along with puffballs and honey-colored mushrooms.

From the overlook continue downhill over a rocky trail to the junction between the hiking trail and a trail to the Cascade Lodge. This is waypoint 25.

Twenty-Six: Cascade Creek

Just past waypoint 25 is Cascade Creek. The bridge across it is waypoint 26. Upstream from the bridge are tons of *cobbles* and boulders, and the outcrop in the creek is sparsely amygdaloidal basalt. On the downstream side Judy discovers *horsetails* and ferns.

Twenty-Seven: Ski Trails and the Ninety Six Steps-Tomorrow!

From the creek it is uphill along, then above the creek to yet another junction. This one is with a wide ski trail called Deer Yard Lake Trail, part of the Cascade River Ski Trails–an interconnected system with 32 miles of trail.

At the junction we can look down into the Cascade River Valley to the infamous 96 wooden steps that lead to the river. These we get to do another day, for this junction marks the end of the hike. Take the spur trail downriver to the parking lot on highway 61. The mosses and Canadian carpet are thick through here and we find large leafed *aster* and horsetails along the spur trail.

For Judy the highlight of this hike was her discovery of Adoxa followed by Lake Agnes and the long, beautiful walk through the maple forest. I loved the rock cedars and nooks and crannies at waypoint 4, the dam crossing, Sawtooth Mountains, and lookout Mountain along with the maple forest. There seems to be lots on this walk for just about everyone.

Superior Hiking Trail
Walk 23: Cascade River Loop

Walk Logistics

Start and End: Cascade River Wayside on Highway 61 or Cook County Road 45 where the bridge crosses the Cascade River

Getting There: Highway 61 north from Lutsen passing Jonvick, Spruce, and Indian Camp creeks to the Cascade River and the wayside parking lot at the side of the highway.

To get to Cook County Road 45, take Highway 61 past the Cascade River and Cascade River State Park to Cook County Road 7. Turn left and follow this to County Road 44. This is about 2 miles from Highway 61 and is where County Road 7 takes a sharp bend to the right with County Road 44 straight ahead. County Road 44 dead ends into County Road 45. Turn left on County Road 45, and it is 2.6 miles to the Cascade River and the parking lot.

Walk Distance: 7.8 miles   **Date Walked:** September 16ᵗʰ, 2004

Worth a Longer Look:

Cascade River Delta: 2, 28   Primeval Forest: 10
Thomsonite: 3, 18   Hidden Falls: 11
Cascades: 4, 5   Ancient River Channel: 13
Sandstones: 6, 8, 25   Slump, Waterfalls: 16, 20
96 Steps: 7   Horizontal Potholes: 21

Waypoint-to-Waypoint

One: Fall Days and Superiors Waves

From the Cascade River wayside the sound of Superior's wild waves, thundering hard against the rocky shore, is a vivid and scary reminder of why this body of water is much more like an ocean than a lake. The constant pounding, a harsh cacophony of drums, cymbals, and horns, is part of the eternal battle between land and water; a battle water always wins.

This morning the wind is blowing steadily inland pushing the grey, patchy clouds away from us at warp speed. The slanting rain that had fallen most of the morning has stopped, and it looks like it is going to clear up and be a nice hiking day after all–about 60 degrees, breezy, and no bugs.

Waypoint 1 is at the Cascade River wayside.

Two: Deltas and Waterfalls

215

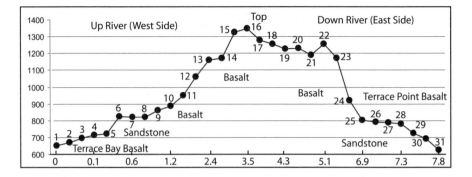

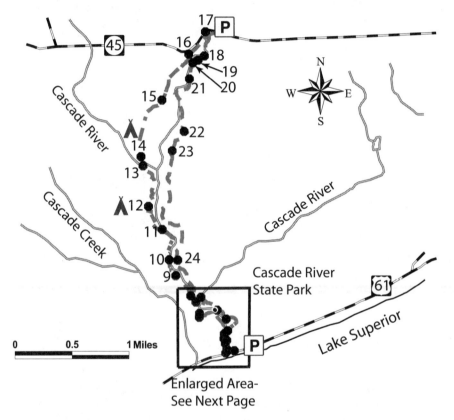

Enlarged Area-
See Next Page

Leaving the parking lot we walk up a wide, gravel trail lined with
thimbleberry plants to the Cascade River Loop Trail, which begins at a
bridge across the river. From the bridge, which is waypoint 2, there is a view
upstream of a small waterfall and, downstream, a gorge carved out of
reddish-colored *basalt*. This lava flow is called the Terrace Point Flow and is
some 160 feet thick; it can be traced from just west of Spruce Creek (walk
22) across the Cascade River to Good Harbor Bay, a distance of about 15
miles.

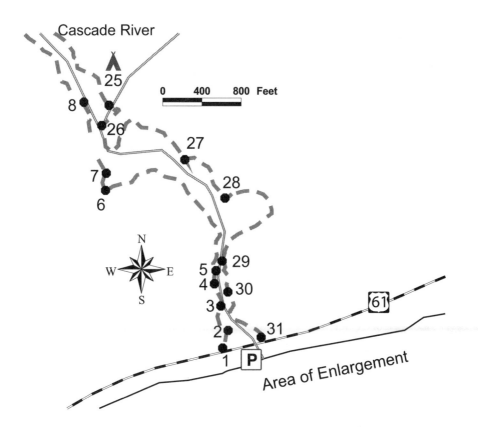

Along this section of the walk the gravel that composes the trail represents part of a *delta* that formed several thousand years ago as the water levels of *Glacial Lake Duluth* fell. The gravel deposits are made up of rounded *pebbles* of varying rock compositions, as well as some *cobbles* and sand. These were derived from the erosion and size-sorting of the *glacial till* by a much younger and more vigorous Cascade River shortly after the ice melted off the land. The gravel forms thin deposits on top of the basalt lava flows from the current level of Lake Superior (about 600 feet) up to an elevation of 900 feet, which marks the shoreline of old Glacial Lake Duluth. As the Cascade River flowed into this ancient lake the velocity of the river water decreased rapidly and the sand to pebble-size material dropped out and created the delta. Locally the gravel deposits are sandy, and these represent beach deposits formed from the reworking of the delta by wave action as water levels in the lake fell.

Judy and I follow the trail on the west side of the river (left bank).

Three: Thomsonite, Potholes, and Rock Trees

Walking up a set of wooden steps we come to waypoint 3, a junction with a short trail to a rail enclosed viewing platform overlooking a waterfall. To the

217

left is an *outcrop* of *amygdaloidal basalt* that weathers reddish-brown. The round *amygdules* of this *pahoehoe* flow are small and filled by pink to white thomsonite (a semi-precious *zeolite* mineral), white *calcite* and clear *quartz*. Good examples of *potholes* can be found in the flow, and dark pools of water seem to reflect the quiet of the forest.

Standing at the edge of the outcrop is a lone warrior in the form of a cedar tree. Looking like it grew right out of the rock, it reminds me of the Little Spirit Cedar tree at Grand Portage. Judy tells me cedars always seem to find crazy places to wind their roots. More cedars line the gorge, and because it is close to the fall season, their needles are turning orange.

Four: Cascades and White Pine

Continuing up the river via a series of wooden steps we cross under a power line, which is waypoint 4. Along the gravel trail and in the river are outcrops of basalt lava; the river forms a series of steps or cascades over these flows. There are large white pine through here along with a lot of mountain ash laden with berries.

Five: Root Beer Water

Just beyond the power line we come to a bridge across the river, and this is waypoint 5. The water is frothy and full of tannins that give it the look of root beer, foam included. From this vantage point, which is 50 or 60 feet above the river, we can see three small step-like falls and a water chute through a narrow basalt gorge. Judy and I take an old stone staircase up to the top of these cascades. Even though this is a bit off the regular trail it is well worth the short side trip! Along this section are white pine zoos (fenced enclosures to protect the pines from deer) and lots of informal overlooks (that is, no human-made structures). *Bunchberry* lines the walking path.

Six: The Sentinel, Sandstones, and the 96 Steps

Continuing upriver and uphill there are nice views of the basalt gorge from three or four short side trails; the white pines are tall and stately and look like they are trying to touch the passing clouds. A large block of basalt, part of a *cooling joint*, hangs over the river and will, in the not too distant future, fall spectacularly into the water. For now, the way it sits above the water gives it the appearance of a lone sentinel guarding the river from unwanted intruders.

Sneaking past the sentinel we continue upriver over a wide gravel and bouldery trail with outcrops of amygdaloidal basalt and stands of large white pine. As we walk along we have nice views down, into the river, and, on the far bank, there are exposures of red *sandstone*. The sandstone formed when the exposed lava flows started to erode during lulls in eruptive activity. Ancient streams then deposited this eroded material as sand bars and channel deposits, which was then buried, compacted, and cemented together to form solid rock. *Cross-bedding* and *ripple marks* are well preserved in these ancient stream deposits. As expected from the erosion of basalt lavas, the sandstones are composed of *plagioclase feldspar, pyroxene, magnetite*, and small basalt rock fragments. Being more easily eroded than the basalt, the sandstones tend to underlie low areas and form coves along the shoreline.

Moving away from the river we continue uphill to waypoint 6, the junction where the Superior Hiking Trail goes west to Lookout Mountain, and east, down to the river by way of the 96 steps.

Seven: 96 Steps and the Flood Plain

Down we go, 96 steps (count them–a long way for just about anyone, but especially so for a small, short-legged dog like Charlie) to get to the river and a junction (waypoint 7) with a side trail that leads to the water's edge. The hiking trail heads upstream along the river's *flood plain*.

Eight: Red Sandstone

The trail climbs above the river passing a large white pine and an opening where we watch the river flow over beautiful red sandstone. The sunlight reflecting on the water gives this scene a kaleidoscope look–a speckled pattern, ever changing, of red, blue, and yellow. The trail then heads back down to the river where there are large *boulders* of basalt, whitish *granite*, and pinkish *monzonite*. Red sandstone outcrops on the river bottom, and downstream is a large, reddish-colored boulder pile left by some long ago flood.

Nine: Drunken Staircase, Snake Tree, and Tiny White Pines

Moving away from the river we climb up a "drunken" staircase, walk past a large white pine, to a cedar grove and the cedar root "snake" tree, a tree with numerous roots across the trail. The various plants through here are full and green and pretty. Moving on we have views of pinkish-colored basalt, which forms tall, impressive cliffs, before coming to an overlook from which we can see a small, lacy cascade of water flowing over reddish basalt. This is waypoint 9.

At this point thick vegetation covers all surfaces. There are also tiny black spruce, cedars, and white pines–and we do mean tiny. These are this year's seedlings, and in the case of the spruce, they have a star-shaped appearance from above with their single needles circling around the small stem.

Ten: Flow Contacts and the Forest Primeval

Staying above the river we walk through a dense cedar forest with a few large white pines and birch mixed in; the trail is crossed by lots of tree roots.

This section feels like the forest primeval: thick-growing lichens, dense trees, mossy carpets, and a warm wind singing through the cloud caressed trees.

Crossing over a basalt lava flow with small plagioclase feldspar crystals, we find an outcrop of reddish colored basalt (red color due to oxidation of iron-rich minerals) with amygdules that are filled by calcite, quartz, and thomsonite; however, many of the amygdules are empty as the minerals filling them have weathered out. This outcrop is at the junction with a small trail that leads to the river, and this represents waypoint 10. Taking the trail we come to the top of a pahoehoe lava flow. Across the river from it is a contact between this flow top and the massive base of the overlying flow. The contact, well exposed, is sharp and undulating and can be followed for a short distance downstream.

Eleven: Hidden Falls and Not So Pleasant Moose

Passing a boulder-filled creek the trail continues above the river to an opening with a view of a water cascade over a basalt lava flow; there is a massive basalt cliff on the opposite side of the river. From here we cross another snake den of tangled tree roots before returning to the edge of the river and an outcrop of reddish basalt with feldspar crystals and sparse amygdules.

Continuing on we walk along the river through a cedar forest over more tree roots; there are large white pine here with birch and spruce. Waypoint 11 is the junction of the hiking trail with a spur trail that goes to the Hidden Waterfalls. The trail to Hidden Falls is 0.3 miles long. Judy walks down it only to find a dead moose in the water along with lots of indicators that a wolf pack has been hanging out there. Needless to say the ravens are busy and noisily protest her intrusion. Oh, by the way, moose or not, Hidden Falls is very pretty.

Twelve: Big White Pine Campsite and Slippery Bridge

The trail heads uphill and away from the river through a cedar, spruce, and birch forest, followed by a ridge walk before heading downhill to a bridge across a small creek. Outcrops in and along the creek bottom are amygdaloidal basalt, and this could be the same flow as the one at waypoint 10. The bottom of the creek is composed of solid rock and would surely make a wonderful water chute, which I am sure it is in the spring. The bridge across the creek is very, very, very slippery–dangerously so.

From the creek our uphill walk continues to the spur trail to the Big White Pine campsite (waypoint 12). The ravens are still talking and I'm pretty sure they are discussing the various ways to serve up moose! Instead of Hidden Falls it could easily be Dead Moose Falls. With this in mind we kind of discuss how local names, like Mystery Mountain, Mike's Rock, Gold Hill, and Judy's Canyon, might be born. There are enormous yellow birch through here.

Thirteen: Thousand Year-Old River Channel

The trail is up and down through a forest of paper and yellow birch with some spruce; the understory is moose maple and hazel. Cross a boulder-jammed creek that represents an old channel of the Cascade River, one that formed when the river was much younger, higher, and fiercer. This river channel is overlain by gravel deposits of the Cascade River delta, indicating it must have formed several thousand years ago.

From the boulder-filled creek the trail heads uphill and becomes relatively flat before descending over wooden steps and tree roots to waypoint 13, a bridge across a small creek. The outcrop here represents the top of a basalt lava flow; it's amygdaloidal with most of the amygdules filled by either pinkish zeolite and/or calcite. This flow top is overlain by a layered, broken rock, one that looks like potato chips. The broken pieces contain small rock fragments that are dominantly basalt and clay-rich sedimentary rocks set in a fine-grained matrix composed of a green clay mineral, plagioclase feldspar, and quartz. Though the origin of this deposit is not known, it most likely represents a *mudflow*.

Fourteen: Cut Log Campsite

The steep ascent up and out of the creek is via wooden steps that appear to have been constructed for someone who is at least ten feet tall! At the top there is a short walk to Cut Log campsite, which is located beside a giant felled white pine; this is waypoint 14. Surrounded by ash trees the campsite contains another large felled pine. The two pine trees appear to have been abandoned after being cut many years ago.

Fifteen: Daisy Plants and Hop Across Creek

From the campsite the trail passes through a maple-birch forest, which changes into one of spruce and birch as we near a small creek.

After the creek it's back into a maple forest with some yellow birch to waypoint 15, a boulder-filled creek that is crossed by walking or hopping on the boulders. However, the creek is small enough so we could simply jump across it.

Sixteen: Elbow Tree, Waterfall, Long Slump, and County Road

We continue on through a dominantly maple forest with big ash trees to another boulder-filled creek after which we enter a more mixed forest of spruce and birch along with maple "elbow" trees. The first is right in the trail corridor, but no one has removed it so there it stands for all to ponder. A bit further down the trail, we find another tree growing horizontally out from a stump before it bends its elbow upwards!

We come to a creek that drops over a dramatic and steep waterfall down to the Cascade River. The drop is close to vertical and well over 60 feet. Below the falls is a deep water pool and here the river cascades over a basalt lava flow; all-in-all it is very, very pretty. From here we pass a major *slump* that extends down to the river. There is a wooden fence along the trail marking the site of the slump, which must be 60-70 feet from the top to the river. The valley floor is filled with maple and pine, and the colors are gorgeous. From the slump it's a short walk to waypoint 16, which is Cook County Road 45.

Seventeen: Cascade River Bridge and Parking Lot

Walk 0.3 miles east on County Road 45 (to the right) crossing the bridge over the river, then continuing on to the Superior Hiking Trail parking lot. Hiking trail signs (waypoint 17) tell us it is 3.8 miles back to Highway 61 on the Cascade Loop trail or 5.5 miles to the Bally Creek Road.

Eighteen: Graffiti and Lavas

The loop trail continues under the bridge, and both the bridge and nearby outcrops are adorned with much "art" work. Walking along the river through a cedar forest we cross over numerous planked sections with lots of tree roots across the trail. Waypoint 18 is beside an outcrop in the river with a small rapids and a nice little waterfall. The outcrop is an amygdaloidal flow with the amygdules varying from 20-50%. These are filled by pale green *epidote*, white calcite, and white, pinkish white, and pink zeolite minerals (thomsonite and/or laumantite). A high cliff of basalt in the distance is composed of the *massive* part of the lava flow that overlies the amygdaloidal flow we are standing on.

There is abundant *wild lettuce*, meadow *rue, sensitive fern, wood anemone, goldthread,* and *cow parsnip* here.

Nineteen: Potholes and Blueberries

Just down the river from waypoint 18 are two spectacular potholes in the basalt; these are located very close to the bottom of the cascade. Satellite reception is terrible through here with accuracy around 100ft. There are two shrubby plants of note through here: the familiar *blueberry* and the less common yew.

Twenty: Falls and Slump

The trail continues along the river to the large slump and waterfall seen at waypoint 16 (waypoint 20). The rock cliff is composed of two lava flows; the flow bottoms are massive and thick, and the tops are amygdaloidal and thin. The outcrop in the river is amygdaloidal basalt.

Twenty-One: Horizontal Potholes

The cedar forest and tree root-lined trail continue past an amygdaloidal basalt outcrop to waypoint 21, four horizontal potholes bored into the basalt lava on the opposite side of the river. The potholes are just above the water level, and there are numerous boulders and cobbles sitting inside them. The potholes occur at or near the contact between the top of an amygdaloidal lava flow and, above it, the massive base of the overlying flow. The contact is sharp and undulating, and you can follow it down river from the potholes. The potholes look like caves or the burrows of large animals. They formed from swirling eddies or whirlpools of water which, with the help of pebbles and cobbles, abraded away areas of the basalt that had large gas holes or abundant, closely spaced small ones. There are more large cedars here, and one-sided *pyrola*.

Twenty-Two: Jumble Creek and Steep Climb

Continue along the river over a root-lined trail to a small creek from which point we again turn away from the water and head uphill. At the top we immediately descend back to the river where there is a basalt cliff on the opposite side and, on this side, a cedar tree growing straight out over the water. Then, like musical topography, it's uphill past an amygdaloidal basalt outcrop to the top and a private property sign near planks that cover the trail.

Remaining above the river we walk through a cedar and spruce forest with numerous planked sections over hillside seeps. Pass a boulder-filled creek clogged with a tangled mess of trees and logs. The creek has to work hard to move all this stuff in the spring before resting during the remainder of the year. From here it is downhill and across a narrow but steep gully with a noticeable slump above it. The boulders in the slumped material are the same composition as those seen in the tangled stream, and this is probably the source of both boulders and trees. Waypoint 22 is at the top of a horrendous steep climb up dozens of poorly spaced wooden steps. As Judy says "This ain't much fun."

Twenty-Three: Murphy Mountain

Passing through a spruce-birch forest the trail has fewer tree roots as it follows the ridge top. There are partial views across the river to the opposite hillside. At waypoint 23 we have a nice view of Murphy Mountain to the northeast through an opening in the forest.

Twenty-Four: Nice Walk

We now have a nice, long walk through a spruce-birch forest with cedar groves as the trail remains away from the river. After passing a Superior Hiking Trail sign and crossing a dry creek, the forest changes to one dominated by cedars, yellow birch, and big pine trees. There are buckets of white pine cones along here–kind of bonanza if you're a squirrel. Continuing the pleasant walk through a white pine woods with cedar and spruce the trail follows the edge of the Cascade River Valley. Along here we find steep drop-offs and have partial river views. Waypoint 24 is at the sign marking the end of private land.

Twenty-Five: Trout Creek and Red Sandstone

Continuing to walk along the edge of the valley we pass the junction with a trail to a not so nice overlook, before entering a dark, cedar-dominated forest with some spruce. It's then downhill to Trout Creek and the Trout Creek campsite. The creek contains little water, but sure has a lot of large boulders and pieces of red sandstone. The campsite is slowly being undercut by the creek, and in the near future there will be no more camping here. Waypoint 25 is at the bridge across Trout Creek. There is sandstone in the creek both above and below the bridge. The sandstone has beautifully preserved ripple marks and *mud cracks*, and is *hematite* red in color. The sandstone is 1.1 billion years old and these preserved textures indicate the sandstone was once a sandbar that formed from the deposition of sand grains in a stream or river. Imagine what this area would have looked like way back then. There would have been no life, which also means no vegetation; it would have been a dark, barren landscape composed of ragged and rolling lava flows criss-crossed by streams and rivers on their way to some far distant sea. Add bubbling hot springs, hissing steam vents, red glowing lava, and the smell of sulfur, and you would have Dante's vision of hell right here in Minnesota.

Twenty-Six: Cascade River

From Trout Creek it is a short walk to the Cascade River (waypoint 26) and an outcrop of red sandstone. The sandstone is well-bedded and breaks into flagstone-like pieces.

Twenty-Seven: Slump and Old River Channel

Once again the trail turns away from the river and heads uphill (there is a bench at the top) where it winds along the ridge top to waypoint 27, a state park sign and a large river slump. The slump occurs right at a bend in the river and has exposed an old river channel, which consists of a layer of large boulders sitting on top of a basalt lava flow. Again this channel is older than the Cascade River delta and represents a younger and stronger river.

Twenty-Eight: You Are Here, Large Slump, and the Delta

Continue above and away from the river along a wide, gravel trail to a "you are here sign" followed closely by a second "you are here sign" which is waypoint 28. At this point the trail really does get hard to follow for it vanishes having slumped away into the river. There is a lot of gravel on the trail, from pea-size to cobbles, and this represents part of the old Cascade River Delta deposit.

Twenty-Nine: Around the Slump

The trail follows a ski trail around the slump area. Waypoint 29 is where the ski trail rejoins the hiking trail just above a narrow gorge in the river.

Thirty: Waterfalls and Basalt Gorge

It's downhill via wooden stairs to a nice view of waterfalls over a lava flow. Pass the bridge across the river (waypoint 5 on the way up) to an overlook of the river and basalt gorge seen earlier in the day. This is waypoint 30.

Thirty-One: Parking Lot

Continuing downhill and down river we come to another rocky, noisy overlook of the basalt gorge. From here it is a short walk back to highway 61 and the parking lot.

This is a grand loop hike although at 7.8 miles it is fairly long. If you don't mind the distance there is a ton to see from sandstones, thomsonite, deltas and pahoehoe lavas to white pine, yellow birch, glorious fall colors, rock cedars, 96 steps, and, in the spring, lots of wildflowers. Most of all, however, this hike is centered on the spirited Cascade River–both its powerful past and busy present.

Superior Hiking Trail
Walk 24: Bally Creek Valley

Walk Logistics

Start: Large parking lot on Cook County Road 45 just before the Cascade River

Getting There: Take Highway 61 past the Cascade River and Cascade River State Park to Cook County Road 7. Turn left and follow this to County Road 44. This is about 2 miles from Highway 61 and is where County Road 7 takes a sharp bend to the right with County Road 44 straight ahead. County Road 44 dead ends into County Road 45. Turn left on County Road 45, and it is 2.6 miles to the Cascade River and the parking lot is on the right.

End: Forest Road 158 (Bally Creek Road)

Getting There: Take Highway 61 past the Cascade River and Cascade River State Park to Cook County Road 7. Turn left and follow this past County Road 44 and 45 to a dirt road to the left which is 4.36 miles from Highway 61. Follow this 0.3 miles to where it dead ends at Forest Road 158 (Bally Creek Road). Turn left and the small parking area is on the left, 1 mile down the road.

Walk Distance: 5.5 miles   **Date Walked:** September 29th, 2004

Worth a Longer Look:
Red Pine Forest: 4, 5
White Pine and Clubmoss: 12

Waypoint-to-Waypoint

One: Parking Lot

Our string of hiking luck continues for the weather, once again, is close to a perfect ten: clear sky, light breeze, temperature about 50 or 55 degrees, and no bugs. I'm coming to agree that fall is the perfect time to hike along the North Shore.

Waypoint 1 is at the Superior Hiking Trail sign post at the far end of the large parking lot on Cook County Road 45.

Two: Northern Half-Dome and Minnow Trap Creek

Leaving the parking lot it's uphill and along a ridge above and parallel to the Cascade River. To the northwest there is a prominent hill that we have named Northern Half-Dome because it looks like the half-dome from Hike

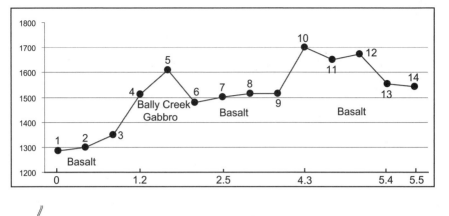

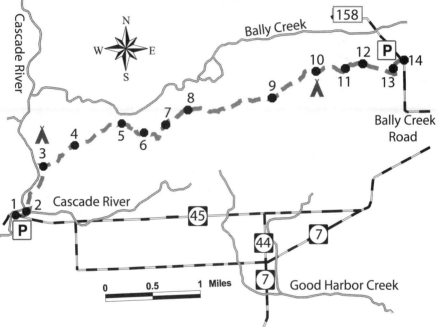

11; the name comes from its shape, which is reminiscent of the great *granite* domes in Yosemite National Park. The shape is due to *exfoliation* and *frost wedging*. Northern Half-Dome is composed of *Star Wars Porphyry*. After enjoying the view descend through an aspen, birch, and spruce forest to Minnow Trap Creek, which is waypoint 2.

The creek name immediately gets Judy going. She quickly points out that a minnow isn't just a small trout or perch–those are called fry or fingerlings. Minnows are actually a species of fish and, I must confess, I never knew that–I thought they were just small other fish.

Three: Fall Colors and the North Cascade River Campsite

It's uphill out of Minnow Trap Creek to an old river *slump* located right above a *meander* bend in the Cascade River. From here we have a great view of Northern Half-Dome, which is brightly lit by the reds of the maples covering it. Speaking of color, along the ridges we can see an abrupt "tree line" that seems to follow the contour of the hills. Conifers fill in one section and maples and aspen the other. In summer, it would be all green and we would have to rely on the subtle differences in textures of the tree types to tell the difference, but in fall, it is striking and easy!

The river is directly below us and there is a bench here for very, very short people.

From the slump it is a 0.5 mile walk along the ridge crest that marks the top of the Cascade River Valley. Views of Northern Half-Dome continue as we enter a trail section where there is a cutover area to the right and a nice, older forest to the left. The forest slopes to the river with the river banks graced by cedar and pine. Waypoint 3 is at the junction of the spur trail that goes to North Cascade River campsite. A "happy" book has been placed at this waypoint. This is a notebook placed here by the Superior Hiking Trail Association for hikers to record their impressions of the hike. Judy and I call these "happy" books because of the happy thoughts usually written on the pages.

Four: Red Squirrels and Red Pines

Turning away from the river the trail continues through an older cutover area with a few large cedar, spruce, and birch left standing; mountain maples, hazel, and alder are thick here. Judy gets a good laugh watching a red squirrel run through the closely spaced cedar branches, nipping twigs and cones and sending them to the ground in a steady rhythm.

We then cross a boardwalked section before heading uphill over a trail littered with *cobbles* that come from weathering of the *glacial till*. These represent a variety of rock types though pink *monzonite* and dark *basalt* dominate. Waypoint 4 is at a National Forest Boundary sign and the start of a more mixed forest. Though we don't see any we are sure moose are not far away for their tracks and scat are here, there, and everywhere. There are lots of hazelnuts on the ground, making us wonder if the bears and squirrels ever have arguments over who gets to eat what? Near waypoint 4 red pines line the trail, so the footpath is covered in soft and springy brown needles.

Five: More Red Pines, Red Squirrels, and a Bearing Tree

Now comes a pleasant 0.4 mile walk along a pine needle covered trail that follows the hilltop. Judy finds red squirrel tunnels and food caches everywhere and she points out numerous stumps of large white pine amongst the red pine trees.

Turning rather scraggly, the red pines begin to thin as the trail follows the Bally Creek Valley. A large swamp is visible to the north and northwest.

Waypoint 5 is at a National Forest property boundary, and there is also a birch "bearing tree" and survey marker placed here in 1937.

Six: Bally Creek Gabbro

We continue along the hillside with partial views of the Bally Creek Valley and accompanying swamp; lots of pin cherry and *Juneberries* with *pipsissewa* are growing on the east side of the trail. There is an outcrop in the trail of medium-grained *olivine gabbro* with about 60% dark *pyroxene*, 35% grey *plagioclase feldspar* and 5% green glassy olivine. On the fresh surface the rock is really dark-colored whereas on the weathered surface it is brown. Since this rock unit is not on geological maps of the area, we have elected to call it the Bally Creek Gabbro.

From here the trail heads gently downhill over and past small outcrops of Bally Creek Gabbro to an old trail that crosses the walking path. This is waypoint 6.

Seven: Hematite-Rich Basalt

It's a short walk to another Bally Creek Gabbro outcrop through an aspen dominated forest with lots of small willows. This trail section is nice because it is very quiet, it's one of the few spots on the trail where we cannot hear the traffic on Highway 61.

The trail goes downhill, crossing a flat area, before heading up again to wind along a rather flat hilltop as it continues to parallel Bally Creek; this section has some large aspen trees. Waypoint 7 is at an outcrop of reddish-weathering basalt lava that is rather nondescript except for the red concentric *hematite* bands through it.

Eight: Quivering Aspen and Banded Valley

Leaving the large aspen trees behind, we enter a cutover area where all the aspens are about the same diameter and height. As we continue through this cutover area we pass outcrops of sparsely *amygdaloidal basalt* which, on the broken surface, has lots of hematite stringers and patches. The *amygdules* are small and filled by thomsonite and *calcite*. Continue on through the aspen cutover with dead birch before arriving at a moss and lichen-covered basalt outcrop from which we have a view across the Bally Creek Valley (waypoint 8). The trees in the valley seem to be arranged in distinct bands: green spruce and yellow aspen seem to alternate back and forth.

Nine: Glacial Erratics, Golden Trees, and D-Uh

We now enter a forest with fairly large spruce and aspen with some birch and balsam. Passing two basalt outcrops we arrive at a clearing ringed by spruce and aspen with a swampy area to the right.

From here the forest vanishes, and it's back into cutover as we go by a Superior Hiking Trail sign with an arrow indicating which way the trail goes–well dah, there is absolutely zero choice here. From the "you have been saved" sign it's a long, easy stroll through an aspen dominated woods with spruce and birch as well as abundant hazel and alder. The aspen and birch are pure golden, and their gently waving leaves shimmer when lit by the sun. The cobbles along and on the trail come from weathering of the glacial till and are a mixture of different rock types. Waypoint 9 is at the junction with an old trail to the left and a large, pink *glacial erratic* of monzonite. The minerals making up this erratic are pink *orthoclase*, gray plagioclase, and needle-shaped *pyroxene*.

Ten: Spur Trail to Northern Parking Lot and the Bally Creek Campsite

Continue to walk through an aspen dominated forest with some spruce and birch. In places the trail comes out into full sun, and Judy tells me these places still smell like summer even though the calendar says something much different. The hillside to the southeast is covered in red maples, yellow aspen, and green spruce.

Waypoint 10 is at the junction with the spur trail that leads to the northern parking lot on the Bally Creek Road. This is a 0.7 mile walk; at 0.5 miles the trail crosses Bally Creek where the Bally Creek campsite is located.

Eleven: Witches Broom, Labrador Tea, and Glacial Erratics

We now have a pleasant walk with gentle ups and downs as the trail follows the hillside through a moist feeling, maple-birch forest with smaller stands of spruce and aspen. The understory is pure green here with *blueberries*, *Labrador tea*, different mosses, and ancient stumps and fallen logs. *Twinflower*, *Canadian mayflower*, *bunchberry*, pipsissewa, and *wintergreen* are abundant and lovely through here. The trail goes past a huge witches' broom (mistletoe fungus) in a low lying area with a few cedar and white pine. We can see the Bally Creek Valley to the west, making this a pretty spot.

Waypoint 11 is at an area where there are large boulders of pink monzonite, pinkish white *granite*, and dark gray basalt.

Twelve: White Pines

We continue on our pleasant walk through the maple-birch forest which now alternates with spruce depending on the side of the hill the trail follows:

maple on the east, spruce on the west. Waypoint 12 is at a stand of white pine with some tiny young white pine mixed in with *clubmoss* and/or princess pine. There are also *Indian pipes* here.

Thirteen: Needle Covered Trail and Red Pines

Our pleasant walk continues though now it's through planted red pines. After a turn to the right at a Superior Hiking Trail sign, it's a short distance to an outcrop of basalt, which is waypoint 13.

Fourteen Downed Trees and the Bally Creek Road

The trail heads down past cedars and the tiny, clover-like *wood sorrel* into balsam and aspen. As it does we encounter many blown down trees all the way to the small parking space on the Bally Creek Road (County Road 158). This is waypoint 14 and the end of the hike.

Judy and I agree this particular hike, after half-dome, was mostly one of long strolls through either a forest of maple, aspen, birch, and spruce, stands of white and red pine, or a cutover dominated by aspen trees. Nice short hike, Judy tells me and the dogs agree for they are still full of energy and want to continue on the trail.

Superior Hiking Trail

Walk 25: Bally Creek, Floating Bog, and Maple Hill

Walk Logistics

Start: Forest Road 158 (Bally Creek Road)

Getting There: Take Highway 61 past the Cascade River and Cascade River State Park to Cook County Road 7. Turn left and follow this past County Road 44 and 45 to a dirt road to the left which is 4.36 miles from Highway 61. Follow this 0.3 miles to where it dead ends at Forest Road 158 (Bally Creek Road). Turn left and the small parking area is on the left, 1 mile down the road.

End: Pincushion Mountain parking lot

Getting There: Take Highway 61 to Grand Marais. Turn left onto the Gunflint Trail (Cook County Road 12) and go north on this paved road to County Road 53. Turn right (marked as scenic lookout) and go 0.25 miles to the parking lot.

Walk Distance: 8 miles   **Date Walked:** September 24th, 2004

Worth a Longer Look:

Bally Creek Pond: 3	Floating Bog: 13
Bally Creek Beaver Dam: 4	Tamarack Woods: 14, 15
Clone of Aspen: 6	Huge Ash Trees: 16
Red Pine Forest: 9	Grand Marais View: 17
Grassland and Pond: 11	Pincushion Lava Flow: 20

Waypoint-to-Waypoint

One: Parking Lot

All good things come to an end, and so it is with the great weather we have recently had for walking. Last night the wind rose up and brought with it a cold, heavy rain. This morning the sky is a troubled grey with pregnant-looking clouds hanging onto the tops of the higher hills. The wind is strong enough to turn the lake into a sea of rolling, frothy white caps, and the temperature is a cool 45 degrees. Hopefully the rain has ended and the only wet stuff falling on us will be from the drippy tree branches and fluttering leaves.

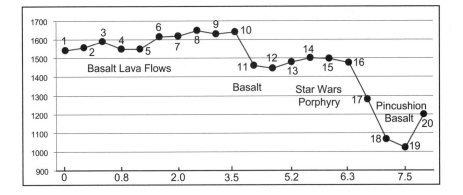

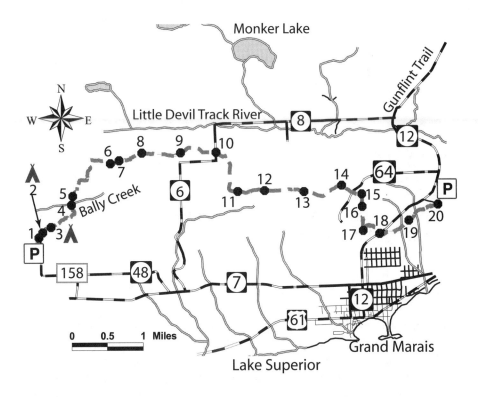

Waypoint 1 is at the small parking lot, really just a pull-off, beside the Bally Creek Road. Possibly the rain last night was a good omen; since we have been standing here three logging trucks have raced by and there is no towering dust cloud following them.

Two: South Bally Creek Pond Campsite

We start with a short walk (350 feet) along a wide, flat trail through a wet, dripping birch forest with balsam and some large, older spruce to the

233

junction with the spur trail that leads to the South Bally Creek Pond campsite. This is waypoint 2.

Three: Bally Creek Pond and Wood Duck House

After the trail junction we cross a small creek (the planks across it are slippery after last night's rain) and pass more large spruce before arriving at the Bally Creek Pond (waypoint 3). The pond has a wide, grassy marsh extending away from it, and there is an old beaver lodge in the pond along with a wood duck house. Wood ducks are cavity nesting ducks so they benefit from all the hard work of the beaver. When beaver dam a creek, water floods the trees and eventually kills some of them. The dead trees then become easy to hollow out, especially if you're a pileated woodpecker and, after the woodpecker is finished, a wood duck has a ready-made, penthouse home.

It's strangely quiet by the pond, as if the water absorbs the noise the wind is making. Higher up the wind rattles the aging autumn leaves and the needles of pine and spruce as it attempts to push away the dark cloud caught on the hilltop just behind the pond. Just past waypoint 3 is the spur trail to the North Bally Creek Pond campsite.

Four: Bally Creek and the Beaver Dam

Leaving the pond we have a short uphill section followed by an easy walk over a *cobble* and tree-root crossed trail that is partially closed in by young alders and mountain maples. Lumpy orange-and-yellow-colored mushrooms are everywhere complementing the carpet of red, brown, and yellow leaves that form a dense quilt upon the landscape.

Passing through an alder thicket we walk by a skinny white pine before heading down the hill to Bally Creek, which is waypoint 4. Dark grey, *massive basalt outcrops* here, and a bench overlooks a substantial beaver dam. The dam, about 200 feet long, is the only way across the creek. Forgoing the resting spot, we step out onto the boardwalk that partly covers the dam. The boards are tilted, broken, and as slippery as a greased pig, but slowly we make our way across walking in water as much as on the planks. The pond is an active one for mud, moss, and twigs of all kinds are pushed up and into the dam, effectively blocking the passage of water out of the pond and giving the planks a decided tilt. Judy spots a fairly new beaver lodge in the creek bank near the end of the dam, and she thinks the bench would be the perfect spot at dusk or dawn to watch the beaver at work.

Five: Safe and Sound

As we make our way across the boardwalk, Charlie falls in twice, and Sammy does the beaver thing–she swims. Waypoint 5 marks the end of our slippery journey across the off-again, on-again boardwalk, and the place one wet dog is waiting for us.

Six: Moose Food, Wood Sorrel, and Clone of Aspen

From the damn dam the trail enters a carpeted forest; we can imagine forest fairies moving about in the mossy plants. The trail then heads up and along a ridge that appears to drop straight off on both sides; mountain maple and alder locally close in the trail. We arrive at a swampy area filled with cedars and ash trees along with *dwarf enchanter's nightshade*, ferns, and *marsh marigolds*. Tons of moose tracks are visible in the mud and these clearly indicate the moose use the trail in both directions. There are also piles of moose scat and Judy, naturalist that she is, picks up some of the kumquat-size pellets and breaks them apart. Showing them to me she points out how they look incredibly like sawdust, as if someone molded these out of debris left behind in a wood shop, and that apparently is exactly what the moose are eating: not sawdust but woody plants like mountain maple. These saw dust pellets are from last winter when much of the moose browse was twigs. During the growing season they also eat softer aquatic vegetation consuming over 30 pounds of plant material in a day.

The trail continues on through more cedar and *wood sorrel*, the leaves of which look a lot like shamrocks, into a clear cut that is obviously recent and extends far to the north. A bend in the trail takes us away from the clear cut into a forest of small red pines mixed in with fir, cedar, willow, and young aspen. Passing a small opening full of *raspberries* and other sun-loving pioneer species, and surrounded by young birch and aspen, we arrive at waypoint 6, the Clone of the Aspen. All the aspen here are the same height and girth. They are tall and skinny with leaves at the very top. Not only that, but the leaves are all the same color of yellow. These trees come not from seeds but from the root system of trees that were cut long ago. This ability to clone themselves makes aspen a very versatile plant and allows it to exist in many habitats across our country.

Seven: Grass Road and Glacial Erratic

From Clone of the Aspen it is a short walk to a grass-covered road (old Forest Road 115) the hiking trail follows for a short way to waypoint 7, the junction between the forest road and the hiking trail proper. A large *glacial erratic* composed of *Star Wars Porphyry* is found here.

Eight: Forest Road 115 Again

It's an easy walk from waypoint 7 to waypoint 8 where we again encounter Forest Road 115. Between the 2 waypoints the trail is lined with mountain maple, willow, and ferns and the forest is composed of aspen, birch, and maple.

Nine: Red Pine Forest

From the forest service road we have a beautiful walk through a red pine forest with large, tall trees. There are also lots of pine stumps along the edge of the trail and through the woods, and Judy thinks these are the result of thinning that took place about thirty years ago. The wind in these tall pines sounds like water rushing through a rocky gorge and, believe it or not, there is actually an Ojibwe word for the sound, Sissiquinod. Pine needles line the trail all the way to waypoint 9 which, for the last time, is Forest Road 115. Active logging occurs near here for there are piles of birch logs stacked along the road side.

Ten: Aspen Clones II and the Dividing Road

From the forest service road the trail enters a cutover area that we name Aspen Clone II. It is filled with small aspen that are all about the same height and size; they even have the same size leaves and make nearly identical noises as they flutter in the wind. The abundant *bracken ferns* have turned yellow and, in many cases, are dried up and brown. From Aspen Clone II it's back into an area of large red pines and the start of another planted pine grove. This is probably part of the same stand we saw at waypoint 9 but the ones in between were removed during logging. The red pine here are not as pretty as the first stand; they are thinner and have aspen trees coming up underneath them. Waypoint 10 is at County Road 6, an interesting spot because the road marks the dividing line between tree species; maple trees grow on one side and aspen and birch on the other. There are several different kinds of *pyrola* here (wintergreen family), including *one-sided, lesser, shinleaf* (most common), and *round-leaved.*

Eleven: Ponds and Wet-Footed Plant Poem

After crossing the county road the trail, littered with cobbles composed of pink *rhyolite* and dark basalt, goes through an aspen, spruce, and birch forest to the North Shore State Trail. The hiking trail turns to the right and follows the wide snowmobile trail, which is lined by plants that like open, sunny places: *fireweed, goldenrod, dogbane*, and raspberries.

Continuing down the snowmobile trail we come to a small pond on the right surrounded by alders with *sphagnum moss, horsetails*, and ferns. Judy reckons this would be a fun place in spring because wildflowers would form a luxurious carpet and the air would be filled with the sound of dozens of croaking frogs. From the pond it's an "exciting" walk down the wet, grassy snowmobile trail under a gray sky with the wind howling and the rain desperate to begin. As we walk Judy points out that the tall green stuff I've been calling grass is not all grass. Mixed in with the real thing are rushes and sedges, all of which are wet-footed plants. Judy goes on to tell me I could tell these plants apart because:

The Sedges have edges,

The Rushes are round,

While the Grasses are jointed

And grow from the ground.

Not bad I tell her, but Dr. Seuss you ain't.

In the middle of this "grass land" is a pool of stagnant water (waypoint 11), and to our right a huge swamp which we are separated from by alder, spruce, and ash trees.

Twelve: Spruce Swamp

As we continue down the snowmobile trail the spruce forms a dense, dark lining which suddenly opens into a large swampy area (waypoint 12) filled with dead spruce and cedar trees.

Thirteen: Floating Bog

Still following the snowmobile trail we have a continuous canal of water to the left and ponds of water separated by alder and spruce to the right. It is wet and "grassy" through here, and we find piles of *calla lilies* that have been dug up by moose. Overall this is a wonderful bog environment and, as it turns out, really unique for the Superior Hiking Trail. Albert's Pond (Walk 14) has a floating boardwalk at the edge where you can see many of the plant types seen here, but here the trail cuts right through a very large bog. So what we see as we stroll along is *Labrador tea, bog rosemary and bog laurel, cranberries, snowberries, pitcher plants, sundew, leather leaf,* and lots of mosses along with spruce and tamarack trees. The abundant cranberries are really SOUR and that's with puckered asterisks! As we get to the end of the bog we notice lots of dead birch.

Waypoint 13 is toward the end of the bog at an outcrop of *hematite* banded basalt. Turning around to look back into the bog we both start to laugh because the tops of the black spruce trees are all lined up and look like feather dusters or toilet bowl brushes on parade. This, as Judy informs me, is an easy way to identify these spindly dark trees. Anyhow, there are small tamaracks near the outcrop, and Judy is amazed by the number of flickers she has seen through here.

Fourteen: Moose Beds and Tamaracks

From the basalt outcrop the trail passes a cattail pond with *wild lettuce* and a variety of tall grasses. In places the tall grasses are molded into large size nests, which Judy claims are just the size of a curled up, sleeping moose. The trail heads up a small rise through a cedar grove and along a grassy stretch to an area where there are five large cedar trees; it's more park-like than grassland here. From the cedars continue on to waypoint 14, a beautiful stand of tamaracks–tall and lacy with drops of water hanging from their needles.

Fifteen: Tamarack Woods and Ash Trees

We find it a pleasant walk through the beautiful tamarack woods to County Road 64. There are big ash trees in here, and this is a wonderful spot for summer and fall wildflowers, especially *asters*, *goldenrods*, and *buttercups*. Crossing the county road we come to the junction between the snowmobile trail and the Superior Hiking Trail proper; this is waypoint 15.

Sixteen: Huge Ash Trees

Being back on the narrow footpath feels kind of nice after the wide, wet, grassy snowmobile trail, but unfortunately this section is dominated by planked areas over wet swampy ground; the wood planks are slippery when wet. Enormous ash trees are prominent in here (Judy tries but she cannot get her arms around a tree), and these must be ancient since ash grows so slowly. The trees are 20-30 inches in diameter and very tall. *Goldthread, bunchberry,* sphagnum moss, *blue flag iris* and Labrador tea are abundant along the boardwalk sections. Waypoint 16 is at the end of the planked area.

Seventeen: Great View and Star Wars Porphyry

Walking downhill through a spruce, birch, and aspen forest we come to a small boulder-filled creek. Here and there along the trail are angular pieces of red rhyolite. As we continue downhill there are partial overlooks of Grand Marais followed by a short downhill section to a spectacular overlook of Grand Marais and the harbor. Today, pushed by the wind, large, rolling, white topped waves crash completely over the breakwater.

The outcrop here is Star Wars Porphyry, the kind with sparse plagioclase crystals. The rock has concentric bands of red hematite, and these appear to outline *cooling joints*. Jack pines grow here.

Eighteen: Jack Pine Ridge, Gunflint Trail, and the Great Lake

We now follow Jack Pine Ridge above Grand Marais walking over Star Wars Porphyry with the percentage of large *plagioclase feldspar* crystals increasing from about 5% to 10-20%; these show up nicely where there is no lichen or moss on the rock. There is a non-maintained spur trail at this point that goes to the west and affords some nice views of the town below. Lots of *Juneberries* and cherries grow along this *talus* slope with the *frost-wedged* rock being pieces of Star Wars Porphyry.

We now have a steep descent down to the Gunflint Trail (County Road 12). On the way down we pass two small outcrops; one is basalt with small plagioclase feldspar crystals, the second is *amygdaloidal basalt*. Waypoint 18 is at the highway.

Nineteen: Pincushion Ski Trail

Crossing the highway we make our way over a bouldery trail crossing a wet planked area and a *boulder*-filled creek to the junction with the Pincushion Ski Trails (waypoint 19). The hiking trail continues to the left, following the ski trial.

Twenty: Pincushion Lava

Walking along the ski trail we come to a bridge over a small creek with a large, flat outcrop of sparsely amygdaloidal basalt in the stream bed. From here we walk past another basalt outcrop and large aspen trees, to an outcrop of what we call Pincushion Basalt. The dark gray matrix of this flow is chock-a-block full of tiny (pinhead size) *amygdules*. Patches of larger amygdules are very distinct; these outline circular areas that represent *vesicle cylinders*. The amygdules are filled by *quartz, calcite*, and a white *zeolite*. A pink banded mineral also fills some of the amygdules and hematite forms red bands through the rock. This outcrop essentially continues up to the parking lot, and here and there can be found large *agate*-filled amygdules. The parking lot and overlook represent the end of a really interesting and, with the floating bog, beaver dam crossing, red pine forest, and Jack Pine Ridge, rather unique and special walk.

Superior Hiking Trail
Walk 26: Pincushion Mountain and the Devil Track River

Walk Logistics

Start: Pincushion Mountain parking lot

Getting There: Take Highway 61 to Grand Marais. Turn left onto the Gunflint Trail (Cook County Road 12) and go north on this paved road to County Road 53. Turn right (marked as scenic lookout) and go 0.25 miles to the parking lot.

End: Cook County Road 58 (Lindskog Road)

Getting There: Take Highway 61 north from Grand Marais past the Devil Track River to County Road 58 (Lindskog Road). Go north (left) on the county road for 0.8 miles to the parking lot.

Date Walked: September 22nd, 2004   **Walk Distance:** 5 Miles (includes spur trail)

Worth a Longer Look:

Pincushion Mountain: 5   Barrier Falls: 15
Devil Track River and Rhyolite: 8, 10, 11, 15   Cathedral Pines: 17
Large Slump and Boulders: 9   Chasm Creek: 18

Waypoint-to-Waypoint

One: Pincushion Parking Lot and Pincushion Basalt

We are in the Pincushion Mountain parking lot just north of Grand Marais. From here we have a great view of the town, Artist Point, and Lake Superior. Today it is cloudy and breezy with the wind straight off the lake. The temperature for this late September hike is 60 degrees and probably will not get much warmer. Over the past two days 2.5 inches of rain have fallen, and it was raining when we left Duluth this morning. Now it appears to be rapidly clearing, and we are very grateful.

The *outcrop* at the Superior Hiking Trail sign (waypoint 1) is pale brown to tan *basalt* that contains numerous pinhead-size *amygdules* filled by *quartz*, *calcite*, and a cream-colored *zeolite*, which is probably thomsonite. *Hematite* bands are seen throughout the rock and these represent differential weathering along *cooling joints*. This particular rock is part of what is called the Pincushion Basalt because of all the pinhead-size amygdules it contains.

240

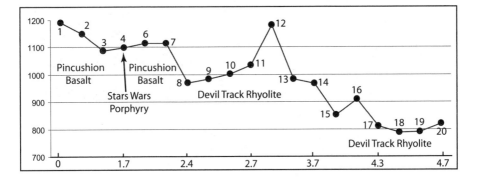

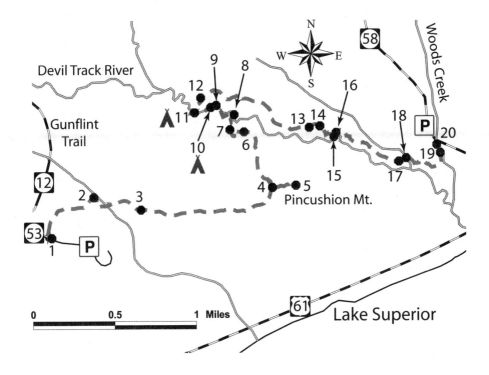

These may well be the reason for the widespread use of this name in this part of the country.

Two: Pincushion Mountain Ski Area

Leaving the parking lot we cross an open field-like area with a ski chalet to the left. The chalet and numerous ski trails throughout this area are used for high school ski races. Cook County High School, below us, has trails that lead up the hill and connect with the trail system through the Pincushion Mountain area.

Proceeding on a wide, grassy ski trail we pass another outcrop of Pincushion Basalt before coming to the Pincushion Mountain ski trail signs. The walking path follows the ski trail to the right and this is waypoint 2. There are some large aspen through here, and they are beginning to turn yellow.

Three: Inky Cap Mushrooms and Dead Birch

Following the ski trail we cross a wide bridge over a small creek; large-leaved *asters* are blooming, and inky cap mushrooms are abundant and in all stages of life from young and firm to old and dripping black ink. From the creek we walk along the ski trail to a junction with another Pincushion Mountain ski trail. The foot path goes to the right, and this is waypoint 3.

Four: Kibbles and Bits and the Layered Forest

Crossing another bridge we walk through an aspen-birch forest with some nice size trees including a few cedar. Looking around the woods this time of year we see a variety of colors, which is far different than the solid green that represents the height of summer. The bracken ferns are now yellowish-brown and look tired and dried out; the large, palm-shaped *thimbleberry* leaves are a dark, soft green and look like they could live forever; and the mountain maples, just above our heads, are on fire, a flaming red color that screams water bomber. If we tilt our heads upwards, the golden yellows of the birch and aspen are distinctive. Together this menagerie of plant life combines to give the forest a multilayered and very "fall" look.

Crossing yet another bridge Judy yells "abracadabra, see how the forest has changed? It is much more dense-looking with the addition of spruce and balsam fir." We continue to follow the ski trail but now, mimicking the forest, there is a distinctive change in the nature of the trail. The material making up the trail is kibbles and bits (see *diabase weathering*) and these are composed of *amygdaloidal basalt* with many of the minerals that filled the amygdules having weathered out leaving round holes behind. We also find two or three *boulders* of distinctive *Star Wars Porphyry* on the trail.

The ski trail turns rocky with the tops of basalt outcrops sticking out, and these are surrounded by kibbles and bits. The basalt is amygdaloidal (5-40%), and again the minerals filling the gas cavities are mostly weathered out. Still following the ski trail we come to waypoint 4, which is the junction with the spur trail that will take us up to Pincushion Mountain.

Five: Pincushion Mountain and Star Wars Porphyry

Taking the spur trail to Pincushion Mountain we find, just a few feet past waypoint 4, that the spur trail splits. Following the left branch we have a steep ascent over a sloping rock face, the top of which provides a nice view of Lake Superior and the surrounding hillside. The rock we just scaled is Star Wars Porphyry, an igneous intrusive rock which, at this outcrop, contains 15-35% large *plagioclase feldspar* crystals. This is the same rock that occurs on Oberg, Moose, and Leveaux mountains, at Maple Hill above Grand Marais, and around parts of Lake Agnes.

We continue along a rocky ridge over Star Wars Porphyry which has had much of the plagioclase feldspar weathered out giving the rock a worm-hole appearance; the holes have rectangular, lath-like, or space-ship-like shapes. As we walk along we have great views of Lake Superior, the Devil Track River Valley, Maple Hill (one with radio towers), and other hills to the north.

It is also hard not to admire the natural landscaping. The rocks have been converted into rock gardens with a wide variety of textures and colors. Growing on them are lichen communities, low ferns and mosses, and *cinquefoils*, with jack pines adjacent to the outcrops. The rock continues to have a wormy weathering pattern and, in places, is criss-crossed with fractures that give the usually massive rock the appearance of large stones set in place to form a flagstone-like patio. Where lichens and moss are not present, we can see large plagioclase feldspar crystals making up 20-45% of the rock.

At the end of the ridge there is an abrupt and steep drop-off. This "wow" spot is at an elevation of 1115 feet and is waypoint 5. The top of Pincushion Mountain is at 1148 feet. There are fantastic views from here of Grand Marais, Artist Point, the rock walled harbor, the north shore of Lake Superior, and 5 mile Rock (five miles north of Grand Marais). Yellow *hawkweed* is everywhere, and the cinquefoil growing here is tiny and white with glassy green leaves sporting 3 teeth or leaf tips. Along with the abundant jack pine are stumpy looking aspens, mountain ash, and willows.

Six: Back Track

Following the ridge back to waypoint 4 we continue down the ski trail to a sign for the Devil Track River (0.4 miles from here). This is waypoint 6 and the start of the Superior Hiking Trail proper.

Seven: Army Aspens and a Place to Sit

Back on the real footpath we once again have to watch for tree roots and boulders. From waypoint 6 it is uphill to waypoint 7, which is at a wooden bench and the start of a long series of wooden steps that lead down the hillside. We can hear the river, and the aspen trees are "army" aspen–tall and ramrod straight.

Eight: Long Steps and the Devil Track Rhyolite

Descending the hill via a steep and really long set of wooden steps (150 of them) we end up on a dirt-packed trail that is covered with yellow aspen and birch leaves. Walking over a red rock outcrop we come to waypoint 8, a nice view down to the Devil Track River which, at this point, flows between high

243

cliffs of pink to reddish-colored *rhyolite*. The river's name in Ojibwe is Manido bimadagakowini zibi, meaning the "spirits walking place on the ice river." The Ojibwe applied the name primarily to Devil Track Lake but, according to their custom, it applies to the outflowing river as well. However, it is possible this wild rocky river gorge, a place full of mystery and beauty, may have suggested the name. The translation to Devil Track dates from 1851 and whoever did it is guilty of turning what was spiritual and mysterious into something scary and evil.

Balsam fir, birch, and cedar trees are abundant along this trail section with the cedar being young and thick indicating a lack of deer to browse on them (definitely not a normal Minnesota happening). The trail is lined with *bunchberry*, *clubmoss*, shinleaf *pyrola*, ferns, polypody fern, *wintergreen*, *twinflower*, and *miterwort*. The whole area reminds both of us of the Split Rock River for there is beautiful greenery, a spectacular river gorge with high rocky cliffs, and a similar-looking volcanic rock.

The rhyolite here is called the Devil Track Rhyolite (see *pyroclastic flows*) and is actually a bit different from the *Split Rock Rhyolite* and other rhyolite units seen so far along the trail. The main difference is that the Devil Track Rhyolite has a much greater aerial extent; it is found up to 25 miles inland from the lakeshore. The origin of this rock is uncertain, and this is discussed in the glossary. Here the rhyolite does mimic the Split Rock Rhyolite as it too has been broken into numerous sub-horizontal fractures that cause it to "split" into rectangular or flagstone-like pieces. This fracturing is due to a process called *exfoliation* or unloading, which with weathering leads to the loose pieces. To avoid confusion with the "split" nature of the Split Rock Rhyolite, we refer to the "fractured" nature of the Devil Track Rhyolite as "sheet" fracturing.

The rhyolite outcropping here is reddish-brown with irregular, small pink patches (*spherulites*?), as well as tiny cream to pink feldspar crystals (*orthoclase*) and rare tiny quartz crystals. A dark prismatic mineral that makes up only a small percentage of the rock is probably *pyroxene*.

Nine: Stranded Boulders and a Large Slump

It's a short walk along the river to a sharp bend where many boulders have been stranded by fierce spring waters; these are a great testament to the power water can have. The boulders are of mixed lithologies, but mostly are basalt or rhyolite. The outcrop here is "sheet" rhyolite, which has small feldspar crystals and a reddish color.

Continue along and above the river over lots of angular and rectangular pieces of rhyolite to waypoint 9, which is opposite a large *slump* on the outside of a *meander* bend in the river. We can see older slumps upstream along with some small waterfalls.

Ten: Rock Pieces and a Really Neat Spot

Waypoint 10 is at the bridge across the Devil Track River. Here the river runs through a deep gorge and we have a great view of a waterfall downstream. Another waterfall upstream cascades, in a step-like fashion, over steps formed from the erosion of the rhyolite along fractures and cooling joints.

Rhyolite is exposed all along the shore and has a definite flat, sheet-like appearance. The loose and broken rock material must be constantly swept away by high waters during the spring or following heavy rains thus keeping outcrops clean and shiny. The exposed rock has two sets of fractures at right angles to each other, and this nicely illustrates why this rock breaks into platy or rectangular pieces.

The bridge has a distinct A-shape and is quite an awesome piece of work in itself. This is a really pretty spot, and a "happy" book has been placed here. This is a notebook provided by the Superior Hiking Trail Association for writing down impressions of the hike. I have come to wonder why we see none of these in the middle of swamps or at some of the more "picturesque" campsites? Interesting entry here says "bear cub ran by us on September 8– scary!" The West Devil Track campsite is on this side of the river.

Eleven: Rhyolite Gorge and the Stone Chair

The trail climbs up the side of the wild and desolate river gorge, over and past rhyolite that seems to stick out everywhere, to the spur trail to the East Devil Track campsite, which is waypoint 11. At the campsite we find a chair built in the shape of an Adirondack chair, and this is quite functional and wonderful to sit in with the only drawback being it is made out of stone! *Harebells* are everywhere, and the rhyolite outcrop has small tabular to irregular areas of pink feldspar with pyrite (fool's gold) in the center. Rare quartz crystals and a yellow colored clay mineral can also be found.

Twelve: Spruce(less) Knob

Uphill, via a steep set of wooden steps, then along a well-packed dirt trail to the junction with a small blocked off (by logs) trail to the left. From here pass a *frost-wedged talus* slope of angular rhyolite boulders, followed by a short uphill to a bench for the little people, at a place called Spruce Knob (waypoint 12). We wonder about the name since there are only balsam fir here! Note the blisters on the tree bark and the flattened needles on the branches. Actually, at the end of the hill, stands one big spruce, so perhaps that is where the place got its name. If that's the case then it should be called One Spruce Knob.

Thirteen: Aspen and Willow Leaves

We have a short walk along the ridge, which winds away from the river, before heading downhill over a steep bouldery trail to a small creek with a split log bridge across it. The creek area is filled with alder and mountain maple, and pieces of rhyolite occur along the creek bottom. From the creek it is a long "just walk and get it over with" section (0.53 miles). As we walk along Judy keeps staring at the willows and aspens, commenting on the shape of their leaves. The willow is long and slender and pointed and contrasts with the rounded, almost heart-shaped aspen leaves.

The trail passes over angular pieces of rhyolite and goes by one large white *glacial erratic* of *granite* to waypoint 13, the start of a downhill section with a view downstream and out to Five Mile Rock in Lake Superior.

Fourteen: Slippery Trail and a Flume Drop

From waypoint 13 we have a short downhill along a gravel ridge that separates the Devil Track River from a tributary stream. The trail down to the creek is rock strewn and slippery. In the creek are lots of large boulders jumbled together, and there is a flume-like drop-off at the far end. In the spring this place would be simply roaring, and watching the water shoot over and down the flume would be awesome. *Dewberries* are abundant here. The creek is waypoint 14.

Fifteen: Barrier Falls Overlook and Large Slumps

Still above the river we have nice views of steep canyon walls. Spruce and balsam fir line the trail and, to tell them apart, Judy points out the balsam is bubbly (round blisters on the bark) and the spruce is scaly (bark looks like scales on a lizard).

Waypoint 15 is at a great upriver view of the steep rhyolite cliffs and nice waterfalls. Large slumps occur on both sides of the river caused by the steepness of the canyon walls. The rocky cliff will continue to crumble and slide under the dual processes of frost wedging and the downward pull of gravity, until a more stable "funnel" or "v" shape is created in the cliff walls. Two large white pines hanging at an angle on the slumped slope block an open view of the falls. We now know why this spot is called Barrier Falls Overlook, and this is waypoint 15. Talus piles of rhyolite can be seen along the base of the cliff.

Sixteen: Wow Spot

A short distance uphill we come to a "wow" spot (waypoint 16), a spectacular view down a rhyolite cliff into the river, which is some 140 feet below. The rhyolite has a nice pink color and exhibits "sheet" fracturing.

Seventeen: Cathedral of Red Pines

Walking along the rhyolite ridge we come to a nice view across the river of a funnel-shaped scar where there has been a large rock slide. Continuing on we pass large aspen trees before coming to an old forest service post and the start of a red pine forest. The post has 5/37 inscribed on it, and that is when these trees were planted.

Staying above the river we walk through red pines with some "scaly" spruce to a virtual cathedral of red pines (waypoint 17) with a lovely carpet of pine needles beneath them. It is a breathtaking spot, for with the red pine are large-leaved *aster, sarsaparilla, thimbleberry*, hazel, *honeysuckle*, alder, and mountain maple.

Eighteen: Chasm Creek

From the red pine cathedral we head steeply downhill over wooden stairs and a gravel-packed trail to a bridge across Chasm Creek (waypoint 18)–a creek with steep rhyolite walls and a highly polished rhyolite streambed. This is a beautiful small canyon and reminds Judy of the Cascade River– what with the steep cliffs, the moss-cover, and everything so lush green. Just downstream from here the creek takes a 90 degree turn (following the right angle fractures in the rock), and after the turn there is a 20-30 foot drop that would be an exciting and spectacular waterfall in the spring.

Nineteen: Coltsfoot and Tiny Aspens

From Chasm Creek the trail follows the creek down to the river, then continues on along and above the river through another stand of red pines, followed by a birch-aspen forest with many of the trees on the river side looking like they can't wait to get down into the water. Tiny aspens are coming up under the birch. *Coltsfoot* and pyrola are abundant here. The trail continues away from the river to a bridge over a small creek (waypoint 19) with ferns, *rue*, and *cow parsnips*.

Twenty: Parking Area (33)

From the bridge it's not far to the parking area on Lindskog Road (County Road 58) and the end of the walk. Pincushion Mountain, the Devil Track River gorge, and the rhyolite the gorge is carved out of are the main highlights of this walk.

Superior Hiking Trail
Walk 27: Woods Creek, Kimball Creek, and the Kadunce River

Walk Logistics

Start: Cook County Road 58 (Lindskog Road)

Getting There: Take Highway 61 north from Grand Marais past the Devil Track River to County Road 58 (Lindskog Road). Go north (left) on the county road for 0.8 miles to the parking lot.

End: Kadunce River Wayside

Getting There: Head north out of Grand Marais on Highway 61. Pass the Devil Track River, Woods Creek, Durfee Creek, and Kimball Creek before crossing the Kadunce River (Highway sign says Kondonce Creek). The wayside is immediately past the river.

Walk Distance: 8.6 miles   **Date Walked:** September 23rd, 2004

Worth a Longer Look:

Pyrola and Maple Hill Rhyolite: 2   Kimball Creek: 14
Magic Corner: 5, 6   Agate Lava: 19
Kimball Creek Rhyolite: 10   Canyon: 21
White Oaks: 11   Kadunce River: 23
Large Aspen: 12

Waypoint-to-Waypoint

One: Woods Creek and County Road 58

For today's hike we have to park on the roadside because the parking lot is full of road construction equipment. In the dense morning fog the power shovel and front-end loader look like prehistoric monsters, jaws agape, waiting silently for something solid to wander past. The fog not only gives the machines an imaginary, monster-like form, but it also makes an interesting carpet of moving white that is speckled with the occasional yellow, green, or red of the nearby trees. The drive down from Nor'Wester Lodge on the Gunflint Trail was kind of scary as dense fog patches steamed up the front and side windows and, once solidly coated, we drove into bright sunshine that led to a few seconds of total blindness. During those moments I imagined a real monster, a large bull moose, stepping out from the close-by woods.

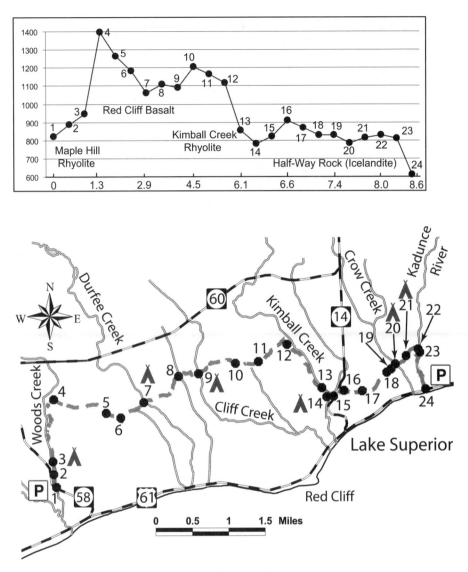

Today's hike includes two more *rhyolite* units, the Maple Hill, a lava flow, and the Kimball Creek, a widely distributed unit whose origin, like that of the Devil Track, is problematic. Both an explosive origin, with emplacement as *pyroclastic flows* (hot mixtures of pumice, gas, and air) similar to deposits at Bandelier National Monument, and Yellowstone National Park, or eruption of lava from extensive fissures are offered as explanations for the widespread nature and uniform composition of the Kimball Creek Rhyolite.

Waypoint 1 is at the Superior Hiking Trail sign next to Woods Creek, immediately north of County Road 58.

Two: Pyrola Plants and the Maple Hill Rhyolite

We head uphill along the side of Woods Creek passing four different *pyrola* species (one-sided, lesser, shinleaf, and round-leaved), coralroot *orchid*, and *wood anemone*, with the forest dominated by birch and balsam fir along with a few red pine. In mid to late July this area would be filled with the waxy, umbrella-shaped flowers of the different pyrola plants.

The *outcrops* along, and in the creek, are part of the Maple Hill Rhyolite. This lava flow has 2-4% square to bi-pyramidal *quartz* crystals and 5-10% pink tabular to lath-like potassium feldspar (*orthoclase*) crystals enclosed by an *aphanitic*, reddish matrix. In places the rock is faintly *flow banded*. This unit can be traced for a distance of 5 miles and is named for exposures in the Maple Hill area. Outcrops of this unit at Nipissing Cliff near the lakeshore are *amygdaloidal* and have well-defined flow bands.

Three: Woods Creek Campsite and Glacial Erratic

We continue to follow Woods Creek finding abundant loose pieces of rhyolite on the trail; rhyolite outcrops in a bend above the creek. This section of the trail is lichen and moss- covered, including some star moss. Come to the junction with the spur trail to the Woods Creek campsite, which is waypoint 3. A lichen and moss-covered *glacial erratic* of *Star Wars Porphyry* can be seen here.

Four: Bench Mark and the Black and White Forest

The walk continues above and parallel to the creek on a root-crossed and *boulder*-covered trail. The boulders come from erosion of *glacial till* and are dominantly *basalt* and rhyolite with some pink *monzonite*, *granite,* and *pegmatite*. Passing through dense stands of spruce followed by more open birch, fir, and spruce woods we come to a small *slump* above a *meander* bend in the creek. The distinct white versus black color of the forest is the result of the white in the birch bark contrasting with the dark, almost black spruce. There are a few ash trees along the creek.

From the meander we have a nice, long walk going gently uphill over a bouldery trail through a dense grove of spruce to waypoint 4, a benchmark near a barb wire fence now on the ground, and a post with 5/39 inscribed on it. This is the date the rows of spruce were planted.

Five: Magic Corner and Unexpected Pleasures

Another "just walk and get it over with" section through a forest that varies from aspen and birch to almost all aspen. At the end of this we come around a magic corner and there before us is a beautiful open meadow of grass, rock, and red staghorn sumac, which is just about everywhere we look. This place, which Judy calls a "Sound of Music" field is waypoint 5. This is a wide open, gorgeous expanse with tons of *snowberries, wild roses, raspberries, Juneberries,* willow, *strawberries, honeysuckle, goldenrod,* and viburnum. A few pine and spruce trees ring this enormous open area, much of which is solid rock.

The rock here is amygdaloidal basalt (locally called the Red Cliff lavas for exposures along the lakeshore) with the round amygdules ranging from pinheads to more than an inch in diameter. These compose from 3-15% of the flow and are filled by either *calcite*, quartz, or a cream-colored *zeolite* (thomsonite); many are empty with the minerals filling them having weathered out. The rock contains small *plagioclase feldspar* crystals and has a reddish-colored matrix with numerous quartz and calcite veins. Locally this *ophitic* basalt is weathered to kibbles and bits (see *diabase weathering*).

From the field we have nice views of Lake Superior, Five Mile Rock, Pincushion Mountain, and Maple Hill.

Six: Microclimate and Old Rocks

Walking to the end of the meadow, which is waypoint 6. Judy and I talk about what a wonderful surprise and special treat this place has given us. For me, walking over this rocky, grassy area is like walking over recent *pahoehoe* lava flows with thin soil and plant development; it is hard to believe the rock is 1.1 billion years old! For Judy it is the variety and abundance of plants along with the sheer beauty and peacefulness.

Seven: Durfee Creek

From the "eye and mind" stretching meadow we return to a birch, aspen, and balsam forest with larger, more massive pieces of ophitic basalt along with basalt kibbles and bits on the trail. Sloughing through a muddy, wet spruce-aspen forest we come to an open field or clear cut. Crossing the field we enter an aspen-birch forest, cross a small creek followed by a short uphill then downhill walk to the Durfee Creek campsite. Just beyond the campsite is boulder-filled Durfee Creek, which is waypoint 7. Today there are lots of dead man's fingers and tall inky cap mushrooms near the creek, as well as the usual creek plants: *cow parsnips*, *horsetails*, and ash trees.

Eight: A Mossy Place

From Durfee Creek the trail goes through an aspen-birch forest with Judy finding turquoise mushrooms of the "green stain fungus" type on most of the dead branches she picks up. Walking over a mossy area with a small creek we cross an old road. After this it is a "just walk and get it over with section" with waypoint 8 at a small creek with a set of wooden planks across it. With all the moss growing on the trees, roots, and ground this could be called Moss Creek.

Nine: Cliff Creek and Campsite

Continuing through a more open spruce, aspen, and birch forest we come to another "mossy" creek, after which it is another 0.25 miles to Cliff Creek and the Cliff Creek campsite (waypoint 9). There are lots of ash trees here, and the boulders in the creek are basalt and rhyolite.

Ten: Spruce, Changing Forest, and Rhyolite

Leaving the creek area we walk through a moss-rich spruce forest. In fact Judy has decided the tree of the day is spruce with moss as the dominant ground cover. Crossing two small planked creeks, we head uphill into a drier area, and a dramatic change in the forest: crispy and dry aspen, willow, and birch instead of wet and moss-rich spruce. The willow have typical diamond-shaped leaf scars, which gives them the name diamond willow.

Moving on through a crispy and dry forest we come to an outcrop of rhyolite which has a large area of broken rock scattered down a gentle slope below the outcrop (waypoint 10). Just before waypoint 10 the trail is littered with pieces of rhyolite, and there are Juneberries, viburnum, and red pine.

The rhyolite consists of about 5% tabular to lath-shaped, pink to cream-colored feldspar crystals (both orthoclase and plagioclase) and abundant tiny worm-like quartz patches that may represent *spherulites*. The matrix is red and aphanitic. The rock has sub-horizontal *unloading* fractures parallel to the flow direction, as well as vertical fractures along *cooling joints*; erosion along these fractures causes the rock to break into flagstone shaped and/or angular pieces. This is the Kimball Creek Rhyolite, which is believed to be over 900 feet thick with a length of at least 32 miles. Because of its widespread nature, its origin, like that of the Devil Track Rhyolite, is problematic. Geologists who have worked on these units postulate a *pyroclastic* origin for both of them and envision them emplaced as high temperature pyroclastic flows (see glossary for further discussion).

Eleven: White Oak

The trail continues over flagstone and angular pieces of Kimball Creek Rhyolite with partial lake views through a forest of spruce with birch, aspen, and balsam fir. Come to an open, rocky meadow with nice views of the lake and shoreline (waypoint 11). The meadow is underlain by Kimball Creek Rhyolite, and weathered pieces of rhyolite cover the trail ranging in size from donut hole on down.

Abundant white oak grows in the open field, with white pine near the end of the meadow. Three-toothed *cinquefoil* and *blueberries* can be found along the trail, as well as the hoof prints of moose followed by those of wolves.

Twelve: Large Aspens and a Craters of the Moon Trail

The hillside we are walking along is composed of rhyolite, and weathered pieces of this material make up the trail. These make the walking rather interesting for I'm reminded of the flanks of volcanic cinder cones I've walked down in Death Valley and Craters of the Moon National Monument. Passing a 1930 survey marker we come to an outcrop of rhyolite, one with small cavities that are irregular in shape and lined by quartz or filled by calcite. These may have formed as degassing features in a high temperature volcanic rock (called *lithophysae*).

From here the trail is boulder-covered (rhyolite and basalt) as it goes through a spruce, aspen, birch forest; the white oak has vanished.

The rock on the trail also vanishes as we start down toward Kimball Creek. Large aspen and cedar trees are all along here, and waypoint 12 is in a grove of very large aspen (up to 30 inches in diameter) with some cedar.

Thirteen: Long Walk

We now have a long walk along and above Kimball Creek passing large, old birch stumps and crossing a small creek as we head gently downhill. Going by some white pine we reach waypoint 13, a hiking trail sign that says we are 59.2 miles from Lutsen.

Fourteen: Kimball Creek, Old Stream Channel, and Holey Rocks

Going steeply downhill, via wooden steps, we cross the bridge over West Kimball Creek, with the creek flowing over fractured and broken red rhyolite. Just downstream from the bridge is East Kimball Creek. There are yellow birch in this area, and a large, white glacial erratic can be seen sitting on top of the rhyolite. A line of subround to round boulders occur along the stream bank. These are perched directly above the rhyolite and are believed to represent the remnants of an old stream channel.

On the upstream side of the bridge we find three round boulders, each with a hole drilled through it, and the three all line up. Are these old bridge supports or something more mysterious and magical like the "key" rocks at Stonehenge?

From this point it is a short walk to the bridge across Kimball Creek East (waypoint 14) and the Kimball Creek campsite. Just downstream from here East Kimball Creek joins West Kimball Creek to form Kimball Creek. The creek has boulders of Star Wars Porphyry in it.

Fifteen: County Road 14

We head steeply uphill from the creek, over wooden steps, to the Superior Hiking Trail Parking lot on Cook County Road 14. This is waypoint 15.

Sixteen: Half-Way Rock

Walking along the parking lot we cross the county road passing a Superior Hiking Trail sign. Then it's over a trail composed of angular to cinder-like pieces of what we call the *Half-Way Rock* to a power line and an outcrop of Half-Way Rock, which is waypoint 16.

The rock gets this name because, in composition and mineralogy, it is half-way between a rhyolite and a basalt. Geologists call such rocks *Icelandites* after similar rocks found in Iceland. Judy refers to this rock as Half-Way Rock On Ice. This particular lava flow can be traced over a distance of 20 miles and is believed to represent the eruption of lava out of an extensive system of fissures or cracks. Here the Half-Way Rock contains cream-colored plagioclase feldspar crystals, and the black spots through the rock are clumps of *pyroxene* crystals with or without *magnetite*. The matrix is aphanitic and red-colored.

From the power line we can see County Road 14 and almost all the way down to the lake.

Seventeen: B and B Trail and More Cinder

It's a 0.25 mile walk from the power line to the junction with the spur trail to the Jaegerhaus Bed and Breakfast. The trail is composed of cinder-like pieces of Half-Way Rock and the forest consists of nice aspen, birch, and spruce. The outcrop at the spur trail is Half-Way Rock with cream-colored plagioclase feldspar crystals, black pyroxene, and magnetite clumps in a mottled pink siliceous (quartz-rich) matrix.

Eighteen: Cinder Versus Kibbles and Bits

We keep walking along and over "cindery" pieces of Half-Way Rock, before going down a set of relatively steep steps. The cindery rock pieces that cover the trail are easier to walk down than the kibbles and bits pieces that form from the weathering of *diabase*. The cinders are more irregularly shaped and stick into the ground unlike the smooth, rounded kibbles and bits that roll like marbles. The rock on the trail vanishes; the trail becomes dirt-packed and root-lined to an outcrop of Half-Way Rock. From here it is once again over and along Half-Way Rock, on a cindery trail, through a young aspen forest with spruce and birch to a small creek with Half-Way Rock exposed in the bottom.

From the creek continue over and along small outcrops and cinder to waypoint 18, an outcrop of amygdaloidal Half-Way Rock. Amygdules are round to elongate and make up 20-35% of the rock; most are empty. The rock weathers a reddish-brown color.

Nineteen: Easter Egg Icelandite

It's a short walk to an outcrop of very amygdaloidal Half-Way Rock. Amygdules are up to four inches long and are mostly weathered out. However, we can still see quartz-filled ones with the quartz standing out in relief above the rest of the rock. In fact some of these might be considered quartz Easter eggs. The weathered out pieces of quartz line the trail. *Hematite* coats amygdules and is abundant in the matrix and along fractures through the rock. In places fragments of amygdaloidal Half-Way Rock are enclosed by a amygdaloidal matrix indicating this may be the kind of fragmental material that typically occurs at the top of such flows (flow top breccia).

Twenty: Crow Creek and Campsite

Continuing over the Easter Egg Flow we walk downhill, via wooden steps, to Crow Creek. The bridge across the creek is waypoint 20, and the spur trail to the Crow Creek campsite is to the right. Amygdaloidal Half-Way Rock outcrops in the creek and along the creek banks. Elderberry and *evening primrose* grow along the banks with the primrose over 7 feet tall.

Twenty-One: Canyon Land

It's a 0.25 mile walk from Crow Creek to the bridge across the west fork of the Kadunce River (waypoint 21). The river has cut a narrow, straight, steep canyon through the Half-Way Rock with the canyon walls rising twenty or thirty feet above the river. The West Fork campsite is to the right, but it is not a very appealing site. It would be a challenge to get water, for this branch of the river is completely dry.

Twenty-Two: Large Aspen

Up and out of the river we continue on a trail composed of angular pieces of you know what, to a dirt packed and root-crossed trail that leads to a small creek with planks over it. From here it is a short distance to a forest service sign and a nice stand of big aspen. From this point it is downhill to a trail junction with the Superior Hiking Trail heading to the right. This is followed by a short walk to a nice view of the Kadunce River, and this is waypoint 22.

Twenty-Three: Kadunce River

The trail follows the river then crosses it to come to the junction of the Superior Hiking Trail (which continues on to Magney State Park) and the spur trail that heads down the river to the parking lot on Highway 61. This is waypoint 23. A "happy" book can be found here, and the undergrowth is typical *Canadian carpet* with lots of blueberries. Written in the "happy" book is this "Kadunce–the sound of a rock thrown in the river." At this spot the river flows through a steep gorge cut into Half-Way Rock by erosion along cooling joints and sub-horizontal unloading fractures. This is similar to the weathering seen in the Split Rock Rhyolite and Devil Track Rhyolite but, since Half-Way Rock is softer it erodes much faster.

Twenty-Four: Wayside

We follow the spur trail down river with nice views into the river gorge.

Pieces of Half-Way Rock, angular to popcorn-shaped, occur along the trail, and nice white pines are scattered through a dominantly spruce-aspen forest. Waypoint 24 is at the wayside on Highway 61.

The highlight of this hike was certainly the "magic corner" followed by "Half-Way Rock," white oaks, large aspen, and the Kadunce River.

Superior Hiking Trail
Walk 28: Lake Walk and Little Brule River

Walk Logistics

Start: Kadunce River Wayside

Getting There: Head north out of Grand Marais on Highway 61. Pass the Devil Track River, Woods Creek, Durfee Creek, and Kimball Creek before crossing the Kadunce River (highway sign says Kondonce Creek). The wayside is immediately past the river.

End: Judge C.R. Magney State Park parking lot

Getting There: Take Highway 61 past the Kadunce River and County Road 14 to Judge C. R. Magney State Park at the Brule River. Turn left into the park and proceed to the parking lot. State Park permit is needed.

Walk Distance: 9 miles   **Date Walked:** September 30th, 2004

Worth a Longer Look:
Halfway and the Half Pothole: 2   Little Brule River: 18
Lake Superior Shoreline: 8, 9, 10,11   Froth Rock: 19
Different Habitats: 12   Jack Pines: 21, 22
Flagstone Creek: 16

Waypoint-to-Waypoint

One: Parking Lot and the Kadunce River

It's a gorgeous day, one of those days when it feels great to be alive, especially if you get to spend it not only on the Superior Hiking Trail, but also on the only section that follows the shore of Lake Superior.

Today is one of the Crossing Borders tour days when artists from Duluth to Thunder Bay open their studios to the public. That is really a nice idea. Judy and I agree that our present studio is open for tours every day–rain, sun, or snow–and the artwork is the very best Mother Earth can provide!

To reach waypoint 1 and the start of today's hike walk up the spur trail that follows the Kadunce River to the bridge across it. At the bridge there is a "happy" book, and on the way to the bridge there is a nice size cave worn into what we call *Half-Way Rock* that forms the river gorge.

Two: Black Tooth Root, Half Pothole, and Half-Way Rock

257

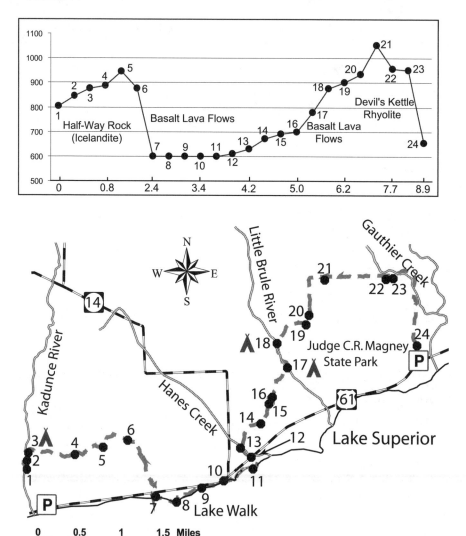

The trail goes up a short hill, parallels the river, then heads back to the water where *outcrops* of Half-Way Rock are exposed. Walking along the river we come to waypoint 2, a large outcrop of Half-Way Rock from which we have a nice view of a series of small cascading waterfalls. Across the river is the "black tooth," a tooth-shaped tree root that is dark black from lack of brushing–well, really it is from a lightning strike.

The reddish weathering Half-Way Rock is *amygdaloidal* and contains small *plagioclase feldspar* crystals that appear to be "clumped" together and gradually decrease in size across the outcrop. The *amygdules* are round, up to an inch in diameter, and largely weathered out. Just upstream from waypoint 2 is a really neat half *pothole* (one side is missing) in which the

258

water swirls around and around over water polished rock. Upstream are numerous pools of water, and each has a small, rocky drop above it.

Three: Kadunce River Campsite

The trail follows the river a short distance before heading inland where we climb a set of wooden steps to the Kadunce River campsite and waypoint 3. *Dewberries* are abundant in this section, and these look like a cross between a raspberry and a strawberry.

Four: Dead Aspen

The trail, with planked sections, continues away from the river through a mixed forest with tall, thin aspen trees, all about the same height and diameter. The understory is dominantly hazel and mountain maple. Crossing an old road we pass through an area with large aspen stumps and some cut trees lying beside them; Judy estimates the trees have been down and rotting for some 30 years.

Waypoint 4 is at a large outcrop of Half-Way Rock similar to that seen at waypoint 2.

Five: Rotten Rock and Blueberries

We travel on through an aspen forest with small ash trees, over amygdaloidal Half-Way Rock with weathered pieces covering the trail in cinder-like chunks. There are a lot of *raspberries* and dogwood along this trail section. After crossing a small creek, with amygdaloidal Half-Way Rock exposed along the bottom, we find abundant *bunchberries* and *blueberries* along the trail, and pieces of cinder-like Half-Way Rock on it. Coming to a large, rocky clearing with lots of spruce trees, both alive and dead, Judy points out all the old man's beard that covers the spruce trees. Judy also finds a ton of blueberries and I find Half-Way Rock so rotten (deeply weathered) I decide to ignore it and pick blueberries. As we look around this particular neighborhood (when we can stop ourselves from picking the blueberries) there is a partial lake view and some nice white pine.

The trail continues over almost solid rock and blueberries to a ninety degree bend, and from here we have a nice lake view; this is waypoint 5. The red leaves of the sumac add yet another dimension to both the color and texture of the forest's fall display.

Six: Timber Wolf Creek

Upon leaving the open hillside the blueberries vanish but bunchberries are blooming. We pass large aspen with birch and spruce before coming to a small creek that has large aspen on one side and dead birch on the other. Boulders in the creek bed come from erosion of the *glacial till* and are dominantly *basalt* and Half-Way Rock

259

From here it is a short walk to an old road, after which we enter a cutover forest with young aspen and some white pine and spruce. The trail is partly composed of kibbles and bits (see *diabase weathering*) all the way to a set of wooden steps that lead down to Timber Wolf Creek and waypoint 6. The outcrop along the creek bottom has been polished smooth by the rushing water (spring time only). The rock is no longer Half-Way Rock but basalt with 1-5% large *hematite*-coated plagioclase feldspar crystals in a fine-grained matrix with lots of hematite stringers and patches. Amygdules compose 2-5% of the rock and are filled by *epidote, quartz,* and *zeolites* (laumantite and thomsonite); many are weathered out.

Seven: Diabase and Basalt

It's downhill from the creek through a spruce-birch forest with white pine. Along the trail we see *curly dock* and small yellow mushrooms as well as lots of kibbles and bits. Passing a basalt outcrop we come to a well-used dirt road and an outcrop of *diabase* with nice needle-like crystals of black *pyroxene* occurring in clusters or single crystals.

After the road we cross a power line and enter a young aspen forest with larger, mostly dead birch trees. Passing an outcrop of *ophitic* basalt, which is weathering to kibbles and bits, we continue downhill to Highway 61. Crossing the road we come to a large outcrop of feldspar crystal basalt, which is waypoint 7. From the power line cut to the highway Judy saw lots of *blue bead lily, thimbleberry,* dogwood, *cow parsnip,* cherries (which have black knots on them so they are easy to spot), and nine bark, the only place on the hiking trail to see it! There is dogwood, lots of mountain ash, alder, *evening primrose,* tamarack trees, willows, *sweet gale,* and black ash. We also walk past typical wetland plants such as *leather leaf, thyme, bog rosemary,* and *Labrador tea.* All this plant life over such a small area– "Wow" says Judy, "Mexico City without pollution!"

Eight: Sorted Rocks and a Long, Rocky Beach

Walk along the lakeshore over *cobbles, pebbles,* and smaller rock particles. The rocks have been size-sorted by Superior's waves with the larger rocks found closer to the water. Between the lake and the highway is a grassy marsh with duckweed. The marsh is surrounded by lovely tamarack trees. Waypoint 8 is at a rocky island that sits just offshore at the point where the beach curves away in both directions. We can see a long way, and today there is no one else here. It's glorious down along the water, sunny and warm with large but gentle waves rolling onto the rocky beach. If it was white sand we could be in Bermuda (but replace the palms with tamarack and balsam).

Nine: Pumice and the Lakes Power

Walking down the rocky beach we find most of the *boulders* and cobbles to be grey, black, or reddish-brown basalt, both massive and amygdaloidal; some have plagioclase feldspar crystals. A few cobbles and pebbles of *rhyolite* are mixed in with the basalt, and many of these contain well-preserved elongated *pumice*. The pumice-bearing material also contains quartz and feldspar crystals along with round white-to cream-colored spots that are *spherulites*. These rock pieces come from a *pyroclastic flow* deposit similar to those at Long Valley California, Yellowstone National Park, or Mount St. Helens.

Looking at the cobbles, pebbles, and sand we can only imagine the awesome grinding and crushing power of Superior's waves as they constantly create fine sand from big pieces of rock. Waypoint 9 is at a large chunk of *massive* basalt, a *glacial erratic* right at the edge of the beach.

Ten: Old Highway, Large Amygdules, and Vesicle Cylinders

We stroll on along the beach to a sign that indicates there is 0.5 miles of beach walk left (waypoint 10). Old Highway 61 is here, and it is being broken into pieces and washed away by the lake. From just past waypoint 10 to a prominent point of land, the shore is solid outcrop. The rock is amygdaloidal basalt with elongate and round amygdules filled by milky to clear quartz, banded quartz, *calcite*, and white to pinkish-white zeolite. The amygdules are up to 6 inches in diameter and make up 5-15% of the rock. This flow also has *vesicle cylinders* more than a foot in diameter. The amygdules increase then decrease in abundance as we walk along indicating we have gone from the top of a flow into the more massive center.

Eleven: Basalt Boulders, Nice Island, and Wild Roses

Our nice walk continues to another point of land. Here the vesicle cylinders in the basalt are being eroded downward by the action of the waves to form potholes

Walking another quarter of a mile we come to an outcrop of amygdaloidal basalt with large vesicle cylinders. This is waypoint 11, and just past here is an area with large boulders of basalt that have been piled between a small rocky island not far off shore and the outcrop. The basalt has red hematite bands through it.

Near the basalt outcrop is a grove of balsam poplar; we find *harebells*, *cinquefoil*s, *strawberries*, and *wild roses*.

Twelve: Happy Dog and Microhabitats

Coming to the end of the lake walk we turn towards the highway. Charlie is certainly happy about this turn of events because he was the only one not impressed with the lake walk. He did not care a paw about walking over all those loose rocks. Pass a hiking trail sign to Magney State Park, and continue over a mostly planked section, through a wet, boggy area to Highway 61 and waypoint 12.

Judy found lots of different habitats on the lake side of the highway; bogs, ponds, and old beaches. Several boardwalks gave her the chance to get close to them for a better look. The purple *asters*, *goldenrod*, and a whole field of *fireweed* are particularly noticeable in this prime spot.

Thirteen: Large Birch and Hanes Creek

From Highway 61 it is gently uphill through a nice birch-aspen forest with some large ash trees and one enormous birch before the power line cut. Crossing the power line we walk over a kibble and bit trail to Hanes Creek, which is waypoint 13. A lot of angular pieces of amygdaloidal basalt occur along the creek banks with the amygdules filled by quartz, calcite, and zeolite. Some of the amygdules are banded. There are a lot of downed aspens along the creek, but young aspens are coming up all around.

Fourteen: Alder Swamp and Yellow Birch

It's gently uphill, through a birch-aspen forest, with lots and lots of young, tall, thin aspen trees. Passing two outcrops of reddish to tan weathering basalt we come to the start of a planked-over section.

This leads us through an alder swamp, with a few large birch, to a private land sign. From here the trail is lined with bunchberries and blueberries as it winds through a forest of spruce and birch with a few old and dead yellow birch and lots of young aspen. Waypoint 14 is at a small boulder-filled creek.

Fifteen: Painted Basalt, and the Sleeping Rock

Continuing on we walk through a birch-spruce forest with a stand of dense balsam fir and spruce; all along here Judy is busy collecting chanterelle mushrooms. We come to an outcrop of basalt that, because of red hematite veins and fracture fillings, has a definite painted look to it.

From here we cross two rock-filled creeks, and walk through a dense grove of spruce and fir back into birch and aspen with alders. Pass a pink-colored glacial erratic with zoned potassium feldspar (*orthoclase*) and large quartz crystals to arrive at Sleeping Rock–a glacial erratic that leans against two dead birch trees. The rock looks peaceful now, but once upon a time it was definitely moved. The question of the moment is–did the birch trees grow up and in doing so move the rock? This is waypoint 15.

Sixteen: Flagstone Creek

Leaving Sleeping Rock we have a short walk to an area where pieces of angular, subangular, and subround amygdaloidal to massive basalt, tons and tons of rock pieces (many of which are flat or flagstone-like), are scattered over what must be an intermittent streambed. Possibly it only has water in it during spring run off. This is waypoint 16. The "stream" is about 20 feet wide, and *wild ginger*, *rue*, and cow parsnips grow along both sides.

Seventeen: South Little Brule River Campsite

Traveling through a birch, aspen, and spruce forest we enter an alder swamp to arrive at a creek with angular rocks all along the bottom and *miterwort* along the sides. The pieces of basalt contain small dark spots, which are *chlorite*-filled amygdules. From here we walk over a basalt outcrop to an old road/ATV trail, then head gently uphill. As we walk upward we first cross a massive basalt representing a flow bottom, then an amygdaloidal basalt representing a flow top. Blueberries and bunchberries can be found in abundance along the trail all the way to waypoint 17, the spur trail to the South Little Brule River campsite.

Eighteen: White Pine, Moss, and Beautiful Colors

The trail now wanders along the edge of a cliff with big spruce, cedar, and pine; there are a few black spruce, and many of the trees have lots of moss on them. A large white pine grows right on the edge of a *slump* in the making, with a steep drop into the Little Brule River. The outcrops in the river banks are ophitic basalt.

Walking along the river we can see ahead of us a large cave cut into the rocky bank, and this gives the appearance of the river emerging out of the bank. In reality the river bends past it. We can also see another large white pine in trouble; Judy thinks the roots will hold it, but without a bank I don't think so.

The gorge exhibits an array of beautiful colors: deep green of the balsam trees, burnt orange of the mountain maple, and yellows of the mountain ash. Old man's beard, a lichen (Usnea) hangs from many of the trees.

We now walk along a relatively dry river to a *meander* bend with a pile of rocks derived from an outcrop in the bank that has been undercut by the stream. The moss growing on the rock suggests the stream has not flowed here for some time. We wonder how long it's been since the river was high enough to reach the top of the outcrop in the bank?

We come to the bridge across the Little Brule River (waypoint 18). The outcrop in the bank is amygdaloidal basalt with round to angular amygdules filled with quartz, *jasper*, zeolite, and chlorite. The North Little Brule River campsite is here.

Nineteen: Froth Rock, Football Field, and Bear Den

Several planked sections, dry now, take us over what, in the spring, is most likely a very wet area. We then travel through a forest with large aspen and spruce scattered amongst smaller birch, spruce, aspen, and fir. Passing two outcrops of reddish-colored basalt we come to a private land sign. A large cedar tree east of the trail is slowly tipping up and looks like it will eventually be a great den site for a hibernating bear!

From here it is not far to an outcrop of Froth Rock. This is the amygdaloidal top to a basalt lava flow. Amygdules make up 55-75% of the rock, ranging from pinhead-size to ½ inch in diameter. They are round to subround and angular to elongate and filled by quartz, calcite, clay, and/or zeolites. It is unusual to see such an amygdaloidal-rich rock because typically they erode away quickly.

From the Froth Rock it is a short walk to waypoint 19, a dirt road to what looks like a large open, grassy football field to the right.

Twenty: Rhyolite and Sunflowers

Just past the football field is more froth rock as we head into an aspen forest with some large trees and stumps. From here there is a short uphill to an outcrop of quartz-feldspar crystal rhyolite (waypoint 20). Quartz crystals are grey to clear, square to triangular in shape, and 3-4% in abundance. Plagioclase feldspar is cream-colored and small. The crystals are in a siliceous pink to salmon-colored matrix with white spots or patches that probably represent spherulites. Elongate and angular cavities in the rock are lined with small quartz crystals and these may be *lithophysae*. Because the rhyolite is the same one that forms the Devil's Kettle on the Brule River (walk 29), we name it the Devil's Kettle Rhyolite.

Twenty-One: Large Aspen and Jack Pine

It's gently uphill over rhyolite outcrops and angular pieces of rhyolite on the trail, through white pine of various ages and older spruce mixed amongst younger birch and aspen to a deer stand in a white pine tree.

We then walk over rhyolite outcrops and through an area of large aspen in a sea of smaller aspen with spruce, birch and white pine. In places the rhyolite forms pink kibbles and bits on the trail. Waypoint 21 is at the beginning of a jack pine stand with *wild geraniums*, *horsetails*, and blueberries.

Twenty-Two: Spherulite Kibbles and Bits

Carrying on we walk through a section of jack pines with white pine and some black and white spruce over a trail composed of either pink kibbles and bits or pine needles. As we walk over rotten (deeply weathered) rhyolite outcrop it becomes obvious it's the weathering of the spherulites in the rhyolite that leads to the formation of the kibbles and bits on the trail. These disappear from the trail as we arrive at a planked area over a low, swampy spot.

The trail becomes dirt-packed and tree root-crossed as it goes through some large aspen and birch with spruce and lots of smaller aspen to an open area and large outcrop of ribbon textured, spherulitic rhyolite with lots of kibbles and bits (this is waypoint 22). The rhyolite is composed of cream-colored feldspar, up to ½ inch long, and smaller quartz crystals, in a spotted grey to slightly pink matrix; the spots represent spherulites. There is also an acicular dark mineral that weathers to hematite and biotite. Fruit trees, mountain ash, and spruce ring the outcrop.

Twenty-Three: Start of State Park

From the rhyolite we have a short walk to an old road that marks the end of private land and the start of the Judge C.R. Magney State Park. This is waypoint 23.

Twenty-Four: Culvert Dog and a Great Day

Traveling through an aspen forest with spruce and birch we arrive at Gauthier Creek where there is abundant black spruce and old man's beard. Following the creek we come to the junction between the Superior Hiking Trail and a park trail. The hiking trail continues to the right.

It's now an easy walk down the creek on a wide grassy park trail/road with large aspen and ash trees, plus some pine, over rhyolite outcrops with kibbles and bits to a small creek with a large Sammy culvert. Sammy has to jump up three feet to get into it (this dog, for some perverted reason, has a passion for crawling through culverts). Continuing down the trail, we turn sharply to the left before entering the state park parking lot.

Wow! That's from both Judy and I. What a great walk and a great day. The lake shore was spectacular. Throw in Half-Way Rock, rhyolite kibbles and bits, and numerous large, old growth trees, and we (dogs included) had quite the afternoon.

Superior Hiking Trail

Walk 29: Devils Kettle, Picnic Hill, and The Flute Reed River

Walk Logistics

Start: Judge C.R. Magney State Park parking lot

Getting There: Take Highway 61 past the Kadunce River and County Road 14 to Judge C.R. Magney State Park at the Brule River. Turn left into the park and proceed to the parking lot. State Park permit is needed.

End: Parking lot on County Road 70 (Camp 20 Road)

Getting There: Take Highway 61 past Judge C.R. Magney State Park to County Road 69 (North Road). Travel 2.75 miles to County Road 70 (Camp Road 20). Turn left onto County Road 70 and go 4.75 miles, passing the junction with Hong Hill Road to the parking lot, which is on the right (0.25 miles past Hong Hill Road).

Walk Distance: 4.6 miles to County Road 70, plus 1.7 mile walk on road to parking lot.

Date Walked: October 6th, 2004

Worth a Longer Look:

Bridge over the Brule River: 2	Meanders and Oxbows: 8
Slumps, Meanders, and Erratics: 4	Picnic Rocks: 14, 15
High Falls and Rhyolite: 5	Flute Reed River: 16
Devil's Kettle: 6, 7	

Waypoint-to-Waypoint

One: Parking Lot

Early October and the nights are getting colder, crisper, and clearer. In fact the sky the last few nights has been so clear the stars have turned into hard diamonds and Jupiter and Saturn look like a pair of faraway headlights. Last evening, sitting around the picnic table at our campsite on Nine Mile Lake, Judy and I played connect the dots–celestial dots, sparkling points of light in a clear dark sky. Between the dots we strung imaginary lines that we used to try and create everything from fishers, beavers, and loons to dippers, dragons, and serpents.

Ours was a confused sky; a sky populated with more Ojibwe figures than the Greek and Roman ones we had been raised with. Overall, we both agreed the

266

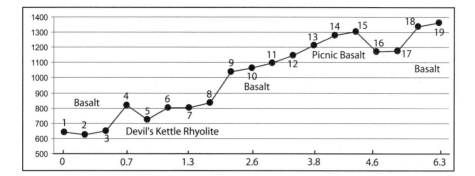

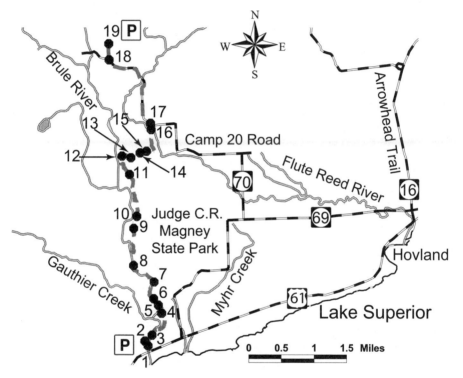

Ojibwe figures, and night sky they gave life to, fit this northern land. They went well with *diabase* ridges, *anorthosite* knobs, *basalt* shores, iron ore pits, rocky portages, ice-covered lakes, and dark pine forests. Living and hiking here, in the North Country, demands a sky filled with moose, fishers, loons, beavers, bears, sweat lodges, and even a "winter maker." How could anyone pitch a tent, light a fire, listen to a wolf howl, or paddle a canoe under a sky full of twins, crabs, lions, winged horses, rams, goats, and bulls. No no, it's got to be a northern lands sky, and the Ojibwe sky fit perfectly.

We are in the parking lot of Judge C.R. Magney State Park on a clear, sunny day with the temperature a crisp 42 degrees, but it is supposed to climb all

267

the way to 70 by this afternoon. Ours is the only car in the parking lot; too bad, for it's a great day to be outside. Hiking up an active and ever-changing North Shore river makers it even better. The park was established in 1957 to preserve three waterfalls on the Brule River; the Lower Falls and Upper Falls, plus the famous Devil's Kettle Falls. Speaking of which, waypoint 1 is at the Superior Hiking Trail sign that directs us to Devil's Kettle.

Two: Bridge Over the Brule River

It's a short walk from the parking lot past a plaque with a brief biography of Judge C. R. Magney to waypoint 2, the bridge across the Brule River. The river was named by the French voyageurs the Bois Brule (burned forest), and this name was apparently a translation from the Ojibwe. The river has also been called the Arrowhead. There is an *outcrop* of dark, *massive* basalt in the river.

Three: Old River Channel and the Cross Rock

Crossing the bridge we head up and along the river on a wide gravel path with a few larger *cobbles*. The line of *boulders* to the right of the trail represents an old river channel formed when the Brule was flowing at a much higher level. The channel was abandoned as the river cut down through *glacial till*, *Glacial Lake Duluth* clay, and volcanic rock during the last several thousand years.

Waypoint 3 is at the start of a large "tree zoo," an area that has been fenced off to protect white pine from browsing deer and hungry rabbits. A *glacial erratic* called the cross can be found here. It gets this name because it contains two intersecting *quartz* and feldspar veins that form a distinct cross shape. The veins are different ages–we know this because one cuts and offsets the other.

Four: Slumps, Meanders, and Glacial Erratics

We continue up the wide path over gravel beach deposits exposed as water levels in Glacial Lake Duluth fell. These gravel beaches represent temporary shorelines of this ancient lake. Boulders seen here have been weathered out of the glacial till that is exposed further up the trail. Come to a fenced area where the river bank is *slumping* into the water. At this point the trail is a hundred feet above the river. A large glacial erratic of tan weathering, massive basalt sits here. It's kind of neat trying to picture this large rock sitting on a barren gravel beach on the shores of Glacial Lake Duluth.

Continuing up the trail we have partial views of the river and small waterfalls. Climbing a set of wooden steps we continue along the wide, gravel trail as it moves away from the river to avoid a large *meander* and the erosion and slumping associated with it.

At waypoint 4 we get a nice view of the meander bend and a small waterfall with a pool at its base. A lot of *bedrock* is exposed in the river because of the low water levels. The forest here contains some nice aspen, birch, and spruce, with a few white pine.

Five: Upper Falls and the Devil's Kettle Rhyolite

It's just a short walk up the trail, past the old steps, to the new steps that lead down to Upper Falls. We go down the long, steep set of wooden stairs, then along a wooden boardwalk to waypoint 5, a short set of stairs that leads down and onto a large outcrop of *rhyolite* lava at the base of Upper Falls. With the low water levels the river has separated into several "fingers," and these flow rather lazily over and down the rhyolite into the pool below. A nicely curved "three-quarter" *pothole* occurs at the base of the falls.

The rhyolite lava flow, pale red in color due to trace amounts of the iron oxide mineral *hematite*, contains small crystals of tabular-shaped, cream-colored feldspar (4-7%) and square to round glassy quartz (2-5%). The rock is pitted where the feldspar has weathered out. The rhyolite has a "hackly" or rough-textured weathered surface and is called the Devil's Kettle Rhyolite.

Six: Devil's Kettle

From waypoint 5 it's up another set of wooden stairs that takes us above the falls; on the opposite side of the river is a cliff of rhyolite. Come to the junction with a hiking club trail and the trail to Devil's Kettle. The outcrop here is similar to the rhyolite at waypoint 5, but here it is breaking into angular to rectangular and/or irregular chunks. The rough weathered surface and the way it breaks apart are due to numerous *spherulites*, the white spots throughout the rock.

There is a great view from here of Devil's Kettle Falls. Above the falls the river divides as it plunges over the rock rim with one branch flowing down and through what was once a sixty foot deep pothole that has had its downriver side eroded away. The other branch fountains into a beautiful round pothole or kettle and is never seen again. How deep the pothole is no one knows, and what happens to all the water is anyone's guess, and there sure have been lots of those. Judy thinks it ends up somewhere in China while I opt for a Disneyworld kind of plumbing system under the pothole that simply recycles it.

Take the hiking club trail to the viewing platform directly above the Devil's Kettle (waypoint 6). The view from here is impressive with water pouring into the cavity; imagine what this looks like in the spring.

Seven: River Bars and Boulder Islands

The wide trail continues up and along the river to a gravel bar with larger cobbles at each end and *pebbles* and smaller cobbles in between. This gravel bar occurs on the inside bend of a large meander and is probably reworked each and every spring. Once past the gravel bar the hiking trail becomes its old self–narrow, bouldery, and root-crossed. Continue up the river past another gravel bar to waypoint 7, the start of a boulder-filled island and a large meander in the river. The island begins on the meander bend and ends where the meander ends. The boulders on the island and in the river come from erosion and slumping of the river banks; some of the basalt boulders have large weathered out *amygdules*. Massive rhyolite lava continues to outcrop on the opposite bank.

Eight: Oxbows, Spill-Over Channels, and a Huge Pine Stump (15)

Continuing upriver through a cedar and ash-dominated forest, we cross a small stream that seems to be in a great hurry to reach the river, and walk through a cedar grove to yet another meander and gravel bar. From this point the trail moves away from the main channel of the river to follow a "spring flood" spill-over channel. The banks of the "spill-over" are crammed with boulders and cobbles that represent glacial till with the finer material, the sand and clay, washed out. These banks are undercut and slump into the river during spring runoff. The trail moves back to the river passing through a cedar grove with pink-looking rhyolite outcropping on the opposite bank.

Once again the trail leaves the river, but this time it follows an old *oxbow* that is filled in with boulders, alders, spruce, and cedar to waypoint 8, the end of the oxbow. An enormous stump of what we call the Three Magi White Pine is found here. We named it this because a large spruce, small birch, and tiny fir are all growing up out of it.

Nine: Glacial Lake Red Clay

From the Three Magi Pine we continue up the river with the banks crammed full of cobbles and boulders that, like the spill-over channel, represent glacial till, with most of the finer silt and clay material washed away. The forest is made up of cedar, spruce, birch, and balsam fir with large white pine stumps scattered throughout. The white pines were cut around 1900 and were part of northern Minnesota's once great white pine forest.

Pass a bench intended for little people, followed by a sharp bend in the trail from which it's uphill and away from the river. As we climb we notice how the trail and hillside change from boulder-rich glacial till to the red clay deposits of Glacial Lake Duluth. The change occurs where the trail makes a sharp turn at a large spruce tree.

Waypoint 9 is at a distinct break in the slope of the hillside and represents an old strand line of the glacial lake (this was once a shoreline).

Ten: Large Aspen and Glacial Till

Continuing uphill, with the trail composed of red clay, we pass an area with large aspen trees and a planked-over wet section to waypoint 10, a nice view back down the river. From here we can see a small meander and a hillside of red maples and yellow aspens and birch. Just before waypoint 10 the trail leaves the red clay deposits and is back in glacial till; the elevation here is 1050 feet.

Eleven: White Pines and the Lightning Tree

From waypoint 10 it is a long walk (0.75 miles) with gentle ups and downs as the trail bends and twists above, but parallel to, the river. This walk is through a nice section of white pines. Cross two boulder-filled streambeds (dry) and come to waypoint 11, an old lightning struck white pine with only the charred black bottom part left.

Twelve: Large Rock Cliff

Crossing a small, boulder filled-stream we head gently uphill through an aspen, spruce, and birch woods with some white pine and one dense, dark grove of small spruce and aspen to waypoint 12, a view of a big hill to the left (1400 feet high). A large exposure of dark grey, *columnar-jointed* basalt is exposed along the front of the hillside. The Brule River is far below us and winds around the bottom of the hill.

Thirteen: Pahoehoe Lava

Continuing uphill we come into a large, open area composed mostly of lichen-covered, brownish-grey to tan-colored basalt. On a fresh surface the rock is grayish green with conchoidal fractures and few amygdules. Down slope, near the end of the clearing, we find a billowy flow surface that may represent the top part of a *pahoehoe* lava flow. The amygdules, hard to see on a weathered surface covered with lichen and moss, are round, up to 0.5 inches in diameter, and quartz-filled.

Fourteen: Picnic Rock

Still heading uphill we come to a large, grassy opening with a great view of Lake Superior and a long exposure of the same lava that is at waypoint 13. Here the rock breaks into flat or square pieces. With white pine trees, the view, and the nice grassy area, this makes a great picnic spot. For this reason the basalt exposed here is called the Picnic Basalt Flow and the opening is called Picnic Rock I.

Fifteen: White Pines and Columnar Joints

Just uphill from here is another large opening. Here the Picnic Basalt Flow breaks into columnar shaped pieces and, at the end of the opening, there is columnar-jointed piece of basalt across the trail. The basalt lava also has 1-

2% lath-like grayish-green *plagioclase feldspar* crystals up to 0.5 inches long.

Waypoint 15 is at an old, white pine lined road that cuts across the opening. This is another nice picnic spot so we name it Picnic Rock II.

Sixteen: Flute Reed River:

From Picnic Rock II it is a long walk (0.5 miles) over angular pieces of Picnic Basalt, along a hillside that parallels the Flute Reed River, before descending down a gentle hill into an alder swamp, with lots of young and a few older aspens, to the river itself. This is a great name for a river, and we wonder if this is a Native American connection to reeds growing along the river's edge and musical instruments? Waypoint 16 is at bridge across the river.

Seventeen: County Road 70

It is a short walk from the Flute Reed River to waypoint 17, which is at County Road 70 (Camp Road 20). At the road there is room to park a couple of cars, had we parked here, we could have avoided the 1.7 mile road walk to the parking lot.

Eighteen: Parking Lot and the Happy Moose

We parked at the parking lot, so we end up walking down the dirt road. Along the way we pass some really large ash trees, cross the Flute Reed River again, smile at the "happy" moose, and see a white pine zoo at the edge of a clear cut on the way to waypoint 18, the junction with Hong Hill Road.

Nineteen: Parking Lot

County Road 70 continues straight ahead, potholes and all, to the parking lot (0.25 miles from the junction) and waypoint 19, which is the end of the hike. The Brule River, with slumps, meanders, oxbows, waterfalls and the Devil's Kettle, along with Picnic Rocks I and II, and the Flute Reed River are the high points of this walk.

Superior Hiking Trail

Walk 30: Clear Cut, Tom Lake Road, Carlson Creek, and Busy Beaver

Walk Logistics

Start: Parking lot on County Road 70 (Camp 20 Road)

Getting There: Take Highway 61 past Judge Magney State Park to County Road 69 (North Road). Travel 2.75 miles to County Road 70 (Camp Road 20). Turn left onto County Road 70 and go 4.75 miles, passing the junction with Hong Hill Road to the parking lot, which is on the right (0.25 miles past Hong Hill Road).

End: Arrowhead Trail (Cook County Road 16)

Getting There: Take Highway 61 north to Hovland. Turn left onto the Arrowhead Trail (Cook County Road 16) and follow this for 3.3 miles to the parking lot on the right.

Walk Distance: 8.2 miles   **Date Walked:** October 4th, 2004

Worth a Longer Look:

Birds and More Birds: 5   Rock Monster: 13

White Pine and the Rove: 9   Carlson Pond: 14, 16, 17

Beaver and Monzonite: 11   Dam and Beaver Runways: 23

Waypoint-to-Waypoint

One: Parking Lot

Snow in the first week of October! Of course it was up on the Gunflint Trail where snow manages to fall 10 months of the year. We spent the night at the Nor'Wester Lodge, and in the morning the ground was covered with two inches of wet, heavy, dripping snow. Here in the parking lot of Camp Road 20 it is cold (40 degrees) and the wind is not pleasant, but at least we are close enough to Lake Superior so that what fell from the heavens overnight was rain. The sun is still below the trees, but with the sky a pasty blue we have hopes it will warm up.

The small parking lot off Camp Road 20 has been hacked out of a swamp and is surrounded by balsam poplar and black ash. Waypoint 1 is in the parking lot.

Two: A Long Day (Maybe)

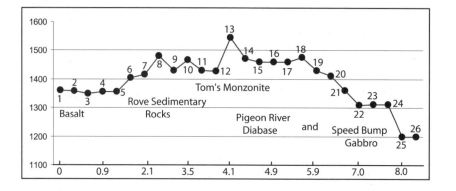

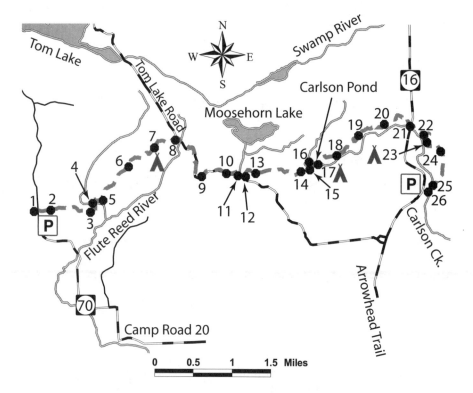

The trail heads off into the swamp passing some large cedars and spruce to a long boardwalk section with more ash trees. So let me see–snow, cold, and now a swamp–I'm getting the unpleasant feeling this may be a very long day!

Three: Clear Cut and Balm of Gilead

Traveling through the ash swamp we go up a slight rise to emerge into an open, grassy area that is not the Pampas or the Serengeti Plain but a recent clear cut. Even with the strong wind, the air has a distinct sweet smell that Judy thinks it's due to all the Balm of Gilead. No, not one of the round table knights (my thought) but a small evergreen tree of the myrrh family, if you are in Africa, or a resin-bearing balsam poplar here in the American cutover.

Crossing a small creek in a narrow alder swamp, we climb a short set of steps to re-emerge into the clear cut. The trail then passes by numerous slash piles with deer tracks all around them. The clear cut contains lots of young spruce but everything else is gone. We can really "stretch" our eyes here and look over to the large spruce, aspen, and balsam poplar trees in the distance.

Going by a large spruce stump with a private land sign nearby, Judy points out all the young red pines and spruce that were planted after the logging was completed. From here the trail winds through tall grass, wet in places, with numerous rotting slash piles and old stumps contributing to the scenic view. It's windy and cold here in the open, and the place reminds me of the tundra. I half expect to look up and see not a moose at the edge of the forest but a wooly mammoth!

Waypoint 3 is at the end of all this openness.

Four: Flute Reed River

The trail heads toward a small pond surrounded by tall, yellow grass with standing dead trees in the water. As we draw closer it becomes more obvious that this is the Flute Reed River dammed by our friendly beaver. Waypoint 4 is at the bridge over the river.

Five: Planted Pines and a Birders Heaven

The trail heads back into the open, grassy clear cut with lots of recently planted red and white pine along with balsam poplar. We wonder how many times this area has been logged, and Judy comments that it appears they took everything but a few token trees to help reseed. Along the boardwalk sections we find lots of moose tracks, as well as *wild ginger*. Walking through another narrow alder swamp we return to the clear cut. This is followed by a long boardwalk section; moose tracks and ginger continue as we pass through yet another alder swamp and back into the cutover (this is beginning to sound like a CD with a big scratch in it–broken record for people my age) to finally (wahoo!) climb a small rise to get a nice view of the beaver pond. This is waypoint 5. There are a ton of purple flowered nettles here as well as *asters*, different grasses, and abundant bull thistle.

The pond is the place to look for ducks, and it would be a fantastic birding spot in the spring.

Six: Forestry Practices, Large Aspens, and Ground Moraine

We follow the edge of aspen woods with the clear cut on the right. The slash left over from logging has not been cleaned up: it's lying all over the place and Judy wonders about this practice. Is it left on purpose to rot in small piles (my vote) instead of being burned or placed in one central spot?

The trail goes over *glacial till*, which forms a deposit here called *ground moraine*, Minnesota's natural carpet. *Boulders* that have weathered out of the till can be seen along the trail. These are of various rock types.

The trail parallels the Flute Reed River as we walk through a stand of large aspen with wide, spreading crowns, and then into an area with much smaller aspen trees. This is followed by a long section where hazel bushes close the trail in on both sides, followed by the appearance of maple trees mixed with ash and more large aspen. Waypoint 6 is at a planked-over area in the maple woods.

Seven: Hazel Campsite and Bears

From waypoint 6 we have a long walk through an aspen, spruce, and birch forest, with an alder swamp to the right that comes and goes. Pass over yet another planked section that crosses a small, swampy stream in an alder swamp.

Continuing through the mixed forest with some cedar we arrive at Hazel campsite. Looking around at the thick hazel we wonder how it got its name! Judy thinks this is the first waypoint today that has not been wet or swampy. Growing with the thick hazel are large birch and maple trees, so at this time of year there are many crunchy leaves underfoot.

Speaking of crunchy there is a bear cable here for food storage. Bears love hazelnuts as do squirrels (faster body and better eyes versus larger size and a louder voice–wonder who gets the hazelnut?). Here at the campsite the bears, in the fall, will be drawn to the hazel, and if there happens to be a human lunch or dinner about–well, what a Kodak moment that would be.

Waypoint 7 is here at the campsite.

Eight: Old Stream Channels and Tom Lake Road

From bear haven, oops I mean Hazel campsite, continue through the forest, crossing two boulder-rich areas that mark old stream channels. From here the amount of maple in the forest increases as we pass yet another stream channel and go up a gentle hill then along the top to Tom Lake Road, which is waypoint 8.

Nine: White Pine and the Rove Sedimentary Rocks

Turn right onto Tom Lake Road, which is now a grass and rock-covered or gravel trail as well as a great place to be on a lovely fall day. Walking down the road with hazel thick on both sides come to a large white pine. Hazel has male and female flowers on the same plant. The tiny red female flowers come out just as the rivers are shedding their ice in the spring. The male catkins grow long and release their pollen. Neither flower part is very large, and yet, they produce rather large seeds that are encased by a prickly, sticky outer covering that looks like a bird's long beak. The seed, or nut, is the familiar looking hazelnut.

Come to a road junction, though the one to the left is more of a bouldery stream bed now. The walking path continues straight ahead down Tom Lake Road through a nice forest of cedar, maple, birch, aspen, and white pine. The sides of the road are composed of boulder-rich till and, for the first time on the hiking trail, these boulders are dominantly sedimentary rocks: *slates, argillites,* and *siltstones* of the *Rove Formation.*

As we continue down the road we have a lovely view of some really nice white pines; waypoint 9 is at the junction with a narrow trail that heads off to the right (southeast).

We decide to see where this trail goes and follow it to an open area where we find oodles of angular pieces of slate, argillite, and siltstone, some of which show nice bedding. The argillite is black with nice curving fractures, the slate breaks into thin slabs, and the siltstone has the nice bedding. *Bedrock* is just inches below the surface, and so where we are standing was once under several hundred feet of water. The sedimentary rocks here are part of what is called the Rove Formation and formed between 1.8 and 1.9 billion years ago in the deep part of an ocean basin. In fact, the sandy shore was some forty miles to the north and west and between it and this spot the iron ore deposits, now mined on the iron range, were forming (see Rove Formation in glossary).

Ten: Rock Works

Retracing our steps we continue down Tom Lake Road. Piles of rock line the roadside and these were most likely hand-piled here when the road was built to make it more passable–I'm glad I was not on the chain gang that had the chore of doing this!

Waypoint 10 is at the junction between Tom Lake Road and an older road that heads off to the left (northeast) toward Moosehorn Lake. There are nice red and white pine here.

Eleven: Beaver at Work and Pink Monzonite

From the road junction it is a short walk to a brand new (2004) beaver pond that makes the Tom Lake Road impassable. The beaver have dammed Moosehorn Creek, and the walking path now goes around the pond to the left.

The rock *outcrop* on the hillside adjacent to the pond is a pinkish-colored *monzonite*, an igneous intrusive rock that lacks *quartz*. Here the monzonite is composed of laths of cream to pink-colored feldspar, which weathers out

277

leaving holes on the surface, and square to needle-like black *pyroxene* in a fine-grained matrix (dominantly potassium feldspar or the mineral *orthoclase*). This rock is very similar to the monzonites seen on Walk 12 north of Egge Lake. The monzonite exposed here is part of the *Mid-Continent Rift* system and was probably a feeder for felsic volcanic rocks at the surface. As this particular rock is not shown on geological maps of the area, we call it Tom's Monzonite.

The trail continues around the pond passing a *talus* slope made up of *frost-wedged* boulders of monzonite: here the rock is more mafic with pyroxene making up about 30%.

Waypoint 11 is at the junction of the foot path and the Tom Lake Road.

Twelve: Pigeon River Diabase

The trail continues down Tom Lake Road and, as Judy and I walk along, we notice that the rock in the hillside changes color from pink (monzonite) to dark grey (Pigeon River Diabase). The *diabase* is a *dike* intrusive into Tom's Monzonite and represents a small part of a large complex of dikes and *sills*. These are similar to the *Beaver Bay Igneous Complex,* but not nearly as much is known about them.

Waypoint 12 is at the junction between Tom Lake Road and the hiking trail, which makes a sharp left turn to head steeply up the hillside.

Thirteen: Rock Monster

Back on the narrow foot path we head uphill over numerous wooden steps and boulders (dominantly diabase, basalt, and monzonite), passing two large red pines before reaching the top. From here we travel through a mixed forest with red pine and lots of downed balsam to a large *glacial erratic* that looks like a great rock monster rising up, out of the forest floor. The erratic is 25 feet long and 4-5 feet high and is composed of *ophitic gabbro*. In the center of the erratic is a circular depression that looks like a water-filled kiva, and we wonder if it was ever used by Native Americans. Small pines, polypody ferns, and caribou lichen grow all over the rock monster.

The forest rock monster is waypoint 13.

Fourteen: Carlson Pond and a Long Walk

The rock monster is followed by a long walk (0.7 miles) that starts off in an open maple-birch forest with lots of large gabbro erratics and frost-heaved boulders, followed by a dense spruce, aspen, and birch forest with boulders of mixed lithologies—*basalt*, gabbro, siltstone, and *pegmatite*. This is followed by a gentle downhill to waypoint 14, a view down Carlson Pond, which is actually a long marsh with ponds or pools of water that contain lots of tall grass. The ponds are surrounded by spruce, birch, and aspen trees.

Fifteen: Carlson Pond

We walk along Carlson Pond; the hillside to the right is composed of gabbro with most of the loose boulders derived from there. The gabbro is a medium-grained, ophitic intrusive rock that forms part of the *Pigeon River Intrusive Complex*. Many outcrops of this rock have a lumpy weathered texture (see *diabase weathering*), and Judy refers to this texture as "speed bumps." I like this analogy, and that's how this rock unit got its name–Speed Bump Gabbro

Waypoint 15 is at the pond's edge by a beaver dam. The yellow leaves of the birch and aspen near the pond, along with the tall brown grass, makes the whole scene very pretty, especially so because the forest away from the pond is dark and dense with spruce and balsam.

Sixteen: Carlson Creek

Continuing around the pond we come to Carlson Creek, which drains the pond. Boulders of coarse-grained Speed Bump Gabbro are seen here. This is waypoint 16.

Seventeen: Wild Rice and the South Carlson Pond Campsite

The trail continues around the pond, which is wide and expansive with open water and lots of wet grassy areas. Waypoint 17 is at the South Carlson Pond campsite. There is a small dock here, and we wonder if it has anything to do with the wild rice (the Ojibwe call it Manomin) that borders this side of the pond. This area contains many soft and mossy plants; some of these are *clubmosses* and young cedars. There is also *blue flag iris*, black spruce, *Labrador tea, pipsissewa,* and *bunchberry* lining the trail. I guess if a swamp could be called pretty this would be it.

Eighteen: Giant Beaver

Walking along a slippery trail we travel through dense spruce-birch woods before finally saying good-bye to the pond. The forest becomes more open and stays that way until we reach a hillside that the trail follows; below us is a long beaver pond. Waypoint 18 is at a large aspen tree that has been gnawed upon by beaver that had to come all the way up the hill to have at it. Judy cannot get her arms around the tree, and so we figure the Pleistocene beaver, the so-called giant beaver, an animal that stood 4 feet tall and was 8 feet long, really never went extinct. They are here, thriving around Carlson Pond, and woe to the logger who messes with their trees.

Nineteen: Active Logging

Going past more beaver downed aspen trees we head downhill to a sign that warns of active logging in the area. We wonder if it's logging by human or giant beaver. The sign says to stay 200 feet away from logging machinery, and again it's not clear if that means beaver teeth, flat tails, or motorized logging equipment.

From this spot we can see the beaver pond below with the trees close to the trail marked with red and blue flags and red paint. The trail then descends into a low-lying area near the edge of the pond where there are lots of alder and elderberry with a few really big aspen trees (beaver food).

Coming to the edge of the pond we find more big aspen and big beaver chews. We have a nice view down the pond thanks to the efforts of these four-legged engineers. This is waypoint 19.

Twenty: Clear Cut and Reclamation

Leaving the pond it is a short walk to a clear cut area that is currently being logged; the clear cut is open and desolate with everything gone. However, even though the logging has only been going on this summer or last, Judy finds lots of balsam poplar sprouting; they must act like aspen and quickly reseed themselves. Near the edge of the cut area, many trees have been blown over. They have lost the support of their neighboring trees and are now in the direct line of winds that they can't stand up to.

We walk along the edge of the clear cut over some boardwalked sections, then up a low hill. As we walk along I tell Judy that it kind of befuddles me how so many people perceive mining as being so detrimental to the environment and then turn a blind eye to this kind of mess. There is no cleanup or reclamation going on here. If this were a mine the DNR, Sierra Club, and other environmentalists would be drawn here like bees to honey.

The trail through this area is not easy to follow, but after the end of the clear cut waypoint 20 is at a planked-over area in an alder swamp with a small beaver pond to the left.

Twenty-One: Arrowhead Trail and Red Pines

Crossing over another boardwalked section the trail moves in and out of an ash, aspen, spruce, birch, and alder forest while paralleling Carlson Creek, which looks swampy and alder-filled. Entering an area of 45 year old red pines with some balsam fir we descend to Carlson Creek and waypoint 21, the Arrowhead Trail or County Road 16.

Twenty-Two: Another New Dam and a Rerouted Creek

Crossing the Arrowhead Trail we head down to the creek then along its edge to another fairly new beaver pond made by damming Carlson Creek for the fourth or fifth time. This has formed new "lake front property," and the creek no longer follows the course shown on the map. Waypoint 22 is at the new, improved beaver dam.

Twenty-Three: Beaver Runways, Huge Dam, West Carlson Pond Campsite, and Sons and Daughters of the Giant Beaver

The footpath continues around the edge of the pond and follows along its opposite side before crossing a planked area with a new beaver dam at the end. Here we find numerous beaver runways into the pond; these are dragging sites where the beaver are literally dragging the wood down to the water's edge. Some pretty impressive logging operations, for some of the larger trees got hung up on the vegetation as the beaver attempted to move them.

From the runways the trail follows along the pond edge to a new beaver lodge at the north end of the pond and the West Carlson Pond campsite. I assume campers share this spot with the beaver–first come first served! There are two huge, "can't get your arms around" aspen that the beavers have gnawed and tried to move! The dam here is at least six feet tall so now I really do believe the giant beavers survived and their sons and daughters have moved here from further upstream. The giant beavers were nocturnal creatures who worked and hunted in the dark, so you won't catch me camping here at waypoint 23!

Twenty-Four: Large Spruce and Alder Swamps

Walking through a stand of young, beaver-chewed aspen we enter an alder swamp before leaving the pond area and heading into a birch-dominated woods with aspen and spruce. Some of the spruce trees are very big. Waypoint 23 is at a planked area in an alder swamp.

Twenty-Five: Yellow Leaf Trail

The trail heads uphill through an area of blown down balsam. The aspen and birch trees on the hillside are golden yellow and their leaves cover the trail, so walking along is like following the yellow brick road. The rock outcropping here is Speed Bump Gabbro with the "speed bumps" composed of clumps of pyroxene.

From here it is downhill, over wooden steps and across a planked area, before again heading uphill to walk along a narrow ridge that separates Carlson Creek from a small tributary. From the ridge it is downhill to boulder-filled Carlson Creek and this is waypoint 25. Ash and fir trees line the creek banks, and hazel is the dominant underbrush. The large boulders in the creek represent a time long ago when the creek was as fast and powerful as the giant beaver who really did live by its banks.

Twenty-Six: Bridge Across Carlson Creek

From waypoint 25 we have a short walk to the bridge across Carlson Creek and the end of the hike. The hiking trail continues on to the Jackson Lake

Road while a spur trail, to the right, goes uphill over wooden steps to the parking lot on the Arrowhead Trail.

I found Tom Lake Road fascinating with the white pines, active beaver, Rove Formation and the monzonite, I also liked the rock monster and the beaver runways along Carlson Creek. Judy thinks Carlson Pond and Creek with their variety of plants along with enterprising beaver were the walk highlights. Neither of us would vote for the clear cut or active logging area.

Superior Hiking Trail
Walk 31: Hellacious Overlook, Isle Royale, and Moose

Walk Logistics

Start: Arrowhead Trail (Cook County Road 16)

Getting There:

Take Highway 61 north to Hovland. Turn left onto the Arrowhead Trail (Cook County Road 16) and follow this for 3.3 miles to the parking lot on the right.

End: Jackson Lake Road

Getting There: Take Highway 61 to Hovland. Turn left onto the Arrowhead Trail (Cook County Road 16) and follow this 4.5 miles to the Jackson Lake Road. Turn right onto the Jackson Lake Road, and it is 3.1 miles to the parking lot on the left side of the road.

Date Walked: October 4th, 2004   **Walk Distance:** 4.7 miles

Worth a Longer Look:
Microclimate and Lake Views: 6   Wow Spot: 10
Little Cedar Overlook: 9   Hellacious Overlook: 13

Waypoint-to-Waypoint

One: Parking Lot

It's a cold blustery day on the Arrowhead Trail. Yellow and orange leaves swirl around us as we listen to the Minnesota Public Radio weatherman tell us we will have sunshine, wind, and a high temperature of 63 degrees to look forward to. Right now, at nine in the morning, it is 38 degrees and we saw snow on passing cars as we drove north.

Waypoint 1 is at the Superior Hiking Trail sign in the small pull-off adjacent to the Arrowhead Trail. With our backpacks and three dogs we seem to be objects of great curiosity for the logging truck drivers as they race by.

Two: Carlson Creek

From the parking lot we walk downhill over wooden steps through an aspen forest to the bridge across Carlson Creek, which is waypoint 2. A hiking trail sign here reminds us of tree branches in late fall because it has a dusting of

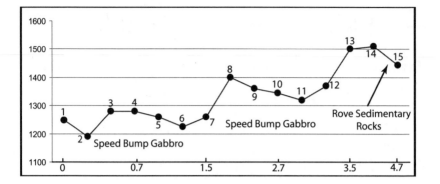

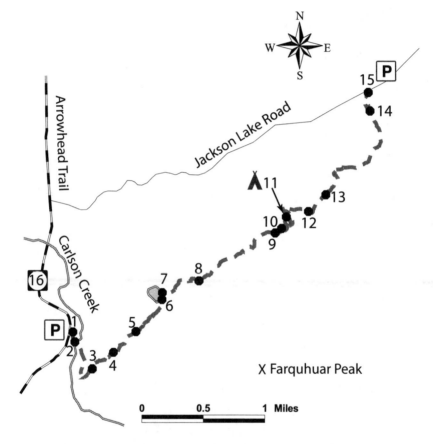

snow on it–"flocked" as some would say. This a new expression for me: I won't even dwell on what my first thoughts are as Judy utters those words.

Brrr, the snow makes us feel colder, but the white on the green and yellow is kind of pretty. Both of us hope it will warm up quickly as we walk along.

Three: Speed Bumps and Farquhuar Peak

The trail follows Carlson Creek for a short distance before turning away to head uphill past some pretty big aspen to an *outcrop* of *ophitic* Speed Bump *Gabbro*, which is part of the *Pigeon River Intrusive Complex*. The gabbro has a lumpy weathered texture, and there are some kibbles and bits (*diabase weathering*) on the trail. Judy calls the lumpy texture of this rock "speed bumps," and that's how this rock unit got its name.

We have a short, steep climb to the hilltop (waypoint 3), from which we have a nice view of Lake Superior, Isle Royale (some 25 miles distant), and Farquhuar Peak, the high hill to the southeast (1254 feet); the Carlson Creek Valley is below us. The outcrop is surrounded by aspens along with the red leaves and berries of the staghorn sumac. Moose tracks are all around the outcrop, and Judy wonders whether they stop here for the view. She says she notices that Sammy often races to the edge of some escarpment or cliff then stops to peer out. Does she take in the view? Or is it just a place to stop and sniff the new smells blowing up the ridge?

As we hike up this section we notice lots of sun-loving species of plants, including *Juneberries* and *honeysuckle*

Four: Island Illusions

It's on over Speed Bump Gabbro with views of Lake Superior and the North Shore landscape to a great view of Isle Royale through a notch in the hills ahead of us; this spot is waypoint 4.

The clouds reflecting off the lake create the illusion of islands on the water— large, small, and floating. There are white pines through this section along with pin cherry trees and *blueberries*. Abundant moose sign continues.

Judy dreams of spending a warm August morning at this spot contemplating the illusionary factors of sky and lake while munching on blueberries and watching for moose.

Five: Boulder seats

Continuing over massive and Speed Bump Gabbro we travel through a mixed forest with white pine and views similar to those at waypoint 4. In the Carlson Creek Valley we see grassy meadows that turn out to be farm fields. Pass over a *dike* composed of *Half-Way Rock* (diorite) with red clover blooming around it and viburnum growing on top of it. Viburnum usually likes south-facing slopes in an open habitat. Another note on this shrub is that it is much broader and taller than honeysuckle, yet it occupies a similar habitat. C*orydalis* leaves dot the outcrop.

From the dike of Half-Way Rock it's back into Speed Bump Gabbro with the trail passing a *glacial erratic* of gabbro with large *pyroxene* crystals that look like lumps of coal, before coming to an open outcrop of gabbro that has large *boulders* sitting around it. These make very nice seats and represent waypoint 5.

Six: Microclimates and Yellow Mustard (13)

Walking on we cross outcrops of Speed Bump Gabbro in various stages of weathering from the normal speed bumps to kibbles and bits. From the outcrops we have views of Lake Superior, Farquhuar Peak, and the rolling landscape. There are lots of yellow mustard plants along here (not the invasive ones) and several large white pine.

The trail heads uphill, with great open views of the lake and landscape, as it passes some nice white pine, to an outcrop of Speed Bump Gabbro. Below are open fields and a farm. The trail continues over numerous outcrops of gabbro before descending to a pond with a grassy marsh on three sides of it. Waypoint 13 is at the pond, which appears to have a climate all unto itself– we name it Little Siberia. There is snow on the ground, it is dark and gloomy, and a cold wind whips around us causing a frantic search for sweaters and fleece. At the last waypoint it was warm and sunny–very strange happenings here, very strange indeed!.

Seven: The Moose

Leaving Little Siberia the trail goes around the end of the pond and up a hillside covered in dense fir trees to a nice, warm sunny overlook. This is followed by a second overlook of the pond and grassy marsh, and here we find a really strange looking rock; one with large white feldspar crystals set in a fine, dark matrix. The feldspars look like paint streaks and this is waypoint 7.

Judy and I are debating what to call this rock when she nudges me rather hard and points toward the marsh. Standing at the edge of the grassy area, a few feet out from the trees, is a big bull moose. He stands in full view and stares in our direction. I tell Judy what an awkward looking creature he is– long spindly legs, a prominent hump behind the shoulders, and a large rack of antlers that make him look top heavy.

Having seen and heard enough of us (more likely it was something in the trees), the moose flicks his head high into the air, snorts, turns, and, to prove my description wrong, vanishes into a thick knot of trees with amazing grace.

Eight: Spruce Budworm

The trail continues uphill into an area that has had a large outbreak of spruce budworm in the past. We find lots of down, dead, and broken balsam strewn about the forest floor. It appears the budworm killed the trees and storm winds then blew them down, breaking many in half or in thirds or even in fourths! Lots of young balsam and aspen are growing up throughout this thicket of branches, stumps, and half or quarter trees. Continuing uphill, over more Speed Bump Gabbro, some cut by *pegmatite* veins of *plagioclase feldspar* and pyroxene, we come to another area of budworm devastation. Waypoint 8 is in the midst of this devastation at an outcrop of Speed Bump Gabbro from which there is a nice view of Lake Superior and the North Shore landscape including farms and fields in the Carlson Creek Valley. The lake is a deep blue color and seems to reflect the sky's generally optimistic mood.

It is interesting to look back up the ridge and study the vegetation. Now that the intense green of summer is gone, the shape, texture, and color of the plants is more apparent. For example, on the open ridges, the pinnate leaves of the sumac stand out from the oval Juneberries and the yellow pointed birch. The willows seem so fresh looking with their lanceolate, waxy, still-green leaves.

Nine: Bearberries and Little Cedar Overlook

We enjoy a long walk (0.85 miles) through a nice spruce-aspen forest now that we have left the budworm behind. The trail moves in and out of open areas with nice views ahead and to the right (northeast-southeast). The open areas are underlain by Speed Bump Gabbro. There are *bearberries* and *thimbleberries* through here, as well as patches of snow. Also lots of hazel and mountain maple.

The nice stroll continues and eventually we come to Little Cedar Overlook. This is apparently named for the lone cedar tree growing on an "island" in an old beaver pond that is now mostly a grass meadow some 200 feet below us. Lake Superior is supreme in the distance, and between the little cedar tree and the big lake are orange and yellow hills. The outcrop at the overlook is the "same old thing" cut by pegmatite veins that have pyroxene crystals up to three inches long. The overlook is waypoint 9.

Ten: First Wow Spot

From Little Cedar Overlook it is just a short walk to the first "wow" spot of the day. Expansive views of Lake Superior, Isle Royale, the rolling hilly landscape, and beaver pond and marsh below. As we look over this ridge the yellow aspen and birch leaves appear to be dancing on the wind as they flutter from the trees, but are kept aloft by updrafts along this rocky cliff. Judy believes this section of the trail might become her newest favorite spot, but of course this is what she says on just about every hike–seems like the one she enjoys most is the one she is on.

Eleven: Rolling Rock and Woodland Caribou Campsite

We head downhill, then along the hillside with continuous views to the north and east as we pass a large gabbro boulder perched on the cliff side (tempting as it is please don't try and send it tumbling down). From here we continue downhill to the junction with the spur trail to the Woodland Caribou campsite. Lots of woodland here in the form of spruce, but alas no caribou. This is waypoint 11.

Twelve: Big Boulder Creek

Continuing downhill we come to a creek filled with really large boulders– way too big for the likes of this small creek. So did they come from the hillside above, or were they here before the creek, or both? Lots of *pyrola* leaves here along with *bracken ferns*, native Canada Rye grass, *miterwort*, and *wild ginger*. Waypoint 12 is on the bridge over the creek.

Thirteen: Hellacious Overlook

The trail heads uphill parallel to the creek before turning away to traverse through a wide flat section with outcrops of the "same old thing." From here it is continuously uphill to a sign for Hellacious Overlook followed by a steep ascent over gabbro to a spectacular view, the second and best "wow" spot of the day. From here we can see the whole length of Isle Royale including the lighthouse on the south end of the island and, closer to us, another beaver pond and marsh. Nice view behind us of the hill we just came from and the hilly terrain to the west.

Looking at Isle Royale I tell Judy that in 1664 a French trader by the name of Pierre Bouchard wrote: "In Lake Superior there is a large island about fifty leagues around in which there is a fine mine of red copper; there are also found several places large pieces of this metal in a pure state. They– traders–have told me that they saw an ingot of pure copper which, according to their estimation, weighs 800 lbs. which lay along the shore."

Native Americans called this island Minong and today we call it Isle Royale, the wolf's eye. Located in the northwest corner of Lake Superior the island is 22 miles by boat from Grand Portage. It is a densely forested, wind-lashed wilderness that is 9 miles wide, 45 miles long, and home to moose and wolves. The island was dedicated as a national park in 1931 to "conserve a prime example of north woods wilderness."

The island is a paradise for people who like solitude because there are few visitors. I think this is due largely to the difficult access, a 6-8 hour trip by ferry, or a shorter trip by float plane. Also 98% percent of the island is designated as wilderness; so there are few modern comforts here.

The island's prominent spine, called Greenstone Ridge, follows the Greenstone basalt lava flow, which runs the entire length of the island. The flow gets its name from the abundant green "stains" that form as native copper is altered by weathering to a carbonate mineral called malachite. The greenstone flow is part of the Portage Lake Volcanic Group and has been traced clear across Lake Superior to the Keweenaw Peninsula in Michigan, making it one of the largest lava flows to be found on earth. The flow is over 1500 feet thick and covers more than 3000 square miles.

From 1840 to 1847 the Lake Superior region produced the vast majority of copper mined in the United States, with the last mine on Isle Royale closing in 1890. In prehistoric times, from about 7000 to 3000 years ago, Native Americans, known to archaeologists as "the old copper culture," mined and supplied copper to Indian bands from Maine to Yellowstone, and from the Gulf of Mexico to Quebec. These early Indian miners were a lot like the savvy gold and copper prospectors and hard rock miners of the 19th and early 20th century–they left no stone unturned, and in so doing missed very little. It turns out that every modern copper mine on Isle Royale and the Keweenaw Peninsula had been discovered and worked by these ancient copper miners. It was written in 1873 that the native miners showed "great intelligence... in locating and tracing the veins and in following them up without interruption."

Why this particular overlook is called "hellacious" we do not know. The climb is not hellacious, but for a geologist it is certainly hellacious to keep looking at the same old ophitic gabbro over and over and over–damn hellacious.

Fourteen: Rove Formation and Surprise Rock

It's now downhill and along the hillside with continuing nice views as we pass the Hellacious Overlook sign and continue down into a dominantly aspen forest. There are lots of boulders of Speed Bump Gabbro with gabbro outcrops in the hillside. At the bottom it seems most of the fir trees are down, and alder and ash become the prominent tree species.

From the bottom of the hill it is an easy, but long, walk through an aspen, birch, and spruce forest to an area where we find lots of angular pieces of rock on the trail. These *siltstones* of the *Rove Formation* are massive, very fine-grained, dark gray rocks that break like slate. The flat angular siltstone continues along the trail, but the only actual outcrops are of the "hellacious" Speed Bump Gabbro. The forest is dominated by birch before giving way to balsam woods that have a cleared-out look because of all the death and destruction caused by wind and disease.

Passing a moss covered outcrop to the right of the trail we cross a bouldery creek and walk through an alder swamp to the "whale" of a rock. It's a gabbro outcrop that rises some 6 feet from the forest floor and has trees growing out of it that look like Ahab's harpoons. This is waypoint 14.

Fifteen: Pyrola, Blueberries, and Parking Lot

Continue downhill over Speed Bump Gabbro to the bottom where Judy finds four species of pyrola and lots of blueberries. Dragging her away from the blueberries we move on through an alder and ash swamp to emerge onto the Jackson Lake Road (waypoint 15). Turn right and walk a short distance down the road to the parking lot.

Judy and I agree that Little Siberia, the moose, and Hellacious Overlook were the best parts of this walk.

Superior Hiking Trail
Walk 32: Jackson Lake, Andy Creek, and the Open Campsite

Walk Logistics

Start: Jackson Lake Road

Getting There: Take Highway 61 to Hovland. Turn left onto the Arrowhead Trail (Cook County Road 16) and follow this 4.5 miles to the Jackson Lake Road. Turn right onto the Jackson Lake Road, and it is 3.1 miles to the parking lot on the left side of the road.

End: Otter Lake Road

Getting There: From the Superior Hiking Trail parking lot on the Jackson Lake Road, continue up the road for 5.2 miles to the Otter Lake Road. Turn left (west) and go 2.0 miles down this road, passing a gravel pit on the left before reaching the parking area (left of the road).

Walk Distance: 8.2 miles   **Date Walked:** October 1st, 2004

August 29th, 2005

Worth a Longer Look:

Pyrola Plants: 2	Highest Point: 10
Cuestas and Tortured Basalt: 3	Wildflower Walk: 11
Clubmoss and Yew: 4	Andy Lake Road: 13
Pipsissewa: 6	Andy Lake Campsite: 16
Migmatite: 7	Red Pine Forest: 17

Waypoint-to-Waypoint

One: Night and Day

Second time around is better, at least when it comes to this particular hike. The first time we walked this section was on October 1st, 2004, and by the time we arrived at the small parking lot the sky had clouded over. In fact it was totally grey and the low clouds looked liked they had eaten a ten course dinner and were desperately seeking gastric relief. As we stood in the parking lot, trying to figure out just where the trail started, the clouds found it–the rain began and did not stop for the rest of the day. To top it off the wind came up and the temperature went down. By the end of the hike my fingers were so numb I could no longer write! Even if they had been warm

291

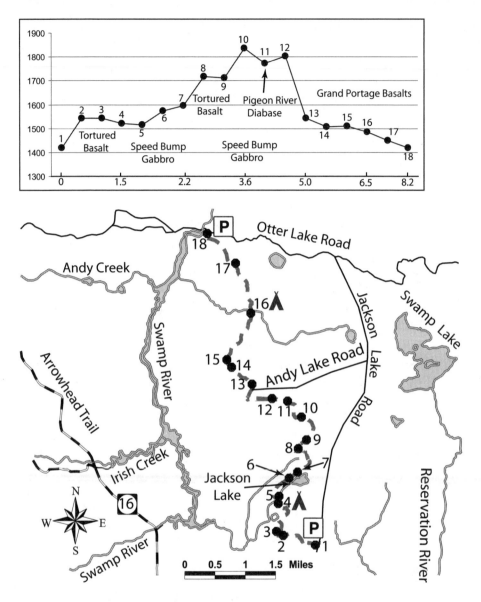

and toasty there was still not a chance in hell of me signing the end of the trail "happy" book.

Second time around is on August 29th 2005, and the difference is like a cafeteria lunch versus a gourmet meal. No rain, no wind, temperature around seventy degrees, and the clouds are big, fluffy stuffed animals, the kind that are perfect for cuddling up with.

The final section of the hiking trail begins at the edge of the Jackson Lake Road some 350 feet south of the parking lot. Waypoint 1 is at the hiking trail sign that marks the trailhead.

Two: Pyrola and Twinflowers

The hike begins with an uphill section that passes through a young balsam poplar forest over a bouldery trail with the rocks made up of *basalt*, *monzonite, diabase, siltstone*, and *shale* that all come from the weathering of the *glacial till* covering the landscape. Pass a really neat boulder of *amygdaloidal basalt* with the *amygdules* filled by pink and white *quartz* (pretty *agates*-to-be).

As we walk along Judy points out a change in the forest: from poplar into a mature maple-birch forest with some spruce and large aspen. The trail, now covered by maple leaves, goes gently up and down and has the look of an old logging road. After the amygdaloidal boulder look for the tiny round-leafed *pyro*la plant, which is only about six inches from side to side and has round, green leaves that spread out, forming a flat circle. This is a pretty plant that is scattered throughout the area with *Canadian mayflower* (wild lily of the valley), and *twinflower*. This section must be a lovely place in late May and early June when all the beautiful green, low to the ground plants are blooming. How different from the three foot tall *goldenrods* and *fireweeds* of late summer!

Waypoint 2 is at an *outcrop* of moss-covered basalt with lath-like *plagioclase feldspar* crystals (up to 1.5 inches long) and lots of red *hematite* along fractures and cracks.

Three: Sandworms and Tortured Basalt

From waypoint 2 the trail is relatively flat as it passes over outcrops of plagioclase-rich basalt. Then comes a short uphill to waypoint 3, an outcrop of *Tortured Basalt*. From the basalt outcrop there are nice views to the south and west of the rolling landscape and a swampy looking stream valley which, aptly, is called the Swamp River Valley. Swamp River or, just as appropriate, Moose Haven, flows slowly toward the junction with the Pigeon River. From here we can see a nice *cuesta* in the distance; in fact there are a whole bunch of these long, sloping hills on the horizon which, with their blunt ends, look to me like sandworms from the planet Dune. Here in Minnesota they are seen as teeth on a saw and are part of what are called the *Sawtooth Mountains*.

The basalt outcrop is crossed by numerous fractures which, with weathering, lead to the formation of flat, angular slab-like pieces that have conchoidal fractures. The name Tortured Basalt comes from the fact that the poor rock ends up looking like it has been given a rough time by planet earth.

The basalt outcrop is surrounded by juniper and its sage-colored berries. The pointed, scratchy needles of the plant can't keep Judy from looking down at the ground cover, which consists of *bearberry*, a waxy looking creeping plant, *blueberries*, and ground cedar, a kind of *clubmoss*. Judy finds a funny-looking cedar tree that is bushy at its base but about three or four feet off the ground it has been chewed back to brown twigs and bark. Above four feet the top is bushy and full of cedar needles. The tree is funny looking because in the winter snow covers the bottom, thus protecting it from the deer that nibble the branches in the middle. They are not tall enough to reach the top branches, so the tree ends up looking like an hourglass.

Four: Clubmoss, Yew, and the Jackson Creek Campsite

Continuing along the edge of the ridge over moss and lichen-covered Tortured Basalt we walk through a maple and birch-dominated forest with large aspen to the start of a short downhill section. The area is carpeted by clubmoss and yew, which is a low-growing evergreen shrub. Just before the start of the downhill there is an outcrop of basalt which contains lath to tabular plagioclase feldspar crystals that make up 25% of the rock.

From the basalt outcrop proceed downhill into a spruce, aspen, maple, and birch forest with some cedar. In places the trail is narrow, closed in, and bouldery. Come to a spruce-cedar swamp with planked over sections (cut logs) before heading uphill into a dark maple, birch, and spruce forest with some large aspen. Pass an outcrop of medium-grained *gabbro* composed of grey to greenish-grey plagioclase feldspar, black *pyroxene*, and some green, glassy *olivine*. This is the Speed Bump Gabbro, which forms part of the *Pigeon River Intrusive Complex*. The gabbro gets its name from the many outcrops that have a lumpy weathered texture (see *diabase weathering*), which Judy thinks look like "speed bumps."

Continue through the same kind of forest over Speed Bump Gabbro boulders and cobbles of basalt, diabase, and yet more gabbro, to the Jackson Creek campsite, which is waypoint 4.

Five: Jackson Creek, Yew, and Balsam

Jackson Creek is just past the campsite with a large gabbro outcrop in the hillside to the left. Both balsam and yew grow here side-by-side. Judy takes this opportunity to remind me of the differences in the color and shape of the needles. She flips the needles over to show me that one has stripes, the other doesn't. The stripes turn out to be the racing stripes on the fir-ari! Just on the other side of the creek we admire a patch of *wintergreen* and a small pool located just upstream.

The wooden logs across Jackson Creek have wire mesh on them, which is a great idea because it gives us footing on what might otherwise be a slippery log. After crossing the creek its uphill to waypoint 5, an outcrop in the trail of Tortured Basalt. To the right is a small beaver pond surrounded by an open grassy area.

Six: Pipsissewa

From waypoint 5 we walk across outcrops of Tortured Basalt as we head up then down a gentle slope to a small creek that is crossed via a large boulder. The forest is maple and birch with some spruce and balsam fir. From the creek it's uphill through a stand of balsam fir followed by gentle ups and downs through a nice birch forest with young maples and some balsam fir. A steep hillside to our left has outcrops of Pigeon River Diabase along it, and boulders from this hillside litter the slope between the trail and the hill. This is followed by an uphill section to an outcrop of Speed Bump Gabbro that weathers a rusty brown color.

From here it is a short walk uphill to another gabbro outcrop (waypoint 6) where the plagioclase feldspar crystals are weathering a chalky white color, which makes them appear to make up more of the rock than they really do. Judy's favorite evergreen is also here, a low ground cover plant called *pipsissewa*. She says she loves its toothed, waxy leaves. Because she hardly ever sees it, she gets pretty excited when it appears–so excited she doesn't even see the gabbro outcrop–imagine that!

Seven: Migmatite or the Roots of a Mountain Range

Continue along the rocky ridge above Jackson Lake over and past outcrops of Speed Bump Gabbro to waypoint 7, a *glacial erratic* of a rock called migmatite. The migmatite has blobby-elliptical areas composed of dark minerals surrounded and cut by white quartz and feldspar. This rock formed deep in the earth's crust by high temperature and pressure metamorphism; it is the kind of rock found in the roots of mountain ranges. This particular "root" probably comes from the Voyageur National Park area where it was part of an ancient mountain range that formed some 2.65 billion years ago when the edge of the North American continent collided with a belt of ocean volcanoes (like those of modern day Indonesia). The eroded remnants of the volcanic belt can today be seen in the area of Tower and Ely, Minnesota.

Eight: Large Maples and the Dark Forest

Just past the migmatite we walk up a short slope to an outcrop of lumpy gabbro and a view of Jackson Lake and the grassy marsh at its north end. Continue on over more lumpy gabbro, with rusty weathering pyroxene and chalky white plagioclase feldspar, through a maple, birch, spruce forest with some really old, big, gnarly maple trees. The spruce is mostly to the right of the trail on the slope down to Jackson Lake.

From here it's downhill past a large white spruce. Overall the forest along this section gives the impression of darkness, which comes from the shade created by the tall maples and the dark color of the bark of both cedars and maples. Pass an outcrop of Tortured Basalt and more yew before heading uphill with a steep final section, including a switchback, over stone steps to a break in slope (flat trail) and waypoint 8. As we climb the steps, Judy points out *blue bead lily*, and *rose-twisted stalk*. Because we are here in August, we get to stop climbing every few steps and eat the blueberries!

Nine: Lots of Gabbro and Lots of Different Trees

Having our fill we continue uphill over numerous outcrops of Speed Bump Gabbro with views of the landscape to the east (right) including Mount Sophie at 1814 feet. Then we follow along the hillside, over outcrops of "you know what" to waypoint 9, a gabbro outcrop with a steep drop-off.. This section isn't very long, but it is kind of magical with everything so soft and mossy and sprucey, and the evergreen leaves of the ground cover plants, like pyrola, pipsissewa, and blueberry, emerging through the mosses. The forest through this section also adds to the magic of the place, for every northern tree we can imagine shows up here.

Ten: Highest Point

The walk along the hillside continues through a spruce, birch, and maple forest with balsam fir, aspen, big yellow birch, and a dark grove of cedars. The outcrops and rocks on the trail are Tortured Basalt. From the cedar grove it's gently uphill where we notice the differences between the mountain maple and sugar maple that grow side-by-side. Beside their size Judy shows me the subtle difference in the shape of the leaves and, at this time of year, the different shades of red and orange they exhibit.

As we near the hilltop there is a large *talus* slope of basalt immediately below the trail, and there are partial views of Swamp Lake in the distance. Continuing on we arrive at waypoint 10, the highest point on the hiking trail at 1829 feet. However, forget about the spectacular view from this "nosebleed" height because we are in the middle of the north woods.

Eleven: Mafic Rock and a Wildflower Walk

From the highest elevation it is a nice, easy, long walk through a maple-dominated forest with some large cedars and spruce to a small stream, which is waypoint 11. Judy thinks this part of the hike would make for an excellent spring wildflower walk and, later in the year, a fall color hike.

At the stream she finds plenty of *jewelweed* and elderberry. Elderberry is a funny shrub because it seems to come to life earlier than anything else in the spring. There are lots of moose tracks here, indicating their interest in the really mafic rock exposed in the creek. Different than the Speed Bump

Gabbro, this rock has a smooth, rich, brown weathering color and is composed of 70-75% pyroxene, olivine, *magnetite*, and *ilmenite* (all dark-colored minerals) and 25-30% grey plagioclase feldspar. We decide that this rock is a *dike*, though exactly which unit it is related to we don't know.

Twelve: Jackson Lake Road

From the creek we walk through the nice forest over more mafic rock before going uphill, over a muddy slope and Tortured Basalt, to the top where we come to a small opening with white pines, mountain ash, and pin cherries. The trail through this section is 5-10 inches deep in maple leaves!

Over smooth weathering basalt we continue along the hillside to waypoint 12, a stand of white pines and a great view to the northeast of the low, swampy landscape and a very straight-looking Jackson Lake Road. A cut log marks the waypoint.

Thirteen: Bagged Dog, Hung Tree, and the Andy Lake Road

Just past waypoint 12 we leave the white pines and enter a maple forest with cedar, birch, and spruce. It is dark in here (even when it is not raining) due to the high, thick maple canopy. A short uphill section is followed by a walk along the hillside to a small opening with views to the west and north; there is an outcrop of Pigeon River Diabase here.

From the opening it is a long walk, generally downhill, over outcrops of *ophitic* Pigeon River Diabase through a mixed forest with cedar becoming more common as we approach the Andy Lake Road (waypoint 13). There is a lot of twinflower, *bunchberry*, and *naked miterwort* in this section. This is the area where, on our first hike, Judy bagged the dog. Rhubarb, the Jack Russell Terrier that has been hiking with us, was shaking so violently in the rain and cold wind Judy was worried she might get hypothermia. So she took a large Ziploc bag, cut four holes in it, put it on the dog, and zip locked it tight. Rhubarb kept it on for the rest of the hike, and her shaking visibly subsided! This was also the place where Judy almost got crowned–permanently. A large maple tree snapped in half right above the spot where she stopped to jot down a few notes. Talk about angels or fairy godmothers, the snapped off half got hung up in a big spruce tree, and there it dangled, some twenty feet above Judy's head! The noise when it broke was something else–sudden, loud, and very scary–CRACK!

Just before reaching the Andy Lake Road there is a large glacial erratic of feldspar crystal basalt and, at the road, a large pile of rock composed of angular pieces of amygdaloidal basalt. These rocks are part of what is locally referred to as the Grand Portage Basalts, a series of lava flows that extend from the Canadian Border down to Hovland. The amygdules are filled by quartz, *calcite*, and a white *zeolite*. White pines and balsam poplar line the road, and *hemp nettle* and *raspberries* grow in the open areas. Later we find out the Andy Lake Road dead ends at the Jackson Lake Road. There is a gate across the Andy Lake Road at the junction of the two, along with a sign saying that hikers may walk on this road to reach the hiking trail.

Fourteen: Ground Moraine and Moose Rubs

Crossing the road the trail becomes closed in on both sides by mountain maple, elderberry, and hazel with a few larger spruce trees rising above the green world. Pass a large glacial erratic of basalt as the trail continues through a cutover area with the landscape made up of deposits of glacial till called *ground moraine*. The trail remains pretty much closed in all the way to a grove of cedar trees (waypoint 14) with some large aspens. The small trees in the grove have part of their bark missing due to friendly moose rubbing the velvet off their horns. *Wild ginger, miterwort, dwarf enchanter's nightshade, dewberry*, and *starflower* are abundant through this section.

Fifteen: Creeks and Interrupted Ferns

Passing through a low, swampy area we enter into another cedar grove where there are two small creeks with plank bridges across them (waypoint 15). The many boulders in the creeks are basalt; interrupted ferns are abundant here.

Sixteen: Sun-Loving Plants, Star Watching, and the Andy Creek Campsite

Continuing in and out of cedar swamps and through cutover areas we enter a more recent cutover just past a large glacial erratic of diabase. The plants in the open area are all sun-loving, dry-foot species, which is typical of clear cuts. Asters, *goldenrod*, raspberries, and aspen trees have moved into the clear cut in full force.

From here we pass through an area where some large aspen and balsam poplar have been spared the chainsaw before coming to a large, open grassy area full of goldenrod and raspberries. Piles of old slash dot the landscape, and these have been overgrown by green plants. From here it is a short walk to the Andy Creek campsite and waypoint 16. The campsite is in the open and is surrounded by *honeysuckle* and *dogbane*. This campsite is reported to be a favorite spot because it provides a 360 degree view of the night sky. On a clear evening, sitting beside a nice fire, campers can watch the constellations rise and set and count how many moose, canoes, bears, fishers, and other Ojibwe constellations can be seen!

Seventeen: Andy Creek, Red Pines, and Bumblebees

Leaving the campsite we walk over amygdaloidal basalt boulders before crossing Andy Creek with its wire-mesh bridge and large cedar tree. From here we walk through a wet, grassy area with alders, black spruce, and fir over numerous planked sections into a planted red pine forest. The red pines line the trail with star moss and *sphagnum moss* abundant below them. Passing an open area, we travel through a grove of red pine and spruce, before entering yet another open area where there is a ton of goldenrod and even more bees. The buzz of the bumblebees is clearly audible, and the motion of their yellow and orange bodies moving from flower to flower is mesmerizing.

From bumblebee corner it's an easy walk through the grassy cutover to a sharp bend in the trail and a couple of Superior Hiking Trail signs indicating the trail direction. This is waypoint 17.

Eighteen: Long Grassy Walk and the Otter Lake Road

From the signs we have a long walk (0.77 miles) to the Otter Lake Road and the parking lot. The walk follows what is clearly an old, grass-covered logging road, which is lined on both sides by tall grass that overhangs the trail–not a fun place when the grass is wet.

At the parking lot we find a "happy" book provided by the Superior Hiking Trail Association to record thoughts or impressions of the hike and/or of the whole trail (which we have just finished walking). There are not nearly the number of entries in this "happy" book as those we have seen further south; this could be because the number of walkers up this far north are fewer, or fewer of them are happy!

Not a bad final walk, and the last bit through the cutover is easy going (if you are not freezing, soaking wet, and numb). On the way back to the Jackson Lake Road parking lot look for a large glacial erratic with a marker on it (right hand side of the road). This was placed here in remembrance of those killed in an airplane crash that occurred just west of here in 1971. The plane vanished and was not discovered until 1983 during scouting trips to plan the route of the Superior Hiking Trail.

Glossary I:
Geological Terms and/or Features

Aa Lava Flow: Aa is one of the two kinds of lava associated with the subaerial part of shield volcanoes. The word is Polynesian for "lava you can not walk on in bare feet" (if you do you say aa a lot). This kind of basalt lava has a jagged and rubbly flow top composed of pieces of angular lava. Such flow tops form because aa lava is very sticky (viscous) and thus flows so slowly it piles up at its front in much the same manner a carpet does when slowly pushed into a wall. This leads to a rough, angular, broken surface. Aa lava flows can also be vesicular, and these gas cavities tend to be contorted indicating volcanic gas was escaping as the lava flow slowly moved over the ground. Aa is much less common along the Superior Hiking Trail than its more fluid relative Pahoehoe lava.

Agate (Lake Superior): A translucent, cryptocrystalline variety of quartz (chert) characterized by a variety of colors arranged either in alternating bands or stripes, irregular clouds, or swirls. Agates occur as the filling of gas cavities (vesicles) in volcanic rocks, dominantly basalt.

Agate Flow: The name given to basalt lava flows along the Superior Hiking Trail that have large (pea to half-dollar size) amygdules filled by jasper, chert, and/or banded chert. Some of the amygdules have hollow centers with edges lined by tiny quartz crystals. In places, these flows weather to knobby, round, and/or irregular gravel-like pieces and so, when walking over these flows, it is fun to search through the "gravel" for agates.

Amygdaloidal: General name for a volcanic rock that contains numerous amygdules.

Amygdule (Greek for almond-shaped): Gas cavities (vesicles) in a lava flow that have been filled by one or more minerals. The holes vary in size from pinheads to the rare watermelon-sized one.

Anorthosite: A rare, coarse-grained igneous rock composed of more than 85% plagioclase feldspar; other minor constituents are apatite, magnetite, ilmenite, olivine, and pyroxene. Most anorthosites are older than 1 billion years; they are also found in the outer crust of the moon (which is why they are often called moon rocks). The origin of these unusual rocks remains controversial. One of the more common explanations is that anorthosite forms in large cooling and crystallizing bodies of hot molten rock (magma chambers) that have the overall composition of basalt. As the magma cools, plagioclase feldspar crystals form. These have a specific gravity (density) that is less than the magma they crystallized from, about 2.76 compared to 3.15. Being lighter than the magma, the feldspar rises or floats to the top of the magma chamber where it collects to form a solid layer of almost pure plagioclase. Later intrusions (like the Beaver River Diabase) can easily disrupt and fragment this layer, picking up pieces (xenoliths) of anorthosite on the way toward the earth's surface. The anorthosite found along the Superior Hiking Trail occurs as inclusions or xenoliths in the Beaver River Diabase.

Aphanitic: A term that means the minerals in a rock are too small to be seen without using a magnifying glass or jewelers loupe.

Argillite: A compact rock derived from the mild metamorphism of mudstone or shale. Argillite is more highly compacted then either of these, but it lacks the planar or thin sheet-like layering of slate.

Banded Gneiss: A metamorphic rock composed of alternating bands or layers of dark (pyroxene, biotite) and light (quartz, feldspar) minerals. The bands vary from less than 1/8 inch wide up to more than a foot; they form due to segregation of light and dark minerals under conditions of high temperature and pressure.

Basalt: A dark-colored (usually dark grey, dark green, or black), extrusive (lava flow) volcanic rock. Minerals commonly found in basalt include plagioclase feldspar, pyroxene, and, less commonly, olivine. Minor minerals are ilmenite and magnetite. Basalt is the most common volcanic rock on earth with most of the oceanic crust (ocean floor) composed of this material.

Beaver Bay Igneous Complex: A series of roughly contemporaneous sills, dikes, and irregularly shaped intrusive masses that are dominantly diabase to gabbro in grain-size (same chemistry and mineralogy). Minor rock types include monzonite and quartz monzonite. These igneous intrusive rocks occur along the North Shore of Lake Superior between Gooseberry Falls State Park and Grand Marais, and can be traced inland for 15-25 miles. These rocks are related to the 1.1 billion year old Mid-Continent Rift and represent magma chambers to, and feeders for, some of the basalt lava flows of the North Shore Volcanic Group.

Beaver River Diabase: This is the most common intrusive rock in the Beaver Bay Igneous Complex. It occurs as sills, dikes, and sheet-like masses from south of Beaver Bay all the way to Grand Marais. These dark rocks are the intrusive equivalents of basalt and are commonly ophitic. They are dominantly fine-grained, but medium-grained varieties also occur; these typically represent slower cooled centers of large dikes/sills or sheet-like intrusive masses. A distinguishing characteristic of this unit is the small to large, round to angular xenoliths of anorthosite and basalt that are found throughout it (also see diabase).

Bedrock: The solid rock that underlies soil, glacial deposits, gravel, and/or other superficial material. Rock that is part of the crust of the earth.

Bird Droppings Basalt: A basalt lava flow with large, tabular to lath-shaped, plagioclase feldspar crystals that make the rock look like a basalt lava flow in a penguin rookery! The feldspar crystals, or bird droppings, compose 15-50% of the rock and are up to 2 inches long. In places, the crystals have been weathered out leaving lath-like or tabular holes in the lava flow. The flow also contains chert-filled amygdules that range from pinhead to quarter-size.

Boulder: A rock fragment greater than 10 inches in diameter (about the size of a volley ball). Typically somewhat rounded as the result of glacial or river transport.

Calcite: Composed of calcium carbonate ($CaCo_3$), this is a common mineral found in amygdules, and it is the main constituent of limestone. Calcite is commonly white or gray, fizzes in dilute hydrochloric acid, and forms rhombohedral-shaped crystals.

Chatter Marks: Wedge-shaped indentations in bedrock formed by boulders in glacial ice gouging or banging against the rock.

Chert: Either a hard, dense cryptocrystalline (crypto meaning hidden) sedimentary rock or a filling in an amygdule. Chert is composed of quartz crystals that are too small to be seen without the aid of a microscope. Typically, chert has a conchoidal fracture (cracks like glass creating smooth, spoon shaped surfaces). Usually white or cream-colored, though it can be black (flint) and red (jasper).

Chlorite: A soft, dark green, iron-magnesium silicate mineral that is a common alteration product of pyroxene and amphibole; also occurs as amygdaloidal fillings.

Cobble: A rock fragment between 3-10 inches in diameter; the fragment is typically rounded or abraded as the result of glacial and/or water transport.

Columnar Joints: See cooling joints.

Cooling Joints: A type of fracture pattern resulting from the thermal contraction of hot volcanic, or near-surface intrusive rocks as they cool and crystallize. Commonly seen as evenly spaced, elongate, pentagonal or hexagonal columns oriented perpendicular to the cooling surface. Columnar jointing is common in all compositions of lava flows, although it is generally best developed in mafic (basalt) lava flows; it also occurs in diabase sills and dikes. Classic examples of cooling joints are Devil's Post Pile in California and Devil's Tower in Wyoming.

Creep: The gradual down slope movement of regolith (soil, sediment, rock debris, and mineral grains) due to the freezing and thawing of the ground. In colder climates the upper part of the ground freezes during winter only to thaw again in the spring. Because water increases in volume by 9.2% when it freezes, the water-saturated soil and underlying rock expand outward perpendicular to the slope they are on. When this material thaws, gravity pulls the material back down vertically and thus a tiny bit down slope. Imperceptible to us, over a long period of time creep causes fences, walls, foundations, grave stones, and trees on hillsides to tilt or actually move down slope.

Cross-bedding: Beds or layers in a rock that tilt at an angle to the original horizontal surface upon which the sediment accumulated. Cross beds form during deposition of sediment (sand-silt) from changing river or ocean currents and are common in deltas, gravel bars, and beach deposits.

Crow Creek Lava Flows: The name given to basalt lava flows exposed along the cliff walls seen from the Crow Creek bridge. Individual flows are easy to identify as they have massive centers and bases, and very amygdaloidal tops that are speckled white to cream-colored from the minerals filling the gas cavities. The amygdaloidal tops weather more rapidly than the massive centers and thus have a "punky" look to them.

The top 2-3 feet of the cliffs exhibit narrow saucer-shaped to horizontal fractures that form by a process called unloading or exfoliation. Great examples of this are Half Dome in Yosemite, Stone Mountain in Georgia, and the cliff faces along the Split Rock River. The ones developed at Crow Creek are poor cousins to these others.

The vertical cracks in the cliffs form by frost wedging along hexagonal cooling joints. The two processes, unloading and frost wedging, produce the blocky pieces of Crow Creek Lava seen on the trail.

Cuesta: An asymmetric ridge with a long, gentle slope on one side (this parallels the tilt or dip of the surrounding or underlying strata) and a steep cliff-like or blunt-nose-shaped face on the other side formed by frost wedging and glacial plucking. The resultant hill ends up looking like one of the teeth on an old wood saw. Examples of cuestas along the North Shore are Oberg Mountain and Leveaux Mountain.

Debris Flow: A dense, cohesive, flowing mixture of sediment, water, and commonly organic debris. The sediment ranges in size from mud to boulders and makes up >50% of the volume of the flow. Debris flows generally move down slope in laminar fashion (not turbulent) due to the force of gravity. Debris flows generated at volcanoes are commonly referred to as lahars. Deposits of debris flows are massive and composed of poorly sorted, fragmental rocks. The fragments are usually of mixed lithologies and vary from house-size to penny-size.

Delta: A fan-shaped deposit at the mouth of a river formed by deposition of sediment (pebbles, sand, and silt) carried by the river. Deposition occurs when the river flows into a larger body of water (lake or the sea) and the velocity of the water dramatically decreases; the water loses its power and the sediment it is carrying falls out.

Diabase: A dark, igneous intrusive rock formed from hot, molten magma that never quite reached the earth's surface. Instead the magma is injected along existing rock contacts and cools below ground, more slowly than if it had flowed onto the surface. A diabase thus forms the middle part of a triumvirate with deeper gabbro and shallower basalt. See diabase formation.

Diabase Formation: Diabase, basalt, and gabbro have similar mineralogy and chemistry, but basalt is a lava flow and cools quickly so it has smaller crystals and a finer grain size; its crystals are visible only with a microscope. Gabbro is a deep intrusion and cools slowly so it has larger crystals and a coarser grain size; its crystals are easily seen with the naked eye. Diabase is a shallow intrusion that cools slower than a lava flow and faster than a deep intrusion; the crystals are between basalt and gabbro in size and can be seen with a magnifying glass. So, like good old basalt and hardy gabbro, diabase is made up of grey to greenish-gray plagioclase feldspar, and a black to greenish-black kind of pyroxene called augite, with or without a little bit of glassy green olivine and black, metallic magnetite and/or ilmenite. "Crossing over" is a good name for this middle rock because it represents a change from deep gabbro to basalt lava and most likely represents direct feeders for surface lava flows.

Diabase Weathering: What gives ophitic diabase, gabbro, and the few ophitic basalt lava flows along the Superior Hiking Trail their character? It's the different looks they take on as they weather or break apart. There is: "smooth and even," "lumpy," "crumbles" and its friends–"kibbles and bits." This last rock material is the size and shape of dry dog food and gives the trail a "gravelly" look and feel. All these types of diabase weathering can be seen along the Superior Hiking Trail.

Dike: A tabular-shaped igneous intrusion that cuts across layers (bedding, flow contacts, etc.) in the country or intruded rock.

Epidote: A soft calcium-iron-aluminum silicate mineral with an apple green color. Epidote is a common mineral in amygdules.

Estuary: An estuary is a "drowned river mouth." These are common along the east coast of the United States with Chesapeake Bay and Delaware Bay being good examples. The Split Rock River estuary is 0.5 miles long and filled by alder thickets. The estuary is the result of the river downcutting through the basalt and rhyolite lavas at the end of the last Ice Age, some 7000 years ago. From that time on, the level of the water in the lake rose and flooded the mouth of the river. Since then the lake has managed to remain high enough to maintain the estuary.

Exfoliation or Unloading Fractures: The process by which horizontal sheets, plates, concentric shells, or pieces of rock, from less than one inch to several feet in thickness, are successively spalled or stripped from the surface of an exposed rock mass. The rock mass ends up with a saucer or onion skin appearance. Exfoliation is the result of differential stresses within the rock, often caused by slight pressure differences between the exposed rock at the surface and the rock lying just below the surface (more pressure on it). This unloading causes expansion and splitting of the rock forming horizontal fractures. These features are most common in rhyolites and granites.

Fault: A fracture or crack along which there has been displacement of one side relative to the other, movement is parallel to the fracture or crack

Flint: A dark grey or black variety of chert.

Flood Plain: The flat part of a river valley that is covered by water when the river overflows its banks.

Flow Banding: Layering in a rhyolite lava that results from shearing of viscous lava during flow. Flow bands are often contorted and folded and are commonly represented by color variations, which are due to differences in mineral content, vesicularity of the layers or alternating layers of volcanic glass (dark) and spherulites (light-colored spots).

Frost-Wedged: See frost wedging

Frost Wedging: This is a process by which water fills fractures and cracks in the rock, freezes, and expands by as much as 10%. This causes the cracks or fractures to enlarge just a tiny bit, and, after hundreds or thousands of freeze-thaw cycles the rock breaks into angular fragments. These fragments then slide, roll, or fall to the bottom of a cliff or hill to produce piles of rock debris called talus.

Gabbro: A dark-colored igneous intrusive rock that, mineralogically and chemically, is the equivalent of basalt and diabase. Gabbro has a coarser grain-size than either basalt or diabase because of slower cooling. See diabase formation.

Gabbro, 3M: A brown-weathering, medium-grained igneous intrusive rock containing more dark minerals (about 55% pyroxene and 5-10% olivine) than normal gabbro (about 40-50% dark minerals). This rock underlies Mystery Mountain and thus its 3M name: Mafic Mystery Mountain Gabbro.

Glacial Erratic: Large boulders (house-size to end table-size) carried in glacial ice and left behind when the ice melts away. These are the "how did that get there" rocks– large rocks sitting on hills, in the middle of swamps, in open fields, or in thick woods. The boulders may have been carried for hundreds of miles, or they may be from just down the road.

Glacial Lake Duluth: This meltwater lake formed about 11,000 years ago when the Laurentide Ice Sheet melted back over the southern and southeastern edge of the Lake Superior Basin. Meltwater became trapped between the edge of the ice sheet and the edge of the basin. This lake was smaller but deeper than present day Lake Superior with shore lines at elevations of 1,000 to 1,100 feet (today's Lake Superior is at about 600 feet). Glacial Lake Duluth drained to the south down the Brule River (in Wisconsin) and the St. Croix Valley into the Mississippi River. The lake lasted until the ice sheet melted back over Sault Ste. Marie and uncovered a topographically lower area, which allowed the lake to drain to the east. This led to catastrophic floods down what today is the St. Mary's River.

Glacial Plucking: A process whereby meltwater at the base of glacial ice (formed from pressure melting) seeps into broken and fractured rock and freezes solid. In doing so the frozen water attaches the broken rock firmly to the bottom of the glacier. As the ice flows forward the stuck piece of rock is pulled or peeled off the bedrock as easily as a tooth is pulled by attaching it by a string to a doorknob then slamming the door shut. This process, over time, creates small and large basins as well as whalebacks.

Glacial Striations: Fine parallel scratches or grooves in bedrock formed by rocks embedded in the glacial ice. As the ice flows over the land, the rocks are dragged across the bedrock leaving fine parallel marks behind. From these you can tell in which direction the ice was moving.

Glacial Till: Till is a wonderful Scottish word that means "stiff rocky ground," which is exactly what the hardy northeastern Minnesota farmers found when they tried to dig into it. Deposits of till are composed of sediment and rock deposited directly from the melting ice; in other words the ice melts away and leaves behind a lot of what it carried.

Deposits of till are not layered or bedded, and they are said to be poorly sorted, meaning large and small rocks occur side-by-side. This gives till a much different look than the other kind of glacial deposit—outwash—which forms from sediment carried in the waters that flow away from the front of a melting glacier. Outwash deposits are layered or bedded and relatively well-sorted.

Landforms composed of till are called moraines. There are three kinds of moraines: end, terminal, and ground. Most of the till along the North Shore is part of a ground moraine, a blanket of till that covers the countryside, fills in depressions, and smooths out the landscape.

The red color of the till is due to finely crushed and pulverized bits of sedimentary material that filled in the Lake Superior Basin when volcanic activity came to an end about a billion years ago. These rocks—sandstones, shales, and siltstones—formed what are called "red bed" deposits, assemblages of continental bedded sedimentary rocks that are red or maroon in color because they contain small amounts of the red iron oxide mineral hematite. During the last Ice Age the glaciers found these rocks to their liking, and not only scooped them out of the basin like children scoop seeds out of a pumpkin at Halloween, but in doing so, pulverized them. The final glacial product was red silt-clay-and sand-size particles distributed throughout the till.

Gooseberry Waterfalls: The location and existence of the numerous waterfalls at Gooseberry Falls State Park is due to the nature of the basalt lava flows that underlie the park. The lava flows within the park are 5 to 25 feet thick and have amygdaloidal tops. When these flows formed the flow tops were frothy, much like the foam that develops when warm Pepsi is poured into a glass full of ice cubes. Such tops are easily eroded, leading to the exposure of sparsely amygdaloidal flow centers which, in these particular flows, have well developed vertical, six-sided cooling joints. The river erodes away the frothy flow tops and then works its way down and along the cooling joints to form a series of widely spaced, step-like features that mark the start of a waterfall. The falls, over time, become higher and steeper as water continues to erode down and through the cooling joints.

Granite: One of the most common kinds of igneous intrusive rocks, and a major component of the continental crust. Granite contains at least 20% quartz and has more potassium feldspar than plagioclase feldspar. It is the intrusive equivalent of rhyolite.

Ground Moraine: See glacial till.

Half-Way Rock on Ice: An extrusive volcanic rock so named because it is half-way between rhyolite and basalt in composition and mineralogy. Officially called andesite, after the rocks that make up a good part of the Andes Mountains. The half-way rocks along the Superior Hiking Trail are special half-way rocks similar to ones found in Iceland. They contain more iron than a normal andesite and have been given the name Icelandite.

Hematite: A common iron mineral (Fe_2O_3) that occurs in two distinct forms:

  1) A soft, brick-red earthy variety (common along the hiking trail).

  2) A much harder metallic black variety with platy crystals.

Hornblende: A vitreous, black mineral that forms six-sided to prismatic crystals. It is found in intermediate to felsic igneous rocks and is composed of sodium, calcium, potassium, iron, magnesium, aluminum, and silicate.

Ilmenite: An iron-titanium oxide mineral that can be mined for titanium. A common minor constituent of mafic igneous rocks. It is black, metallic, and forms elongate crystals.

Iron Formation: A sedimentary rock that contains at least 15% iron. The iron can occur as oxide minerals (magnetite and hematite), as carbonate minerals (ankerite and siderite), or as sulfide minerals (pyrite). The main silicate minerals in iron formations are chert and jasper.

Lithophysae: Radial aggregates of fibrous crystals that form around an expanding gas cavity in magma or hot flowing lava. Lithophysae are commonly the result of vapor-phase crystallization within a rhyolitic magma. They should not be confused with spherulites, which are similar-shaped structures formed from devitrification of volcanic glass.

Magnetite: A common iron mineral (Fe_3O_4) that strongly attracts a magnet. Magnetite has a metallic luster, is black in color, forms small octahedral crystals, and is relatively hard (6) on the Moh's scale.

Massive: A term applied to rocks of any origin that are more or less featureless in texture and fabric.

Meander: Pronounced sinuous curves or bends in a river that look much like switchbacks on mountain highways. These form most commonly in rivers that have gentle stream channels flowing across fine-grained sediment and/or glacial till.

Mid-Continent Rift: Some 1.1 billion years ago, when Minnesota was truly the center of the continent, the west got sick and tired of the east and tried to separate, much like

306

Africa and South America did 200 million years ago. Hot molten magma rose upward from deep with the earth, and as it approached the surface, it caused the crust to arch or bow upward, and then split open like an overcooked sausage. A great crack formed, one that spread from the Lake Superior region down what is now the St. Croix River Valley and on through Minnesota, Iowa, and clear to the edge of the continent, which was somewhere in Kansas. This great crack or rift is referred to as the Mid-Continent Rift.

Hot molten rock poured out of this growing crack year after century, lava flow upon lava flow, thicker and thicker until a pile of basalt lava some 2-10 miles deep covered the Lake Superior Region. You would not, however, have needed to strain your neck or use high-powered binoculars to see the top of the lavas, for the rift widened and deepened at about the same rate lava was being extruded. Overall the topography remained pretty flat. The volcanic eruptions went on for about 23 million years and, since lava is about as sticky as wet cement, the greatest amount of lava piled up close to the eruptive source (the rift). The tremendous weight of this rock pile caused the land to sag downward for hundreds and hundreds of feet. This tilted the lavas some 10-20 degrees to the southeast (in Minnesota) and led to the formation of the Lake Superior Basin.

The lavas are dominantly basalt (pahoehoe and aa) with lesser amounts of rhyolite and the half-way rock on ice called Icelandite. Overall, the lavas can be likened to pancake batter spreading out over a hot grill, and this kind of eruption gave rise to stacked pancakes or sheets of lava called plateau or flood basalts.

The eruptions were not continuous, and during quiet periods streams and rivers flowing into the basin carried sediment that blanketed the surface of the flows with sand, silt, and clay. With resumed volcanic activity the sediment was covered up, and eventually became what are called interflow sedimentary rocks (sandstones and siltstones).

Not all of the magma erupted at the surface as lava; much of it remained below ground to form igneous intrusive rocks. Erosion has partly exposed many of these, with the three largest intrusive groups being the Duluth Complex, the Beaver Bay Complex, and the Pigeon River Complex.

After 23 million years rifting came to a halt, probably because the heat source in the earth's crust had expended its energy, and/or because a great continental collision started along what was the east coast. Called the Grenville Orogeny (mountain building event), it produced the ancestral Appalachian Mountains, and possibly the pressure of this collision prevented the rift from continuing to widen. In effect it may have squeezed the rift to death.

The basalts and rhyolites and half-way rocks seen along the Superior Hiking Trail are generally called the North Shore Volcanic Group, and all formed during this rifting event.

Monzonite: A relatively rare igneous intrusive rock that contains no quartz and has just about equal amounts of plagioclase feldspar and potassium feldspar.

Mud Cracks: Irregular fractures in a crudely polygonal pattern that formed by shrinkage of clay, silt, or mud, generally during drying under surface conditions.

Mudflow: A flowing mixture composed of water and mud (clay-and silt-sized sediments) with or without a small percentage of rock pieces. The term should be used exclusively for mud-dominated mass flows, and should not be used as a substitute for the term debris flow. Mudflows are common in both volcanic and non-volcanic environments.

Mudstone: A dark, fine-grained sedimentary rock composed of compacted clay and silt.

North Shore Volcanic Group: The name given to a thick (2-8 mile) sequence of 1.1 billion year old lava flows with minor interflow sedimentary rocks that occurs along the North Shore of Lake Superior from Duluth to Pigeon River. All of the volcanic rocks exposed on the Superior Hiking Trail belong to this group. These rocks range in composition from basalt (most common) through icelandite (half-way rock) to rhyolite. The volcanic rocks were all erupted from the Mid-Continent Rift.

Obsidian: Volcanic glass, typically black in color and of rhyolitic composition. Glass is characterized by conchoidal fractures. It forms from the rapid cooling or quenching of magma or hot lava, leaving no time for individual minerals to nucleate and grow.

Olivine: A vitreous, olive green mineral that is a minor component of gabbro, diabase, and basalt. It is composed of iron, magnesium, and silica.

Ophitic Texture: From the Greek meaning a stone spotted like a serpent, ophitic is a texture seen in mafic igneous rocks (basalt, gabbro, or diabase) in which large pyroxene crystals (augite) enclose much smaller crystals of plagioclase feldspar. The large pyroxene crystals are separated from each other by fine-grained areas of plagioclase feldspar with some olivine and magnetite. This gives the rock a mottled black and gray look. The larger pyroxenes are more resistant to weathering than the intervening feldspar-rich areas and so end up as "raised lumps" throughout the mafic rock. It is this texture that gives many of the diabases, and some of the basalts seen on the trail, their interesting weathering characteristics.

Orthoclase Feldspar: A white or pink potassium feldspar ($KAlSi_3O_8$). Orthoclase is a common rock-forming mineral in granitic rocks.

Outcrop: Bedrock exposed at the earth's surface.

Outwash: Melting glaciers let loose enormous volumes of water that carry away and deposit sedimentary material. Water-deposited glacial sediments are called outwash. Unlike till, outwash is layered (bedded) much like a lasagna, and the pieces of rock found within each layer are said to be sorted, because they are all about the same size.

Landforms created by outwash include:

1) Eskers, which are snake-like ridges of sand and gravel.

2) Kettles, which are small lakes that form at the margins of fast melting glaciers.

3) Kames, which are steep-sided, conical hills that look a lot like giant muffins and are composed of sand and gravel. They form when sediment, deposited from meltwater, fills holes in the stagnant ice at the front of a melting glacier.

OxBows or Cut-Off Meanders: Once a meander forms in a stream the curvature of the meander grows until it becomes so extreme that only a narrow bit of land is left between the two arms of the meander; in other words, a gooseneck forms. In the spring, when the water is high and fast, a stream can erode through the gooseneck, cutting a shorter, straighter channel for itself. The new channel is referred to as a cut-off, and the abandoned meander, because of its curved or horse shoe shape, is referred to as an oxbow. Over time the oxbow is filled in by sediment and vegetation. Cut-offs are important; over the last 176 years the Mississippi River has become 242 miles shorter because of its ability to cut off meanders.

Pahoehoe Lava: Pahoehoe, Polynesian for "lava you can walk on in bare feet," is associated with the subaerial part of shield volcanoes and with plateau lavas. Pahoehoe lava flows are distinctive because, being less viscous than aa, they have a billowy or ropy to shelly upper surface. As pahoehoe lava flows over the ground, the upper part of the flow is air cooled and becomes stickier, or more viscous, than the center part. The hot center then drags or pulls the sticky part, and this action forms either a billowy or curving rope-like surface. At times so much gas is escaping from the lava that it builds up under the sticky top and exerts enough upward force to break the top into shell-like slabs (shelly pahoehoe). Both billowy and ropey pahoehoe lava flows can be seen along the North Shore.

Palisade Rhyolite: A rhyolitic unit exposed from Palisade Head northeast through Tettegouche State Park to Highway 1. See pyroclastic flows and rhyolites for its origin.

Pebble: A rock fragment between 4 and 64 mm in size (about the size of peas to dumplings). Typically rounded during ice or water transport.

Pegmatite: A very coarse-grained igneous rock that typically occurs as dikes or veins. Commonly composed of quartz, feldspar, and biotite.

Phenocrysts: The term refers to large crystals in a much finer-grained rock. Phenocrysts form when lava begins to cool well beneath the surface. Crystals start to form and, as they grow larger, the magma, due to a sudden pressure release, rises rapidly toward the surface where it begins to cool quickly. The end result is large crystals (phenocrysts) in a very fine-grained rock (called a porphyry). This kind of rock occurs as either lava flows or near-surface intrusions.

Pigeon River Intrusive Complex: The term refers to a series of diabase dikes and sills, along with larger gabbroic masses, that have intruded the Rove Formation (sedimentary rocks), the Gunflint Iron Formation, and the rocks of the Beaver Bay Igneous Complex. These rocks outcrop from just south of Hovland to the Canadian border and are responsible for the waterfalls on the Pigeon River.

Pipe Amygdule: Elongate, cylindrical zones of amygdules that extend vertically up through a lava flow ending in a vesicle cylinder. These reflect the rise of gas bubbles through a cooling lava, most commonly basalt. May be caused by the flow of lava over wet ground with the water flashing to steam and rising up through the flow.

Plagioclase Feldspar: This cream to gray-colored mineral is one of the most abundant minerals in the earth's crust and is therefore an important rock-forming mineral. It is composed of sodium, calcium, aluminum, and silica. The ratio of calcium to sodium leads to several different varieties of plagioclase feldspar. Crystals are usually tabular to lath-shaped.

Potassium Feldspar: See orthoclase.

Potholes: Potholes are bowl-shaped depressions "carved" into the bedrock floor of a stream. The flowing water performs this feat by abrading the bedrock, especially when it is moving fast and there is lots of it. It uses sand grains and pebbles as its major grinding and cutting tools. Where there is a combination of a natural depression in the rock (such as a fracture, joint, or gas cavity) and eddies or swirling water, there is an opportunity for sand and pebbles to get into the depression and be rapidly spun around and around by the water. This turns the sand and pebbles into effective drills. Over time the depression grows larger and deeper. In a lot of potholes beautifully polished and rounded pebbles and cobbles can be seen, many of which represent the drill bits that help make the hole.

Pumice: Solidified fragments of cooled, highly vesicular (>60% gas holes) rhyolitic magma or lava generally formed during explosive eruptions. The highly vesicular nature of pumice (looks like Swiss cheese) results from large volumes of gas rapidly expanding within a depressurized magma. The low density of pumice permits it to float on water for extended periods of time. Size is highly variable, though the vast majority is ash-size (dust). Pumice is the main component of explosive volcanic eruptions.

Pyroclastic: From Greek meaning fire-broken, this refers to processes resulting from the explosive fragmentation of a magma or lava. Pyroclastic eruptions occur because magma is much like Pepsi Cola. The plastic pop bottle sitting on the store shelf contains a dark liquid with a cap on it. By looking at it there is no way to tell there is a lot of gas (carbon dioxide) dissolved in the liquid. However, pick the bottle up, gently shake it, and a few small bubbles form. If you shake it vigorously then take the top off, you have a frothing, foaming mess spewing everywhere.

An explosive volcanic eruption is much the same. Magma has a lot of gas dissolved in it and, like the pop, the gas is held in the liquid because of pressure; the bottle cap on the Pepsi and the overlying column of rock on the magma. As magma rises up to shallower levels of the crust, pressure decreases (like gently shaking the bottle), and small gas bubbles begin to form. The higher and faster the magma rises, the quicker and more rapid the gas comes out of solution, much like vigorously shaking the pop. Remove or breach the cap and there is instantaneous pressure release, and the gas froths out, tearing the magma apart and generating an explosive eruption. The torn-apart bits of magma are called pumice,

Pyroclastic Flows and the Devil Track, Kimball Creek, and Palisade Head Rhyolites: The Devil Track, Kimball Creek, and Palisade Head rhyolites are enigmatic units that have characteristics of both lava flows and pyroclastic flow deposits. Though evidence exists for both origins, the widespread distribution of these units (compared to other rhyolites the trail crosses), the lack of flow breccias and vesicles (gas cavities or, in older rocks, amygdules), and the presence of pumice at the base of the Devil Track and Palisade Head rhyolites, and top of the Kimball Creek Rhyolite, is more characteristic of high temperature pyroclastic flow deposits.

Pyroclastic flows are mixtures of pumice, gas, and air that are dense enough to travel over the ground (flow) at high speeds (60 mph up to >300 mph) for great distances (up to 200 miles from source). A large part of the deposit is composed of pumice, which ranges from bread loaf through donut hole to peanut-size with most fragments the size of breadsticks that have been run over several times by a semi-truck (volcanic ash). If the eruption temperature is high enough, the pumice can be so hot on deposition that, in the center of the flow, this material welds or fuses together to form a homogenous

310

glass. The temperatures may actually be hot enough to cause this glass to flow during final cooling. It is thus possible for flow bands and folds to form in this kind of pyroclastic flow.

The only evidence of the pyroclastic origin of such rocks is preserved in the much more rapidly cooled tops and bottoms of the deposit. Though very poorly exposed, this is where relict pumice is found in the Kimball Creek, Palisade Head, and Devil Track rhyolites.

It should be stressed that temperatures high enough to cause this "welding" phenomena and flow folding are far from the norm; most pyroclastic flows retain ample evidence of their origin.

Pyroxene: A common dark-colored mineral found in basalt, diabase, and/or gabbro. Forming four-and eight-sided prismatic crystals, it is composed of iron, magnesium, and silica (Si_2O_8). Pyroxene is another of the rock-forming minerals. It comes in several varieties depending on the iron/magnesium ratio. The most common of these is augite, from the Greek meaning "bright," for its shiny, black crystal faces.

Quartz: Crystalline silica (SiO_2); one of the most common minerals in the earth's crust. Quartz occurs as clear, purple (amethyst), pink (rose), and/or black (smoky) hexagonal-shaped crystals and as irregular masses. It also occurs in microcrystalline form which, depending on color, has been given the names flint (black), chert (cream), and jasper (red). Quartz is the main constituent of Lake Superior agates.

Quartz Monzonite: A common igneous intrusive rock with 10-20% quartz and about equal amounts of plagioclase feldspar and potassium feldspar. Its mineralogy and chemistry are between those of diorite and granite.

Rhyolite Lava Flows: Rhyolite is the extrusive equivalent of granite and the complete opposite of the basalts seen along most of the trail. Where basalt is dark-colored and composed of dark minerals such as pyroxene and olivine, rhyolite is light-colored (pink to gray) and composed of light-colored minerals such as quartz, potassium feldspar, and plagioclase feldspar. The rhyolite lavas seen along the North Shore are the same age as the basalt lavas, but they make up only a small percentage of the rocks the hiking trail crosses. Rhyolite lava is much more viscous than basalt lava, and is erupted at a much lower temperature. The combination of these two factors means rhyolite, as a lava, does not travel far from where it is erupted–0.5 to a few miles at most. In fact, rhyolite is often so viscous it piles up right over the volcanic opening to form inverted bowl-shaped feature called a lava dome. Rhyolite flows are thick, may have cooling joints, spherulites, and flow banding.

River Terrace: A level or step-like surface breaking the continuity of the slope above a river or creek, the terrace represents an old flood plain.

Ripple Marks: Elongate ridges of sand spaced at a uniform distance from each other. Ripples form in shallow water by wave action or currents and are preserved in sedimentary rocks.

Rove Formation: A group of sedimentary rocks that formed between 1.9 and 1.8 billion years ago, at the same time and in the same narrow elongate basin as the iron ore deposits on the Mesabi Iron Range. The Rove Formation is composed dominantly of greywackes, siltstones, shales, and mudstones that formed over a 100 million year time span.

These sedimentary rocks, as a group, go by several different names. Along the North Shore they are called the Rove Formation, on the Mesabi Range they are known as the Virginia Formation, and near Duluth they are the Thompson Formation. In Wisconsin, they become the Tyler Formation, and in Michigan they are the Michigamie Formation. Though they are all the same kind of rock, all the same age, and all deposited in the same environment, they did form in three different basins: the Animikie, Marquette and Huronian. Because of this, and because different people were mapping the different basins, it took geologists some time to realize the rocks were all the same. Since there was no Internet back when these rocks were being mapped and described, they got different names and the names have stuck.

Think back 1.9 billion years ago, back to when the iron formations were forming in warm shallow water off shore from sandy beaches. These beaches were about 30-40 miles from what is now the hiking trail. The iron ore was forming on a continental shelf, which is the submerged part of a continent on the edge of an ocean basin. The east coast of the US is a good modern example, a place with sandy beaches, barrier islands, and warm shallow water.

Seaward of the continental shelf is something called the continental slope, the place where the seafloor begins to dip more steeply and water depth increases. Beyond the continental slope is the continental rise the transition zone between the continental slope and the ocean basin proper, called the abyssal plain. It was on the continental rise and part of the abyssal plain where turbidity currents carried the sediment that ended up forming the rocks of the Rove Formation. In the Animikie Basin these sedimentary rocks vary from about 1000 feet to more than 10,000 feet in thickness, but they never formed a great range of mountains. Instead some quirk of plate tectonics caused the bottom of the basin, the continental rise, slope, and shelf, to subside at about the same rate the sediments were being deposited. So the actual thickness of sediment covering the seafloor was never very great. Most of it was buried soon after it was deposited. This particular process of planet earth, the continuous and slow subsidence of the continental rise and deposition of sediment, went on for tens of millions of years. So, as North America's first supercontinent, which has been named Kenoraland, rifted apart, a basin named the Animikie formed. Layers of iron ore and chert, now known as the Biwabik, Cuyua, and Gunflint Iron Formations, were deposited close to the newly created shore, while the greywackes and siltstones of the Rove, Virginia, and Thomson Formations were deposited in the deeper parts of the ever widening rift.

Sandstone: A sedimentary rock composed of sand-size grains that are most commonly quartz. In the North Shore Volcanic Group, the sand-size grains are dominantly plagioclase feldspar and pyroxene.

Sawtooth Mountains: The name given to prominent hills along the North Shore of Lake Superior from about Tofte to Grand Marais; the hills have long, gentle slopes in the direction of the lake (the way the lava flows dip), and steep cliff-like or blunt nose shapes on the opposite side. This gives the hills the profile of teeth on a wood saw. The hills that make up the Sawtooth Mountains are composed of either Star Wars Porphyry and/or basalt lava flows.

Schist: A medium- to coarse-grained metamorphic rock that exhibits a parallel alignment of platy or prismatic minerals.

Shale: A fine-grained sedimentary rock composed of clay flakes. Shale forms due to lithification (hardening and compaction) of mud.

Sill: A tabular-shaped igneous intrusive rock body that parallels the planar structure (flow contacts, bedding, or layering) of the surrounding rocks.

Silt: A particle finer than sand and coarser than clay

Siltstone: A sedimentary rock composed of silt-size grains of feldspar, quartz, and clay.

Slate: A metamorphosed shale that tends to break into thin planar pieces.

Silver Creek Diabase: The Silver Creek Diabase is an igneous intrusive rock, one geologists call a sill. Take the word sill, add the word diabase, which comes from German and translates into "crossing over," and what you get is a wanna-be-lava flow; magma that did not quite make it to the surface. The Silver Creek Diabase forms a prominent ridge that extends from Silver Cliff on Highway 61 to the headwaters of the Gooseberry River.

Slumps: Slumps are one of the more common forms of "mass wasting," which is defined as the down slope movement of rocks and/or soils, especially soft, loose stuff like clay or silt, under the influence of gravity. Slumps can be identified because the head, or beginning, of the slump has a crescent-shaped scarp. Trees hanging over the edge of the scarp and big cracks in the trail also help. Slumps usually involve several separate blocks which, together, look like giant steps going down a hillside. Each block is composed of unconsolidated material that moves as a single mass but only about as fast as a lazy turtle. The material never goes very far–unless it reaches a river, that is.

The slumping along rivers on the North Shore typically occurs above meanders. The velocity of the flowing water is not uniform around a meander. In meanders the higher velocity water, as well as the more turbulent water, is on the outside of the curve, which, in this case, is the slump side of the stream. This higher velocity water erodes away the glacial till at the base of the slope, most often during spring run-off, leaving the material in the stream bank unsupported. It eventually gives in to the pull of gravity and slumps downward. This loss of slope stability happens in stages leading to a kind of domino effect that, in the end, produces step-like blocks. As long as there is a meander and the stream is actively eroding its banks, the slumped area will continue to grow.

Sonju Lake Intrusion: This 3,800 foot (1200 meter) thick sheet-like intrusive body is composed dominantly of various layered gabbroic rocks that, in places, contain anomalous amounts of platinum and palladium (anomalous for these precious metals means more than 1 part per million). The layering in this intrusion varies from rocks composed of almost all dark minerals (olivine and pyroxene), through ones containing abundant magnetite and ilmenite, to ones composed mostly of plagioclase feldspar. The youngest and uppermost layer of this intrusion is monzonite. The Sonju Lake Intrusion is limited to the Finland-Sonju Lake-Manitou River areas.

Spheroidal Weathering: Chemical weathering that turns an angular, block-shaped rock into a rounded rock. Weathering is more intense on the edges or corners of block-shaped pieces than on the smoother rock faces and thus, over time, the edges and corners are worn away, leaving a round shape.

Spherulite: Typically rounded, radiating arrays of crystal fibers produced by the high temperature devitrification of volcanic glass. These form in rocks that cooled from hot magma to solid rock so quickly that individual minerals had no time to form and grow. When that happens an amorphous glassy mass called obsidian or volcanic glass is formed. With time glass slowly changes or devitrifies to form fine-grained minerals or crystal fibers. In rhyolitic rocks the crystal fibers are generally composed of potassium feldspar and quartz, whereas in mafic rocks the fibers commonly consist of plagioclase feldspar and/or pyroxene. Spherulites typically have diameters of 0.1-1 inch, but they can be much larger (commonly up to 8 inches). Isolated spherulites are generally spherical, but adjacent spherulites may impinge upon one another to produce long chains that are often aligned with flow foliation.

Split Rock Rhyolite: The Split Rock Rhyolite is a pink to red, fine-grained lava flow that may contain 2-5% easily visible, tabular-shaped, white plagioclase feldspar crystals. The pink or red color comes from the abundance of potassium feldspar in the rock. This lava flow forms steep cliffs on the shore of Lake Superior south of the Split Rock River, along and in the Split Rock River, and in nearby streams. The cliffs and high towers are largely the result of weathering of the rhyolite along vertical cooling joints and numerous, closely space horizontal fractures that give the rock a "flagstone" look. These horizontal fractures occur in the upper 5 to 15 feet of the rhyolite and are due to a process called unloading or exfoliation. This characteristic feature of the rhyolite has given rise to many names including "shingle parting," "stacked saucers," and "split rock." Locally there are also 2-8% quartz-filled, elongate, and contorted amygdules near the top of the flow. Spherulites (small whitish spots) can be seen in some outcrops.

Star Wars Porphyry. These tan to brownish weathering, coarsely porphyritic rocks get their name because some of the large white and gray plagioclase feldspar crystals look like the space ships from the Star Wars movies. Overall, these rocks form a near-surface, sill-like intrusion that is up to 300 feet thick and has a dip or slope of 15-20 degrees towards the lake (this is the same as the basalt lava flows). Partly eroded and glacially sculpted, the intrusion now occurs as a series of cuestas that include Oberg Mountain, Moose Mountain, the hills north of Lake Agnes, part of Maple Hill above Grand Marais, and Pincushion Mountain. It is believed that at one time the sill formed a continuous body that extended from just south of Leveaux Mountain to just north of Grand Marais! These cuestas are mostly responsible for the topographic features along the North Shore known as the Sawtooth Mountains. The white to gray plagioclase feldspar crystals in this rock vary from 0.1 to 2 inches in diameter and make up 10-50% of the rock. They are enclosed in a fine-grained matrix that is composed of pyroxene, magnetite, ilmenite, biotite, and apatite.

Taconite: Low grade iron formation (25-30% iron) composed of quartz, jasper, magnetite, and/or hematite. Taconite is suitable for concentration of the iron minerals by grinding and magnetic treatment. From this concentrate pellets can be made that are 60-65% iron and suitable for steel making.

Talus: An apron of rock rubble at the base of a slope. Along the Superior Hiking Trail the most important process that causes the rocks to break loose and begin their down slope journey is frost wedging.

Tortured Basalt: A name given to distinctive basalt lava flows along the Superior Hiking Trail that break into angular or flagstone to step-like surfaces. These form due to weathering along numerous fractures that crisscross the rock at various angles. The name comes from the fact that the rock ends up looking like it has been given a very rough time by planet earth.

Unconformity: A break or gap in the geological record; this gap may represent a month or a billion years or longer.

Unloading: see exfoliation.

Vesicle: See gas cavity.

Vesicle Cylinder: Round to irregular-shaped areas in the tops of lava flows that contain abundant amygdules. These features form from concentrations of gas rising up through a cooling lava along cylindrical-shaped pathways.

Whaleback: A tapered, blunt-nosed hill formed when pieces of rock (in a highly fractured rock) are pulled away by overriding ice (see glacial plucking). Generally this process is most pronounced on the down ice side of irregularities on the outcrop surface. So named because the bedrock exposure ends up looking like the back of a whale headed out to sea.

Xenolith or inclusion: As magma (hot molten rock) is injected into, through, and around pre-existing rocks, much like cream is injected into doughnuts, the intruded rocks are bent or arched upwards, as well as being shouldered aside. As this takes place, small to very large pieces of the pre-existing rocks are broken off and completely surrounded by the intruding magma. Depending on the composition and temperature of the magma, some of these pieces will be assimilated or completely melted by the intruding magma, but many will be preserved as alien (strange) pieces of rock, totally different in appearance and composition than the material they are entombed in. The name xenolith comes from the Latin words meaning xeno for stranger and lithos for rock. They have been compared to raisins in oatmeal, only these raisins vary in size from dimes to larger than football stadiums.

Zeolites: A group of more than 40 hydrous silicate minerals composed of varying amounts of sodium, potassium, calcium, and aluminum. Zeolites are best known for their occurrence in holes in volcanic rocks where they have precipitated out of warm groundwater at low temperature. The most common zeolite minerals seen along the Superior Hiking Trail are: thomsonite (white to cream-colored or pink, often fibrous or radiating), laumantite (massive and white or pink), and white stilbite.

Glossary II:

Common Wild Flowers

Found Along the Superior Hiking Trail

Adoxa Moschatellina (from Greek for obscure or insignificant): This plant is also called muskroot due to its musky odor. To some Adoxa is a symbol of Christian watchfulness with 5 tiny white-green flowers pointing to the 4 cardinal directions plus one toward heaven. The plant has 3 parted, lobed leaflets on a long stalk. Leafs are similar to those of the corydalis. This is a relatively rare and threatened plant that likes shady, moist forests. Blooms May to July.

Aster, Large-Leaved: (Aster macrophyllus): Daisy Family, also called "lumber jack toilet paper," because the basal leaves are large (4 to 8 inches wide), rough, and heart-shaped. The plant is 1 to 5 feet tall with violet or whitish ray flowers. Plant stems are a pale purple color. Blooms late July to late August and is part of the Canadian carpet. Ojibwe hunters are said to have smoked the leaves before embarking on a hunt because they believed the smoke attracted deer and moose.

Aster, New England (Aster novae-angliae): This member of the Daisy Family has deep violet flowers and crowded, toothless leaves clasping the hairy stalk. Rays numerous (40 to 100). Plant 3 to 7 feet tall. Likes thickets, meadows, wet places. Blooms late summer and fall.

Aster, Purple (Aster patens): Daisy Family with lobes of short, oblong, toothless leaves. The purple flowers occur at the ends of slender branchlets and have 15 to 25 rays. Grows 1 to 3 feet tall. Blooms August and September

Aster, Purple-Stemmed (Aster ciliolatus): This 2 to 7 foot tall plant has blue or purple-rayed flowers, a bristly, purple stem, and rough, toothed leaves. Found in swamps and wet thickets. Blooms July through September.

Aster, White (Aster umbellatus): This 2 to 7 foot-tall plant of the Daisy Family has flat-topped clusters of white flowers with relatively few rays. Disks are yellow. Leaves are lance-shaped with rough edges.

Baneberry: (Actaea rubra): A member of the Buttercup Family, this 1 to 2 foot-tall plant has white, 4 to 10-petaled flowers that occur in tight, oblong clusters. Leaves are divided and then subdivided into sharply toothed leaflets. The fruit consists of a cluster of red or white berries, each with a red stalk and a black or purple "eye," which leads to the nickname of doll's eyes. Berries, leaves, and roots are poisonous. Blooms late May to early June.

Bearberry: (Arctostaphylos uva-ursi): Uva in Latin means "a bunch of berries" and ursus is "bear," and yes bears do love to eat bearberries. This plant is a trailing shrub of the Heath Family and has reddish bark and small, paddle-shaped, evergreen leaves. The egg-shaped, white to pink flowers are in terminal clusters. Berries are red. Native Americans used the dried leaves for tobacco; they called it kinnikinnick. Bearberry tea was used to treat kidney stones, inflammation of the urinary tract, and headaches. Blooms mid-May into early June in dry, often sandy soils. Look for it on outcrops, rock ledges, and beneath pine trees.

Bedstraw, Sweet-Scented: (Galium triflorum): This 3 to 4 foot-tall plant has small, greenish-white flowers with 4 petals; flowers in open clusters. The leaves are oblong and in circles of 6; sweet-scented when dried. Blooms June through July.

Bedstraw, Northern: (Galium boreale): Similar to above, but 1 to 3 feet tall with leaves in whorls of 4, each with 3 prominent nerves. Likes rocky soil. Blooms late June through July.

Bellwort, Large-Flowered: (Uvularia grandiflora): This 6 to 18 inch plant of the Lily Family has nodding, bell-like, 6-pointed bright yellow flowers. Leaves clasp stem with flower stems looking like they pierce the leaves. Often blooms alongside sessile bellwort. Blooms late April through May.

Bellwort, Sessile: (Uvularia sessilifolia): Also known as "wild oats," this 4 to 12 inch-tall plant has nodding pale yellow flowers. Leaves are attached directly to the stem. Blooms late April through May. The young plant shoots are a good substitute for asparagus, and Ojibwe hunters carried the root as a charm to attract white-tailed deer and moose.

Bindweed: (Convolvulus arvensis): Part of the Morning Glory Family, this trailing vine has white or pinkish, funnel-shaped flowers; leaves are "lance-like."

Birdfoot Trefoil: (Lotus corniculatus): A member of the Pea Family, this 6 to 24 inch-tall plant has clover-like clusters of yellow flowers. The leaves are in 5 parts: 3 clover-like leaflets and 2 that look like a large appendage at the base of the leafstalk. Slender seed pod suggests a bird's foot and thus the name. Blooms mid-June through August.

Bloodroot (Sanguinaria canadensis): One of the earliest spring flowers to bloom. The plant has a large lobed-leaf that wraps itself like a shawl around the 6 to 12 inch stalk, which bears the very pretty 8- to 10-petaled, white flower. The leaf remains long after the flower has vanished. Broken stem emits an orange juice that the Ojibwe used as a dye for baskets and clothing. The juice does contain alkaloids and can be toxic. Blooms from late April to late May.

Blue Bead Lily or Clintonia (Clintonia borealis): Also known as "corn lily," this 6 to 14 inch-tall plant has 2 or 3 shiny, parallel-veined basal leaves and yellow, bell-shaped flowers on a leafless stalk. Has poisonous blue berries, but young leaves taste like cucumber. Blooms from mid-May through June; berries conspicuous from July to August.

Bluebell (Campanula rotundifolia): See Harebell.

Blueberry, Low Bush (Vaccinium angustifolium): Low, woody shrub some 10 to 20 inches tall that can be found in open, rocky areas, especially in old burn areas. The leaves are shiny, alternate, and without teeth, while the urn-shaped white flowers hang down in loose clusters. Blooms late May to mid-June with berries ripe in early to mid-July.

Blue-Eyed Grass (Sisyrinchium montanum): This plant is not really a grass but a member of the Iris Family with blue flowers that open only in the afternoon. Buds of the blooming plant look like thin strands of grass with blue-tipped ends. The blue flowers have 5-7 petals with a yellow "eye" in the center. Blooms May to June in open meadows.

Blue Flag Iris (Iris versicolor): Also called wild iris, this 2 to 3 foot-tall plant with graceful, sword-shaped leaves (very distinctive) has curved, violet-colored flowers that are deeply veined. Found in marshes and along the edges of lakes. Blooms from mid-June to mid-July. The Ojibwe always carried a small bit of the plant with them when they went berry picking for they believed it would keep snakes away.

Bog Laurel (Kalmia polifolia): A member of the Heath Family this 2 foot tall evergreen shrub has a terminal cluster of pink to purple, bell-shaped flowers with leathery, shiny dark green leaves that are white on the undersides. Blooms late May to Mid-June

Bog Rosemary (Andromeda glaucophylla): A member of the Heath Family, this evergreen shrub is a 6 to 18 inch-tall plant that has pink, urn-shaped flowers in drooping clusters with thick, long, narrow leaves. The leaves are bluish-green and kind of white underneath. Blooms from early May through June.

Bracken Fern (Pteridium aquilinum): This fern can grow over 3 feet tall with fronds that branch once or twice giving the appearance of compound leaves. The triangular-shaped fronds have many spatula-shaped leaflet-like segments that have their edges rolled under. The stem at the base is dark brown and hairy becoming straw-colored and hairless toward the top. Found in acid soils in both old-growth and new pine forests as well as in abandoned pastures and along forest margins.

Buckwheat (Fagopyrum sagittatum): White or pink flowers in branching sprays, the 1 to 2 foot-tall plant has arrowhead-shaped leaves and swollen sheaths where attached to the reddish stem. Blooms June through August.

Buckwheat, Climbing False (Polygonum scandens): Similar to above, but the plant is a twining vine.

Bunchberry (Cornus canadensis): Part of the Dogwood Family this 3 to 8 inch plant has 4 white bracts (modified leaves adjacent to the flower) that surround the center cluster of tiny greenish flowers giving the appearance of a single pretty blossom. Leaves are in a whorl of 6, and the fruit is scarlet-colored and pulpy with a slightly sweet taste. The root was used for infant colic and the leaf for tea to ease aches and pains. Blooms from late May to late June, berries appear in mid-July.

Buttercup, Common (Ranunculus acris): This is the most familiar and most common of the 36 buttercup species. The 2 to 3 foot-tall plant has 5 to 7 glossy, overlapping yellow petals (buttercups) with bushy stamen. The leaves are deeply cut into 5 to 7 unstalked segments. Fields and meadows; blooms late May through July.

Calla Lily (Calla palustris): A member of the Arum Family this 8 to 10 inch-high water plant has flat, shiny, white flowers, and an open petal around a short, cylindrical spike. Leaves are heart-shaped with long stalks. Fruit is a cluster of red berries. Found in bogs and on the edges of ponds. Blooms mid-May to late June. Name means "beauty of the marsh."

Canadian Carpet: Refers to a small number of plant species that comprise the vast majority of ground cover in a boreal forest. Species include blue bead lily, Canadian mayflower, bunchberry, twinflower, pyrola, starflower, Indian pipe, wintergreen, aster, pipsissewa, ladyslipper, spotted coral root, and large-leaved aster.

318

Canadian Mayflower (Maianthemum canadense): The Latin name means May blossom of Canada, plant also known as "wild lily of the valley." This 3 to 6 inch-tall plant has 2 to 3 heart-shaped leaves and clusters of 4 pointed white flowers. Berries are white with spots but turn pale to ruby red in the fall. Likes moist woods and commonly found in spruce-fir forests. Flowers from mid-May to June. Native Americans used the plant to cure headaches, sore throats, and kidney problems.

Chickweed (several varieties): Chickweed is a 4 to 16 inch-tall plant with small, white flowers that have 5 petals. The petals are so deeply cleft that flowers often seem to have 10 petals. Leaves are in pairs. An excellent source of vitamin B.

Cinquefoil, Dwarf (Potentilla canadensis): This 2 to 4 inch-tall plant has cream-colored to yellow 5-petaled flowers with radially, 5-parted leaves that are wedge-shaped and toothed. Flowers and leaves rise from runners that are on separate stalks. Runners can be 6 to 20 inches long. Stems are silver and hairy. When chewed, the leaves are an excellent source of vitamin B. Blooms May to June.

Cinquefoil, Rough-Fruited (Potentilla recta): A member of the Rose Family this 1 to 2 foot-tall plant has pale yellow 5-petaled flowers in a flat, terminal cluster. These are attached to an erect, very hairy stalk with many-branched leaves. Leaflets are 5 to 7 and relatively narrow. Native Americans made a tea of the leaves and used it to treat diarrhea. Blooms mid-June through July.

Cinquefoil, Shrubby (Potentilla fruticosa): This is a bushy, 1 to 2 foot-tall shrub with silky leaves (whitish underneath) and woody stems; leaf segments are toothless, and the yellow flowers have 5 petals. Blooms July to mid-August and likes cold, exposed rock ledges.

Cinquefoil, Tall (Potentilla arguta): A member of the Rose Family, this 1 to 3 foot-tall plant has white or cream-colored 5-petaled flowers that occur in flat-topped clusters. Leaflets 7 to 11, toothed and downy underneath. Blooms late June through July.

Cinquefoil, Three-Toothed (Potentilla tridentata): A member of the Rose Family, this 1 to 10 inch-tall ground-hugging plant has white 5-petaled flowers, and 3 shiny leaflets with 3 rounded teeth at the tip. The leaves turn deep red in the fall. Common in rocky crevices. Blooms mid-June through July.

Clematis, Purple (Clematis verticillaris): A member of the Buttercup Family, this climbing vine has pretty, bell-like purple flowers with 4 sepals. Flowers are "downy" inside and out; leaves are in groups of 3. Rocky woods and open slopes. Blooms late May through June.

Clubmoss, Ground Cedar (Lycopodium complanatum): This kind of clubmoss looks like a small cedar tree. The stem branches are made up of scale-like leaves, flatted and fanned out in one direction. Cones (1-4) occur on 3 inch stems looking like the arms of a candelabra.

Clubmoss, Shining (Lycopodium lucidulum): Bright green stems up to 10 inches tall. These may branch 3 times. Leaves are of unequal size and toothed at tips.

Clubmoss, Stiff (Lycopodium annotinum): A common ground cover in the boreal forest. These are short (up to a foot tall), stiff, evergreen plants with straight, sharply pointed leaves at right angles to the stem. Likes acid soils.

319

Clubmoss, Running (Lycopodium clavatum): Also known as "running pine," this plant has long, forking horizontal stems that create a maze over the ground. Straw-colored strobiles (a group of modified leaves at the end of a stem) occur in pairs atop a single stalk. Leaf tips end in threadlike hairs. Found under aspen and fir trees. Spores were used to stop bleeding.

Coltsfoot (Tussilago farfara): This 6 to 15 inch-tall plant has a stalk with reddish scales and a bristly yellow flower that looks like a dandelion. Flower appears before the leaves. Blooms mid-April through June.

Columbine (Aquilegia canadensis): A member of the Buttercup Family, this plant has drooping red bell-shaped flowers with 5 long, curved spurs (they look like Bung's hat in the Wizard of Id). Very distinctive, have been called the "eye candy of the wildflower world." Blooms early May through June, and likes rocky or gravelly areas with partial to full sun.

Coralroot, Spotted (Corallorhiza maculata): This 8 to 20 inch member of the Orchid Family is entirely purplish-red; the hooded flowers have a purple-spotted lip. Grows in clumps beneath balsam fir and white cedars. Blooms mid-June through mid-July.

Corydalis (Corydalis): Small (6 to 16 inches) plants of the poppy family that have finely cut leaves and narrow, yellow, tubular flowers with a hollow spur. Several varieties grow along the trail, but all love sun, grow on rocks, and in sand and gravel. Native Americans placed the root on wood coals and inhaled the smoke to "clear the head." Blooms in June.

Cow Parsnip (Heracleum maximum): This large (4 to 10 foot-tall) plant is a member of the Carrot Family and has leaves commonly over a foot wide that are divided into 3 maple-shaped segments. Stem is hollow and may be 2 inches thick at the base. White flowers occur in umbrella-like clusters, are woolly and rank smelling. Likes moist ground. Native Americans ate the cooked root to relieve upset stomachs; the root, when dried, can be used as a salt substitute. Blooms late June through August.

Cowslip See Marsh Marigold.

Cranberry (Vaccinium species) : Two species of cranberry are found in bogs along the Superior Hiking Trail.

> **Large Cranberry** (Vaccinium macrocarpon): A creeping shrub with small, alternate, oval leaves. Flower is pink and has 4 petals on a long stem. Fruit is an edible red berry. Plant is 1 to 6 inches high. Blooms late June through July.

> **Bog Cranberry** (Vaccinium oxycoccus): Similar to above but shrub is 1 to 4 inches tall with pointed leaves that are white underneath and have rolled edges. Blooms mid-June through mid-July.

Dewberry or Dwarf Raspberry (Rubus pubescens): This 3 to 6 inch-tall plant has 3 leaflets that resemble strawberry leaves. The red fruit is a cluster of juicy droplets that resemble a raspberry. These are edible but not great tasting; also fruit is not easy to remove from the plant. Blooms early May to early June.

Dogbane: see Spreading Dogbane.

Dutchman's Breeches (Dicentra cucullaria): A member of the Bleeding Heart Family, this 5 to 9 inch-tall plant has white or pink nodding flowers with long, triangular spurs.

320

The spurs resemble the legs of tiny "pantaloons" or "breeches" that appear to hang upside down as if on a clothesline. Leaves are finely dissected and bluish-green. This is a close relative of the bleeding heart. Native Americans used the leaves to make tea (possibly because of its repute as a powerful love potion). Blooms mid-April to mid-May.

Dwarf Enchanter's Nightshade (Circaea alpina): A 3 to 8 inch-tall plant with tiny white flowers that have 2 deeply notched petals. Leaves are paired and coarsely toothed; they have a heart-shaped base. Blooms July to September.

Evening Primrose (Oenothera biennis): Also known as "evening star" and "night light," this plant's flowers open fully in the evening and wilt the next day. The yellow flowers have 4 showy petals on a 1 to 5 foot-tall stalk; leaves are long and tapering. The reddish stem is rough, hairy, and branched. Used by Native Americans to treat sore muscles. Blooms July through August.

False Solomon's Seal (Smilacina racemosa): A member of the Lily Family, this plant has oval, pointed leaves that alternate along the stem, which is tipped with a cluster of creamy-white flowers. The fruit is a white berry that is speckled with brown turning ruby-red. Blooms early May through June.

Field Pussy Toes (Antennaria neglecta): A member of the Daisy Family with leaves at the base, this plant often forms dense mats. Leaves have only 1 main nerve. The stem is long and woolly with terminal white flower clusters.

Fireweed (Epilobium angustifolium): A member of the Evening Primrose Family, this 3 to 5 foot-tall plant has slender spikes of many purple-pink, roundish flower petals, drooping flower buds, and reddish seedpods angling upwards. Leaves alternate. Flowers open from the bottom of the plant upward and, as the saying goes, when "fireweed blooms at the top, summer is over." Loves disturbed soil, roadsides, gravel pits, burn areas; blooms July through mid-August.

Goatsbeard (Tragopogon pratensis): A member of the Daisy Family with dandelion-like flowers. Plant has grass-like leaves that embrace the smooth stem, and long pointed bracts that support the yellow rays. Juice of stem is milky. Flowers close up in mid-day. 1 to 3 feet tall. Blooms June through September.

Golden Alexander (Zizea aptera): Part of the Parsley Family, this 1 to 3 foot-tall plant has small yellow flowers in compound umbrella-like clusters. Lower leaves are heart-shaped and un-divided; upper leaves are divided into 3 to 5 leaflets. Blooms April through May.

Goldenrod (Solidago species): over 10 varieties of goldenrod along the trail, but all have yellow-rayed blossoms in clusters with either plume-like leaves that are parallel veined or feather-veined. Blooms July to late August.

Ground Cedar: See Clubmoss, Ground Cedar.

Goldthread (Coptis groenlandia): A member of the Buttercup Family; 3 to 5 inches tall. The plant has 5 to 7 white petal-like sepals and 15 to 25 stamens. The plant has shiny, dark, evergreen leaves with 3 leaflets and bright yellow roots. Blooms in May; prefers cool woods and bogs.

Hairy Rock Cress (Arabis hirsuta): A member of the Mustard Family, this 1 to 2 foot-tall plant has oblong to paddle-shaped basal leaves in rosettes; stem leaves are narrow and clasping. White 4-petaled flowers occur in small clusters. Blooms May to June.

Harebell (Campanula rotundifolia): Also called bluebell, this 6 to 18 inch-tall plant has blue-violet, bell-shaped flowers that are ½ to ¾ inch long. The leaves are narrow or hair-like. Blooms from late June to mid-August.

Hawkweed, Orange (Hieracium aurantiacum): A member of the Composite Family, orange hawkweed is also called "devil's paintbrush." The 8 to 24 inch-tall plant is very hairy with leaves forming a basal rosette. Plant has deep orange flat-ray flowers with yellowish centers. Called hawkweed because it was once believed hawks ate the flowers to improve their vision. Blooms mid-May through July. There is also a yellow-flowered variety.

Hemp Nettle (Galeopsis tetrahit): This alien plant of the Mint Family has hairy white or pale magenta flowers in the axils of leaves; lower lip of flowers is striped purple and there are bumps on the lower lip. Square stem bristly; 1 to 2 feet tall. Roadsides and waste places; blooms June through mid-September.

Hepatica (Hepatica americana): This 4 to 6 inch-tall plant of the Buttercup Family has rounded, 3-lobed leaves, hairy stalks, and 6 to 10-petaled white, pink, or blue flowers. Blooms from mid-April to late May; can be seen blooming amongst patches of melting snow.

Honeysuckle (Lonicera): Honeysuckles are mostly 1 to 5 foot-tall woody shrubs and vines with oblong to heart-shaped or oval opposite leaves. Flowers are bell-shaped or funnel-like, yellow to orange, with 5 stamens (male organs tipped by pollen). Several different varieties. Blooms May to August.

Honeysuckle, Bush (Diervilla lonicera): This 1 to 4 foot-tall plant has sharp-pointed, toothed leaves and yellow funnel-shaped flowers that are tinged in red. Blooms June to August.

Horsetails (Equisetum species): Also called "Indian Tinker Toys" (because the stem can be pulled or popped apart at nodes) this non-flowering plant has reddish-brown, scale-like leaves (called teeth) at nodes that are clumped together in threes. The stiff, hollow stem has a ridge-like surface with spicules of silica on the ridges. This makes the plant rough enough to file fingernails or scrub pots. The stem is topped by a spore-producing cone. The plant name comes from the vegetative shoots that appear feathery. Moist, wet areas.

Indian Pipe (Monotropa uniflora): Also called "corpse plant" and "ghost flower," this is a member of the Wintergreen Family. It is 4 to 10 inches tall and has waxy, translucent stems from which a nodding white or pink flower hangs. Leaves are scale-like. The plant has no chlorophyll and obtains its food like a mushroom. The clear sap was used by Native Americans to help clear up cloudy vision. Blooms July and August.

Jack-in-the-Pulpit (Arisaema triphyllum): A member of the Dragon Arum Family, which includes philodendron, this unique plant has a fleshy, club-shaped spike (Jack) that is gracefully covered by a flap-like green or purplish-brown sheath (the pulpit). There are 1 or 2 long stalked leaves that are 3-parted; the fruit is a cluster of scarlet berries. Blooms mid-May to mid-June. The Ojibwe tell a wonderful story about this plant and the little people who inhabit the forest.

Jewelweed, Pale (Impatiens pallida): Similar to Spotted Jewelweed, but flowers are pale yellow.

Jewelweed, Spotted (Impatiens capensis): Part of the Touch-Me-Not Family, this 2 to 5 foot-tall plant has spotted orange flowers, each one shaped like a horn-of-plenty. Flowers hang, pendant-like, from a thin stem that exudes juice when broken. Ripe seed pods explode at a touch. Jewelweed can help cure the itch from poison ivy-rub the leaves on the itchy spot for fast relief. Blooms mid-July to mid-August; likes wet, shady places.

Joe-Pye Weed (Eupatorium purpureum): Daisy Family, 3 to 5 feet tall, with pinkish-purple flower heads in round-topped clusters. Narrow, short-stalked leaves in whorls of 3 or 4. Gives off vanilla odor when bruised or crushed. Named after Joe Pye, a Native American doctor who treated early colonists for typhoid fever with this plant (or so the story goes). Blooms July through mid- September.

Juneberry (Amelanchier species): Member of the Rose Family, also known as serviceberry, this shrub is 5 to 15 feet tall and has spectacular white drooping flower clusters that turn many parts of the hiking trail into virtual "gardens." The flowers have 5 long petals, and the leaves are oval and toothed. Also slender reddish buds. Blooms late May into June. Huckleberry-like fruits ripen in July.

Labrador Tea (Ledum groenlandicum): This evergreen shrub, a member of the Heath Family, is a 1 to 3 foot-tall plant with white or pinkish flowers in terminal clusters. The leaves are leathery with rolled edges and are "rusty-woolly" on the under surfaces. Native Americans used the leaves for tea, and they also chewed the leaves. Likes bogs; blooms from late May through June.

Leatherleaf (Chamaedaphne calyculata): A member of the Heath Family, this 1 to 2 foot-tall shrub has pinkish-white, bell-shaped flowers in one-sided clusters. Evergreen leaves are leathery with dot-like scales on both upper and lower surfaces. Blooms May through early June.

Leek, Wild (Allium tricoccum): This 8-12 inch tall plant forms bunches of green leaves in early spring in hardwood forests. The leaves smell strongly of onions while the bulb or leek grows beneath the ground. Lilac-colored flowers generally bloom in July after the leaves have disappeared.

Lupine (Lupinus perennis): This 18 to 30 inch-tall plant of the Pea Family has blue-violet, pink, or purple pea-like flowers on a long, terminal axis. The leaves are round and divided into 7 to 11 leaflets. Has long, bean-like seed pods. Grows in dry soil, open woods, and clearings. Blooms June through mid-July.

Marsh Marigold (Caltha palustris): Part of the Buttercup Family, also known as "cowslip," this is an early spring flower found in wooded, swampy areas and along the edges of creeks. The 8 to 24 inch-tall plant has large yellow flowers (1 to 2 inches) with 5 to 9 petals and round or kidney-shaped glossy leaves. Native Americans mixed the root with maple sugar and used this concoction to relieve coughs; they also used the raw root to heal minor wounds. However, eating the plant can cause heart inflammation. Blooms late April through May.

Mertensia (Mertensia virginica): Part of the Forget-Me-Not Family, this plant is also known as "Virginia Bluebells." It is 1 to 2 feet tall, and has blue, trumpet-like flowers that are pink when in bud. The leaves are oval, smooth, and well-veined. Found in moist woods and bottomlands; blooms from late April through May.

Miterwort (Mitella diphylla): A member of the Saxifrage Family, this 10 to 18 inch-tall plant has a pair of stalkless leaves on the stem below a terminal cluster of beautiful, fringed white flowers.

Miterwort, Naked (Mitella nuda): This 3 to 8 inch-tall plant lacks stem leaves (thus the name naked) and has a terminal cluster of delicate white flowers with threadlike fringes. Has basal leaves on stalks.

Mullein, Common (Verbascum thapsus): A member of the Snapdragon Family, this 2 to 7 foot-tall plant has a club-like flower head with yellow, 5-petaled flowers and large "flannel" textured leaves that look like they flow into the stem. Blooms July through mid-September in fields and along roadsides.

Oak Fern (Gymnocarpium dryopteris): This 5 to 8 inch-tall fern is identified by its delicate triangular-shaped fronds, which are usually held horizontally. The plant likes cool, moist woods and rocky soils. The leaf stalk is striped green to brown and is nearly black at the base.

Orchid, Bog (Arethusa bulbosa): This 10 to 12 inch-tall orchid has 3 erect pink sepals and a hood that partially covers over a spotted, crested lip. Grass-like leaves form after flower matures. Blooms late June through July.

Orchid, Coralroot (Corallorhiza species): several different varieties of Coralroot orchid grow along the trail; all have "lipped" flowers and parallel-veined leaves. They lack green pigment and bear their pink, red, and white flowers on a leafless stalk. Most varieties bloom June to late-July.

Orchid, Ladyslipper, Pink (Cypripedium acaule): Also called Moccasin Flower, this member of the Orchid Family is a 6 to 15 inch-tall plant with a distinctive heavily veined, pink "pouch." The plant also has 2 oval basal leaves with parallel veins. Likes cool, shady, mossy, or rocky areas. Blooms mid-May to late June. The root was used to ease tooth pain.

Orchid, Ladyslipper, Showy (Cypripedium reginae): A member of the Orchid Family this 2 to 3 foot-tall plant has white petals in striking contrast to its rose-colored pouch. Stem is thick and hairy and leafy at the top. Found in swamps, wet woods, and roadside ditches. Minnesota State Flower. Blooms June and July.

Orchid, LadysSlipper, Yellow (Cypripedium calceolus): Another member of the Orchid Family, this is a 1 to 2 foot-tall plant with an inflated yellow lip (slipper) and 2 lateral petals that are long, twisted, and brownish-green. Likes bogs, wet woods, shady swamps. Blooms June through mid-July.

Orchid, Purple Fringed (Habenaria fimbriata): A 1 to 4 foot-tall plant with numerous purple flowers that have a "3-part" fringed lip. Lower leaves are large; upper leaves are small. Blooms June to August.

Ostrich Fern (Matteuccia struthiopteris): Named for the frond's resemblance to the plume of an Ostrich. This fern grows to heights of 3 to 8 feet; the fronds increase in width at the top. In the spring rootstalks send up tightly coiled new leaves that resemble the head of a violin; these are called "fiddleheads."

Ox-Eye Daisy (Chrysanthemum leucanthemum): A white daisy with a yellow disk; leaves are dark, narrow, irregular; and bluntly toothed. Grows to heights of 18 to 30 inches. Plant was used by Native Americans as a stimulant. Blooms June to mid-August.

Pearly Everlasting (Anaphalis margaritacea): This 1 to 2 foot-tall plant, a member of the Daisy Family, has white flowers in tubular heads and terminal clusters. Numerous silver-white bracts surrounding single flowers give the plant its name. Leaves are long and narrow. Blooms from late July into August.

Pipsissewa (Chimaphila umbellata): This 6 to 12 inch plant of the Wintergreen Family has a terminal cluster of waxy white to pinkish flowers, each with a ring of reddish anthers (enlarged part of the stamen that holds the pollen). Dark, shiny toothed leaves radiate in whorls from the stem. Pipsissewa is Cree for "breaks into small pieces." Grows in dry woods; blooms mid-May to late June. Used by Native Americans to treat sore eyes and skin irritations.

Pitcher Plant (Sarracenia purpurea): This 12 to 18 inch-tall bog plant has red, pitcher-like, heavily veined leaves that are usually half-filled with water. The flaring lips are lined with downward pointing bristles that help trap insects. The nodding, globular red flower is on a separate stalk. Insects fly or crawl into the pitcher and fall into the water at the bottom and drown. Then they are ingested by the plant. Blooms June to early July.

Purple Vetch (Vicia americana): Part of the Legume Family, this 2 to 3 foot-high vine has violet-purple, pea-like flowers that occur in loose racemes (long cluster of flowers arranged singly along a stalk). Blooms mid-May through early July.

Pussytoes (Antennaria canadensis): A member of the Daisy Family, this 5 to 12 inch-tall plant has small white, woolly flowers in a cluster at the top of the stem. Basal leaves, which have 1 main nerve, are larger than leaves on the stem. Blooms late April to early June.

Pyrola (Pyrola species): There are several different species of pyrola to be found along the hiking trail. The leaves of this plant have analgesic properties and Native Americans used it to treat cuts, sores, and rheumatism.

1. One-Sided Pyrola (Pyrola secunda) is an 8 inch-high plant with all the flower stalks attached to one side of the long stem. White flowers are small, waxy, and cup-shaped. Basal leaves are rounded and not toothed. Blooms mid-June through July.

2. Round-Leaved Pyrola (Pyrola rotundifolia) is an 8 to 18 inch-tall plant with fragrant white to rose-colored flowers that occur at the end of the long stem. Leaves are shiny and round. Blooms May through July.

3. Shinleaf Pyrola (Pyrola elliptica) is a 5 to 10 inch-tall plant that has large (up to 3 inches), elliptical leaves that are flattened at the end, and not pointed. Bluish white, cup-shaped flowers at the top of the long stalk. Blooms mid-June through July.

4. Lesser Pyrola (Pyrola minor) is a 4 to 8 inch-tall plant that has small leaves with the leafstalk often longer than the leaves. Green-veined white or pinkish flowers are small.

Raspberry (Rubus idaeus): This tall bush has 5-petaled white flowers and prickles or sharp spikes on the canes. Blooms June to early July; berries typically ripen late July and August.

Rose-Twisted Stalk (Streptopus roseus): A member of the Lily Family, this 1 to 3 foot-high plant has a zigzag stem, parallel-veined leaves, and six-pointed pink, bell-like flowers that hang singly from leaf axils. The fruit is cherry red and translucent. Blooms mid-May through June; likes acidic soils. Another name for this plant is "scootberry," because eating the berries makes you "scoot" to the bathroom a lot.

Rue, Early Meadow (Thalictrum dioicum): A member of the Buttercup Family, this 1 to 2 foot-tall plant has drooping or dangling clusters of 4 or 5-petaled greenish-white flowers with purple tips. Blooms late April to May.

Rue, Tall Meadow (Thalictrum polygamum): Taller (3 to 8 feet) and later blooming (June through July) than early meadow rue. Leaves are divided, then subdivided into many roundish, 3-lobed leaflets. Plumes of white flowers lack petals.

Running Pine: see Clubmoss, Running.

Sarsaparilla, Wild (Aralia nudicaulis): Part of the Ginseng Family, this plant has large, 3-branched leaves (each with 3 to 5 leaflets) with white, round, umbrella-like flower clusters below the leaves on a separate stem. Leaves start off a burgundy color then slowly turn green. Has blue-black berries that ripen in mid-July. This is a close cousin to wild ginseng and, supposedly, was the root used in the original root beer, or the drink called sarsaparilla. Blooms mid-May through late June.

Sensitive Fern (Onoclea sensibilis): So named because it is sensitive to cold, the fronds of this fern wither rapidly after a frost or after being cut. This is a 15 to 30 inch-tall fern with a single blade that is deeply cut, but not all the way to the stem. Has a lacy network of veins that covers the single blade. Tips of leaflets are blunt. The hollow structure in which spores are produced is on a totally separate stalk, which is much shorter than the fronds. Likes wet areas.

Sheep Sorrel (Rumex acetosella): A member of the Buckwheat Family, this 4 to 12 inch-tall plant has small, arrow-shaped leaves with spreading lobes. Flower heads are tiny and green to pale brown. Found along roads, in acid soil, and in fields with thin soils. Blooms from mid-June to September. Native Americans used the leaves as a seasoning in meat dishes and for making tea.

Snowberry (Gaultheria hispidula): A member of the Heath Family, this low, creeping plant has small, alternate, oval leaves along the stems. Flowers are white, tiny, 4-lobed, and bell-shaped. Fruit is a white berry tasting of wintergreen. Blooms May through July. Ojibwe name for this plant is waaboozaba, and they used it for cuts, burns, and to cure tapeworm.

Solomon's Seal (Polygonatum biflorum): A member of the Lily Family, this 1 to 3 foot-tall plant has paired, greenish-yellow flowers that dangle beneath the elongate leaves. Flowers are arranged alternately on the stem. Berries are blue-black. Blooms early May through June.

Sphagnum Moss: Called peat moss or the "shag carpeting of the Canadian Shield," these are stout, thick-leaved mosses that vary from red to pink to dominantly green in color. The stems may be 8 inches long with 5 branches at each node. This particular moss can absorb up to 27 times its weight in water. Found in floating bogs, cedar swamps, sedge mats, and spruce swamps.

Spreading Dogbane (Apocynum androsaemifolium): This 2 to 3 foot-tall, shrub-like plant has clusters of small, pink, bell-shaped flowers and paired, ovate leaves. Flowers are striped inside with a deep rose color. Plant has milky juice. Blooms June to mid-August.

Springbeauty (Claytonia virginica): A member of the Purslane Family and also called "fairy spuds" (the tubers resemble a small potato with many protruding eyes). This plant has smooth, linear leaves halfway up the 4-10 inch-tall stem. Flowers have 5 petals and are white to pink with darker pink veins. Found in moist woods blooming from mid-April through May.

Starflower (Trientalis borealis): A member of the Primrose Family with two 6 to 7-pointed, star-like, white flowers on thin stalks above a whorl of 5 to 9 shiny, tapered leaves. Found in wooded areas blooming from mid-May through June. Also called "Star of Bethlehem" and, in Sweden, "wood star."

Starry Solomon's Seal (Smilacina stellata): This 1 to 2 foot-tall member of the Lily Family has small, star-like flowers, 3 to 14 in plume-like clusters at the tip of the stem. Leaves alternate and are smooth, shiny, and clasp the stem. Blooms May into June.

Strawberry, Common or Meadow (Fragaria virginiana): A member of the Rose Family, this wild strawberry is similar to the domestic version. The 3 to 6 inch-tall plant has hairy, 3-toothed leaflets on a slender stalk. The 5-petaled white flowers occur in a flat cluster on a separate stalk. Plant spreads by runners. Blooms late May through June; berries ripen mid-June into July. Seeds are embedded in pits in the red fruit.

Strawberry, Wood (Fragaria vesca): Similar to the common strawberry, but flowers and fruits are smaller and on stems that are taller than the leaves, which are more pointed. Fruit is more elongate and the seeds are on the surface of the fruit, not in pits. Blooms May to mid-July.

Sundew (Drosera rotundifolia): This 8 to 10 inch-tall plant has small, white flowers on one side of a long stem. Round basal leaves have reddish, glandular bristles that exude a sticky juice. When the sun shines on this plant, the leaves look like they are covered with sparkling dewdrops. When an insect lands on one of these, the bristles close to capture the unwary creature. Blooms mid-June through July. Native Americans used the leaves to treat different kinds of coughs as well as asthma.

Sunflower, Common (Helianthus annuus): This 7 to 10 foot-tall plant of the Daisy Family has a yellow flower head with reddish-brown disk florets. The leaves are heart-shaped, toothed, and resinous with slender stalks. The stem is rough and hairy. Blooms July through September. There are many varieties and sizes of sunflowers including wood sunflowers, which are 2 to 6 feet tall.

Swamp Saxifrage (Saxifraga pensylvanica): This 1 to 3 foot-tall plant has a sticky, hairy stem and lance-shaped toothless leaves. The flowers may be white, greenish, yellowish, or purplish with 5 petals and 10 bright yellow stamens. Likes swamps and low meadows. Blooms mid-May to mid-June.

Sweet Cicely (Osmorhiza claytoni): Part of the Parsley Family this 1 to 3 foot-tall plant has a round stem and wide, fern-like leaves. Both leaves and stem have soft, white hairs. The leaves are bluntly toothed, and the lower ones are large (a foot or more in length). The white flowers are small and occur in flat-topped clusters. The roots have a sweet licorice odor. Blooms May to June.

Sweet Gale (Myrica gale): The flower of this 1 to 3 foot-tall plant is a catkin on a sweet smelling, branched shrub. The leaves are leathery and fern-like with yellow glandular dots. Fruit is nut-like. Blooms late May through June.

Tansy (Tanacetum vulgare): This member of the Daisy Family grows 2 to 3 feet tall and has many small button-shaped, yellow flower heads in a flat-topped cluster. Fern-like leaves are finely divided. Strongly scented plant (sometimes called "stinkweed"). Likes waste areas, roadsides, and open fields. Blooms from late July through mid-September. The Ojibwe used the root for ear drops and the leaves as a fever suppressant, and the dried leaf was chewed for sore throats.

Thimbleberry (Rubus parviflorus): This is a waist-high bush (2 to 4 feet) with large, maple-like leaves and big, fragile, 5-petaled, white flowers. The raspberry-like fruit develops in August. The berries easily fit over the end of your finger like a thimble. Also called salmonberry. Blooms mid-June to mid-July.

Trillium, Large-Flowered (Trillium grandiflorum): Trillium is Latin for "three." Same as nodding trillium, but the flowers are much larger and stand upright between the 3 leaves. Blooms May to early June. Flower turns pink as it ages.

Trillium, Nodding (Trillium cernuum): Three broad leaves and 3 showy white or pink petals. The single flower dangles below the leaves. The plant is 10 to 18 inches tall and likes acid woods. Blooms from late April to early June.

Turtlehead (Chelone glabra): This 2 to 3 foot-tall member of the Snapdragon Family has white to pink flowers in a spike, or closed cluster, at the top of the stem. The upper lip of the flower is broad and arched over the lower one, and it is notched at the apex. The lower lip is 3-lobed and woolly. Leaves opposite. Blooms late July through August.

Twinflower (Linnaea borealis): Part of the Honeysuckle Family this fragrant, dainty plant has small, pink, bell-shaped flowers that occur in pairs at the top of thin, 3 to 6 inch-tall stalks. The leaves of this creeping plant are small, paired, and rounded. Likes mossy areas; flowers in June.

Violet, White (viola incognita): This 1 to 5 inch-tall plant has white 5-petaled flowers atop a bare stem. The leaves arise from the base of the flower stem. Blooms May to mid-June.

Violet, Wooly Blue (Viola sororia): This 3 to 8 inch-tall plant has blue or violet, 5-petaled-flowers with white centers. There are numerous leaves with blades up to 4 inches wide. Found in damp woods and meadows. Blooms May to early June.

328

Violet, Yellow (Viola Pubescens): This 4 to 10 inch-tall plant has 5-petaled yellow flowers. Both leaves and flowers arise from the main stem. There are 1 to 5 basal leaves, which are broad and smooth. Blooms May through early June. The flowers and leaves may be eaten raw in salads.

Wild Geranium (Geranium maculatum): A member of the Geranium Family, this 1 to 2 foot-tall plant has showy, rose-colored flowers with 10 stamens (male flower organ tipped by the pollen-bearing anther). Fruit is a long pod (called a crane's bill) that splits at the base. Leaves are compound and on long stalks. Blooms May to June.

Wild Ginger (Asarum canadense): Wild ginger has large, heart-shaped leaves with hairy stalks. The reddish-brown flower is found in the crotch between 2 leafstalks. The flower is at ground level and is commonly hidden beneath last year's dead leaves. The root of this plant can be used as a substitute for the ginger you buy in grocery stores. Blooms late April through May

Wild Lettuce (Lactuca canadensis): A tall (4 to 10 feet) branched plant with many small, pale white, dandelion-like flowers in long, narrow clusters. Blooms late June through August.

Wild Onion: See leek, wild

Wild Rose (Rosa species): Two varieties are found along the hiking trail. Flowers are 5-petaled white or pink, with many stamens. Prickly variety has pink flowers on a bush that is waist high and covered by prickles. Smooth variety has a smooth stem. Rose hips are the fruit of the rose plant; these ripen to a deep red or orange color in August. Rose hips are a great source of vitamin C.

Wintergreen (Gaultheria procumbens): Part of the Heath Family and also called teaberry, this 3 to 6 inch-tall plant has waxy, pinkish-white flowers that are urn-shaped. Leaves are oval, thick, waxy, and dark green. The edible red berries form in late summer but ripen in the fall. Berries taste and smell of wintergreen, and the crushed leaves are the source of oil of wintergreen. Blooms mid-July to late August.

Wood Anemone (Anemone quinquefolia): Also known as windflower, this member of the Buttercup Family has deeply cut, dark green leaves divided into 3 or 5 leaflets. The plant is 4 to 8 inches tall and has a 5-petaled white flower that closes up on cloudy, cool days (hence one of its other names—"drops-of-snow"). An early spring flower blooming late April through mid-June. Native Americans made a tea of the roots and used this to ease headaches and prevent dizziness.

Wood Sorrel (Oxalis montana): This 6 inch-high plant has pink or white flowers, strongly veined in pink, with 5 petals. The leaves are divided into 3 inversely heart-shaped leaflets that look like shamrocks. Blooms May through July with the young leaves having a lemony flavor.

Yarrow (Achillea millefolium): A member of the Daisy Family, this 12 to 20 inch tall plant has aromatic, fern-like leaves and white to pinkish flower heads in flat-topped clusters. Although it is a composite, the 5 rays give each head the look of a 5-petaled flower. Blooms July through late September. The plant is also called bloodwort because the plant can be used to speed up the formation of blood clots.

Yellow Vetchling (Lathyrus pratensis): This alien plant of the Pea Family grows to a height of 1 to 3 feet and has yellow flowers in a long cluster. These occur from the point where the leaf and stem connect. The plant has a pair of pointed leaflets accompanied by a tendril, and a similar pair of leaves at the base of the leafstalk.

References

Bates, R.L. and Jackson, J.A., 2004, *Dictionary of Geological Terms*. American Geological Institute, 3rd edition,

Boerboom, T.J., Green, J.C. and Miller, J.D., 2003, *Bedrock Geology of the Castle Danger Quadrangle, Lake County, Mn.* St. Paul, Mn., Minnesota Geological Survey, Map M-140.

Boerboom, T.J., Miller, J. and Green, J.C., 2004, *Geological Highlights of New Mapping in the Southwestern Sequence of the North Shore Volcanic Group and in the Beaver Bay Complex.* In Severson, M. and Hein, J., eds., Field Trip Guidebook, Institute on Lake Superior Geology, Duluth, Mn., p. 46-85.

Fitz, T. III, 1988, *Large Felsic Flow in the Keweenawan North Shore Volcanic Group in Cook County, Minnesota.* Unpublished M. Sc. Thesis, University of Minnesota-Duluth, Duluth, Mn.

Green, J.C. and Fitz, T.J. III, 1993, *Extensive Felsic Lavas and Rheoignimbrites in the Keweenawan Midcontinent Rift Plateau Volcanics, Minnesota: Petrography and Field Recognition.* Journal of Volcanology and Geothermal Research, V. 54, 177-196..

Green, J., 1996, *Geology on Display, Geology and Scenery of Minnesota's North Shore State Parks.* State of Minnesota, Department of Natural Resources.

Joslin, G.A., 2004, *Stratiform Pd-Pt-Au Mineralization in the Sonju Lake Intrusion Near Finland, Minnesota.* Unpublished M. Sc. Thesis, University of Minnesota-Duluth.

Marotta, Juanita, 1971, *Minnesota's Wildflowers of the Forest, Field and Wetland.* Published by the Author.

Marshak, S., 2004, *Essentials of Geology.* New York, N.Y., W.W. Norton Company.

Miller, J.D., 1988, *Geologic map of the Silver Bay and Split Rock Point NE Quadrangles, Lake County, Minnesota.* St. Paul, Mn., Minnesota Geological Survey, Map M-65.

Miller, J.M., Green, J.C., and Boerboom, T.J., 1989, *Geology Map of the Illgen City Quadrangle, Lake County, Minnesota.* Saint Paul, Mn., Minnesota Geological Survey, Map M-66.

Miller, J.D., Green, J.C., Boerboom, T.J. and Chandler, V.W., 1993, *Geologic Map of the Doyle Lake and Finland Quadrangles, Lake County, Minnesota.* St. Paul, Mn., Minnesota Geological Survey, Map M-72.

Miller, J. and Chandler, V. W., 1997, *Geology, Petrology, and Tectonic Significance of the Beaver Bay Complex, Northeastern Minnesota;* in Ojakangas, R.W.O., Dickas, A.B., and Green, J.C., eds., Middle Proterozoic to Cambrian Rifting, Central North America, Geological Society of America Special paper 312.

Miller, J.D., Jr., Green, J.C., Severson, M.J., Chandler, V.W., and Peterson, D.E., 2001, Geologic map of the Duluth Complex and related rocks, northeastern Minnesota. Minnesota Geological Survey Miscellaneous Map Series, M-119, scale 1:200,000, 2 sheets.

Morton, R., 1996, *Music of the Earth: Volcanoes, Earthquakes, and Other Geological Wonders.* New York, N.Y., Plenum Publishing. 2004, Perseus

Morton, R. and Gawboy, C., 2000, *Talking Rocks: Ten Thousand Years of Native Americans and Geology in the Great Lakes Region.* Duluth, Mn., Pfiefer-Hamilton.

Ojakangas, R.W.O. and Matsch, C.L., 1982, *Minnesota's Geology.* Minneapolis, Mn., University of Minnesota Press.

Peterson, R and McKensey, M., 1968, *A Field Guide to Wildflowers.* New York, N.Y., Houghton–Mifflin Co..

Stensaas, M., 1996, *Plants and Trees of the North Woods and Boundary Waters.* Duluth, Mn: Pfiefer-Hamilton.

Stensaas, M., 2003, *Wildflowers of the BWCA and the North Shore.* Duluth, Mn., Kollath-Stensaas Publishing.

Superior Hiking Trail Association, 2004, *Guide to the Superior Hiking Trail.* Duluth, Mn.: Ridgeline Press.

Tekiela, S., 2001, *Trees of Minnesota, Field Guide.* Adventure Publications Inc..

Water, T., 1987, *The Superior North Shore, A Natural History of Lake Superior Northern Lands and Waters.* Minneapolis, Mn., University of Minnesota Press.

Ron Morton is a professor in the department of Geological Sciences at the University of Minnesota-Duluth where he teaches introductory geology, volcanology, Precambrian geology, and other earth science courses. An advocate of geology for lay people, Ron enjoys translating technical scientific concepts and terminology into everyday language and experience. Ron is also the author of "Music of the Earth" (Perseus, 1996, 2004) and, with Carl Gawboy, "Talking Rocks" (University of Minnesota Press, 2000).

Judy Gibbs has worked as a naturalist for a variety of organizations including Wolf Ridge Environmental Learning Center and Hartley Nature Center; she also has been the on-site coordinator for many of the University of Minnesota-Duluth Elderhostel programs. Through her work as a naturalist, and her love of hiking and the out-of-doors, Judy has become intimately familiar with the natural history of the North Shore of Lake Superior. Judy is the author, with Larry Weber, of "Backyard Almanac" (University of Minnesota Press, 1995). She is presently supervising the building of the Superior Hiking Trail through Duluth.

Ron and Judy are currently working on a walking guide for the hiking trails in the state parks located along the North Shore of Lake Superior.